STUDIES IN LABOUR
AND SOCIAL LAW

GENERAL EDITORS

B. A. HEPPLE
Sometime Fellow of Clare College, Cambridge

PAUL O'HIGGINS
Fellow of Christ's College, Cambridge;
University Lecturer in Law

VOL. 1

Administrative Justice and the Unemployed

JULIAN FULBROOK
London School of Economics and Political Science

Administrative Justice and the Unemployed

MANSELL 1978

Mansell/Information Publishing Limited
3 Bloomsbury Place London WC1A 2QA

International Standard Book Number: 0 7201 0555 2

Printed and bound in Great Britain by
Ebenezer Baylis and Son Limited, Worcester

British Library Cataloguing in Publication Data

Fulbrook, Julian
Administrative justice and the unemployed. —
(Studies in labour and social law; vol. 1).
1. Insurance, Unemployment – Great Britain – History
I. Title II. Series
368. 4' 4' 00941 HD7096. G7

ISBN 0-7201-0555-2

CONTENTS

PART III
THE TRIBUNAL PROCESS

PREFACE

This study of the British welfare system is concerned with the machinery set up to provide cash benefits for the unemployed. In particular, it focuses on the system of local administrative tribunals set up to hear appeals on the initial administrative determination of claims. It also attempts to relate that modern framework to its historical and social context.

At the start of the twentieth century, there existed for the relief of the indigent only the partial aid offered by the Poor Law authorities and various forms of spasmodic charitable assistance. The intervening years have, however, seen the rapid growth of a whole network of social mechanisms for income maintenance, including the introduction of National Insurance, which Professor Titmuss characterized as 'one of the great social inventions of the twentieth century'.[1] The problems connected with the relief of the unemployed have always been a central preoccupation of welfare systems, and in any study of unemployment benefits it is important to recognize the often critical impact of past experiences. In the British system, many of the old structures and procedures have remained through successive changes in the framework of social security, and in examining modern practice it must be noted that, as Professor Crick has written, the best explanation 'of why a thing is as it is, is that things happened in the past to make it so'.[2]

Although unemployment relief has always existed within a structure of law, there has until recently been little recognition or study of the legal issues involved in the determination of claims. This has been due partly to what can be characterized as the legacy of charity in relation to welfare questions, but more importantly it is due to the setting up in 1911 of a unique appeal system set aside from the courts, and combined with a conscious attempt by social welfare administrators to 'keep lawyers out'. The complete absence of lawyers was never in fact

For notes see p. ix

achieved, nor entirely intended, as lawyers served both as Umpires and as chairmen of the Courts of Referees in the original National Insurance appeal system. They continue to hold key positions in the modern structure as top-level administrators, as National Insurance Commissioners, as chairmen of Local Appeal Tribunals adjudicating on insurance claims, and as chairmen of a small number of Supplementary Benefit Appeal Tribunals. In terms of advocacy before the local tribunals, however, it should be noted that up to the time of reforms following the 1957 Franks Committee Report, there was a complete bar on lawyers representing appellants before the social security tribunals. Undoubtedly, the reasons for setting up a tribunal system for unemployment claims, rather than leaving such questions to be settled by the ordinary courts, and the precise composition and powers of the tribunals, have had a considerable effect on the way in which the present system operates.

Social security, it will be argued, should very properly be the concern of lawyers. Benefit is decided in the main by the application of rules laid down by statute and delegated legislation, with a potential appeal to tribunals exercising judicial functions. In insurance cases, there exists a further potential appeal to the National Insurance Commissioners, who determine cases by the application of statutory rules and by their own system of precedents. And in all social security cases there exists the ultimate possibility of review by the courts. Such a system, exercising considerable power over the lives of many citizens, must be open to full scrutiny and to an examination of its justice and efficiency.

No attempt has been made here to compile a definitive textbook on the substantive aspects of social security law. Professor Calvert's recent pioneering work is, as he describes it, 'a start' in unravelling the substantive legal issues involved in what has up to now been an academic vacuum.[3] Rather, this study concentrates on the procedural aspects of the present adjudicatory system, attempting to place them within the wider context of the substantive law and the workings of the administrative machinery. Professor K. C. Davis has written that legal scholars involved in administrative law

> ought to be digging into the details and the realities of the administrative process in operation in the ministries and in the tribunals, the major problems ought to be identified, solutions ought to be proposed, the pros and cons ought to be debated and developed both orally and in writing, and the administrators and judges ought to be drawing from the enlightenment that would thus be made available.[4]

Such has been the aim here.

I am most indebted, in the writing of this study, to the numerous officials of the Department of Employment and the Department of Health and Social Security who gave freely of their time to talk with me about their work. They must of course remain anonymous, but I am most grateful to them for their co-operation and patience; in particular, my thanks are due to those members of the Departments connected with the social security tribunals which I was able to observe.

My first observation of Supplementary Benefit tribunals was as an advocate for the Cambridge Law Surgery, whose members have given me much helpful advice. I am also indebted to Sir Robert Micklethwait, the former Chief National Insurance Commissioner, and Commissioner R. S. Lazarus for their assistance and observations.

One important source of information was trade unionists serving as wingmen on social security tribunals and as advocates before them, whom I met in the course of lecturing for the Workers' Educational Association. I also wish to thank the social insurance officers of the Transport and General Workers' Union and the General and Municipal Workers' Union, and the Assistant General Secretary of the Sheet Metal Workers' Union.

My thanks are due to a number of individuals with whom I discussed my research. In particular I should like to mention: Peter Archer; David Bebbington; Rosalind Brooke; Anne Frost and her colleagues at the Nuffield Legal Research Unit; Larry Grant; Ruth Lister; Tom Rivers; Kenneth Scott; David Vincent; John Veit Wilson; and Michael Zander. Arthur Wilson helped immensely by obtaining source materials for me at short notice. Tony Lynes, Howard Mason, Tony Rees, Adrian Sinfield and Albert Weale gave me the benefit of their critical comments on successive drafts; however, I alone am responsible for the remaining errors. I wish also to thank my wife, Mary, for her unstinting advice, support and patience.

My special thanks are due to Bob Hepple and Paul O'Higgins for the discussions we have had and for their unfailing help with my research. Mrs Dorothy Tanfield typed the manuscript meticulously, and coped with the difficulties of transatlantic communications, for which I am most grateful.

JULIAN FULBROOK

Cambridge, Mass.
April 1976

NOTES

1. R. M. Titmuss, *Commitment to Welfare* (1968), p. 59.
2. Bernard Crick 'Introduction', in Maurice Bruce (ed.), *The Rise of the Welfare State* (1973), p. xxiii.
3. Harry Calvert, *Social Security Law*

(1974) p. vii. Although not dealing with industrial injury benefit and only sketchily with Supplementary Benefits, the importance of the breakthrough which Professor Calvert's book achieves can be seen by the fact that an earlier commentator contrived to discuss the misconduct disqualification of social security law without any mention of Commissioners' decisions, but solely in terms of the Common Law; A. Harding Boulton, *The Law and Practice of Social Security* (1972).

4. K. C. Davis, 'English Administrative Law—An American View', *Public Law* (1962), p. 139.

INTRODUCTION

Unemployment is predominantly a question of economic forces. In the twentieth century it has been perhaps *the* major social and political problem in the organization of industrial life. However, this study is not an economic analysis of the causes or cure of unemployment, but rather an attempt to focus on the administrative mechanisms which have grown up in Britain to ameliorate the financial position of the unemployed. That this relief function is 'second best' to the initial prevention of unemployment is clearly obvious. But the nature of the relief structure is of importance, not only because it is the major source of income for the individual who is unemployed, but also because the social security system as a whole has become an integral, and expensive, part of our social fabric. The form and development of that system, and in particular how decisions on the eligibility of the unemployed are made by the adjudicatory machine set up under it, forms the subject of this study.

Part One of the book is concerned to give a concise overall view of the present unemployment relief system and how it seeks to aid the unemployed. An initial chapter deals with the question of how social security benefits fit into the total picture of income available to the unemployed. Chapters Two and Three are an attempt to outline briefly the substantive law of the National Insurance and Supplementary Benefit schemes as related to the unemployed, and to probe specifically the kind of issues most often raised in the adjudicative system. Chapter Four investigates the workings of the administrative machinery which handles initial claims and from which appeals are made to the local appeal tribunals, and, in the case of insurance claims, on a second appeal to the National Insurance Commissioners.

Part One, then, gives a perspective on the modern system of social security. Part Two explores in detail how these legal and administrative

For notes see p. xvii

structures have developed. The Webbs, writing on the Poor Law system of 1910, made the suggestion that 'nothing of today . . . can be really understood without its history'.[1] And although the history of unemployment relief mechanisms makes an interesting study in its own right, it is suggested here that no realistic appraisal of the modern social security system can be made without knowledge of its derivation from past schemes of social welfare and income maintenance. The old forms and rules have not only shaped the present structures, but in many significant respects are identical with them, except in name and title. Although on the surface the system seems to be changing all the time with loudly-heralded reforms, the fundamental concepts have had enormous staying power. Similarly, the underlying philosophy of the present relief system, and the views of those paying for or using or administering it, are often paralleled by those of the past.

Chapter Five chronicles the themes of Poor Law relief for the unemployed, followed in Chapter Six by a discussion of the seminal introduction of compulsory unemployment insurance in 1911. Chapter Seven deals with the slough of the inter-war period when the insurance system foundered under the weight of mass unemployment, and then goes on to discuss the post-war Beveridge reorganization. As Professor Handler has stated, if in any way we can understand the historical roots and consequences of our present social welfare schemes, then perhaps future change can be planned for without 'the traditional process of gimmicks, slogans and insufficient funds'.[2]

Part Three examines the system of tribunals which hear appeals on claims for unemployment benefits. The aim here is to look beyond a superficial commentary on their theoretical form in an attempt to understand their operation in practice and what this means to appellants. Chapter Eight deals with the present structures of the two kinds of local tribunals and the Commissioners, and how they fit into the British administrative tribunal system. It also examines a key dispute on the role of 'discretion' in welfare adjudication. Chapter Nine discusses the role of participants in the tribunal process. Chapter Ten is concerned with the nature of tribunal adjudication and the conduct of hearings, examining this in terms of the rules of Natural Justice. It further considers the question of advice and representation, and makes suggestions for structural change so as to secure more impartial and effective adjudication.

A philosophy of individualism pushed to its logical conclusion would mean that only those who contributed to production could obtain any share in the benefits of production. The ancient Poor Law reflected this view in its axiom that 'If a man will not work he shall not eat'. But the harshness of such a doctrine has always been somewhat mitigated in the British experience by a contrasting concern for the welfare of the unemployed man and his family. At first, individuals in society provided sustenance for the needy as a felt moral obligation, but this unofficial charitable formula has developed into a social structure of wide powers and full State regulation. Nevertheless, the paradoxical nature of its origin continues to be reflected in the present structure, which, in the words of one theorist, 'symbolizes an unstable compromise between compassion and indifference, between altruism and self-interest'.[3] A similar dichotomy exists in society's attitude towards the individuals using the system. Are they to be treated sympathetically as hapless victims of economic forces? Or are they to be regarded as personally and morally responsible for their own predicament? The present structure again mirrors the conflict. There is an attempt to provide full supportive relief, but only through the administrative sieve of regulatory controls which will exclude or provide a work incentive for the type of stereotypical claimant renowned in social mythology, and once characterized by a prominent trade union leader as 'the loafer, the lazy, and the undeserving'.[4] Emotion, myth and partisan political views have of course all played a considerable part in determining structure. As Peter Kaim-Caudle has commented, 'Public discussion of social policy in all countries is generally ill-informed, tendentious and based on misconceptions'.[5] Nevertheless, such conflicts and misconceptions have not unnaturally played a considerable role in shaping the form of welfare legislation, and prevailing attitudes and beliefs have similarly been important factors in the way relief has been administered.

One danger in taking a historical view of the present social security system is that it may be seen as a steady rational progression towards what is sometimes termed 'the comprehensive Welfare State'. The same danger exists in viewing the tribunal system in a similar light. But such views are to read into administrative development the inevitability of hindsight. It also presupposes a present structure in perfected form. An attempt has been made to avoid both pitfalls, and to give an impression of the existing system as a malleable framework, which has been created in a context of polemical debate, short-term reforms which became permanent, legislative and administrative expedients and, in particular, by the impact of individual personalities.

Social Security Law?

Social security questions have not generally been thought of in Britain as legal questions, despite their often baffling complexity. Ten years ago only a small minority of lawyers would have accepted such a view, although the intervening period has seen a radical change, largely brought about by the activities of a number of pressure groups concerned with the rights of the poor and the apathetic response of the legal profession to them. It is clear that such awareness is by no means shared by many of those concerned with the administration of the welfare system, and certainly not by most of the clients using the system. And yet the decision-making process as to who is eligible for benefit takes place through the application of legal rules laid down in large part by the Social Security Acts or by delegated legislation under them, with the possibility of appeal from an initial administrative ruling to a formal system of administrative tribunals.

In relation to contributory benefits, initial insurability problems, known as Minister's Questions, are determined by lawyers working for the Department of Health and Social Security (the D.H.S.S.), in the light of their own past decisions and by the use of Common Law principles. These decisions can be appealed on points of law to the High Court. Adjudication on the statutory disqualifications and other questions of eligibility are decided at first instance by an Insurance Officer, who although without formal legal training is nevertheless necessarily immersed in the legal rules and Commissioners' precedents applicable to determination. Appeals from his decision lie to a Local Appeal Tribunal, whose chairman is normally a lawyer, and at a second stage to the National Insurance Commissioners who are appointed from the ranks of senior barristers. Further review by the High Court using a prerogative order is rare, but possible.

Given this analysis, a number of commentators are willing to admit that the insurance sector of social security involves use of the legal process, even though lawyers, because of the present legal aid position, do not often appear before the Commissioners and even more rarely before the appeal tribunals. Without experience of what goes on in this part of the legal system it is of course unlikely that lawyers will build up knowledge and expertise. However, beyond this point, few commentators feel able to recognize the impact of law on the 'poor relation' of National Insurance, the long-stop system of Supplementary Benefits. For example, Tony Lynes, whose extensive work in this area as a non-lawyer has been instrumental in illuminating what he has described as a 'backwater of British justice', has stated that 'the fields of national insurance and industrial injury . . . bristle with questions of law'. Nevertheless, in the same article, he clearly assumes that Supplementary Benefits is not a parallel field of legal endeavour, in that legal training and skills may only be marginally useful 'in cases where the evidence is confused'.[6]

A view as to whether or not a matter is a fit subject for lawyers to deal with depends a great deal on definition. But it also depends on social policy considerations as to whether lawyers can help or hinder the effective working of an administrative process. One long-standing theme of the twentieth century administration of unemployment relief services has been a determination to 'keep lawyers out'. This has been a major factor in shaping the present position of the social security system, and also in determining the attitudes of those administering and using the system. A comparison of the adjudicatory process of both contributory and non-contributory social security, while pointing to important distinctions, nevertheless reveals a broad similarity. Eligibility for Supplementary Benefits is determined initially by officers of the Supplementary Benefits Commission (the S.B.C.) in accordance with the rules laid down by the statute, delegated legislation under it, and also by internal regulations such as the A Code which, while repeating much of the statutory rules, also forms an additional 'quasi-law' based on departmental policy directives. What is in the A Code is supposed to be secret and purely for the direction of S.B.C. officers in an attempt to gain some consistency of decision through the use of what can be regarded as internal case-law.[7] But it is important to realize that, however, potent its regulation of the initial determination of claims, the A Code should theoretically have no effect on the decision of the Supplementary Benefit Appeal Tribunals, which must adjudicate principally on the grounds of the statute and statutory rules. Supplementary Benefit Appeal Tribunal members are not normally legally qualified; indeed, that this is so forms a major criticism of a final appeal body which has considerable legal powers. There is, however, a right of review by the courts, but this right has been largely dormant until recent years when it has been exercised in a few cases by the efforts of pressure groups with lawyers on their staff. In one recent case appealed to the Divisional Court from a Supplementary Benefits Appeal Tribunal, the Presenting Officer from the S.B.C. is reported to have remarked, 'Oh, that's the law. It's nothing to do with us.'[8] In summary, unless one defines law as solely in terms of cases in the High Court, legal problems and questions are at the heart of social security administration.

Why then is there a reluctance to have lawyers involved? And why have lawyers for so long ignored this vital area of jurisdiction? The answers to these separate but related questions stem partly from the present legal aid system but mainly from the response of legislators to the legal profession when setting up the social security structure. The 1911 Unemployment Insurance scheme was established with the seemingly incessant litigation over Workmen's Compensation firmly in the minds of the draftsmen at the Board of Trade, and with the addition of William Beveridge's personal disillusionment at the actions of the courts in industrial matters.[9] With efficient dispatch as the main criterion in the setting up of the appeal process, the full use of lawyers was thought to be too unwieldy. And for a number of reasons, the need, in setting up the additional structure of appeal tribunals under the Unemployment Assistance Board in 1934, was for a low-profile system very much under the control of the U.A.B. bureaucracy, in an endeavour to 'keep Unemployment out of politics'.[10] Thus in both sectors, the contributory and non-contributory schemes of social security, the initial tribunal framework purposefully excluded lawyers in a representational role. A recent echo of the need to keep welfare law insulated from the full effects of representational lawyering, because of a danger of an 'avalanche' of appeal cases as with Workmen's Compensation, has come from Lord Denning, who believes that, even where there has been a clear error in law, the Court of Appeal should not intervene in case it becomes swamped with appeals.[11] But apart from these considerations, it is important to realize the original character of the welfare system under which the tribunal structures were set up, for, as Professor Tawney stated, 'the services establishing social rights can boast no lofty pedigree. They crept piecemeal into apologetic existence, as low-grade palliatives designed at once to relieve and to conceal the realities of poverty'.[12]

One significant reason for the unconcern of lawyers over questions of social security in Britain has been the Dicey legacy of a refusal to countenance administrative justice. Although this clearly no longer inhibits academic lawyers from investigating the administrative process, its effect is still at times discernible in the attitude of both administrators and practising lawyers. And it must be remembered that the Dicey view of the Rule of Law was the prevalent attitude when the tribunals were set up as a 'cut price' legal system away from the courts. Moreover, despite the Beveridge watershed and the post-war reforms, it is suggested here that these had minimal effect on the administrative and adjudicative machinery of social security. In other areas of health and social welfare, the changes have certainly been immense, but in the field of tribunal adjudication little more was done in the post-war era than to change the original sports-derived names of Courts of Referees and Umpires to that of Local Appeal Tribunals and Commissioners. All the fundamentals of the 1911 Unemployment Insurance system and the 1934 Unemployment Assistance Board system modelled on it, remain today.

Deciding disputes is the basic legal function. The rules of procedure and evidence built up by lawyers are means of assessing rights between parties, and by the application of consistent principles to particular situations the determination of questions is made in an orderly manner and without prejudice to the parties. No one would claim, of course, that lawyers perform this function impeccably. But where tribunal adjudication may very well involve substantially more cash flow than cases in the High Court, and in marginal terms may be of very great importance to the individual claimant, such a system of legally established rights cannot be left to those possessing well-intentioned commonsense.

NOTES

1. Sidney and Beatrice Webb, *English Poor Law Policy* (1910), p. v.

2. Joel F. Handler, *Reforming the Poor* (1972), p. v.

3. Robert Pinker, *Social Theory and Social Policy* (1971), p. 211.

4. John Burns, *The Unemployed* (1892) p. 7. See also the statement of the Fisher Committee that current public opinion towards abuse is 'volatile'; *Report of the Committee on Abuse of Social Security Benefits* (1973) H.M.S.O. Cmnd. 5228, p. 12.

5. P. R. Kaim-Caudle, *Comparative Social Policy and Social Security* (1973), p. 3.

6. Tony Lynes, 'A Chart to Social Security', Legal Action Group *Bulletin* (1973), p. 38.

7. Cf. the private law-making of commercial contracts. This is of course subject to review by the courts and to alteration by the legislature.

8. Frank Field, *New Society*, **24** (31 May 1973), p. 497. See *R.* v. *Greater Birmingham Appeal Tribunal, ex p. Simper* [1973] 2 All E. R. 461.

9. See later discussion at p. 140.

10. See later discussion at pp. 165–6.

11. Lord Denning MR. in *R.* v. *Sheffield Supplementary Benefits Appeal Tribunal, ex parte Shine* [1975] 1 W.L.R. 624, at 631. See later discussion at pp. 297–8.

12. R. H. Tawney, *Equality* (1931), p. 127.

PART I

The Legal and Administrative Framework

I

Sources of Income for the Unemployed

The major sources of income for the unemployed in the British system are contained in two specialist social security schemes: the contributory scheme under the National Insurance Fund and the assistance scheme of Supplementary Benefits.[1] However, further income may be derived by some of the unemployed from the Redundancy Payments scheme, as a result of successful litigation for wrongful or unfair dismissal, as a by-product of the taxation system, from occupational severance and benefit schemes, and from other private sources. The economic effects of wider government policy may also play a considerable indirect role; for example, the security of the unemployed may be protected by measures such as import tariffs or bank regulations designed to safeguard savings which the worker may have to rely on in a period of crisis. Similarly, in a wider context, the socialization of services such as health care or education or subsidized housing has lifted major burdens which previously exerted considerable pressure on the poor and unemployed.

The Beveridge model for social security was that unemployment insurance should play the major role in assisting the unemployed, and certainly the contributory scheme is normally the initial means of relief. Behind this front line of social security is a second defence of Supplementary Benefits which 'as a general safeguard . . . gives help to those whose income falls below the level of their requirements as approved by Parliament'.[2] Both schemes have a long history: unemployment insurance originated as a state scheme in 1911, and the Supplementary Benefits system is the successor to schemes of assistance which have their roots in the Elizabethan Poor Law.

Between them, the National Insurance and Supplementary Benefits schemes provide the bulk of cash assistance to the unemployed. The payment of benefits in kind, which was the norm under the Poor Law

For notes see p. 10

system of out-relief, is continued only in special circumstances under Supplementary Benefits. But the relationship of the schemes is complex. For the five-year period up to and including 1973, for example, there were over three million claims for unemployment insurance benefits.[3] Complete data on social security benefits are notoriously difficult to obtain, despite the new annual D.H.S.S. *Social Security Statistics;* but based on figures in the 1972 Annual Report that there were 22½ million insured contributors for the purposes of unemployment benefits, and allowing for repeat claims in separate spells of unemployment, an estimate can be made that approximately one worker in twelve claims benefit at some point in the year.[4] However, little more than half of the unemployed at any one time are in fact receiving unemployment insurance benefits. This has been so for the period since 1960, when details were first given of this phenomenon, but the proportion has probably existed as far back as the start of the 'dual' system and certainly since the reformulation of the present insurance scheme in 1946.[5] The 'residual' scheme of Supplementary Benefits is therefore charged with the complete support of about 24 per cent of the total unemployed at any one time.[6] Moreover, it gives substantial supplementary aid to a significant number of those in receipt of unemployment insurance benefits. The overlap is due to the fact that those receiving insurance benefits are also entitled to Supplementary Benefits if, in relation to other resources, their income is not sufficient to meet their requirements as laid down by the Supplementary Benefits Commission scale rates; this is generally known as 'topping up'. In November 1974, such allowances were paid to 262,000 men and 39,000 women, with an average payment of a £5.04 supplement to their flat-rate unemployment benefits; where the claimant was in some way ineligible for insurance benefits, because of a low contribution record or through disqualification, the average weekly payment was £13.84.[7]

The character of the two schemes is that the first is an insurance scheme for the short-term unemployed, who in the main quickly find other employment and rebuild a contribution record; and Supplementary Benefits is a scheme for the long-term unemployed, who have exhausted their contribution record, or those who have been temporarily disqualified from insurance benefit, or those whose needs are greater than the allocation of insurance benefit to them. About 20 per cent of the unemployed are receiving no benefits at all; this is partly due to administrative time-lag, complete disqualification of the beneficiary but not his dependants because of a trade dispute, withdrawal of Supplementary Benefits by an Unemployment Review Officer after interview, or ineligibility for Supplementary Benefits after exhaustion of insurance benefits because of excess capital or, more usually, because of a spouse's income. There is a possibility too that those who consider themselves 'temporarily unemployed', or who dislike applying for welfare benefits, may not make claims to which they are entitled even after registering for notification of vacancies with the Employment Service Agency; an estimate made by the D.H.S.S. in 1973 was that there were 40,000 families (comprising 80,000 individuals) living below the Supplementary Benefit level, where the family had been unemployed for over three months and yet had not made a claim with the S.B.C.[8]

A picture of the relative importance of the various categories of unemployment benefits can be seen from the table below, compiled from figures for the seven year period 1968–74 from those who were registered as unemployed. This is clearly not a complete guide to those seeking employment; for example, many pensioners would prefer to work if they could find jobs, and, at the other end of the labour market, young people prolong their formal education because of a shortage of suitable job opportunities. As is well known, many married women do not bother to register when work is difficult to find. Further unreliability comes from the long-term unemployed being assigned to casual or seasonal work which takes them temporarily out of the unemployed category. The General Household Survey in 1971 showed that in fact 23 per cent of people who are not working but seeking work were not officially registered as such. From those in the G.H.S. sample it was possible to estimate that 8 per cent of unemployed men were not registered, 36 per cent of unmarried women, and 66 per cent of married women. However, levels of unemployment in 1971 were 3.1 per cent and there were only 451 unemployed people in the entire survey.[9] A P.E.P. survey in conjunction with a Department of Employment Survey of one in thirty of the registered unemployed showed only one in seven of those who are unemployed as women, whereas the General Household Survey shows one in three of all unemployed workers as women.[10]

Special considerations apply to groups of beneficiaries, such as women and young people. More women than men have no support from either National Insurance or Supplementary Benefits—approximately one third of those registered for work. This was interestingly only a little more pronounced among married women than among single women.[11] Such figures are explicable in the case of married women in that many do not pay the full rate of insurance contributions and are therefore not eligible for unemployment insurance benefits; and when unemployed they are normally not eligible for Supplementary Benefits, as their husbands are generally in full-time work which is an immediate bar to benefit. It has also been the case that until recent years many married women have chosen to stay at

TABLE 1. *Entitlement to Benefit 1968–1974 (in thousands and percentages)*

	MALES over 18 years		*ALL GROUPS*	
National Insurance flat-rate benefit only	107	20.6	139	21.8
Flat-rate benefit plus earnings-related supplement	93	17.9	103	16.2
Flat-rate benefit, earnings-related supplement and Supplementary Benefit	9	1.7	9	1.4
Flat-rate benefit and Supplementary Benefit	55	10.6	63	9.9
Contributory benefits TOTAL	263	50.8	314	49.1
Supplementary Benefit only	155	29.8	182	28.5
Others registered for work but not receiving benefit	100	19.4	142	22.3
TOTAL	518	100%	638	100%

SOURCE: Based on D.H.S.S., *Social Security Statistics 1974* (H.M.S.O. 1975), Table 1.32, from counts of a 5 per cent sample on the first Monday of May and November of each year. The form used here is derivative from that used for quarterly figures in the Department of Employment *Gazette*, a series discontinued in January 1973. The figures for 'All Groups' are compiled from figures for males under and over 18 years, and females under and over 18 years.

home when made redundant rather than search actively for a new job immediately, and also many women have traditionally resigned themselves to taking only low-paid short-term seasonal work.[12] In the case of single women, the explanation may be that many live at home and do not claim, or are not eligible for, Supplementary Benefits, or, as in the case of young people, there has been little time to build up a full contribution record. Sixty per cent of younger workers on average who are registered for work in the month of August are ineligible for insurance benefit, but this figure varies considerably with the school year, as in February the percentage drops to around 40 per cent, and the unemployment figures generally among young people are halved. It is clear that younger workers are particularly vulnerable to cyclical economic change, and that also there are many of them who fail to obtain settled employment.[13] Special National Insurance rules apply to young workers under which those who have just left school can qualify more quickly for unemployment insurance benefits, but the numbers of such people still on the register and without job opportunities has been a cause of concern for some time.[14]

Sources of income for the unemployed other than social security are extremely difficult to quantify. Redundancy payments are, strictly speaking, not 'unemployment benefit', but are, according to one widely held theory, analogous to compensation for a 'property right' in a job which has disappeared. However, as part of a wider manpower policy to facilitate the effective use of labour, they form a valuable financial cushion for those who may have difficulty in obtaining another job and, in particular, to older workers nearing retirement.[15] Older workers are also more likely to be unable to find suitable jobs, so that while it appears that some are 'doing well' out of redundancy payments, the lump sum is often quickly dissipated by a long spell of unemployment before retirement. The Oxford Unemployment Study shows that the extent to which redundancy payments 'mitigated poverty among the unemployed was quite limited'.[16]

The law on entitlement to these payments is exceedingly complex and beyond the scope of this study.[17] Little is known about the proportion of those at present unemployed who have received a redundancy payment, but this clearly forms a helpful supplementary addition to income for those who are eligible for it, as redundancy payments are not deductible from insurance benefits. In relation to Supplementary Benefits, they are regarded as a 'resource' available to the cliamant, and if over £1,250 they will be subjected to a tariff scale for percentage reduction. In the last quarter of 1972, redundancy payments to dismissed workers amounted to nearly £23 millions, involving 63,315 individual payments, which is an approximate average of £360 each.[18] In one study of the effects of the legislation in 1971, it was found that although the average payment then was £260, this varied dramatically when linked to occupational level, so that senior managers received payments averaging £430, whereas unskilled workers with less than three years service averaged only £60.[19] A number of redundant workers also received back their pension fund contributions, which when workers came under an official redundancy scheme, averaged £60, as well as £20 for an employers' severance scheme payment, £20 holiday pay, £10 in lieu of notice, and £10 from miscellaneous sources such as benevolent clubs or related to incentive bonuses or removal expenses. For those not covered by the official scheme, or who had not pursued the possibility of entitlement, these additional sums only amounted to £20 on average.[20] Although not part of the official Redundancy Payments scheme, other small amounts, usually going to redundant workers, may be paid in such ancillary labour service schemes as retraining allowances and expenses for job-hunting expeditions and interviews.[21]

Coupled with this Government scheme, there must be consideration of private compensation and benefits because, in the words of one study, 'very few firms adhere rigidly to the minimum obligations [of the official Redundancy Payments scheme], and the amount of the compensation varies from that basic figure to one month's pay for every year's service, plus 10% of your current annual salary'.[22] However, such 'golden handshakes' are not the total picture, as numerous fringe benefits may sometimes be kept on dismissal— for example, a company car bought on favourable terms—and in general it can be said that the higher the status and salary, the more generous will be the terms of compensation.[23] Definitions vary as to what constitutes a 'fringe benefit'; some commentators narrow it to only those assets which an employee can convert into cash, whereas elsewhere it involves all expenditure on labour other than the basic wage.[24] The most important 'fringes' today for the general worker are matters such as long service payments, and *ex gratia* or seasonal bonuses; however, these will often be legally unenforceable against the employer.[25] For the salaried worker, occupational pension schemes have become an increasingly important fringe benefit, particularly those known colloquially as 'top hat' schemes. Other fringes such as subsidized canteens, playing fields, sport and social clubs, and cheap holiday trips are generally becoming, as one authority remarks, 'vestigial remains of the attitude of management in a different age'.[26] Another fringe 'benefit' which was historically important, but is now fortunately rare in Britain, was the 'tommy shop' and other duplicitous schemes outlawed by the Truck Acts.[27] However, the 'service agreements' of company directors are still of course a highly prized 'unemployment benefit', with the object of securing both financial security after dismissal and also creating an obstacle to discourage potential take-over bids.[28]

One important source of income, for those who have been paying income tax up to the time of their unemployment, is in the form of income tax rebates. These usually become available after four weeks of unemployment. Their size depends on the amount of salary taxable under the P.A.Y.E. scheme, but also on the time in the financial year at which the unemployment occurs. An Appendix to the Donovan Commission estimated that, in the tax year 1967–68, a worker with average earnings of £20 a week would receive in the first few weeks of rebate (provided unemployment began some considerable time after the start, and some way before the end, of the tax year) approximately £3.50 weekly, if the worker were married with two children under 11 years of age.[29] However, there seems to be no definitive study at present on the importance of this source of income, although it was clearly taken account of in the drafting of the Social Security Act 1971. Before the passage of the legislation, any strike pay or income tax refunds which a striker received were ignored up to a level of *personal* requirements of £4.35, in assessing the claim of any dependants. Following the Social Security Act, only £1.00 has been disregarded.[30] The Secretary of State, Sir Keith Joseph, pointed out, but not with complete accuracy, that prior to this legislation it had 'for many years . . . been customary to ignore the tax refunds and strike pay (and any other personal income) available to the people involved'.[31]

Compensation for unfair or wrongful dismissal depends on the breach of a legal right by the former employer. Unfair dismissal was a new concept in Britain introduced by the Industrial Relations Act 1971, and continued with modifications in the Trade Union and Labour Relations Act 1974.[32] In practical terms of how much a worker will receive from an award, a comment made in 1972 is still apposite, in that it is 'a matter of the utmost difficulty to predict the way in which claims of unfair dismissal will be handled by industrial tribunals'.[33] Damages are limited by the Act to a maximum of 104 weeks pay or £5,200, whichever is the less, though tribunals must determine an amount which is just and equitable in all the circumstances of the case, showing on the face of the record any reason for a reduction.[34]

Wrongful dismissal is of an earlier vintage, and consists of unjustified breach of contract by the employer with regard to Common Law rules governing the employment relationship. Breach, which goes 'to the root of the contract', by the worker may justify summary dismissal, although the law is in some respects uncertain on the degree of misconduct needed; in the leading case Lord Evershed stated: 'one act of disobedience or misconduct can justify dismissal only if it is of a nature which goes to show (in effect) that the servant is repudiating the contract'.[35] Damages for wrongful dismissal are quantified, in most cases, by the payment of wages in lieu of notice, which is determined by reference to Common Law rules, but in most cases this will now be the minimum period laid down by a statutory sliding scale in relation to length of service by s. 1, Contracts of Employment Act 1972. Such sums will be most important to the unemployed worker, who will almost certainly have been in 'double jeopardy' before the hearing of his case, in that he may have been disqualified from insurance benefits by reason of 'industrial misconduct', judged by the rules laid down in the National Insurance Commissioners' decisions; 'triple jeopardy' occurs if, as is standard, the S.B.C. reduces his benefit by 40 per cent.[36] Special damages over and above ordinary damages can be awarded in exceptional circumstances, as, for example, where there was the loss of enhancement of reputation and loss of publicity for an actor.[37] However, there is always at Common Law an overriding duty 'reasonably to mitigate' damages. Such sums can be not inconsiderable forms of income-maintenance for the unemployed worker, particularly if he has long service, or is eligible for a greater period of notice under Common Law rules, although in relative terms they are small in comparison with severance payments and other benefits under private schemes.

However, such damages will be taken into account when assessing benefit, if available when a claim is first made; this is not only for purposes of available capital under Supplementary Benefit, but also because insurance benefits are not available until after wages in lieu have been exhausted. Complications can arise here if an employer does not make clear whether a payment to a worker is for wages in lieu of notice or is merely a generous 'golden handshake'; the Insurance Officer is likely to regard it as the former, although it is possible for the worker to show that the amount due to him on the basis of his contractual notice was less than the amount given him by the employer, and that the excess should be treated as severance pay.[38]

There is certainly 'inequality in adversity' under the British system when these extra 'unemployment benefits' are taken into account. Generally speaking, however, such extras are a comparative rarity, and the primary source of income for the majority of the unemployed is contained in the social security system which, although divided in theory and in administrative control, is nevertheless an attempt to provide an overall structure of social assistance.

NOTES

1. Although the 1975 Social Security Act changed the name of the previous consolidating Acts known as the National Insurance Acts, possibly to be in line with European practice, there are many vestigial remains of the former nomenclature; for example s. 1 (1) (a) Social Security Act 1975 refers to the National Insurance Fund; s. 97(3) Social Security Act 1975 to the National Insurance Commissioners; and s. 138 Social Security Act 1975 to the National Insurance Advisory Committee. Although some commentators now refer to contributory benefits as 'Social Security' (see Legal Action Group *Bulletin* (1975), p. 122), the term National Insurance is still used both officially by the D.H.S.S. and in common parlance, and will be so used subsequently in this book.

2. D.H.S.S., 'Social Security in Britain' (1972), a report prepared by the Department of Health and Social Security for the *International Social Security Review* **3** (1972), p. 146.

3. Figures for claims in 1973 were 2,233,000 men and 560,000 women; D.H.S.S. *Social Security Statistics 1973* (1975), p. 25. Table 1.05 gives a regional analysis which shows marked differences in levels; *loc. cit.* A total of 15,671,000 insurance claims for all categories of benefit were made in 1974; D.H.S.S., *Annual Report* 1974 (1975), H.M.S.O. Cmnd. 6150, p. 101.

4. Insured contributor figures from D.H.S.S., *Annual Report* 1972 (1973), H.M.S.O. Cmnd. 5352, p. 112.

5. See Table 175, Department of Employment, *British Labour Statistics, Historical Abstract 1886–1968* (1969), and subsequent quarterly figures contained in the Department of Employment *Gazette*. It appears that, despite transitional benefits and the hostility at the time towards the Poor Law, about 2

per cent of men on unemployment insurance benefits actually received poor relief in 1930; Appendices to Minutes of Evidence, *Royal Commission on Unemployment Insurance* (1932), H.M.S.O. Cmd. 4185, Part V, p. 283. See also on the similar experience of the Unemployment Assistance Board, Polly Hill, *The Unemployment Services* (1940), p. 78.

6. D.H.S.S., *Annual Report 1972* (1973), p. 116. These were the last complete figures given. The replacement of concrete figures by vague diagrams, as in recent Annual Reports, would seem a retrograde step.

7. D.H.S.S., *Annual Report 1974* (1975), p. 32.

8. *Hansard*, **895**, H. C. Deb. (14 July 1975), cols. 371–2.

9. See generally, General Household Survey, *Introductory Report* (1973).

10. W. W. Daniel, *A National Survey of the Unemployed* (P.E.P. 1974), p. 10.

11. See, for example, figures given in the Department of Employment *Gazette* **LXXX** (November 1972), p. 1032. See for a discussion, Brian Showler, 'Who are the Unemployed?' *New Society* (23 July 1970).

12. See the interesting study of redundant married women after the partial shutdown of an American textile mill in the late forties; Charles A. Myers and George P. Schultz, *The Dynamics of a Labor Market* (1951), chapter six.

13. See for a general survey of the problems, National Youth Employment Council, *Unqualified, Untrained and Unemployed* (DE 1974).

14. In general the effect is to qualify them for full benefit once they have paid 26 Class One contributions; see generally, D.H.S.S., *Guide for School leavers*, Leaflet NI 29A.

15. Approximately 10 per cent of all workers aged 60–64 are unemployed and registered for work at any one time; Department of Employment *Gazette.*

16. M. J. Hill, R. M. Harrison, A. V. Sargeant, and V. Talbot, *Men Out of Work, A Study of Unemployment in Three English Towns* (1973) p. 139.

17. See generally, Cyril Grunfeld, *The Law of Redundancy* (1971); K. W. Wedderburn, *The Worker and the Law* (1971) pp. 125–37; B. A. Hepple and Paul O'Higgins, *Individual Employment Law* (1971) pp. 149–61.

18. Department of Employment *Gazette* **LXXXI**, (February 1973) p. 172. The 1965 and 1969 Acts lay down a maximum of twenty years' service and £40 wages per week on a computation scale: for each year of service between 41 and 64, one and a half weeks' pay; between 21 and 40, one week's pay; and between 18 and 20, half a week's pay. There is a tapering-off provision reducing the payment to zero at retirement age when redundancy is declared after 64 (59 for women); see generally Department of Employment, *The Redundancy Payments Scheme, A Revised Guide* (1969).

19. S. R. Parker, C. G. Thomas, N. D. Ellis and W. E. J. McCarthy, *Effects of the Redundancy Payments Act* (H.M.S.O. 1971), p. 81

20. *ibid.*, p. 84.

21. The latest scheme allows for a living allowance for up to two weeks in duration at any one time, plus travelling expenses, as well as receipt of regular benefits; see 'Worker Tramps', *New Society*, **26**, No. 574, (4 October 1973), p. 3.

22. R. P. Wright, *For Men Must Work* (1969), p. 96.

23. See generally, Alex Rubner, *Fringe Benefits* (1962), whose survey proceeds from the point of view that 'fringes are affecting the moral fibre and the material norms of our society'; *ibid.*, p. 173.

24. See H. H. Macaulay, *Fringe Benefits and their Federal Tax Treatment* (1959) p. 5. See for American experience with Supplementary Unemployment Benefits, later at p. 181.

25. See on the contractual position of annual Christmas bonuses, which were held to be unenforceable against the employer, *Grieve* v. *Imperial Tobacco Co.* Bristol County Court, *The Guardian* (30 April 1963) quoted in K. W. Wedderburn, *Cases and Materials on Labour Law* (1967), p. 118.

26. G. L. Reid and D. J. Robertson, *Fringe Benefits, Labour Costs and Social Security* (1965), p. 300.

27. See generally, G. W. Hilton, *The Truck System* (1960).

28. See M. G. McBeath and D. N. Rands, *Salary Administration* (1969), p. 244.

29. *Royal Commission on Trade Unions and Employers' Associations* (1968) Cmnd. 3623, p. 345. See generally Appendix 8. These sums were even lower for unmarried workers and slightly higher for married men with no children: £2.70 and £3.65 respectively; *loc. cit.*

30. See later discussion on p. 43.

31. *Hansard*, **814**, H. C. Deb. (29 March 1971), col. 1151.

32. See generally, Sched. I, Part II. See also ILO *Recommendation* 119 (1964).

33. M. R. Freedland, 'The Burden of Proof in claims of Unfair Dismissal', *Industrial Law Journal* (1972), p. 20.

34. *Morrish* v. *Henlys* (*Folkestone*) *Ltd.* [1973] 2 All E.R. 137. The maxima are contained in para. 20(1) Sched. I. Part II of the Trade Union and Labour Relations Act 1974. See generally, Dudley Jackson, *Unfair Dismissal: How and Why the Law Works* (1975) and S. D. Anderman, *Unfair Dismissal and the Law* (1973).

35. *Laws* v. *London Chronicle* [1959] 1 W.L.R. 698. The Industrial Relations *Code of Practice* also suggested that an oral or written warning is the appropriate disciplinary for a first offence. Cf. *Sinclair* v. *Neighbour* [1966] 3 All E.R. 988; *Pepper* v. *Webb* [1969] 2 All E.R. 216. See as illustrative of Victorian attitudes, *Turner* v. *Mason* (1845) 14 M. & W. 112

36. See later at p. 44. For Commissioners' decisions, see generally, Edgar Jenkins, *Index and Digest of Decisions given by the Commissioners under the National Insurance Acts* (1964). It is important to note here the relationship of admission by an employer that he has wrongfully dismissed a worker, and that worker's disqualification for industrial misconduct under the insurance scheme. In one case observed by the author, an appellant at an oral hearing before the National Insurance Commissioner made a successful application, largely on the basis that in reply to a solicitor's letter threatening action for wrongful dismissal, his former employers sent a payment representing wages in lieu; unreported decision, C. U./115/1973.

37. *Clayton and Waller* v. *Oliver* [1930] A.C. 209.

38. See for example R(U) 5/73.

2

National Insurance and the Unemployed

Contributory benefits from the National Insurance Fund have been since 1911 the immediate recourse for the unemployed eligible worker. It is usually stated that the difference between social insurance and social assistance is that in the former the worker makes specific contractual contributions to guard against lack of income associated with certain risks which may imperil the worker's ability to take care of himself and his dependants; whereas in the social assistance scheme, finance is by way of general taxation. However, National Insurance no longer relies on actuarial considerations, if this was ever really true except in theory, and it is more helpful to view all contributions and benefits as economists view them, as transfers in the circular flow of the national economy, whatever their precise form.[1] In this light, any differences between social insurance and social assistance must be seen in terms of function rather than in attempting to find specious differences in funding. One immediate difference is that National Insurance payments are fixed by statute at specified flat rates in relation to contributions, and, although the administration has power to disqualify from benefit subject to appeal, it has no power to augment or reduce benefit. There is therefore a precision about the nature and amount of benefit which is public and largely statutorily determined. As a general rule, National Insurance benefits are quickly dealt with and involve little reflection on the part of Insurance Officers administering the claims. Furthermore, difficult points are authoritatively determined by the National Insurance Commissioners, whose decisions form a body of precedent to which Insurance Officers can refer.

Secondly, and more importantly, National Insurance because of its quasi-contractual nature does not require a test of need; as is often pointed out, 'a major objective of such a no-means test system is to relieve recipients of the embarrassment and humiliation of the means

For notes see p. 28

test'.[2] In Britain, as will be discussed, there have been a number of attempts to reduce 'stigma', but it is difficult to see how this can be done in a welfare system based on a test of need in the present social climate.

Social insurance schemes are by nature more predictable, have established routines and are easier to administer. The objective criteria on which determination is made are often available to the client and his representative, further speeding the process by ensuring a claim fitting into the correct administrative slot. Because of these factors, National Insurance is able to deal with large numbers in a relatively automatic manner, prompting Professor Lafitte's remark that 'the real distinction is between a *routine* service and a *needs* service . . . the alternative to social insurance is an army of officials and an avalanche of forms and records'.[3]

Since the setting up of the Unemployment Insurance scheme in 1911, there has always been a 'dual system', and at times in the inter-war period a 'triple system'. The distinction between social insurance and social assistance has occasionally appeared negligible, and certainly there has been some movement in many other countries towards amalgamation; however, in most major western systems they remain theoretically separate. An ILO Report of 1942 thought it helpful to view the schemes as 'tendencies' in historical terms which could easily coalesce,[4] but whether or not an insurance system is merely an intermediate stage in a transition to universal benefit coverage paid for by general taxation, its role as a pioneer in adequate benefits and non-arbitrary adjudication has been decisive.

The initial question as to entitlement for unemployment insurance benefits is whether a dismissed worker comes into the insured category eligible for such benefit. All British citizens are classified into four groups under the National Insurance scheme, but only Class One contributors qualify for unemployment benefits.[5] This group comprises all those who are 'gainfully employed in Great Britain either under a contract of service, or in an office (including elective office) with emoluments chargeable to income tax under Schedule E'.[6] Other categories are Class Two for the 'self-employed' or those working under a contract for services,[7] Class Three for those voluntarily paying reduced contributions to achieve certain benefits,[8] and Class Four contributions payable by those coming under Case I or II of Schedule D for tax purposes.[9] Class One contributions are collected through PAYE, Class Four by the Inland Revenue, and Classes Two and Three through the traditional method of purchasing stamps to paste on a card. Primary Class One contributions are paid from the gross earnings of the worker at a rate equivalent to 5.5 per cent of his wage, while

Secondary Class One contributions come from the employer at the rate of 8.5 per cent of weekly earnings.[10] This is a significant change from the pre–1975 position, where there were standard flat-rate contributions, forming by nature a highly regressive tax; however, the employer's contribution still remains as a payroll tax inevitably passed on to the consumer, or taking the form of lowered wages for the firms' workforce.[11]

The rationale for confining unemployment benefit to Class One contributors is usually expressed as being that 'only those who have been employed can be unemployed'. But, in the words of Judy Reid, the 'argument, though neat, does not always fit the facts'.[12] This delineation in National Insurance classification touches on a central problem of employment relations, as to who in legal terms is a 'servant'.[13] The traditional legal criterion of 'control'[14] has become increasingly unwieldy in modern circumstances, and is extremely difficult to apply in situations where 'self employment' has come to be used, in the words of a Report on the 'lump' problem, as 'a device to avoid the many duties the law places on employers'.[15] In this way, the legal divide between the 'employee' under a contract of service and the 'independent contractor' having a contract for services has become blurred; and in recent decisions, particularly on vicarious liability, some commentators have detected a 'policy' element in that judges apportion damages to those best able to afford them, rather than follow the intricacies (and occasional absurdities) of the control test.[16] In other situations, however, it is not a question of where blame should fall, but one involving a substantial sum of money under revenue law[17] or in relation to an employer paying National Insurance contributions.[18] Moreover, one must note that on the individual level in regard to National Insurance, the determination of category may be vital for an injured or unemployed worker, although the sums involved may be considerably smaller. Prediction of category is unfortunately a difficult task in the light of the existing case law. Earlier cases in social security adjudication tended to follow a modified control test formula,[19] but in recent cases there has been some considerable confusion. In one decision, the judge thought that 'the nature of the control which is required in order to bring the employment within the scope of the contract of service varies almost infinitely with the general nature of the duties involved'.[20] And in another case, the judge—presumably to be quite safe—referred to all possible tests including 'what in modern parlance is called economic reality'.[21] But perhaps the most difficult social security case to reconcile with industrial reality has been the *Ready Mixed Concrete* decision, where a complicated contract for 'owner drivers' in a cement company was clearly designed on the facts to defeat the intentions of a number of regulatory statutes. However, the 'self-employment' of the drivers was upheld, although the decision cannot be regarded as helpful in an area of serious difficulty.[22]

'Lump' workers are not covered for a wide variety of benefits including unemployment, industrial injury and redundancy payments when paying only Class Two contributions. But often they escape contribution requirements altogether and are therefore not eligible for sickness, invalidity, or pension benefits. Over 200 men were killed on construction sites in 1973, yet over half the workers in the industry are estimated to be lumpers; where the husband was a non-contributing 'lumper' no form of widow's benefit can be paid. The Inland Revenue believe that there is a £10 million tax loss each year from the 'lump', but most workers in the construction industry believe it to be much higher.[23]

It is important to realise that disputes on National Insurance categories are primarily decided as 'Minister's Questions' and not by the courts.[24] Together with questions of contribution liability, they are initially referred by the Secretary of State to a member of the Department's legal staff, normally a qualified solicitor. In 1974, Minister's decisions were given on 164 cases of liability classification and on 744 contribution cases.[25] But from this number there were no appeals on points of law to the High Court, although this varies; in 1972, for example, there were four appeals, of which three were dismissed and one allowed.[26] In general, however, about 25 per cent of Minister's Decisions are decided wholly or partly in favour of the claimant; 29 per cent in 1974.[27] The appointed solicitor in the Department's legal office may, if he thinks it necessary, hold an oral enquiry at which counsel are often briefed; the Minister's delegate can also subpoena witnesses and compel the production of documents.[28] These decisions together make up an important body of jurisdiction on entitlement, although the Secretary of State is not obliged to give reasons for his decisions or publish reports, and are particularly important in dealing with the insurability of workers in special groups. However, the D.H.S.S. publish a wide range of leaflets based on the decisions explaining the law in relation to these groups. Readers of them are specifically warned that they 'must not be treated as a complete and authoritative statement of the law', but they give valuable (and in some cases unique) guidance.[29] Important decisions were at one time issued as special pamphlets, with the helpful addition of extracts from the resultant High Court decision if the case was appealed. This practice was unfortunately discontinued in 1958, although the published decisions form departmental precedents for the adjudication of emerging disputes.[30] Professor Calvert's opinion, however, is that the decisions are not 'reasoned decisions' and therefore there was no great loss in discontinuing publication.[31]

But even if the standard of decision-making is not particularly high, it is suggested that it is unsatisfactory when so much important jurisdiction, and one relied on by Insurance Officers as precedent in subsequent Minister's Question cases, should go unreported. Subsequent appeal to the High Court of course may bring about a proper exposure of the case in the Law Reports, but only a tiny fraction of such cases are appealed. It would be the recommendation of this author that the whole matter be eventually taken out of Departmental hands and given back to the National Insurance Commissioners who had the jurisdiction until 1920.[32] Questions on contributions also frequently arise in the course of other legal proceedings, such as a bankruptcy case, an action for the recovery of unpaid contributions as a civil debt in the County Court, or through a prosecution in the Magistrates' Court for failure to pay contributions, and these provide further precedents.[33]

Contribution requirements

The 1975 legislation replaced the former system of flat-rate contributions, which dated back to 1911, with a continental-style percentage system linked to a lower weekly earnings limit.[34] Similarly, the old stamp-counting eligibility system has been replaced by a more sophisticated model based on an 'earnings factor', which is the aggregate sum of Class One Primary contributions, so that the first eligibility condition is that insured workers must have an 'earnings factor' in the current year above the lower earnings level multiplied by twenty-five.[35] This enables workers earning well above the lower earnings level to qualify more rapidly than with the older weekly stamp method. The second condition is that, in the previous benefit year, the worker must have either paid or been credited with contributions which were above that year's lower earnings limit multiplied by fifty.[36] Previously the benefit year commenced five months after the termination of the contribution year, and on a quarterly basis, to facilitate the ledger system at the National Insurance Headquarters at Newcastle. Now, however, with a more stream-lined system aided by a computer, the benefit year is based on the previous calendar year starting with the first Sunday in January.[37] Certain reduced contribution requirements allow those who have just joined or re-joined the system to be advanced to benefit when they are unemployed; with younger workers this is done by waiving the second contribution condition.[38]

All four classes of contributor pay contributions to the National Insurance Fund which also includes a small contribution towards the cost of the National Health Service. But for those in Class One, their percentage contribution also includes a notional contribution to the Industrial Injuries' scheme, now operating from the same Fund, and, for those over 18, the employer's Class One Secondary contribution includes a contribution for the Redundancy Payments scheme. Only Class One contributors are eligible for unemployment benefits.[39]

While a worker is unemployed, the Department of Employment normally records a credit on his insurance contribution record, usually during weekly visits to the exchange; this is now done even during a period of disqualification.[40] Credits count only for the second contribution requirement. Generally, a Class Three contribution at least must be paid for any week when a contributor's card is not credited. However, certain groups are exempt from paying any contributions. These include full-time students and unpaid apprentices;[41] married women, who can elect to pay Class One contributions at a reduced rate;[42] and persons with small incomes under £11 a week.[43]

Benefits

Claims for unemployment benefit must normally be made in person on the first day of unemployment at the Employment Exchange. Otherwise, benefit will be disqualified up to the date of full claim, unless good cause can be shown. A limitation period prevents any claims earlier than twelve months before the date of full claim from being considered.[44] Although there are numerous instances of late claims for National Insurance sickness benefits,[45] these occur less frequently in unemployment claims, perhaps because registering for a new job at a local office of the Employment Service Agency, or Labour Exchange as it is still called in common parlance, is so much a feature of daily life. Since 1974, unemployment benefit has been paid by post with a Giro cheque rather than in cash at the 'exchange', but registration at periods determined on an individual basis by the employment officer is still a condition for its receipt. Benefit cannot be paid for an isolated day of unemployment, but only for two or more days within a period of six consecutive days. However, this is subject to the overriding rule that benefit cannot be paid for the first three 'waiting days' of any spells of unemployment.[46] The reason given for this is that of administrative convenience, rather than an attempt to administer an industrial discipline penalty to hold workers in their jobs, but it is interesting to note that in, for example,

West Germany and in a number of schemes in the United States, benefit is paid immediately.[47] Until 1971, benefit for the 'waiting days' was refunded if unemployment continued beyond twelve days.[48] Single days can be combined if they fall within a period of thirteen weeks.[49] For the supplementary earnings-related Benefit scheme, the waiting day period is twelve days. Before the Social Security Act 1971, unemployment benefit was refunded for any 'waiting days' if unemployment lasted for more than twelve days,[50] but this is no longer available; the only possibility is to apply for emergency Supplementary Benefits during this period. The Secretary of State, Sir Keith Joseph, calculated that this change would save £22 millions annually from the Insurance Fund. The forecast for the increased burden on Supplementary Benefits was only £3 millions, involving therefore a net saving (or reduction of income for unemployed and sick people) of £19 millions. Although some of those who lost benefit for the waiting days may have been ineligible for Supplementary Benefit on other grounds, this still presupposed that only about one in seven people potentially eligible for Supplementary Benefits will in fact apply for them.[51]

In order to receive benefit, the claimant must first show that he is 'capable of work and he is, or is deemed in accordance with regulations to be, available to be employed in employed earner's employment'.[52] There must also be no unreasonable restriction on the type of employment which the claimant will take up, although there is nowhere a precise definition of the term 'unemployment'; it is clear from regulations that some employment of a part-time or low-paid nature is not incompatible with the status of unemployment.[53] No benefit can be given for days on which wages or wages in lieu of notice have been paid, and only days on which the claimant normally works can be considered for calculation. It is possible, however, to earn trivial sums without being adjudged to be 'gainfully employed'.[54] However, the claimant must be available at all times for full-time employment and his part-time job must not be the same as his normal occupation. The top rate for earnings is now the figure of 75 pence a day, which is scarcely more credible than the figure existing in 1972 of 33 pence a day. From a general economic perspective, Professor Robinson has remarked that 'regulations calculated to prevent him from doing himself any kind of good are harmful to [the worker] and not beneficial to the rest of society, while regulations that deprive him of the dole on a slight pretext are deleterious to the rest of society as well as himself'.[55] In Germany, for example, forfeiture of benefit is only made after earnings equal that of past employment. Substantial part-time earnings can be made up to twenty hours a week, and thereafter benefit is not forfeited but paid at a reduced rate.[56] Such an approach, while involving more administrative time, would seem much more equitable, as well as providing incentive to work and considerably reducing the motive and opportunity for fraud.

Flat-rate benefits are exhausted after 312 days or one calendar year.[57] However, a claimant may requalify when he has paid thirteen new Class One contributions, and worked for more than twenty-one hours in each week.[58] Cut off points are necessarily arbitrary, but Tony Lynes argues that the 312 day limit has become 'the most blatant discrimination against the unemployed', in that the new invalidity benefit payable after twenty-eight weeks on sickness benefit gives far more generous treatment.[59] The sick as a group are often better off to start with because of their employers' sick pay schemes, but just when the earnings-related benefits of the unemployed are cut off to reduce net benefit, so the sick will have their flat-rate benefit increased to invalidity benefit level. Perhaps what is most worrying is that the definitional line between the sick and the unemployed is very blurred. All studies of the unemployed show a considerable proportion of sick people, and it is a basic finding of empirical research that 'the unemployed are less fit and in a poorer state of health than the working population generally'.[60] How a worker losing his job perceives his condition and how the administrative machinery categorizes him can have therefore a very considerable effect on his benefit level after six months.

The relation of exhaustion and erosion of benefits to levels of unemployment is somewhat paradoxical. With low levels of unemployment, the low proportion of those still entitled to insurance benefits is explained by the number of marginal workers in and out of jobs without time to build up a contribution record. Conversely, with high unemployment levels, a number of the unemployed will exhaust their benefits while unable to find a new job. Very little is known about what Adrian Sinfield has estimated to be the 49 per cent or so who have exhausted or are not entitled to benefit.[61] About 20 per cent at any one time, of the 'off-insurance' group, have exhausted their benefit, and another 8 per cent are awaiting a determination of their claim, although three-quarters are likely to receive it later. Other categories include school-leavers who have not gained the minimum contributions requirement, married women who opt not to pay full contributions, and those disqualified from benefit. This still leaves approximately 100,000 persons unaccounted for, with the explanation that many of these are men who have exhausted their benefit and yet have failed to requalify, as their new job lasted less than three months.[62] As with so many other problems in social security, the data are simply insufficient to permit anything other than informed guesswork.

An earnings-related supplement is paid to claimants aged 18 to 65 (60 for women) who are entitled to flat-rate unemployment insurance benefits, up to a maximum of 156 days from the thirteenth day of unemployment.[63] This was introduced as a result of improvements to social security announced in 1965,[64] and implemented by the National Insurance Act 1966.[65] Assessment of the amount of earnings-related benefit is somewhat complex: the amount is one-sixth of a weekly rate which is equivalent to one-third of the reckonable weekly earnings above £30 or the lower earnings limit, and 15 per cent of those earnings above £30 and not exceeding the upper earnings limit.[66] A claim for flat-rate benefit automatically includes a claim for earnings-related benefit where there is eligibility; claimants were until recently asked at their initial interview to bring their P.60 Inland Revenue form showing earnings in the previous tax year, but this is now done automatically through computer records. The whole supplement is, however, subject to an overriding 'earnings stop' with a maximum total benefit of 85 per cent of average weekly earnings.[67] It seems that only a relatively small number of beneficiaries are affected by this 85 per cent 'cut-off'—about 2 per cent of those claiming benefit.[68] The earnings-related benefit is certainly a significant addition for those who receive it, with payments for one-half of these beneficiaries averaging over £4 a week. By March 1974, the proportion of insurance beneficiaries receiving an earnings-related supplement had risen to 57 per cent, 8,000 of whom were subject to the 85 per cent earnings stop; however, 10,000 of those receiving earnings-related supplement in December 1974 were also receiving Supplementary Benefit to bring their income up to the SBC poverty level.[69] However, there are a number of practical drawbacks, as well as theoretical objections, to a graded scheme carrying over the inequalities of the labour market into social security.[70]

First, no allowance is made for previous breaks in the contributions and income record due to unemployment, sickness or self-employed work, which may reduce the annual reckonable earnings or make the claimant ineligible for benefit. Inflation is also rapidly eroding the value of the supplement, in that the claim will be calculated according to average earnings in a period up to thirty-two months previously, and it can be argued that the scheme is not flexible enough in changing personal circumstances of promotion or wage increase. However, the present maximum would be regarded by many as perfectly adequate, if not over-generous. The concept of earnings-related benefit is also open to the objection that the long-term unemployed in fact have greater needs than those who have been earning high salaries and may have substantial investments and savings. For the long-term unemployed, any stocks of clothing and household goods, together with goodwill from neighbours and relatives may well have long been used up.

Theoretically, the scheme also suffers from the fact that it was introduced as an adjunct to the Redundancy Payments Act to aid labour mobility; this is plausible in relation to unemployment benefit, but hardly in relation to sickness, industrial injury or widow's benefit. As mentioned, the new Invalidity Benefit payable after twenty-eight weeks of sickness means that a sick person categorized as such and incapable of work has an increase in flat-rate benefit at the time when someone on unemployment benefit takes an often considerable reduction. One critic of the earnings-related benefit law, in both its theory and practical effect, describes the present situation as 'a complicated mess'.[71]

In addition to flat-rate and earnings-related benefits, a claimant may be eligible for allowances for certain categories of adults and children dependent on them for support.[72] This follows the original example of dependants' allowances paid in the out-of-work donations schemes after the First World War.[73]

Disqualifications

A beneficiary eligible for National Insurance unemployment benefits can be disqualified from benefit under rules laid down in the 1975 Social Security Act, which attempts to provide some sort of work discipline on workers who may otherwise 'throw themselves onto the Insurance Fund', as the National Insurance Commissioners often term it. They also serve as an incentive for the unemployed to find work or to take jobs offered to them by the Employment Service Agency, and also provide some inducement to general labour mobility by encouraging workers to move to areas of greater work opportunities. These provisions for disallowance were laid down in the original 1911 framework, partly by statute and partly by internal Ministry regulations. The present disqualifications are under four heads:

(1) where the worker is connected in certain specified ways with a trade dispute;

(2) where he was dismissed from his previous job through his own misconduct; or

(3) where he left voluntarily without just cause; and

(4) where he has refused without good cause to apply for or take up a suitable job or training opportunity properly notified to him by the Employment Service Agency.

These rules provide the bulk of the cases in the statutory appeal system, although many such cases take little time to hear and often seem to be *pro forma*. The misconduct and voluntarily leaving provisions are the clauses most often litigated, but it must be remembered that a trade dispute case is frequently a 'test case' upon whose result may depend the benefits of many thousands of workers. No figures are available on the relative proportions of those disqualified who appeal, but the proportions of those disqualified appear to be about 60 per cent for voluntarily leaving and 35 per cent for industrial misconduct. This is from an average disqualification of 48,000 claimants each month.[74] It is clear that the conditions of the labour market have an important effect on these proprtions. In a period of high unemployment and shortage of vacancies such as the present, where the Employment Service Agency estimates there is one vacancy for every nine workers unemployed, there will be few refusals to take employment notified by the Agency. Similarly, the 'voluntary quit rate' is much reduced when there is little opportunity of alternative employment.[75]

Trade dispute

The trade dispute disqualification in social security law was until recently perhaps still one of the most complicated sections in any piece of British legislation.[76] In relation to National Insurance it is an absolute bar to any benefit. From the start of the unemployment insurance scheme, the legislature has attempted to exclude entirely those workers who are unemployed because of their own strike action. There are few commentators who would argue with such a principle. But the scope of the present rule extends far beyond the exclusion of the strikers themselves.

The rationale of the disqualification in 1911 was the desire of the Board of Trade to maintain a posture of 'neutrality', but such a description of the rule has been frequently questioned, in that it has considerable effect by *not* intervening; as Professors Hepple and Kahn-Freund remark, 'What is the denial of unemployment benefits, of supplementary welfare payments or of tax refunds if it is not an indirect compulsion to return to work?'[77] In fact, a precedent had been laid down by the Court of Appeal a number of years before the formulation of the clause as a statutory measure in 1911, which was invariably followed by the Boards of Guardians. This was the *Merthyr* case, brought by coal owners fighting a strike, who objected to paying the rates which supported the payment of strike relief; the Court of Appeal laid down the general principle that strikers could not gain Poor Law relief while able 'to obtain and perform work at wages sufficient to support themselves (and their wives and families if any)'.[78] However, this disqualification did not extend to 'relief given *to* or for the wives and children of such men'.[79] The principle of the case resulted from a basic Poor Law injunction which stated that 'guardians are bound to relieve proved destitution from whatever cause it arises'.[80] Scottish practice differed, and in the 1926 General Strike the Parish Councils in charge of poor relief refused to grant relief even to the destitute dependants of strikers. The trade unions mounted a campaign fund to challenge the decision in the courts, but legislation was speedily passed to pre-empt the case[81] However, from this origin, the trade dispute disqualification has gathered ramifications which go well beyond refusing welfare payments to strikers; for example, according to the National Insurance Commissioners, the trade dispute disqualification's 'manifest object is to prevent the insurance fund from being used for financing *employees* during strikes.[82]

Under the present law, a worker is disqualified from National Insurance unemployment benefit if he is unemployed 'by reason of a stoppage of work which was due to a trade dispute at his place of employment.[83] To escape the ambit of this clause, a worker who is laid off by a strike must prove that 'he is not participating in or financing or directly interested in the trade dispute which caused the stoppage of work'.[84] The interpretation of these words has caused acute difficulty. 'Trade dispute' has been considered by the National Insurance Commissioners in the light of the general case law on the 1906 'golden formula',[85] but over the years the Commissioners have frequently developed their own extensions. For example, the clause has been held by them to include a stoppage on the right of workers to become members of a trade union,[86] but also to include a situation where seamen went on strike because of the exclusive eating habits of other crew members who were members of the 'Close Brethren'. This, according to the Commissioners, was a 'personal matter', but it also concerned the conditions of employment.[87] And in one case, where a worker was totally out of sympathy with a strike organised by his fellow workers who manhandled him at the picket lines, he was nonetheless held to be having a 'trade dispute' with the strikers, even if not with his employers.[89]

Stranger results came from the wide interpretation of other parts of the disqualification clause, existing until 1975, but the law has now been finally changed in accordance with the recommendations of the Donovan Commission who had made a detailed analysis of the history and effect of the trade dispute section.[89] However, in another respect, the ambit of the abuse has widened in recent years. This is because disregard in Supplementary Benefits for the 'personal requirements' of a striker, or other worker caught by the trade dispute clause, has been considerably reduced from £4.55 to £1.00 per week. For, although a striker is in normal circumstances barred from benefit for his own requirements, the disregard of 'personal requirements' is taken into account when assessing the Supplementary Benefits paid to any dependants.[90] Furthermore, the practice of 'subbing' workers with tax-free supplementary allowances until their first pay packet following a period on strike is now stringently curtailed.[91] It must be noted, however, that a striker is generally always debarred from receiving any Supplementary Benefit himself. If he is childless but has a working wife, similarly he receives nothing. The only possibility for a single man is to request Supplementary Benefit under the emergency provisions of s. 13 Ministry of Social Security Act 1966, which gives overriding discretion to the S.B.C. to make payment in urgent cases regardless of other regulations or statutory rules.[92]

The claimant's conduct

The second category of disqualification, under s. 20 Social Security Act 1975, is concerned with the individual conduct of the claimant, either in the way he left his previous employment or in his attitude towards future employment. Unlike the trade dispute disqualification, these are limited disallowances 'for such period not exceeding six weeks as may be determined.'[93] The six week period has however become standard through the judicial legislation of the Commissioners:

> 'The period of six weeks should not be treated as though it were the maximum penalty for an offence to be reserved for the gravest causes, but as a limited application of the principle of insurance law that the insurer is not responsible for losses which the insured person voluntarily brings upon himself.'[94]

As has been noted, the adjudication of these controls forms the major case load of local appeal tribunals in the National Insurance appeal system, and a substantial part of the work of the National Insurance Commissioners. In relation to the labour discipline element in these disqualifications, it is interesting to note that, according to a former Russian trade union leader, one of the central factors in setting up the Soviet social insurance scheme was to use it 'as a weapon in the struggle to attach workers to their enterprises and strike hard at loafers, malingerers, and disorganisers of work'.[95]

Dismissal for misconduct at Common Law involves a breach of the Contract of Employment which entitles the employer to treat the contract as at an end. If the breach is sufficiently serious, then the employer can summarily terminate the contract without notice or payment of wages in lieu. The precise legal rules depend, in the time-honoured legal phrase, 'on all the circumstances of the case'. For, as one judge pointed out in a case before the Privy Council, 'there is no fixed rule of law defining the degree of misconduct which will justify dismissal'.[96] However, although the systematic precedents built up by the Common Law[97] have clearly had an effect on the minds of the Commissioners,[98] they have nevertheless built up their own body of interpretation for National Insurance cases, based on a different concept of 'industrial misconduct'. For instance, one Commissioner has remarked that it was their duty 'to make up their own minds on what constitutes misconduct, in an industrial sense . . . irrespective of the conclusions which may have been reached by the employers or by a court of law'.[99]

In some cases 'industrial misconduct' is considerably wider than the Common Law,[100] and may involve conduct outside the place of employment and arguably outside the contract of employment, as in the case of an airline fitter whose evening drinking habits might have caused (although this was not proved) some embarrassment to his employers.[101] Inefficiency on the job is, however, not 'industrial misconduct',[102] although this may entitle the employer summarily to dismiss the worker at Common Law.[103] On reading Commissioners' decisions and observing hearings, one is struck by the expertise and knowledge which they have built up in this specialized field of work discipline,[104] and there has clearly been recognition of the role of trade unionism in the workplace situation, which has not been an outstanding feature of the High Court.[105] This has not, however, extended to full rights of union membership: in one case a trade unionist, who failed to gain recognition for his union from his employers, left in disillusionment and was immediately held to have 'voluntarily left without just cause'.[106] And similarly, an electrician, who refused to join a union after the initiation of a closed shop agreement with the employers and who then left 'voluntarily', was held to have had 'just cause'.[107]

The interpretation of 'just cause' is, understandably, a difficult matter to assess in other than subjective terms.[108] If the employer himself breaches the terms of the contract of employment, then this will normally be seen as 'just cause' for leaving,[109] but other cases have to be decided simply on their individual merits.[110] For example, in a recent decision, the Commissioners upheld the appeal of a former trainee manager, who quickly realized in his probationary period that he was not suited to the job, and therefore left to save his employers the further expense of training him.[111]

In general, the refusal of 'suitable' employment seems to be less of a subject of appeal to the Commissioners, perhaps because it seems to be used by Insurance Officers as a 'long stop' provision where disqualification under the other heads is not possible; in figures available for 1971, it occurred in 0.5 per cent of all unemployment benefit claims, in contrast to 7.8 per cent for 'voluntary leaving' and 4.4 per cent for 'industrial misconduct'.[112] This is particularly so when an unemployed worker is thought by employment officials to be 'idling'. For example, in one unusual case, an unmarried labourer living in the Shetlands, but not a native of the islands, and who had been unemployed for seven months, was held to have refused a 'suitable' job in Bletchley, Buckinghamshire, 750 miles away.[113] Although the Act is careful to state qualifications on the word 'suitable'—for example, an offer of a job to break a strike is unsuitable[114]—it is nonetheless a difficult question to determine, and may lead to some injustice.[115] However, employment officials also claim that the low use of the sanction is because workers who are reluctant to take work do not 'refuse suitable employment', but are able to persuade employers that they are unsuitable for a suggested vacancy;[116] this is not supported by any data. In any case, data in this area are highly suspect because of the aura of informal interchange between officials and clients. Peter Blau has graphically displayed the effects of this in the operation of an American public employment exchange; for example, one 'successful' filling of a vacancy was as a result of an agency official stating, 'even if it doesn't pay 30 dollars, and the man says he would take you, I would advise you to take it. You don't want anything to happen to your insurance, do you?'[117]

Phrases such as 'suitable work' will of course mean differing things to the claimant and as between a variety of Insurance Officers who make the initial determination. American studies show also that job suitability as a concept varies dramatically with the general economic climate, in that the rates of disqualifications for not accepting suitable work drop considerably during recession years.[118] With this disqualification there may at least be tangible proof of jobs offered and refused, but in other areas of the law there is ample room for widely varying subjectivity. As Professor Dunlop has pointed out in relation to the American statutory requirement that a worker to draw unemployment benefit must be 'able to work and be available for work', such phrases 'have no ready counterpart in the complexities of the labour market'.[119] Studies also show that the law has little relevance to the actual social mechanisms through which the unemployed find jobs, and is also unrelated to a man's desire for obtaining work when so much depends on a 'large element of chance and the role of the family and friends'.[120]

The disqualification clauses are therefore a highly imprecise tool for providing work incentives in an area of the labour market where jobs are rarely intrinsically fascinating or satisfying. Given the origins of the system in a time when the work ethic was dominant, and the nature of present public opinion towards the unemployed, there is probably little chance of immediate reform to the present controls to make them more selective and better suited to social actuality.

NOTES

1. See generally, M. S. Gordon, *The Economics of Welfare Policies* (1963).

2. Lewis Meriam, *Relief and Social Security* (1946), p. 565.

3. Francois Lafitte, *Britain's Way to Social Security* (1945), pp. 23–4.

4. International Labour Organisation, *Approaches to Social Security* (1942) Studies and Reports Series M (Social Insurance) No. 18, p. 84.

5. s. 13(1) Social Security Act 1975, hereafter 'SS Act 1975'.

6. s. 2(1)(a) SS Act 1975. See for judicial interpretation of 'gainfully employed', *Vandyk* v. *Minister of Pensions* [1954] 2 All E.R. 723, where an L.S.E. research assistant was held to be inside the ambit of the sub-section, even though his work was financially unrewarding owing to heavy transportation costs because of a disability. See for the similar position of an articled clerk, *Benjamin* v. *Minister of Pensions* [1960] 2 All E.R. 851.

7. s. 7 SS Act 1975.

8. s. 8 SS Act 1975.

9. s. 9 SS Act 1975.

10. s. 4(6) a) and (b) SS Act 1975. This is 8 per cent of profits or gains in the range £1,600 to £3,600 a year, and should more properly be regarded as taxation rather than as an insurance contribution.

11. There is some argument among economists on this question, although many believe that a major share of any payroll tax is borne by the wage-earner, and some believe that all of it rests on him; see Joseph A. Pechman, Henry J. Aaron, and Michael K. Taussig, *Social Security: Perspectives for Reform* (1968), pp. 175–8.

12. Judith Reid in Olga Aitken and Judith Reid, *Employment, Welfare and Safety at Work* (1971), p. 239.

13. See generally, K. W. Wedderburn, *The Worker and the Law*, pp. 52–67; B.A. Hepple and Paul O'Higgins, *Individual Employment Law*, pp. 12–22.

14. See for examples of its use: *Yewens* v. *Noakes* (1880) 6 Q.B.D. 530, per Bramwell B. — 'a servant is a person subject to the command of his master as to the manner in which he shall do his work', at pp. 532–4; *Performing Rights Society* v. *Mitchell* [1924] 1 K.B. 762, per McCardie J. — 'the final test . . . lies in the nature and degree of detailed control over the person alleged to be a servant'.

15. *Reports of the Committee of Inquiry* under Professor E. H. Phelps Brown into *Certain Matters concerning Labour in Building and Civil Engineering* (1968), H.M.S.O. Cmnd. 3714, p. 240; see, in particular, Appendix III on the legal position by Professor Rideout.

16. For example, *Cassidy* v. *Minister of Health* [1951] 1 All E.R. 574; *Roe* v. *Minister of Health* [1954] 2 All E.R. 131. See generally, P. S. Atiyah, *Vicarious Liability in the Law of Torts* (1967).

17. See for the dramatic effect on the income tax position of a ballet dancer held to be under a contract of service, *Fall* (*Inspector of Taxes*) v. *Hitchen* [1973] 1 All E.R. 368. See also *Household* v. *Grimshaw* (*Inspector of Taxes*) [1953] 2 All E.R. 12; *Inland Revenue* v. *Brander & Cruikshank* [1971] 1 All E.R. 36; and *Mitchell and Another* (*Inspector of Taxes*) v. *Ross* [1961] 3 All E.R. 49.

18. See *Global Plant* v. *Secretary of State for Social Services* [1971] 3 All E.R. 385; *Market Investigations Ltd.* v. *Ministry of Social Security* [1968] 3 All E.R. 732; *Ministry of Social Security* v. *John Bryant & Co.* [1968] 3 All E.R. 175; and *D.H.S.S.* v. *Walker Dean Walker* [1970] 1 All E.R. 757.

19. For example, in the leading case of *Gould* v. *Ministry of National Insurance* [1951] 1 All E.R. 368, Ormerod J. used a 'multiple' test'.

20. *A.E.U.* v. *Minister of Pensions* [1963] 1 All E.R. 864, Magaw J. at p. 871.

21. *Argent* v. *Ministry of Social Security* [1968] 3 All E.R. 208, Roskill J. at p. 216.

22. *Ready Mixed Concrete Ltd.* v. *Minister of Pensions* [1968] 2 Q.B. 947. See notes by Charles D. Drake, (1968) *Modern Law Review* **31**, p. 408, and B. A. Hepple, *Cambridge Law Journal* (1968), p. 227; see also G. de N. Clarke, 'Industrial Law and the Labour Only Sub-Contract', *Modern Law Review*, **30** (1967), p. 6.

23. See generally, Robert Taylor, 'On and off the lump', *New Society*, **31**, No. 650, (20 March 1975), p. 709.

24. Under s. 93 SS Act 1975.

25. D.H.S.S., *Annual Report 1974* (1975) H.M.S.O. Cmnd. 6150, p. 103.

26. D.H.S.S., *Annual Report 1972* (1973) H.M.S.O. Cmnd. 5352, p. 128. In Scotland the appeal lies to the Court of Session, similarly on points of law only.

27. D.H.S.S., *Annual Report 1974* (1975) p. 103.

28. s. 93(3) SS Act 1975.

29. Examples are *Guide for Shipowners and Masters*, Leaflet NI 25; *Caretakers and Other Persons in Charge of Premises*, NI 33; *Employment in or about Places of Public Entertainment*, NI 34; *Company Directors*, NI 35; *Employment at Places of Worship*, NI 36; *Unemployment Benefit for Seasonal Workers*, NI 55, etc, New rulings are issued from time to time, usually in smaller one-page leaflets: for example, *Office or Industrial Cleaners*, NI 162; *Office Staff Employed Through Agencies*, NI 173, etc.

30. The reported decisions ranged over a wide field: for example, M.49 BARRISTERS' CLERK, held to be 'employed'; M.55 MEMBER OF EXECUTIVE COUNCIL OF TRADE UNION, not 'employed', even when visiting a factory as conciliation officer in a dispute—but cf. *A.E.U.* v. *Ministry of Pensions and National Insurance* [1963] 1 All E.R. 864, where a sick steward was held to be 'employed' outside working hours and outside factory premises; M.56 POSTGRADUATE RESEARCH STUDENT, 'non-employed'—but *quaere* if he undertakes supervisions and outside lecturing; M.20 PART-TIME LECTURER and M.39 TUTORIAL RESEARCH ASSISTANT, both 'employed'; M.28 FILM ACTRESS, 'employed'—'for the period of the actual making of the film she was under, to put it neutrally, a measure of control'; M.48 BBC INTERVIEWER, 'not employed' —perhaps overruled now by *Market Investigations* v. *Ministry of Social Security* [1968] 3 All E.R. 732.

31. Harry Calvert, *Social Security Law* (1974), p. 18.

32. See later at pp. 138–9.

33. ss. 149–153 SS Act 1975. See for example, *D.H.S.S.* v. *Wayte* [1972] 1 All E.R. 255, an application for summary judgment arising out of default on payment of arrears amounting to £21,177 after a company had gone into liquidation.

34. At present £11.00. An upper earnings limit of £69.00 is the maximum taken into account for the percentage contribution; see generally, s. 4 SS Act 1975.

35. Or £275 at the present rate; s. 13 and para. 1(2)(b), Sched. 3, SS Act 1975.

36. Or £550 at the present rate; para 1(3)(b) SS Act 1975.

37. s. 13(7) SS Act 1975.

38. s. 13(8) and para. 8, Sched. 3, SS Act 1975.

39. Class One beneficiaries are also entitled to the following: unemployment benefit; sickness benefit; injury benefit; disablement benefit; industrial death benefit; and Redundancy Payments, as well as the universal benefits. Class Two contributors are entitled to sickness benefit.

40. s. 13(4) SS Act 1975. See generally, *Excusals and Credits* NI 43, and *Your Liability for Contributions when Credit cannot be given*, NI 56.

41. s. 8(1) SS Act 1975. See generally, *A Guide for Students*, Leaflet NI 30; *Information for Students*, NI 30A; and *Guidance for Apprentices*, NI 31.

42. See generally, *A Guide for Married Women*, NI 1. Their anomalous position is partly due to Beveridge's somewhat quaint belief that their primary work was to ensure 'the adequate continuance of the British race and of British ideas in the world', *Report of a Committee on Social Insurance and Allied Services* (1942), H.M.S.O. Cmd. 6404, para. 117.

43. s. 4(1)(b) and para. 1(3)(b) Sched. 3, SS Act 1975. A report of the National Insurance Advisory Committee in 1955 estimated that about 90 per cent of those exempted under this provision were non-employed persons, and 75 per cent were women; 'Liability for Contributions of Persons with Small Incomes', *Report of the National Insurance Advisory Committee* (1955) H.M.S.O. Cmnd. 9432; see generally, *Persons with Small Incomes*, Leaflet NI 27.

44. s 82 (2)(c) SS Act 1975.

45. Medical certificates proving sickness must be sent within six days of the start of

incapacity; see generally, *Sickness Benefit*, NI 16.

46. s. 14(3) SS Act 1975.

47. See P. R. Kaim-Caudle, *Comparative Social Policy and Social Security* (1973), p. 219. However, as a general rule, the systems in most states are very much sterner than those in Europe.

48. Changed by s. 7 SS Act 1971.

49. 'Days' under National Insurance are full working days, not including Sundays; see generally, s. 19 SS Act 1975. For the complex borderline situations which sometimes occur between employment and unemployment, see reg. 7, The National Insurance (Unemployment and Sickness Benefit) Regs. (1967) SI 1967 No. 330. See generally on the 'linking' rules, A. I. Ogus, 'Unemployment Benefit for Workers on Short Time', *Industrial Law Journal* (1975), p. 12.

50. s. 7 Social Security Act 1971. The Act effected a return to the pre–1946 position where there was a 'waiting days' period but no refund; s. 11 NI Act 1946.

51. See generally, Sir Keith Joseph, *Hansard*, **814**, H. C. Deb. (29 March 1971), col. 1153.

52. s. 17(1)(a) SS Act 1975.

53. para. 7, The Social Security (Unemployment, Sickness and Invalidity Benefit) Regs. (1975) SI 1975 No. 564.

54. See for interpretations of 'gainfully employed' by the National Insurance Commissioners, R(U) 16/64 and R(U) 13/58.

55. Joan Robinson, *Theory of Employment* 1938), p. 101.

56. See P. R. Kaim-Caudle, *op. cit.*, p. 219.

57. Calculated on a six-day week; s. 18 SS Act 1975.

58. This amounts generally to three months back at work; s. 18(2)(a) and (b) SS Act 1975.

59. Tony Lynes in Michael Young (ed.), *Poverty Report 1974* (1975), p. 77.

60. W. W. Daniel, *A National Survey of the Unemployed* (1974), p. 18.

61. Adrian Sinfield, *Unemployment Compensation and Employment Security* (Fabian Society Seminar paper, 1972), p. 6. An ongoing study of three British towns which has recently published its preliminary findings, discovered that more than 90 per cent of the unemployed registered for work in Newcastle and Coventry were manual labourers, compared with 70 per cent in Hammersmith; see generally, M. J. Hill, R. M. Harrison, A. V. Sargeant and V. Talbot, *Men Out of Work* (1973).

62. See generally, Adrian Sinfield, 'Benefits and the Unemployed', *Poverty* **32**, (1975), p. 12.

63. s. 14(7) and Sched. 6, SS Act 1975.

64. In the Labour Government's *National Plan* (1965), H.M.S.O. Cmnd. 2764, p. 33.

65. See generally, Minister of Pensions and National Insurance, *Memorandum on Earnings-Related Short-Term Benefits* (1965), H.M.S.O. Cmnd. 2887.

66. para. 3(1)(a)(i) and (ii), Sched. 6, SS Act 1975. See for quick reference the table of reckonable earnings in *How your Earnings-Related Benefit is Worked Out*, NI 155A.

67. para. 3(1)(b), Sched. 6, SS Act 1975.

68. D.H.S.S. estimate quoted by Adrian Sinfield, *Unemployment Compensation and Employment Security*. However, there are other serious difficulties in that 'at best, less than half of those one might expect to be eligible are receiving the earnings-related supplement', *ibid.*, p. 8.

69. *Hansard*, **883,** H.C. Deb. (18 December 1974), cols. 459–60 and **885** (14 February 1975), cols. 244–5.

70. See later discussion on pp. 179–80.

71. John Mesher, 'Earnings Related Benefit', *Industrial Law Journal* (1974), p. 118.

72. See for full details, ss. 41–44 SS Act 1975.

73. See later discussion at p. 179–80.

74. Figures provided by the Department of Employment. In the author's survey of one Local Appeal Tribunal 1970–3, out of 180 cases observed, 25 per cent dealt with voluntarily leaving work without just cause; 23 per cent with misconduct; and 25 per cent of cases dealt with a miscellaneous range of problems from repayment of benefit after proved fraud to eligibility questions which were promptly referred to the Secretary of State. Industrial Injury Cases were markedly low in relation to the national average as the tribunal was sited in a predominantly agricultural and white-collar worker area, but also perhaps because unionization is fairly weak. See generally for the effect of lack of advice on social security matters, and in particular industrial injury benefit, Brian Abel-Smith, Michael Zander and Rosalind Brooke, *Legal Problems and the Citizen* (1973), pp. 150–1, 185–6 and 218–19; a survey of a random sample drawn from three London boroughs which found a substantial unmet need for legal advice.

75. This also has wider repercussions in terms of collective bargaining and industrial relations as unemployment levels bring

about a decisive shift of bargaining power: see for an American study, Fred Slavick, *Voluntary Quit Disqualification in Unemployment Insurance* (1954). See also generally, Katherine Kempfer, 'Disqualifications for voluntary Leaving and Misconduct', *Yale Law Journal*, **55**, (1945), p. 147 *et seq.*

76. See for comparative American experience, Leonard Lesser. 'Labour Disputes and Unemployment Compensation', *Yale Law Journal*, **55**, (1945) p. 167 *et seq.*

77. Otto Kahn-Freund and Bob Hepple, *Laws Against Strikes* (1972) p. 8.

78. per Lord Lindley MR in *Attorney-General* v. *Guardians of the Poor of the Merthyr Tydfil Union* [1900] 1 Ch. 516, at 540.

79. my italics. *loc. cit.*

80. Quoted in Sidney and Beatrice Webb, *English Poor Law History* (1929), Part Two, p. 835.

81. The Poor Law Emergency Provisions (Scotland) Act. See generally, Helen F. Hohman, *The Development of Social Insurance and Minimum Wage Legislation in Great Britain* (1933) pp. 340–1.

82. my italics; R(U) 17/52.

83. s. 19(1) SS Act 1975.

84. s. 19(1) SS Act 1975, and s. 111 Employment Protection Act 1975. In 14 jurisdictions in the United States, benefit is available if the stoppage is termed a 'lockout'.

85. 'in contemplation or furtherance of a trade dispute.' The precise National Insurance definition is: 'any dispute between employers and employees or between employees and employees, which is connected with the employment or non-employment, or the terms of the employment or the conditions of employment of any persons, whether employees in the employment of the employer with whom the dispute arises or not'; s. 19(2)(b) SS Act 1975. This is subtly different from the now repealed s. 5 Trade Disputes Act 1906.

86. R(U) 12/60.

87. R(U) 12/62.

88. R(U) 2/53; but see now R(U) 3/69 which narrows its scope considerably. It is interesting to note that the General Strike of 1926 did not come within the ambit of the trade disputes clause for National Insurance purposes, as it was not a dispute between employers and employees, but between the TUC General Council and the Government; see the discussion by Clara D. Rackham in William Robson (ed.), *Social Security* (1948) p. 131. But see also the discussion of wider implications in A. L. Goodhart, *Essays in Jurisprudence and the Common Law* (1927) Chapter 11.

89. *Royal Commission on Trade Unions and Employers' Associations* (1968) H.M.S.O., Cmnd. 3623, pp. 246–56.

90. s. 1(2) Social Security Act, which creates a new s. 10A Ministry of Social Security Act 1966.

91. s. 2 Social Security Act 1971. See generally, the speech by Sir Keith Joseph, *Hansard*, **814**, H. C. Deb. (29 March 1971), cols. 1151–3, and subsequent questions and answer to col. 1161.

92. For a provocative account (complete with line drawings) of the relationship between s. 10 and s. 13, see the section on 'single strikers' in the Claimants' Union *Handbook for Strikers* (1972) pp. 12–16.

93. s. 20(1) SS Act 1975.

94. R(U) 17/54. In Canada the disqualification was changed from six to three weeks in 1971, whereas in the United States disqualification is often a complete bar to benefits until the worker returns to employment and requalifies all over again; see generally, William Lloyd Mitchell, *Social Security in America* (1964), Bryce M. Stewart, *Unemployment Benefits in the United States* (1930) and Paul H. Douglas, *Standards of Unemployment Insurance* (1933).

95. N. M. Shvernik, later chairman of the All-Union Central Council of Trade Unions, speaking in 1933 to the Central Trade Union Council, quoted in Gaston v. Rimlinger, *Welfare Policy and Industrialization in Europe, America and Russia* (1971), p. 279. See for an attack on Swedish social security as a similar 'instrument of control', Roland Huntford, *The New Totalitarians* (1972), pp. 182–203.

96. per Lord James in *Clouston* v. *Corry* [1906] A.C. 122. The Judicial Committee of the Privy Council upheld the decision of a New Zealand jury that a worker who had absconded from his employment to go on a 'three day drunk' had not acted unreasonably or broken his Contract of Employment in the circumstances. The Judicial Committee nevertheless sent the case back for retrial because of certain 'unsatisfactory' elements.

97. See generally, the massive collection in Alfred Avins, *Employee's Misconduct* (1968).

98. This is hardly surprising in that National Insurance Commissioners are senior barristers or advocates with at least ten years practice at the bar, usually in the Common Law field; s. 97(3) SS Act 1975.

99. R(U) 10/54.

100. See generally, for example, R(U) 24/55. Theft is always taken as 'industrial misconduct', even where only alleged and not proven, R(U) 8/57; also when it is theft from fellow-workers and not from the employer, R(U) 10/53. But for the operation of mitigating circumstances, see C.U. 190/150, and R(U) 27/52, where disqualification was reduced to one day as the claimant had already been 'punished' by criminal conviction for receiving stolen property. However, misconduct cannot be carried over into the next job; R(U) 26/56.

101. R(U) 14/57: 'What a man does in his spare time is not necessarily his personal concern alone'. See also R(U) 20/59 in comparison with the Common Law rule in *Hivac* v. *Park Royal* [1946] Ch. 169, on 'damaging' activity to the employer outside working hours. See also R(U) 8/57; R(U) 2/60 and R(U) 1/71, where gross indecency outside working hours justified immediate dismissal.

102. R(U) 34/52, where a thread tapper was dismissed because he could not improve his output though no fault of his own. But see R(U) 8/57, where after an employee had been acquitted from a criminal charge of embezzlement, a disqualification for industrial misconduct was upheld because the worker 'should have taken more care'. Cf. R(U) 10/54.

103. For example, *Jupiter General Insurance* v. *Schroff* [1937] 3 All E.R. 67. See also the redundancy case of *North Riding Garages* v. *Butterwick* [1967] 2 Q.B. 56. See for a fuller treatment of 'self-induced unemployment' in the Commissioners' decisions, Harry Calvert, *Social Security Law* (1974), pp. 149–72.

104. Disentangling the facts from the feelings in such an area is of course extremely difficult—for example, 'it appears from the evidence, including that of Mrs. J., that Mrs. J. approached the claimant and challenged him with having called her to another employer 'a f . . . old cow'; and that following this challenge the claimant shouted to Mrs. J. "bring your f . . . husband up". The claimant denies using the language attributed to him'. Unreported decision C.U./115/1973. The Commissioner upheld the appeal, stating that 'the brief episode which led to the claimant's summary dismissal seems to me to have been trivial, not to say childish, and of no significance for the contractual relationship'.

105. See for a survey of trade union cases, Paul O'Higgins and Martin Partington, 'Industrial Conflict and Judicial Attitudes', *Modern Law Review* **32** (1969), p. 53. See also where a shop steward, who ignored the use of negotiating machinery which his union had agreed to observe, was held 'undoubtedly guilty of industrial misconduct'; R(U) 41/53.

106. R(U) 18/52. 'What the employers chose to do in their own establishment was a matter for them to decide'.

107. R(U) 38/53.

108. See, for example, the letter written to an employment exchange by an irate father, quoted in Sir Ronald Davison, *British Unemployment Policy* (1938), p. 6: 'My daughter, Gladys, has paid into your scheme for four years and every time she tries to draw a bit of benefit, you find her a job. It isn't fair!'

109. R(U) 15/53.

110. See R(U) 14/52 for the firm offer of another job, and R(U) 31/59 for 'personal reasons'.

111. R(U) 3/73.

112. See *Unemployed Statistics: Report of an Inter-Departmental Working Party* (1972), H.M.S.O. Cmnd. 5157, p. 35.

113. R(U) 34/58. But contrast a 'deserving' case, R(U) 15/62: 'the question whether a claimant would have been worse off financially by accepting a situation is not in itself relevant to the question whether he is disqualified'.

114. s. 20(4)(a) SS Act 1975.

115. See generally, R(U) 14/54; R(U) 10/61; but with qualifications in R(U) 5/68. See also R(U) 9/64 on 'usual' occupation in relation to s. 22(5)(b) NI Act 1965. Cf. industrial tribunal decisions on 'suitable alternative employment' under the Redundancy Payments Acts, such as, for example, *Collier* v. *Smith's Docks Ltd.* (1969) 4 ITR 338.

116. Michael Hill, *Policies for the Unemployed: Help or Coercion?* (1974), p. 6.

117. Peter M. Blau, *The Dynamics of Bureaucracy* (1963), p. 102.

118. Joel F. Handler, *Reforming the Poor* (1972), p. 20.

119. John Dunlop in Ralph Altman, *Availability for Work* (1950), p. ix.

120. Adrian Sinfield in Peter Townsend (ed.), *The Concept of Poverty* (1970), p. 224.

3

Supplementary Benefits and the Unemployed

The administration of the National Insurance system is clearly based on a legal entitlement to benefit, with a hierarchy of adjudication based on legal concepts and administered in the main by those with legal training. But in the second-rank scheme of Supplementary Benefits clear-cut legal niceties are difficult to find. There is certainly an officially-stated legal 'right' to Supplementary Benefit, but it is sometimes hard to recognize in the amorphous mass of delegated legislation and partly secret internal administrative rules which govern entitlement; and the feeling of claimants and adjudicators is often that 'law' is a phenomenon entirely unrelated to Supplementary Benefits. Tony Lynes, commenting on the take-up of benefits, states that, although the Supplementary Benefit Act 1966 gives a legal right of entitlement, there is nonetheless

> a wide gap between the wording of the Act and the spirit in which it is administered. And that gap has very little to do with the viciousness of officials, most of whom are neither more nor less vicious than the rest of us. The fact is that *nobody*—except a few cranks in the Child Poverty Action Group—really thinks of Supplementary Benefits as a legal right as, for example, wages or even National Insurance benefits are a legal right. Certainly the average British lawyer doesn't.[1]

Supplementary Benefit is payable to anyone over sixteen and not in full-time work, based on an assessment of their requirements in relation to their resources.[2] It is important to note from the outset that the role of the scheme is now not merely a residual one for a declining minority, as propounded by the Beveridge Report, but a permanent agency dealing with a substantial and increasing sector of the population. The two-fold function of the scheme is to assist those without any resources

For notes see p. 50

and also to supplement the resources of those in receipt of National Insurance benefits but not living at the current Supplementary Benefit 'poverty line' level. To accomplish this, the Supplementary Benefits Commission (the S.B.C.) pays cash benefits which are termed supplementary pensions for those over pension age, supplementary allowances for people under pension age, and single payments to meet 'exceptional needs'.[3] The scale rate of benefit is based on two principal components, that of a basic scale which varies according to the number of dependants and the ages of any children, and according to whether the claimant is a long-term case, of pensionable age or blind; and a special allowance to cover housing or rent expenditure.[4] Housing expenditure is normally paid in full where it is rent, together with the rates, although this may be reduced if there are non-dependent members of the household or if it is considered 'unreasonable'. For owner-occupiers, the 'rent' addition covers rates, an allowance for repairs and insurance, as well as any mortgage interest which is being paid.

Resources

The Supplementary Benefit system is based on the arithmetical calculation of a person's 'resources' and 'requirements'.[5] These sums are then set off against each other and the benefit payable is normally the amount by which the resources fall short of the requirements. One significant change from the Poor Law is the abandonment of a 'destitution test', whereby a claimant was forced to exhaust all his personal assets before applying for relief. The first step in the abolition of this test was the Outdoor Relief Act 1894, which authorized the Boards of Guardians to disregard sick pay given by friendly societies. Further disregards grew largely by internal regulation until codified in 1948. Clearly if a claimant must exhaust his savings before becoming eligible then all incentive to save while in work is lost. The present system is based on a complex system of 'disregards', which are specified amounts of income or savings which can be held without loss of benefit. The disregards are laid down partly by statute and partly by internal administrative rules and are under three heads:

(1) resources taken fully into account, such as National Insurance benefits;[6]

(2) resources wholly disregarded, such as an owner-occupied house;[7] and

(3) resources partially disregarded, such as £4 net weekly earnings for those not required to register for work, and £2 net weekly earnings for those required to register.[8]

The primary disregard is of course that of a claimant's house, and this extends to any reserves which might be acquired from the sale of a person's 'dwelling';[9] however, capital assets from a prior sale will not usually be disregarded. Partly this is due to the natural resentment which would accrue from the forced sale if a full 'destitution test' were imposed, as it still is in some parts of the United States, but also presumably because of the potential aggravation such sales would cause to the already serious problems of housing and homelessness. Careful planning may mean that a Supplementary Benefit claimant, with a capital sum from, for example, a marriage settlement, will be best advised to buy a house rather than continue in rented accommodation.[10]

All other capital assets, including such sums as savings, investments, redundancy payments and bequests are added together and tested on a sliding tariff scale. Total capital amounting to less than £1,200 is ignored, but instead of the former clumsy fixed upper limit on capital, as under the 1948 Act, the tariff scale for Supplementary Benefits calculates a theoretical yield from capital. This assumption that all capital yields (and at such high rates) is of course erroneous, but the alternative of assessing actual net income was thought to be administratively impossible.[11] Figures for 1970 showed that in fact only 0.5 per cent of claimants come into the capital tariff scale, and of these most were making applications for supplementary pensions;[12] with the 1975 change from a limit of £300 to one of £1,200 this number will probably be even more reduced. Unfortunately, like so many terms in Supplementary Benefits adjudication, neither 'capital' nor 'income' are defined in the Act, and this leads to considerable difficulty in borderline cases.[13] The rationale of the tariff provision is, according to the S.B.C. Handbook, 'because, in a means-related scheme, a person with appreciable capital must be expected to spend some of this on day-to-day living expenses'.[14] However, it is clear that in a situation where so few claimants know their legal rights unwise planning of available resources often leads to a reduction in benefit.[15]

The reasons for the partial disregard on earnings are shrouded in mystery. If a person is unemployed, his obvious need is for a full-time job and not a minor incentive to take part-time work. However, taking a pragmatic view, some of those on Supplementary Benefits have long been judged 'unplaceable',[16] and a part-time job, even with a ceiling of £2 a week, is often a practical answer, often involving an attempt at gardening for a long-suffering philanthropist found through such organizations as the Cyrenians. A great deal of administrative discretion is given the S.B.C. by the statute and regulations under it, and in the last analysis, when wages are not immediately ascertainable, they may calculate net weekly earnings 'in such manner and on such basis as the

Commission consider approrpiate, having regard to all the circumstances of the case'.[17]

Requirements

The other calculation in the Supplementary Benefit equation is that of 'normal weekly requirements', as laid down periodically in the scale rates. The basis of the original National Assistance Board scales in 1948 was Beveridge's study of Rowntree's pre-war social surveys.[18] Beveridge's ideas were also clearly moulded by the period of mass unemployment in the inter-war period, and consequently the rate echoed his view that social assistance should meet minimum needs for everyone. But by the introduction of overall social insurance, Beveridge also believed that the assistance scheme would soon wither away into a small-scale residual system.[19] The idea, however, of a nationally enforced uniform scale had first been introduced by regulations under the machinery of the Unemployment Assistance Board in 1934.[20] These scales were originally only to apply on a temporary basis to the 'off-insurance' unemployed who had been catered for by various schemes of 'extended' and 'transitional' benefit for the previous decade, and until 1948 local authorities continued to give Poor Law relief on the basis of widely varying scales. The chief variable was of course rent; and the schemes since 1948 have continued to deal with this assessment on a localized basis.

The appropriateness of cash payments for the needs of the long-term unemployed has often been questioned, in that in a society geared to the work ethic and all that this implies in terms of social relationships, the stronger need is for work opportunities. However, experience with work programmes for the unemployed has had a chequered past, with the workhouse test and roundsman system of the Poor Law the nadir of such attempts to provide work. The difficulties of organizing a viable programme which will provide an adequate income for workers who will thereby retain job skills or learn new ones are of course immense, and only the United States has made major use of such a system during the New Deal years.[21] Experiments were also made in the 1930s in Australia, New Zealand and Sweden, but apart from sporadic work relief programmes to build specific projects, such as town by-passes, the concept has not been conspicuously successful, and certainly not in Britain.[22]

Considerable academic and political criticism has been directed at the calculation of the scale rate, and also at its slow and jerky rise in comparison with the rapid rise in the cost of living. Exactly how the figures 'are arrived at is a closely guarded secret. They are certainly not based on scientific estimates of subsistence needs.'[23] A sharp distinction is made between a householder and someone living as part of another person's household. However, a person who is responsible for rent and household necessities is entitled to the householder rate regardless of his age,[24] although in cases before the Supplementary Benefit Appeal Tribunals there are frequent disputes over claims made by those living in shared accommodation or what S.B.C. Presenting Officers before the tribunals will often characterize as 'communes'. This is a particularly acute problem in an area of housing shortage, where many tenants will share a communal kitchen and a rent book. Such an arrangement is the rule rather than the exception amongst students and other young flat-sharers. In a number of cases observed on this point before Supplementary Benefit Appeal Tribunals, the issue of the rent book seems to be the decisive factor. One little known internal regulation is that where a non-householder claimant under 18 has to provide for a dependent child, the Commission may make a special addition to bring the supplementary allowance up to the full over-18 rate 'where required to enable family commitments to be met'.[25]

Lord Collison, formerly Chairman of the S.B.C., thought that the householder/non-householder distinction should remain because it was 'of very long standing in this country's successive schemes for means-related benefits', and that 'it provides a reasonable and acceptable way of dealing with a situation where one person, often an elderly relative, shares accommodation for which rent and other outgoings are paid by someone else'.[26] Perhaps with elderly relatives this is a reasonable solution, but the rule is applied by the S.B.C. across a wide spectrum and is certainly unjust when depriving one-parent families of adequate benefit just because they happen to share a kitchen with others in the same building.[27] Unfortunately, in the one case on this point appealed to the courts, Lord Denning in the Court of Appeal stated that 'as a strict point of law' there was much to be said for the appellant's contention that he was a householder for Supplementary Benefit purposes while a co-tenant in a student flat, but nevertheless for 'policy' reasons refused to take jurisdiction.[28] Such an attitude would appear highly undesirable for the proper formulation of welfare law, but also very unjust in the particular case dealt with by the Court.

The basic scale rate is meant, according to the S.B.C. Handbook, to cover 'all normal needs which can be foreseen, including food, fuel and light, the normal repair and replacement of clothing, household sundries (but not major items of bedding and furnishing) and provisions for amenities such as newspapers, entertainments and television licences'.[29] This is based on Beveridge's proposal for a margin to cover 'any diversion of expenditure from things which are necessary to things which, though not necessary, may appear preferable to the individual'.[30] Many surveys, however, seem to discover that claimants subjectively feel themselves narrowed into a lower standard of general living, and do not regard the essentials of their normal life-styles to be covered by the S.B.C. list. This was of course the conscious policy of the old Poor Law, to place welfare beneficiaries into a 'less eligible' class, but that it should still seem to be the effect of the modern system of social security is perhaps unfortunate.[31]

Beveridge's view was that it was impossible to fix a standard rent addition scale rate[32] and, although he acknowledged that regional variations would apply to many other necessities, such as food and fuel, he nevertheless thought that administrative recognition of them would not be feasible. But the hope of his Plan was that there would be a parallel 'determined and successful effort to deal with urban congestion and shortage of housing',[33] which would go a considerable way towards redressing the inequalities and regional variations of rent. However, the Assistance Board had already adopted at that time the Beveridge approach of a flexible rent addition to a national standard scale[34] and, with the lack of an effective policy to equalize national rent standards, the addition has remained. Originally, the local advisory committees of the Assistance Board were given the task of drawing up 'local rent rules', but this experience in grass roots participation was none too successful in that rents often varied dramatically within the locality covered by the committee. Added to this was the need for constant revision, and the fact that local advisory committees were voluntary and unpaid often meant that the system was not nearly efficient and speedy enough. Nonetheless, the system survived through the 1948 reforms,[35] and until 1959, when amending regulations abandoned the concept of local rent rules and left the calculation of rent scales entirely in the hands of the National Assistance Board.[36]

A small proportion of claimants are 'rent stopped' in that the S.B.C. refuse to pay the full rent charged to the claimant because it is 'unreasonable'. The last full study, in 1962, showed that almost all cases involved privately rented accommodation, and in particular so-called 'furnished' accommodation. Nine out of ten cases were in large urban areas, and less than one-third concerned people above pensionable age; 50 per cent involved single persons living alone.[37] A number of cases which involve the use of the 'rent stop' have drawn considerable criticism, as the claimant is in effect being penalized for an exorbitant rent over which he has no control. The present policy is for S.B.C. officers to ask themselves two traditional questions—'whether the rent is reasonable for the accommodation provided' and 'whether the accommodation is reasonable for the claimant'.[38] Normally rent is regarded as 'reasonable' where it has been fixed by the local authority, or been determined through the Rent Officer or Rent Tribunal process, but in the latter case a claimant may hesitate to appeal to such a tribunal if he feels there may be difficulties with the landlord, perhaps leading to an eviction. In certain cases, there may also be strong family or community ties between the landlord and tenant which would prohibit recourse to an outside authority.

Adjustments to the rent addition are normally made if 'rent' includes heating and lighting. Similarly, any proceeds from sub-letting are also deducted.[39] And unless the claimant or his wife are blind, the rent addition will be reduced by an amount 'reasonably attributable' to persons who are not dependent on the claimant.[40] Rent allowances and rebates have become supremely important to the Supplementary Benefit claimant since the present scheme may in some cases extinguish the entire rent commitment.[41] An application to a Local Housing Authority for a rent subsidy will generally constitute a simultaneous claim for a rate rebate, although Supplementary Benefits claimants are not eligible for rate rebates and can only receive rent rebates or allowances for their first eight weeks on benefit. A 1972 Child Poverty Action Group study in Islington showed that there is considerable wastage in the take-up of such benefits; even after an extensive advertising campaign, only 19 per cent of those eligible for rate rebates were actually applying for them.[42] Possibly take-up is higher among Supplementary Benefit clients than among other groups who are eligible for some form of rebate, because of advice given to them by S.B.C. officers, under departmental policy, and various advice agencies; but aside from such initial problems of application, there are also serious complexities with the present scheme, with occasional cases where claimants have to suffer because the public bodies involved cannot reach agreement. Local authorities maintain that it is unfair to expect local ratepayers to subsidize the rents of claimants, and the S.B.C. clearly cannot regard itself as a national rent and rate subsidy organization. Unfortunately, there seems to be little sign of such conflicts, described by Professor Donnison, the Chairman of the S.B.C., as 'frontier problems',[43] being adequately resolved at Government level.

Adjustment for exceptional circumstances

As with a number of Supplementary Benefit regulations, the special discretionary additions to the basic rates have their origin in the regulations of the Unemployment Assistance Board set up in 1935. The

Holman Gregory Royal Commission on Unemployment had felt that 'any rigid definition of the household must result in anomalies and hardships to the individual claimant',[44] and so the Board's officers were given wide discretionary powers to make additional payments on the basis of need. These powers were modified in 1948 to create two categories of discretionary payment: a weekly addition to the basic rate, given for 'special circumstances',[45] and an exceptional needs grant, payable as a single lump sum 'as is reasonable having regard to all the circumstances of the case'.[46] This has formed the basis of the present Supplementary Benefits system, and such payments are of crucial importance to a number of claimants. In November 1974, 34.1 per cent of Supplementary Benefit claims included an Exceptional Circumstances Addition, the amount of which ranged from a few pence to £3 or more. The number of claimants receiving additions has doubled since 1972. In addition, 830,000 lump sum payments were made in the year as a whole for 'exceptional needs'; this amounted to a total cost of £11,504,000, which also represents an increase over previous years.[47] Over half the total of Exceptional Needs Payments in recent years have been made for clothing or footwear, although the *Supplementary Benefits Handbook* specifically notes that these items should be regarded as a recurring and continuing expense provided for in the basic scale rates; however, the *Handbook* makes an exception where there are no reserves of capital or where families have been living at or below Supplementary Benefit level for some time.[48]

The S.B.C. may increase but not reduce a supplementary pension; but they may increase, reduce or even withhold a supplementary allowance. The purpose of this widespread discretion is ostensibly to 'ensure flexibility in the administration of the Supplementary Benefits scheme',[49] although it is normally administered only after an interview at the claimant's home. In granting an additional amount of benefit, the S.B.C. used to take into account the long-term addition where it was paid,[50] and, despite a High Court decision in 1973 giving a contrary interpretation of the Act, the S.B.C. continue to set off discretionary additions in taking what they regard as an 'overall view';[51] subsequently legislation overturned the court decision.[52] In statutory terms, *any* exceptional expense can be considered by the S.B.C. for the grant of a discretionary award. However, the *S.B.C. Handbook*, in its curious role of giving 'in a readable manner the material of importance to claimants and their counsellors free from the mass of procedural and other detail which is necessary in staff instructions such as the A Code',[53] lists the most frequent expenses as domestic assistance, a special diet recommended by a doctor, extra heating or substantial expenditure on laundry.[54] Calculations are made on the basis of actual expense, 'known

Departmentally as a reckonable expense', but more often by the use of standard rates drawn up, in the case of special diets, 'on the basis of expert medical advice'.[55] Unfortunately, these rates, as well as being shrouded in anonymity of calculation, also have the habit of remaining static for considerable periods of time.

Exceptional Needs Payments are made in lump sums 'where it appears reasonable in all the circumstances'.[56] These are special needs arising on single occasions, although the S.B.C. in exercising its discretion may take account of any capital or other resources which the claimant has at his disposal.[57] Capital is normally ignored up to a level of £150, although a further internal regulation disallows a claim if a beneficiary has a disregarded income of over 50 pence per week which would meet his special need if taken over a four week period.[58] Sometimes cash payments are not made if the S.B.C. can arrange second-hand bedding, cast-off clothing and furniture through voluntary organizations such as the W.V.S. or charities such as the Church Army, or through the surreptitious advertisement of local jumble sales.[59] This reliance on voluntary and charitable sources has of course a long history, but, as one critic states, there is 'something peculiarly offensive in a public department distributing other people's clothes and using the Salvation Army as a second arm of the State'.[60] Some of the furniture is also decidedly sub-standard. It would certainly seem that, in this area of the work of the S.B.C., a number of the worst features of nineteenth century private charity, in attempting to differentiate between the 'deserving' and the 'undeserving', remain an integral part of the modern system.

The Supplementary Benefit Controls

Unlike practice in the field of sickness or industrial injury payments, the 'genuineness' of unemployment cannot be tested by a simple medical examination.[61] The social security system has therefore built up a series of controls, of which the basic test for both National Insurance and Supplementary Benefits for the unemployed is attendance and registration for work at a local office of the Employment Service Agency. But this initial check is by itself insufficient, so that the unemployment benefit schemes have found it necessary to institute further controls, which regulate in certain specified ways the conduct of the unemployed claimant.[62]

The modern extension of the Poor Law's 'less eligibility' rule was the application of the 'wage stop' to those on Supplementary Benefits but this was finally repealed in 1975.[63] Before the start of the Family Income Supplement for working families in 1971, it reduced the payments of one in three of the unemployed families claiming Supplementary Benefit, affecting 33,000 families; but by April 1974 this had been reduced to 8,300.[64] The wage stop rule was designed to ensure that the income of an unemployed (or temporarily sick) claimant was no greater when receiving Supplementary Benefit than it would be if the claimant were in full-time work in his normal occupation, and the application of the rule was mandatory on those required to register for work.[65] A further 'invisible' number of those who were in receipt of National Insurance benefit was also subject to the wage stop which prevented their benefit from being 'topped up'; but their numbers did not appear in the official statistics.[66] The S.B.C. collected evidence on previous earnings from past wage slips and the P60 tax form, but in the absence of these, the potential wage rate had been fixed in recent years by reference to the scale established by the National Joint Council for Local Authority Manual Workers. This rate seemed in fact to determine the potential wage rate of the majority of those who were wage-stopped.[67] An Official Report on the administration of the wage stop in 1967 rejected demands for its complete abolition, but made recommendations 'to ensure that claimants who are subject to the wage stop are dealt with as sympathetically and equitably as possible',[68] Interestingly, the 1967 Report also stated that the wage stop was not a method 'to provide an incentive for a man to get work',[69] although, as Laurie Elks discovered, the internal A Code directed that officers should not normally raise benefit above the wage stop level using discretionary powers 'since this could well lead to a voluntary unemployment problem'.[70] The Government's new Child Benefit scheme, which will pay taxable family allowances to every child in 1977 should substantially ease a number of problems connected with low pay and poverty caused by large families if they are set at a sufficient standard and social security benefit levels are upgraded to keep pace with inflation. Unfortunately, the repeal of the wage stop cannot yet be regarded as a permanent feature of the British welfare system following a change of Government, and it is still pertinent to ask why a supposed 'welfare' law should at any time be utilized to keep welfare families below the official estimate of poverty.

The major cause of a depression in a family's Supplementary Benefit income below the level of normal entitlement, which still exists, is the extension of the s. 19 and s. 20 Social Security Act controls into the Supplementary Benefits system. For example, the Supplementary Benefit Trade Disputes disqualification[71] was, according to the 1972 Supplementary Benefits Handbook, 'in broadly the same terms as the unemployment benefit disqualification in s. 22(1) of the National Insurance Act 1965'.[72] This was hardly surprising, since unlike any other appeals on Supplementary Benefits questions an appeal on the Trade Disputes disqualification clause goes to the National Insurance Local Appeal Tribunal.[73] The decisions of the National Insurance Commissioners are therefore followed, although there is provision in the Ministry of Social Security Act, as has been noted, for the overriding payment of Supplementary Benefits in cases of emergency.[74] However, an important practical change was made by the Social Security Act 1971, in that the 'personal requirements' of the individual striker (or other person caught by the ambit of the trade dispute clause) were reduced from £4.35 weekly down to £1.00.[75] In practical effect, this measure has been entirely counter-productive, as most trade unions immediately resolved to pay no strike benefits but to increase unofficial benefits in kind, particularly in terms of providing hot meals for strikers and 'supporters' on the picket lines, and 'take-home gifts' of various kinds. Generally workers are paid anything up to two weeks in arrears, so that in many cases a short stoppage will not greatly affect the men and their families. However, the current trend seems to be towards more protracted disputes and such strikes now account for over 90 per cent of days lost through strikes.[76] A private member's Bill in 1973 proposed that any payment of benefit to a claimant for his dependants while on strike should be discontinued, but this radical proposal has not been implemented, although it seemed to have considerable support at the time from those not likely to be affected;[77] Brian O'Malley, until his recent and untimely death the Under-Secretary responsible for social security questions, characterised these proposals for reform as a means to 'use the withdrawal of supplementary benefit as a weapon against men on strike through starving their wives and children'.[78]

In fact, benefit paid to strikers and their families has varied considerably over the past ten years, reaching a record £8 million in 1972, but dropping to £698,775 in the first eleven months of 1973.[79] Unpublished studies done at Warwick University show in any case that undue emphasis on Supplementary Benefits, often described as 'the biggest strike fund of all', is misplaced. Personal savings are by far the largest source of support for the average striker who will draw over £10 a week from this source, and it would seem a reasonable hypothesis that many strikes falter or are quickly negotiated to a conclusion when savings are exhausted.[80] Another source of income comes from the earnings of a spouse, increasingly more important nationally now that over half of all families have more than one wage-earner, but always important in areas where women have traditionally worked full-time.[81] Tax rebates can also be a significant factor; they are normally paid by non-striking staff on each pay day following the receipt of the last pay packet; the 1971 Act clearly took such sums into account, but their amount is at present largely a matter of conjecture. However, an employer can refuse to handle rebates, and this will entail an application to the local tax office, which in some cases has involved delay sufficient to break the strike.[82]

One group overlooked in much of the discussion is that of the unmarried striker. The 1974 *Supplementary Benefits Handbook* formalises their position by applying a destitution test combined with a household means test in the traditional manner. Single strikers are assessed as using their savings at the rate of £6.50 a week until exhausted. At that point, the S.B.C. may under its s. 13 powers and 'providing he has no parents or relatives to whom he could reasonably look for temporary help', bring the single striker's income up to a maximum of £5 a week.[83]

In relation to the 'industrial misconduct' and 'voluntarily leaving without just cause' disqualifications under National Insurance, the position until 1971 was that, in a subsequent claim for Supplementary Benefits to cover the period of disqualification, a reduction of approximately 75 pence a week would be made. But by the Social Security Act 1971, this 'discretionary' reduction under regulations has been changed to a statutory reduction of 40 per cent of benefit in all cases,[84] although the *Supplementary Benefits Handbook* states that where there are such factors as sickness, unmet rent or pregnancy, the deduction should be reduced, although it should be at least 75 pence in order to 'preserve the principle' of the disqualification.[85]

For purposes of Supplementary Benefits, reduction for industrial misconduct and voluntarily leaving without just cause are linked with the refusal to take up employment under the label 'voluntary unemployment'. Again there must be considerable doubt about the definition of such a broad category. Particularly in relation to the refusal of a 'suitable' job, factors such as prior work experience, capacity and health are crucial, and before an insured worker can appeal an adverse administrative ruling to the Local Appeal Tribunal, he will have faced double jeopardy by having his secondary claim for Supplementary Benefits reduced by 40 per cent. Only weeks later after his appeal is heard can he recoup his loss if the original determination was wrong.

However, in the case of refusal to take up employment, the claimant may be subject also to further administrative controls, known collectively as the 'unemployment review' rules, which centre on the now rescinded 'four-week' rule. This 'four-week' rule was introduced in 1968, apparently because of considerable publicity in the Press and on television about allegations of abuse by young men living on Supplementary Benefits and making no attempt to find work.[86] Its primary effect was against unemployed single men who were fit and under 45 years of age, and was applied when there was thought to be suitable available employment for them in the surrounding locality.[87]

In June 1974 the S.B.C. announced its intention to allow the rule to lapse, although it had been suspended from December 1973 at the time of the 'black-out' and also in February and March 1972 at the time of the miners' strike. A principal reason seems to have been Molly Meacher's study which discovered 'the apparently indiscriminate use of the rule against skilled man, often men with mental and physical handicaps and men with dependants who suffer bitterly when benefit is withdrawn'.[88] Twenty per cent of the sample had had the four week rule applied at the outset of their claim, although twenty-eight of the ninety-eight men interviewed suffered from some form of mental or physical disability or illness, and more than a third were skilled workers or had academic qualifications. Aptly, four weeks after the study was made available to the D.H.S.S., an announcement was made that the four-week rule would be amended.[89] As an alternative, the S.B.C. proposed that the same group of single, fit unskilled men between 18 and 45 should have their claims reviewed after four weeks on Supplementary Benefits by an Unemployment Review Officer who will normally interview the claimant during his assessment. If the URO feels that the claimant has 'not made any serious attempt to find work', then benefit is cut off.[90] Although there is a right of appeal to a Supplementary Benefit Appeal Tribunal, benefit is not continued to the hearing, but cut off immediately, with applications for 'urgent need' under s.13 the only possibility of support.[91] Other fit claimants under 45 who are married or skilled, including women, will still be subject to the old procedure, whereby they have their cases similarly reviewed by the URO after three months. The S.B.C. states that the modified controls will initially be introduced in a limited number of areas, where there are good employment prospects, although in fact the old four-week rule only operated in a quarter of S.B.C. local offices. The Fisher Report, while reporting the S.B.C. claim of 'success' with the four-week rule, nevertheless gave figures which showed it had become less and less utilized; in 1970 the rule was in operation at 284 local offices, in 1972 at 105, and by early 1973 at only 88.[92]

Potentially the modified system is more threatening than the old four-week rule under which the claimant was at least warned that his benefit would be stopped after four weeks; this enabled him if properly advised to put in an immediate appeal to the Supplementary Benefit Appeal Tribunal with a chance of being heard before the cut-off, although Tony Lynes claims that, in such circumstances, most local offices saw to it that the appeal never reached the tribunal, intercepting an appeal on the basis that no decisions had been made to withdraw benefit and therefore there was no decision to appeal against.[93] Unemployment Review Officers were first introduced as an experiment by the National Assistance Board in 1961, but now number 120 and are specially assigned to administer these controls. Considerable confusion and some bitterness was caused by the practical operation of the old administrative rule, and recognition of this by the Fisher Committee probably led to the modification of the test.[94] In particular, the Fisher Committee recommended that a suitable vacancy should be regarded only as one available in the area *for the particular claimant* and not just simply as a general possibility of 'vacancies available'.[95] This problem should not arise because in theory the UROs operate 'in close consultation with the Department of Employment, the Manpower Services Commission, the Regional Medical Officers of the S.B.C. and social workers'.[96] The local office of the Employment Service Agency ought necessarily to be contacted for an up-to-the-minute report on the labour market for jobs geared to the individual claimant's requirements before the claimant is called for interview, but unfortunately such liaison is not always made in practice; this is partly attributable to a heavy work load in both agencies dealing with the situation, but also to an uneasy relationship between government agencies in many localities.[97] An additional factor is that the URO is generally based at the Regional Headquarters of the S.B.C. and often cannot be expected to be fully cognizant of rapidly changing local variations and also changes in employment personnel who can give him detailed information on employment conditions.

The S.B.C. have claimed considerable success with the use of these controls, and their figures at first glance seem to substantiate the claim. In 1972, 14,423 claimants were given an initial award of four weeks by Unemployment Review Officers, and of these only 1,871 renewed claims at the end of the period; 1,548 of these were allowed. Of 323 claimants refused, 142 appealed to a tribunal, but the S.B.C.'s decision was reversed in only eighteen cases. A further 1,124 allowances were 'curtailed' after three months; there were a consequent twenty-five appeals, but only three reversals.[98] Because of the level of unemployment, the new scheme is not yet fully operational, but in 1974, 162,000 claimants were called for interview by UROs and almost 89,000 'subsequently ceased to draw benefit'.[99]

In the absence of any proper study of the practical effect of the controls on the search for work by individual claimants, it cannot be stated categorically that there is a direct causal link between the interview with a URO and a subsequent return to work, although this is the hypothesis on which the S.B.C. works. Even if there is such a link it would seem to be a dubious attitude on the part of a welfare agency to frighten a claimant into any job rather than to retrain or place the claimant in a suitable job, a process which may take time but will be better suited to the long-term needs of both the claimant and the community. One claimant in a survey of tribunal appellants conducted by the author gave a vivid account of his repeated attempts to get a job when subjected to the four-week rule. He failed, and for a month relied on borrowing from friends while awaiting an appeal hearing. The appeal was disallowed, but he subsequently hitch-hiked around until he found a job in aother area. In effect ,the control revived in his case the law of 'removal' as under the Poor Law.[100] One commentator, Frank Field, believes that the practical effect of the control is such as to drive claimants to 'live off their wits . . . and to dossing and petty crime'.[101] Additionally, however, there is a negative effect on those who do not actually have their benefit stopped; as Michael Hill points out from his experience as a former officer of the NAB, this group may 'have to face official suspicion and hostility, affecting their chances of obtaining discretionary additions and making encounters with officials unpleasant and stigmatising'.[102]

Possibly one further reason for the 'abolition' of the four-week rule was its doubtful legality, in that the only statutory authority seems to give no express right to cut off benefits for a whole class of claimants or to reduce benefits to a fixed duration.[103] In the light of the *Simper* decision, where the Divisional Court insisted on a claimant-by-claimant judgment when there was a similar standard reduction governed by the internal A Code, the S.B.C. was probably wise to change to an individual interviewing rule rather than apply routinized standards. However, it should be noted that the S.B.C. still retains a back-up 'no-week rule' which can be used to refuse outright any claim 'where the insurance officer [*sic*] decides that a claimant has left, lost or refused work without good cause, and it is known that a particular job is immediately open to and suitable for him'.[104] Under the S.B.C.'s internal code this means that technically an Insurance Officer must first make a disqualification for purposes of National Insurance unemployment benefit before the S.B.C. refuses Supplementary Benefit. However, because of the sheer amount of unemployed workers, the UROs are only able to interview a small fraction and these are inevitably those claimants who have long exhausted any insurance benefit rights. In such a case, it is the URO who determines whether the 'no-week' rule should apply, often after an unsuitable temporary job has been foisted on the claimant who gives up after a day or so.[105] The 'no-week' rule could perhaps be described as the high point of the S.B.C.'s powers to enforce work ethics, although in addition they have the right to bring prosecutions as a last resort.[106] These are handled by Headquarters and are only pursued after careful investigation of a number of incidents and a reference to a Senior Medical Officer who may order a psychiatric examination. About 100 prosecutions have been made each year since 1957, and an internal S.B.C. study in 1968 found that 24 per cent of those prosecuted worked less in the year after prosecution, 25.5 per cent about the same, so that half worked more than before, including 25 per cent who worked considerably more.[107]

Keynes seems to have been the first economist to make the distinction between 'voluntary' and 'involuntary' unemployment, although in a somewhat different context, but all the empirical studies on unemployed workers show that the distinction is highly artificial. Firstly, this is because the unemployed are often the victims of an industrial system where their inability to earn is due to the structure of the job market, technological change, a poor educational system for them or their parents, or lack of a conducive social environment in their formative years. Secondly, as the famous Pilgrim Trust Report pointed out, many of the long-term unemployed 'become diffident owing to continual unemployment, [finding] it more and more difficult to face repeated failures and finally give up looking for work'.[108] This syndrome is confirmed by the more recent Oxford study,[109] and by Adrian Sinfield's ten country study; the latter states that, as a general principle, 'the longer unemployment has lasted the less chance there is of escaping from it'.[110] Possibly a sympathetic URO has here the chance to support unemployed workers in their search for a suitable job before the diffidence sets in, but there is also the danger that working outside the normal employment referral scheme the UROs are becoming a kind of second class employment exchange for unskilled manual labourers, or those who are deemed to be in that category. In the drive to place workers, including the married and skilled, the URO's work may be counter-productive in the long-term. As the Oxford study shows, the lower down the occupational scale a worker is classified, the more intense the competition is for a limited number of jobs.[111] The evidence of claimants and their advisers is that all too frequently they are pushed into taking 'any' job rather than the 'right' one. And this is exacerbated by an over-cautious classification of skills which then 'creates a self-fulfilling prophecy . . . [and] downgrading may turn a difficult situation into an impossible one'.[112]

Compounding the difficulties of classification among the unemployed is the high incidence of ill-health and disability among the long-term unemployed. Many clearly need prolonged medical care and reconditioning to make them fully employable, and the Oxford study comments that 'many of the elderly unemployed are in practice "pensioners" who have been forced to retire early, while the disabled men on the register are sometimes only there because they refuse to give up hope of getting work and join the "sick list"'.[113] It would seem to serve nobody's interest to have someone who is unemployed because of an industrial injury (or even an accident at home) pushed into a menial job with little chance of regaining his former classification and occupation. Conversely, many sick or disabled workers are capable of doing some kind of work, though not their usual work, and special work under medical supervision may often be the best way to help them back to full capacity. A more flexible approach has undoubtedly been taken in recent years, but a considerable amount of imagination, determination and money needs to be injected into the rehabilitation and training services before they can properly cope with the problems.

If the UROs can see their role as a referral agency rather than as disciplinarians, then it is argued that the drive to push marginal workers into employment may well be seen as unnecessary as well as demeaning. There is certainly evidence to show that workers in dull tedious unsuitable jobs come to regard unemployment as a temporary respite from the difficulties of the marginal work situation.[114] British practice has certainly not been as predatory as is, for example, the case in the United States, where State Welfare Agencies may suddenly declare a period of 'full employment', or just announce 'budget cuts', and then stop all welfare payments to the unemployed. This occurs regularly in many localities at harvest time, where there is agricultural 'stoop' labour available, or it may simply be an attempt to push men into 'work programmes' such as cleaning courthouse washrooms or picking up gum wrappers in city parks.[115]

Qualitatively, it is sometimes difficult to see the distinction between such obviously humiliating devices and the more refined approach of the S.B.C. Much of the difficulty is simply that we have so little information about the psychological motivation and condition of welfare claimants on a broad scale, and even less about the effects of social security mechanisms on their perception of employment and unemployment. However, even a National Assistance Board survey in 1956 concluded after a useful, although insufficiently detailed, study that 'wilful idleness as distinct from an understandable lack of keenness arising from physical or mental disability or other causes would seem to account for the lengthy unemployed in very few cases indeed'.[116] And despite the seemingly ever-present mythology of the 'work shy'—for example, the former Secretary of State, Sir Keith Joseph, stated when he appointed the Fisher Committee that it 'would be after the layabouts and work shirkers'[117]—it is clear that extremely complex social mechanisms are involved.

Dependants' allowances mean that for some married men there is little or sometimes no differential between their income through benefits and any wage they could normally expect. Yet unemployment studies contradict accepted folklore in that married men with children are the least likely to stay out of employment for long.[118] This whole question points again to the inadequacy of family allowances which the Government may hopefully rectify somewhat in its Child Benefit proposals; as Barbara Wootton has stated in relation to dependants allowances, 'children do not spring into existence when their father falls sick or out of work and vanish when he returns to work: to provide for them in emergencies is only to call attention to the absurdity of ignoring them at other times'.[119] Social and personal factors, including religious views, are sometimes more important than economic controls in determining such questions. For, as Professor Townsend points out,

> The structure of society exerts powerful constraints on men both to work and to adjust to different types and earnings-levels of work. A man works to preserve the respect of his wife, children, friends and neighbours, to fulfil the psychological needs induced by the customs and expectations of a life-time and to occupy time fruitfully and replenish the stock of information, cautionary tales and anecdotes which he requires to maintain his participation in the web of social relations.[120]

It is perhaps remarkable, and a powerful commentary on human personality, that in an economic situation where frequently low wage earners could gain more by 'living on the dole', it is clear that only a small fraction attempt to do so.

NOTES

1. Tony Lynes, *Welfare Rights* (1969), p. 5.

2. s. 4, Supplementary Benefit Act 1966 (hereafter referred to as 'SB Act 1966'); s. 8 excludes persons in full-time employment by reference to National Insurance regulations.

3. Under s. 7 SB Act 1966.

4. The Long Term Addition, formerly given to pensioners and others under pensionable age but not required to register for work, after a period of two years, was included in the basic scale rates from October 1973.

5. See the precise sectors of calculation on the reverse side of the S.B.C. form, the B/O 22.

6. para. 25(1), Schedule 2, SB Act 1966. However, death and maternity grants are 'wholly disregarded'. para. 20, Schedule 2, SB Act 1966. The reason for this is that they are lump sums designed to meet a specific need over and above daily income needed for subsistence.

7. para. 19, Schedule 2, SB Act 1966. The exact rationale for this group of disregards is somewhat curious; for example, the section

—presumably for patriotic reasons—includes a disregard on any sums payable to holders of the Victoria Cross or George Cross; para. 20(c), Schedule 2, SB Act 1966.

8. s. 11 and para. 4, Schedule 3, Social Security Benefits Act 1975. Rules for computing 'net weekly earnings' are contained in reg. 4(2), The Supplementary Benefit (General) Regs. (1966) SI 1966 No. 1065. See also para. 24, Schedule 2, SB Act 1966.

9. 'Dwelling', however is not defined; para. 19, Schedule 2, SB Act 1966.

10. See Jo Tunnard, 'Mortgages and Supplementary Benefit', Legal Action Group *Bulletin* (1975), p. 184, and Clare Whately, 'More on Mortgages and SB', Legal Action Group *Bulletin* (1975), p. 237.

11. As from November 1975, each £50 amount of capital above £1,200 is reckoned by the S.B.C. as yielding 25 pence which is a considerable improvement on the previously existing rate of 5 per cent for capital resources over £300 and 12 per cent for capital over £800; the Social Security Benefits Act 1975 (Commencement No. 2) Order (1975) SI 1975 No. 1336, activating s. 11 and paras. 2 and 3 of Schedule 3, Social Security Benefits Act 1975.

12. D.H.S.S., *Annual Report 1970* (1971), p. 350: 51,000 claimants were assessed at having over £800, which included a majority (43,000) over retirement age.

13. See, for example, *R.* v. *West London Supplementary Benefits Appeal Tribunal ex parte Taylor, The Times* (13 May 1975) and *K.* v. *JMP Co.* [1975] 1 All E.R. 1032. See generally, Henry Hodge, 'Income or Capital?', Legal Action Group *Bulletin* (1975), p. 158, and Notes on 'Tax and Welfare Benefit Planning', Legal Action Group *Bulletin* (1975), pp. 209–12, 240–4.

14. *Supplementary Benefits Handbook* (1974), p. 12.

15. Cf. advice and planning for the avoidance of tax liabilities. In one case before a Supplementary Benefits Appeal Tribunal observed by the author, an elderly couple who had sold their house, and were now living in a thatched cottage using the balance to effect repairs, were told by the Chairman to come back and see the S.B.C. in a year's time as by then their tariff cut-off would have been considerably reduced by expenditure on the cottage. No one, however, advised them immediately to 'plough back' their resources into the property so as to gain benefit. It should nevertheless be noted that 'planning' of income in such circumstances cannot extend to deliberate abandonment of property such as, for example, by giving it away; the S.B.C.'s wide power of review in such cases is contained in para. 27, Schedule 2, SB Act 1966.

16. Generally those in the all-embracing 'casual labourer' category; see M. J. Hill, R. M. Harrison, A. V. Sargeant and V. Talbot, *Men Out of Work* (1973).

17. para. 4(2), the Supplementary Benefit (General) Regs. (1966) SI 1966 No. 1065. There is a similar long-stop clause relating to all disregards in that 'any resources not specified in the preceding provisions of this Schedule may be treated as reduced by such amount (if any) as may be reasonable in all the circumstances of the case', para. 26, Schedule 2, SB Act 1966.

18. See later at p. 175.

19. *Report of a Committee on Social Insurance and Allied Services* (1942), H.M.S.O. Cmd. 6404, para 27.

20. The Unemployment Assistance (Determination of Need and Assessment of Needs) Regs. (1934) S.R. & O. 1936 No. 776. See generally for a full discussion, p. 167.

21. See Donald S. Howard, *The WPA and the Federal Relief Policy* (1943).

22. See generally for an account of British schemes at the start of the century, José Harris, *Unemployment and Politics* (1973).

23. Tony Lynes, *The Penguin Guide to Supplementary Benefits* (1972), p. 35. See generally, Tony Lynes, *National Assistance and National Prosperity* (1961) and Brian Abel-Smith and Peter Townsend, *The Poor and the Poorest* (1965).

24. para. 9(b), Schedule 2, SB Act 1966.

25. *Supplementary Benefits Handbook* (1974), p. 15.

26. Quoted in Laurie Elks, 'Householders', *New Society*, **31**, No. 640, (9 January 1975), p. 70.

27. See Julian Fulbrook, *The Appellant and his Case: The Appellant's View of Supplementary Benefit Appeal Tribunals* (Child Poverty Action Group, 1975) p. 10. See also generally, Stuart Weir, 'Householders, Non-Householders and Boarders', Legal Action Group *Bulletin* (1974), p. 181.

28. *R.* v. *Sheffield Supplementary Benefits Appeal Tribunal ex parte Shine* [1975] 1 W.L.R. 624, at 631. See later discussion at p. 298.

29. *Supplementary Benefits Handbook* (1974), p. 15.

30. *Report of a Committee on Social Insurance and Allied Services* (1942), *op. cit.*, para. 217.

31. This is of course not the view of everyone; see, for example, the opinions of members of the Institute of Economic Affairs in Rhodes Boyson (ed.), *Down with the Poor* (1971). See for contrasting views to the I.E.A. approach, the various publications of the Child Poverty Action Group, including the periodic *Poverty*. See also for a 'grass roots' viewpoint, Tony Gould and Joe Kenyon, *Stories from the Dole Queue* (1972) and Mervyn Jones, *Life on the Dole* (1972).

32. *Report of a Committee on Social Insurance and Allied Services* (1942), para. 202.

33. *ibid.*, para. 213.

34. By regulation in 1943: 'add the net rent payable so far as is reasonable in view of the general level of rents in the locality'; para. 1(2)(a), Schedule 1, The Assistance (Determination of Need and Assessment of Needs) Regs. (1943) SI 1943 No. 1759.

35. As did so many other existing practices; Schedule 1, The National Assistance (Determination of Need) Regs. (1948) SI 1948 No. 1334.

36. para. 4(1)(a) The National Assistance (Determination of Need) Regs. (1959) SI 1959 No. 1241.

37. The Report suggested two reasons for such a reduction: firstly, where 'satisfactory evidence of the true amount is not forthcoming', and secondly, where 'a rent, which is not excessive in an aboslute sense may nevertheless be considered to be unreasonable in relation to the kind of accommodation provided'; *Annual Report of the N.A.B.* (1962) H.M.S.O. Cmnd. 2078, pp. 22–3. See also Walter Merricks, 'Furnished or Unfurnished?', Legal Action Group *Bulletin* (1973), p. 94, and Laurie Elks, 'Supplementary Benefit and the Rent Stop', Legal Action Group *Bulletin* (1974), p. 134.

38. *Supplementary Benefits Handbook* (1972), p. 15.

39. para. 13, Schedule 2, SB Act 1966. An extra allowance is made for expenses connected with sub-letting, varying from 90 pence per week, where the accommodation is furnished and light and heat are provided, to 15 pence a week for unfurnished and unserviced accommodation; *Supplementary Benefits Handbook* (1974), p. 17. This hardly seems much of an incentive if the aim is to alleviate housing shortage.

40. para. 13(2), Schedule 2, SB Act 1966. 'Dependence' is not defined, and seems not to include emotional dependence; see Julian Fulbrook, 'How the Means Test brought Tragedy to the Phillips's Home', *Tribune* **36**, No. 35, (1 September 1972), p. 1.

41. See s. 11 Rent Act 1974; s. 16(2) and para. 15, Schdule 2, SB Act 1966. See generally, Laurie Elks, 'Rent Rebates and Allowances—Some Legal Problems', Legal Action Group *Bulletin* (1975), p. 233.

42. See generally, Molly Meacher, *Rate Rebates* (CPAG 1972).

43. David Donnison, 'Dear David Bull . . . ', *Social Work Today* **6** (1975), p. 622.

44. *Final Report of the Royal Commission on Unemployment Insurance* (1932), H.M.S.O. Cmd. 4185, p. 133.

45. para. 3, The National Assistance (Determination of Need) Regs. (1948) SI 1948 No. 1334.

46. para. 6, *ibid.*

47. D.H.S.S., *Annual Report 1974* (1975), H.M.S.O. Cmnd. 6150, p. 31. There were 743,000 exceptional needs payments in 1972, and 560,000 in 1970; D.H.S.S. *Annual Report 1972* (1973), H.M.S.O. Cmnd. 5160, p. 31, and D.H.S.S. *Annual Report 1970* (1971), H.M.S.O. Cmnd. 4174, p. 95.

48. See generally S.B.C., *Exceptional Needs Payments* (1973), para. 5, D.H.S.S., *Families Receiving Supplementary Benefit* (1972), pp. 43–9, and Laurie Elks, 'Exceptional Need', *New Society* **33**, No. 665, p. 23.

49. *Supplementary Benefits Handbook* (1974), pp. 19–20. See also para. 4(1), Schedule 2, SB Act 1966, for upward adjustment 'where there are special circumstances'.

50. Under powers in para. 4(2)(a), Schdule 2, SB Act 1966.

51. See the extraordinary letter by the Principal Information Officer of the S.B.C. in which the 1966 statute is preferred to its subsequent judicial interpretation in the Queen's Bench Division; *New Society* **24**, (14 June 1973), p. 636. See generally, *R.* v. *Greater Birmingham Appeal Tribunal, ex p. Simper* [1973] 2 All E.R. 461, an order of certiorari to quash a Supplementary Benefit Appeal Tribunal's decision that an exceptional circumstances addition of 35 pence should be automatically set off against the award of a Long Term Addition, on a construction of the 1966 Act. The Court consisted of the Lord Chief Justice, Lord Widgery, Cusack and Croom-Johnson JJ.

52. para. 4(2), Schedule 4, National Insurance and Supplementary Benefits Act 1973.

54. *Supplementary Benefits Handbook* (1974), p. 20.

55. *ibid.*, p. 21. This is £1.12 a week in most cases. See generally, Tony Lynes, *The Penguin Guide to Supplementary Benefits* (1972), pp. 74–82.

56. s. 7 SB Act 1966.

57. para. 6, Schedule 2, SB Act 1966.

58. *Supplementary Benefits Handbook* (1974), p. 26.

59. s. 14 SB Act 1966 allows payment of benefits in kind. See also *Supplementary Benefits Handbook* (1974), p. 27.

60. Howard Glennerster, *National Assistance, Service or Charity?* (1962), p. 21.

61. See for a classic study on workmen's compensation and sickness benefit fraud, Sir John Collie, *Malingering and Feigned Sickness* (1913).

62. Although 'cohabitation' is a control which sometimes affects unemployed women, its impact is normally on women who are not required to register for work under s. 11 SB Act 1966. For a full study of the cohabitation rule in social security law, see Ruth Lister, *As Man and Wife?* (1973).

63. See para. 2, Supplementary Benefit (General) Amendment Regs. (1975) SI 1975 No. 1335. See also s. 19 Child Benefit Act 1975.

64. See generally for figures of preceding years, Hansard 870, H. C. Deb. (22 March 1974), Cols. 211–13 and (11 July 1974).

65. para 5, Schedule 2, SB Act 1966.

66. In one sample, six out of eleven families 'wage-stopped' fell into this 'invisible' catetory; see Adrian Sinfield, 'Poor and Out of Work in Shields' in Peter Townsend (ed.), *The Concept of Poverty* (1970), p. 233.

67. See generally, Ruth Lister, *The Administration of the Wage Stop* (1972), a study of 18 wage-stopped families. See for the annual rates, *Circular No NM 207, National Joint Council for Local Authorities' Services*. See also Laurie Elks, *The Wage Stop: Poor by Order* (1974), p. 15.

68. Published by the S.B.C., *The Administration of the Wage Stop* (1967), para. 45; this was a survey which involved visiting fifty-two families to discover 'what living on the wage stop meant in everyday terms . . . the general impression derived from the visits was not so much one of grinding poverty in any absolute sense as one of unrelieved dreariness with, in some cases, little hope of improvement in the future'. Cf. the CPAG survey of eighteen wage-stopped families which found 'more than just "dreariness" . . . evidence of considerable financial hardship and in most cases very real deprivation'; Ruth Lister, *op. cit.*, p. 7.

69. *ibid.*, para. 4.

70. Quoted in Laurie Elks, *op. cit.*, p.10.

71. s. 10 SB Act 1966. See generally, *Supplementary Benefits and Trade Disputes*, D.H.S.S. Leaflet SB2 on strikers' benefits.

72. *Supplementary Benefits Handbook* (1972), p. 37.

73. Under s. 18 SB Act 1966. The phrase in the 1974 edition is now 'corresponds closely'.

74. s. 13 SB Act 1966.

75. See the discussion in *Labour Research* (1971) **LX**, p. 88, where a headline from the *Sunday Telegraph* ('£16 benefit for postmen'), with a following comment that a married postman with four children received over £16 weekly while on strike, is analysed: 'It happens that such a striker *could* get over £16 Supplementary Benefit, but only if his four children were sixteen-year-old quadruplets still at school'. *ibid.*, p. 89. See also Tony Lynes, 'Taxing Strikers' Savings', *New Society* (4 March 1971). For another viewpoint, see Robin Page in Rhodes Boyson (ed.), *op. cit.*, p. 26: 'for a number of years the striker, so far from facing financial hardship and embarrassment during a strike, actually receives substantial financial featherbedding from the State in the form of tax-free cash benefits'.

76. See Richard Hyman, 'Living with Strikes', *New Society*, **26**, No. 577 (25 Octtober 1973), p. 204.

77. The Bill was proposed by Ralph Howell, Conservative MP for Norfolk North. The Bill failed to obtain a Second Reading. See for a discussion of its proposals, Judith Reid, *Industrial Law Journal* (1973), p. 111. See generally, the Society of Conservative Lawyers' pamphlet, *Financing Strikes* (Conservative Political Centre 1974).

78. *Hansard*, **883**, H. C. Deb. (10 December 1974), col 223.

79. *Hansard* **883**, H. C. Deb. (10 December 1974), col. 225, for tables on the amounts from 1964–73.

80. Richard Hyman, *op. cit.*, p. 205.

81. See Roger Lasko, 'The Payment of Supplementary Benefit for Strikers' Dependants—Misconception and Misrepresentation', *Modern Law Review* **38**, (1975), p. 31.

82. See earlier for the Donovan Commission figures at p. 21. See generally, John Gennard and Roger Lasko, 'Supplementary Benefit and the Striker', *British Journal of Industrial Relations* **12**, (1974), p. 1, and Armand J. Thieblot and Ronald M. Cowin, *Welfare and Strikes: The Use of Public Funds to Support Strikers* (1972), a Wharton School of Business study which takes an unsympathetic view to anyone in a striker's family receiving any benefit from a Government agency.

83. *Supplementary Benefits Handbook* (1974), p. 45.

84. para. 11, Schedule 2, SB Act 1966 inserted by s. 1(2) Social Security Act 1971.

85. *Supplementary Benefits Handbook* (1974), p. 52.

86. D.H.S.S. *Annual Report 1968* (1969), p. 251. See for a discussion of the Labour Government's attitude, Michael Hill, 'Selecttivity for the Poor', in Peter Townsend and Nicholas Bosanquet (ed.), *Labour and Inequality* (1972), p. 239 *et seq.*

87. D.H.S.S. *Annual Report 1968* (1969), pp. 251–2.

88. Molly Meacher, *Scrounging on the Welfare: The Scandal of the Four Week Rule* (1974), p. 39.

89. *ibid.*, pp. 45, 62, 66 and 116.

90. D.H.S.S. *Annual Report 1974* (1975), p. 32. See generally, Chris Smith, '"Abolition" of the four-week rule', *Industrial Law Journal* (1975), p. 249, who believes that the only change to the claimant will be the absence of the B663 Form warning him of a cut-off after four weeks; *ibid.*, p. 251.

91. *Supplementary Benefits Handbook* (1974), p. 53.

92. *Report of the Committee on Abuse of Social Security Benefits* (1973), H.M.S.O., Cmnd. 5228, para. 262.

93. Tony Lynes, *Penguin Guide to Supplementary Benefits* (1972), p. 142.

94. See *Report on the Committee on Abuse of Social Security Benefits* (1973), H.M.S.O. Cmnd. 5228, pp. 107–8.

95. *ibid.*, p. 236.

96. D.H.S.S., *Annual Report 1974* (1975), p. 33.

97. In one Supplementary Benefits Appeal Tribunal hearing, where an appellant claimed that he did not deserve the four-week rule cut-off because he had never refused an offer of employment from the employment exchange, the S.B.C. Presenting Officer's response was: 'Oh, they are quite happy to let these kind of people sit around and just draw benefit'; Julian Fulbrook, *The Appellant and his Case* (CPAG), p. 10.

98. D.H.S.S., *Annual Report 1972* (1973), p. 121.

99. D.H.S.S., *Annual Report 1974* (1975), p. 33.

100. See later for the law of removal p. 90; Julian Fulbrook, *op cit.*, p. 12. See also Jeremy Bugler, 'Workshy, eh?', *New Society*, **12**, No. 323 (5 December 1968), p. 842, and the subsequent letter from Professor Titmuss, at that time Vice-Chairman of the S.B.C., *New Society*, **12**, No. 324 (12 December 1968), p. 891.

101. Frank Field, 'Four Week murder', *New Society*, **27**, No. 587 (3 January 1974), p. 19. This is backed up by Molly Meacher's study, where 12 per cent of her sample committed crimes for the first time in their lives because of the rule; *op. cit.*, p. 76.

102. Michael J. Hill, 'Policies towards the Unemployed', *Social Work Today*, **6** (1975), p. 390.

103. para 4(1)(b) Sched. 2, SB Act 1966.

104. *Supplementary Benefits Handbook* (1974), p. 52.

105. One appellant in the CPAG survey, whose husband had left her was 'ordered' to take a shop assistant's job, although she possessed A levels. She reluctantly agreed under pressure to 'try it out', while insisting that she wanted 'something more long-term'. When she left the job as 'utterly impossible' after a day, she was declared by the S.B.C. to have 'voluntarily left employment without just cause' and immediately suspended from benefit; this would last, she was informed by the visiting officer, until such time as she took action against her husband for maintenance; Julian Fulbrook, *op. cit.*, p. 15.

106. Under s. 30 SB Act 1966.

107. Quoted in Olive Stevenson, *Claimant or Client?* (1973), p. 121.

108. Pilgrim Trust Report, *Men Without Work* (1938), p. 173.

109. M. J. Hill, R. M. Harrison, A. V. Sargeant and V. Talbot, *Men Out of Work* (1973), p. 74.

110. Adrian Sinfield, *The Long-Term Unemployed* (1968), pp. 16, 80.

111. M. J. Hill *et al.*, *op. cit.*, p. 148.

112. M. J. Hill *et al.*, *op. cit.*, p. 136.

113. M. J. Hill *et al.*, *op. cit.*, p. 140.

114. M. J. Hill *et al.*, *op. cit.*, p. 5.

115. For extreme work controls in a racist environment, see U.S. Commission on Civil Rights, *Welfare in Mississippi* (1969), at p. 132

and elsewhere. See also for discriminatory welfare practices of an earlier era, Gunnar Myrdal, *An American Dilemma* (1944), pp. 359–60.

116. *Annual Report of the N.A.B. for 1956* (1957), p. 72. See also on the physical deterioration of the unemployed. Sir John Collie, *Fraud in Medico-Legal Practice* (1932), p. 32.

117. *Report of the Committee on Abuse of Social Security Benefits* (1973), p. 93.

118. See for commentary on American studies, Eveline M. Burns, *Social Security and Public Policy* (1956), p. 58, and for a British study, M. J. Hill *et al.*, *op cit.*, pp. 54–5.

119. Barbara Wootton, 'The Impact of Income Security upon Individual Freedom', in James E. Russell (ed.), *National Policies for Education, Health and Social Services* (1955) p. 392.

120. Peter Townsend, *Social Services for All?* (1968), p. 27. See also a follow-up survey of the workers made redundant by Rolls Royce; Dorothy Wedderburn, 'Working and Not Working', *The Listener* **87**, (25 May 1972) pp. 669–71.

4

The Administrative Machinery

The administrative system determining social security benefits in Britain has been described by Professor Marsh as 'an Administrative Juggernaut'.[1] Certainly the size of the machinery involved in the determination and payment of claims is that of a heavy industry. And yet in practical terms of the impact on individual claims, this administrative process has as much if not more to do with the amount of benefit given to welfare clients as with the character of the substantive law or the appeal tribunal process, for it is a truism that the effectiveness of any law is determined by the quality and nature of its administration.

With 900 local offices of the Department of Health and Social Security and nearly 1,000 of the Department of Employment directly utilized in this process, the total number of D.H.S.S. staff employed is over 76,000, with a central headquarters at Newcastle employing over 10,000 workers. About 12,500 staff are employed by the Department of Employment to deal with unemployment insurance matters.[2] Every insured person is the subject of an individual ledger sheet in the Newcastle complex, representing 38 million ledgers.[3] Approximately one million 'deficiency notices' are sent out each quarter requesting payment. Full accounts of contributions paid or credited are kept by means of a computer in the Graduated Records Branch, and each day some 30,000 to 120,000 'shuttle cards' are received from local offices requesting individual contribution details. The enormous daily variation in this figure depends on such transient factors as influenza epidemics. The bureaucratic problems connected with this system are immense; for example, over 600,000 index slips are registered in the name of 'Smith'. But the Supplementary Benefits system, which has to assess each individual claim on the basis of need and without help from a computer checking contribution records, is no less complex. In 1974, the S.B.C. dealt with nearly 5 million separate claims,[4] and the insurance side of the D.H.S.S. with 16 million claims, of which 3,221,000

For notes see p. 75

were for unemployment benefits.[5] In any one week, the average total number of all welfare benefits and allowances paid is approximately 18 million. In 1974 the total annual cost of all benefits was about £6,929 millions, of which £360 millions went on all Supplementary Benefits awards and £380 millions on National Insurance awards other than for retirement pensioners. The cost of administering the D.H.S.S. schemes in 1974 was about £270 millions, which represents a fairly rapid increase in recent years, although this is partly due to inflation; nevertheless the figure still remains less than 5 per cent of the total budget.[6]

However, despite the scale of these operations, the critical test of the efficiency of any welfare scheme is at the point of contact between claimant and administrator. It is hardly surprising that, given the enormous work load, and the obvious need for routinization, 'a local Supplementary Benefits office is organisationally more akin to a factory production line than to a social work department'.[7] Unfortunately, as in any large bureaucratic organization, this mass production philosophy may occasionally spill over from the way administrative problems are tackled to the way in which claimants are dealt with, although it is the stated aim of the D.H.S.S. that 'all the Department's staff [should] be humane, helpful and sympathetic when dealing with people'.[8]

Opinion on whether this standard is achieved is of course largely subjective. Almost by definition, the welfare machinery of any country deals with clients undergoing some degree of emotional disturbance, whether this is due to acute poverty, unemployment, illness or bereavement. Certain critics, such as members of the Claimants' Union, view the 'S.S.' as a large-scale Establishment conspiracy, whose operations are 'designed to keep working people under control and underpin the system's low wage levels . . . harassment, discrimination and intimidation are inherent in a system of means-tested benefits'.[9] Collecting the information necessary to administer a welfare system partly based on a personal means test will perhaps inevitably involve some resentment on the part of the claimant, involving as it necessarily does 'an investigation into private business and the completing of complicated forms'.[10] However, the minimization of such resentment through the proper training of officials, and the adaptation of the administrative system itself, raise important questions of policy.

Personnel and Training

A primary question is the extent of power possessed by administrative officials. In a widely-quoted definition, Professor K. C. Davis has said that 'a public officer has discretion whenever the effective limits of his power leave him free to make a choice among possible courses of action'.[11] In such a light, what precisely is the nature of action for an individual officer in the social security framework? In insurance adjudication, the answer is probably very little. Certainly on the unemployment benefits side, the Insurance Officer's job is often regarded as routine in the sense that, if an official reads the circulars from Headquarters on recent Commissioners' decisions and Departmental policy, nothing much can go wrong.[12] In comparison with the prestige of Insurance Officers dealing with sickness and industrial injuries benefit, both of whom are based in the local D.H.S.S. office, the Insurance Officer dealing with unemployment claims is often perceived to be of a lower rank. Yet in terms of Professor Davis's definition, the unemployment Insurance Officer has as much power and because of the nature and number of cases he gets, often more scope for its exercise. Possibly the isolated position of the unemployment Insurance Officer is not conducive to interest in the job, and this is not helped by the fairly rapid changeover of personnel. Difficult cases can and often will be referred to Regional Insurance Officers, who have a considerable impact on policy by contact on individual cases and at regional conferences of Insurance Officers. The National Headquarters' staff similarly lay down extensive policy guidelines through loose-leaf folder supplements interpreting or pointing out Commissioners' decisions and new legislation.

Such clear-cut hierarchies of authority are more difficult to perceive in the more diffuse administration of Supplementary Benefits. It is often stated that in insurance adjudication there is very little room for manoeuvre, but any acquaintance with Supplementary Benefits in practice shows that its much vaunted 'discretion' is in most cases strictly controlled by a legalistic web of internal policy regulations. It is interesting to note here that, when asked, Insurance Officers make available Commissioners' decisions supporting a disqualification to claimants visiting the office, and a number will often show policy directives too if appropriate, although these are often simply an analysis of Commissioners' decisions tied in with the administrative intake procedure. No S.B.C. officer can of course show the written instructions on which his decision is based, other than possibly a reference to the imprecise *Supplementary Benefits Handbook*, which few claimants will possess or have the money to buy.

However, as in any intake process, the nature of S.B.C. interviewing and home visit enquiry can have a considerable effect on defining the original nature and scope of a claim, for example, in notifying the claimant of the possibility of a claim for Exceptional Needs Payments.

It is here that S.B.C. officers have their greatest opportunities for creativity. Unfortunately, this is also the area where, without a standard checklist to work through and report back on, there is some possibility for abuse and domination. The BO/40 clothing list only covers a small part of the interview process, and there is evidence too that its use is by no means automatic. In one study on the take-up of Exceptional Needs payments, the failure of Visiting Officers to itemise all possible sources of help meant that 'ignorance was an effective rationing device'.[13] Home visiting is often the crucial point at which benefit is assessed, although visits are also used to review ongoing allowances, to investigate changes in situation, and as a check on suspected fraud. In theory, these visits have both an 'assessment' and a 'welfare' function under the 1966 Act,[14] although the case-load involved means that little time can be spent on anything but a cursory examination of the claimant's needs and circumstances. Approximately 8 million home visits are made annually, and each Visiting Officer is expected to make from six to ten such visits in a working day, often covering a wide 'territory'. Consent is of course necessary on the part of the claimant before any entry can be made, but the knowledge that the Visiting Officer has the power to withdraw order books or deny benefit makes this consent notional. Again, by definition, welfare recipients are in a dependency situation, often desperately needing benefits and not able to take the risk of offending an S.B.C. officer. As Professor de Schweinitz pointed out, 'even where there is no conscious intent to dictate behaviour to the beneficiary, the pervasive power of money dispensed under the means test may cause the slightest suggestion to have the effects of compulsion'.[15] One partial answer here may be to attempt to get rid of home visits as far as is possible; for example, telephones should be installed free for those claimants who have serious difficulty reaching the local office, but who do not fall under the provisions of the Chronically Sick and Disabled Act. At present telephone installation is possible through the mechanism of an Exceptional Needs Payment, but this is only when it is needed as a 'lifeline'; such difficulties as poor transportation and lack of facilities for child care should also be included. Every claimant should also be asked as a matter of course when it would be convenient for a first home visit, if this is necessary to check items such as bedding or furniture. Automatic issuance of a checklist of possible claims would, it is suggested, make this whole area of operation more congenial and effective.

However, the difficulties on the part of the Visiting Officer performing such a task should not be minimized, and in situations calling for extreme diplomacy and tact, it is hardly surprising that criticism occurs. British experience of welfare officers 'having a look round' in contravention of basic privacy is on the whole probably better than comparable systems, although in the United States what was previously a deplorable situation has in some areas been somewhat changed by the internal administrative directives of Welfare Departments, caused by a fear of litigation from capable neighbourhood attorneys funded under the Legal Services Programme.[16] To make visiting an effective check on fraud within the present structure, and yet to respect individual rights of privacy, is probably in the final analysis an impossible task.

However, further criticism has been made of the analytical approach of Visiting Officers to the task which, despite their training including a course on 'human relations', seems often to amount to little more than an attempt at a Victorian-style delineation between the 'deserving and the 'undeserving'. A 1971 newspaper investigation reproduced an extract from D.H.S.S. form B6A on which examining officers make a diagnosis on a standard list whose lowest appraisal is 'workshy'.[17] Olive Stevenson, the former Social Worker to the S.B.C., while rejecting what she regards as antiquated notions of 'deserving' clients, has nevertheless called for a considerably greater use of social work techniques in welfare administration, believing that 'the problems of some individuals are so interwined as to make a total separation of financial from other social services not only impracticable but undesirable if their welfare is to be genuinely safeguarded'.[18] Facing up to the possibilities for social control implicit in welfare administration, and particularly where home visits are made, she believes that it should be used in controlled circumstances to obtain what she terms 'socially desirable behaviour' by 'bargaining' on 'extras', and that awareness and open discussion of such powers will prevent exploitation of welfare clients. Her proposal is that 'certain officials, suitably selected, trained and deployed [should be] given designated responsibility to co-operate with social workers on matters involving the exercise of discretion—*positive* and *negative*—in relation to the social worker's clients'.[19]

Perhaps it depends on one's personal orientation, but such a view seems anachronistically coercive. It also has echoes of the failure of what can be described as the Kennedy Administration policy of the early 1960s, which was that the answer to most welfare administration problems was to inject more 'social work' and more trained personnel. Unfortunately, changing welfare phrases such as 'interviewing' to 'budget counselling designed to improve family functioning', meant little change to the system, except to increase its coercive possibilities. The traditional Poor Law view, that fear of starvation was an essential weapon of industrial and social discipline, has, according to Professor Handler, its modern equivalent in a social work approach to welfare administration, where there is manipulation of clients, leading to 'an ingratiating, embarrassing type of dependency'.[20]

Much of the criticism of introducing more social work concepts into welfare administration is that this may mean more 'Freudian' pseudo-psychoanalysis by amateurs in an attempt to find, as in many parts of the United States, the 'real reasons' behind a welfare claim, other than poverty. Olive Stevenson counters that American experience is poor because case workers are 'not fully qualified professionally'.[21] However, it is interesting to contrast this with an American lament that only 4 per cent of caseworkers in public assistance programmes have M.A. degrees in Social Work;[22] a standard qualification in many states is that caseworkers possess a degree with a major in Social Work. What is a more cogent point is that even where social workers are 'fully qualified professionally', they often appear unduly judgemental, which can be ascribed more to the nature of their training than to the lack of it.[23]

It would seem that in many welfare systems sub-psychological categorization has euphemistically replaced the old analytical approach of deserving and undeserving, and even Olive Stevenson deplores the frequent use in home visit reports of the omnibus term 'inadequate'.[24] Similar comments could be made about other common jargon, such as 'emotional disturbance', 'the problem family', 'the female-centred family', or, as Richard Elman points out, 'the poor man's propensity toward schizophrenia, which reduces our common human squalor to an exotic psychological squalor defined by class'.[25] A New York City Department of Welfare survey in 1962, done by the caseworkers themselves, diagnosed over 60 per cent of its caseload as 'emotionally disturbed'.[26] Because of such difficulties, a number of American commentators, including Elman, who object to larding the payment of benefits with social work analysis, point to the British system as a model for non-judgemental courtesy and efficiency!

Olive Stevenson is probably right in her analysis that a complete divorce of the welfare administration of benefits and social work expertise would be counter-productive to those clients who might be channelled, for example, towards psychiatric help. Her own attempts to ensure that S.B.C. officers know what referral services are available to them are a valuable contribution, although this author would object if they became part of the 'extras' to be 'bargained' over. Unfortunately, there is reason to believe that what passes for 'social work' in the British system still, despite the efforts of the Commission and its Social Work Adviser, consists largely of 'some very rudimentary attempts at amateur psychology' as in the Parris case, where a claimant obtained her confidential S.B.C. file and passed it to the National Council for Civil

Liberties to publicise. One editorial commentator thought that

> The whole dossier reveals a general hostility and doubt towards claimants, which can only add to the stress that many are under because of poverty. But one is finally left chiefly with the thought of what a waste of staff time is represented by all these psycho-analytic sessions, fruitless unnotified visits and detailed observations of the irrelevant.[27]

Most comments on welfare administration centre on the question of abuse. It often seems that a person's view on whether welfare benefits should be expanded is determined by their view of how much claimant fraud there is. Virtually no research has been done on the quantity or quality of abuse in the British system, and the terms of the Fisher Committee were specifically geared to an examination of abuse controls and not abuse itself.[28] Molly Meacher's study on the four-week rule rule and her analysis of D.H.S.S. surveys in 1969, 1970 and 1971 mentioned in the Fisher Report, show that the amount of abuse is probably less than one per cent; she notes wryly that a 1971 survey on undiscovered over-payment cost eight times the amount initially overpaid. It is also perhaps sobering to note that the Exchequer reclaimed nearly £94 millions in the decade 1963–72 after illegal evasion of full payment of tax, as opposed to an estimated £3 millions overpaid to Supplementary Benefit recipients in the same period either through negligence or by means of fraudulent claims.[29] Clearly the precise amount of fraud in any welfare system will depend on factors such as the efforts of administrators to man the system's checking devices and the malicious or negligent efforts of claimants to slip by those administrative defences. Administratively, the use of computers and improved filing systems has almost certainly reduced the extent of abuse on the insurance side in terms of benefits, although there are still many difficulties with contributions, shading off into questions of tax fraud.[30] In the Supplementary Benefits field, there has probably also been some tightening up due to increased administrative organisation and efficiency, although, as the Fisher Committee pointed out, there is room for improvement, particularly in the utilization of computer technology for rapid checking of repeat claims. However, care should be taken to subject expensive remedial devices or increases of special investigative manpower to full cost-benefit analysis; and as David Piachaud has pointed out, this should take into account any social costs involved, such as increased personnel anxiety among benefit recipients and 'the fact that people genuinely in need may be, and are, deterred from applying for benefits.[31]

Real problems exist in a needs testing system, however, of how regulations can be devised which will not, in the words of Professor Burns, 'expose people to irresistible temptations to profit at the public expense and how to do so without penalizing the vast majority of people of high initiative and strong work attachment in order to protect the system against marginal malingerers'.[32] However, in terms of the personal intent of claimants, we have virtually no information, and the prevailing social myths are based largely on conjecture. As a term, abuse embraces everything from claimants who tell deliberate lies in order to receive both wages and benefits simultaneously to those who honestly but blamelessly transgress the law; in other words, a spectrum of attitudes of mind from full *mens rea* to blameless inadvertence. American, studies, particularly those of Father Becker, indicate that the bulk of abuse may be in the latter category, but the information is highly incomplete.[33] In Britain, certain folkways are probably more responsible than malicious intent for the failure to disclose a wife's earnings, which is a common reason for a repayment order; in a CPAG study of fifty S.B.C. appellants, two cases of 'fraud' arose from a husband's patently honest confusion over the law and his belief that wives go out to work for their own 'pin-money' and not for the household budget.[34] Similar difficulties occur because of the common practice of not disclosing the amount of a pay packet, even to one's spouse.

Claiming at the counter, common to both National Insurance and Supplementary Benefit determination, is similarly a matter of complex personal and social factors, coupled usually with the difficulties of a 'bad' atmosphere, lengthy queues, poor seating and lighting, and an overworked staff who not unnaturally are occasionally hostile. With insurance claims, basic information on a checklist is taken down by the counter clerk and referred to the Insurance Officer who then makes a determination. This may involve investigation by, for example, telephoning the former employer in an unemployment case, and an interview with the claimant if there are special circumstances. If there is an adverse determination followed by an appeal, then the Insurance Officer will send out a standard form checklist letter to former employers to get full details on the reason for termination. On the Supplementary Benefits side, counter interviews are done by those in the Executive Officer grade supervising a number of Clerical Officers assigned to the 'caller' section. Following an initial claim, Territorial Executive Officers do a preliminary home visit in which an assessment of need and calculation of benefit is done; Clerical Officers make home visits for cases considered to be 'routine'. Unfortunately, staff shortages mean that many Clerical Officers are 'acting up' as Executive Officers without the higher pay or the necessary training.

Training of counter clerks in interviewing techniques is of course only part of a short course designed to familiarize them with a host of departmental and administrative regulations. Although recent innovations, such as the use of tape-recorders and video-tape to increase personal sensitivity, have considerably altered the traditional training method of standing behind an interviewer on the job,[35] many commentators both inside and outside Government service believe that much more should be done to equip a 'rater' before he starts to interview claimants on crucial questions which may affect their whole life-style. A considerable part of present training is by programmed learning using material referred to universally in the Departments as 'Noddy Books'. A Civil Service College exists to train managers of local offices of the Employment Service Agency and local social security offices, but the bulk of instruction is carried on at regional centres. Executive Officers, who form the major part of the executive staff, have generally a thirteen-weeks basic tutelage course, and a refresher course every two years. Clerical Officers have a three weeks course at the end of a ten-weeks tutelage period. For both grades, however, a preliminary period is spent at a local office 'on the job', and this initial exposure to attitudes, habits and methods not unnaturally plays a considerable part in shaping their view of the job and its requirements. As Professor Blau has pointed out in a classic study on the organization of a public employment office, 'when the section supervisor explained the work to a new interviewer . . . the procedures he described were quite different from those discussed in the training course'.[36]

Factors such as the adaptability (or non-adaptability) of certain staff members, and the huge turn-over in personnel,[37] all create extra difficulties; it must also be remembered that the poor promotion and pay prospects of this branch of the civil service are not conducive to the attraction of highly qualified or highly motivated officers. The tensions and dangers of the job should also not be underestimated; as one anonymous claimant stated in an article in *Poverty*,

> The strain of poverty allied to recognised or unrecognised emotional trouble in some claimants can cause a tense atmosphere in social security offices, and the acid tongued official runs the risk of getting his nose punched in the heat of the moment.[38]

As Olive Stevenson puts it, 'officials of the S.B.C. may not have chosen this field of work when entering the Civil Service and may find such contacts quite uncongenial', although elsewhere she writes that those who are enthusiastic to join the S.B.C. 'may be social workers manqué'.[39] In the long run perhaps more could be done for the improvement of the morale and standards of S.B.C. officials if selection was less random, rather than in upgrading training methods. This would of course depend on considerably brightening employment characteristics. As for the time spent on existing training, Olive Stevenson, who was actively involved while Social Work Adviser to the S.B.C., regards it as 'pitifully small in relation to the depth and complexity of the issues involved'.[40] She also warns that differences in perception between insiders and those outside with a professional orientation 'should be borne in mind when, as in the Commission's recent paper on cohabitation, references are made to "intensive training"'.[41]

Staff shortage is of course a permanent worry, and indeed it is not unknown for a claimant to be asked if he would like to apply for a job in the Department.[42] Possibly chronic staff shortage is partly due to the criticisms of 'excess bureaucracy' which would arise if there was adequate coverage; critics of the American system often point to the situation in New York where the ratio of welfare officials to welfare clients is far greater than the ratio of police to the general population. The Fisher Committee, following their lengthy investigation of the work of the D.H.S.S., summarized all these problems by stating that 'we have become painfully aware of the handicaps imposed on local office staffs by inadequate accommodation, shortage and rate of turnover of staff [and] the additional burdens created by changes in legislation'.[43] Until these burdens are lifted, no matter how willing welfare administrators are to assist their clients in a sympathetic courteous manner, such strains will continue to ensure less than quality service in the administration of benefits.

Physical facilities

Closely related to management problems in the welfare administration are, as we have seen, problems relating to cramped accommodation which leads to problems not just with personnel but also difficulties with the way clients entering social security offices perceive the system. A number of attempts have been made recently to alleviate the physical conditions of the counter situation by clearing up and brightening the surroundings. This policy is of course not helped by the pre-fabricated or converted nature of many D.H.S.S. and Department of Employment buildings; the Peterborough D.H.S.S. offices, for instance, consist of a converted billiard hall, a fact which is all too easily discernible.

It is important to realize that, although much of the following discussion centres on the poor image of S.B.C. offices, much the same criticisms are made by clients of Department of Employment premises. Over half of one sample of redundant workers agreed that their exchange was 'a place for layabouts'.[44] The result of this attitude has been that employers of professional workers do not notify such jobs to the Employment Service Agency, and as a result such workers do not approach the agency for help. The Department of Employment has attempted to break out of its 'Labour Exchange' syndrome with a register for professional jobs and the payment of benefit through the post, but many inside the service feel that there should be a total break from the original Beveridge 1911 structure where unemployment benefits and an employment service are part of the same administrative system.[45] This, its proponents urge, would ensure that professional and middle-range jobs would be channelled through the public registries rather than being diluted into the separate files of the various private agencies. However, as Michael Hill has pointed out, the concentration on a new image and the 'Job Centres' purely concerned with placement, may mean that 'the traditional clientele of the service are to be regarded as some sort of handicap'.[46]

A *New Society* editorial in 1971 criticized 'labour exchanges' [*sic*] as being 'dingy, depressing and inconveniently located', with staff lacking 'the time, skills and training to do anything other than a clerical task'.[47] Much of this is due to the usual problems of poor finance and staff shortage, but one answer to the 'professional-job-drain' difficulty may be to follow the practice in other countries and make it a statutory requirement on employers to notify all vacancies to the public employment service.

As well as being housed in uncomfortable or unsuitable accommodation, many Department of Employment and D.H.S.S. offices lack adequate seating and have little or no opportunity for privacy. As a general rule it can be said that there is a gradation from sometimes reasonable arrangements in contributory benefit offices to rarely reasonable arrangements in Supplementary Benefit offices, depite the optimistic statement in 1966 that 'in the future there will no longer be the sharp distinction which now exists in the administration of contributory and means-tested benefit'.[48] An interesting study of all D.H.S.S. offices in Birmingham, after one of the periodic attempts to brighten up offices, still revealed a minimum of comfort in many. In S.B.C. offices, the hard benches were conspicuously bolted to the floor, whereas on the insurance side in another part of the same building there were freestanding upholstered chairs; only one local office had identical furnishing in both benefit sections. Given that S.B.C. officers often have to deal with difficult clients, who may go through the trauma of being refused benefit, it may well be a reasonable precaution to have immovable furniture, but this does not mean there has to be a distinction made between sections, or that any furnishings should be tawdry.[49] The total amount of decorations in all of the Birmingham offices consisted of two plants, no pictures, but the usual array of leaflets. Only seven out of twenty-two offices provided cigarette bins, of which six were insurance sections, yet there were buttts strewn on the floors in the others. Given Government policy on smoking and health, the provision of bins and also of separate smoking areas might reduce levels of discomfort all round.

Only three out of twenty-two offices had directions to toilets, which unfortunately seems to be the case at many tribunal hearing locations too. Further difficulties were that in one office the nearest toilet was in a nearby park, and another was 200 yards away in an underground tunnel down steps. This latter difficulty of steps was a common problem with access to toilets, and it was also necessary in some cases to ask for keys at the counter. One office had absolutely no toilet facilities for clients.[50]

It is axiomatic that stigma is closely related to questions of privacy. The threshold of publicity acceptable to people clearly varies with such factors as personality, age and social situation, but often in welfare offices the price of receiving benefits seems for the claimant to be a loss of dignity. Disclosing assets and resources, revealing names of past employers, friends and associates, submitting to investigations and questioning, and accounting for expenditures and social behaviour is embarrassing to many claimants, and yet this often has to be done in an open waiting room or semi-private cubicle. In S.B.C. offices the tension is perhaps heightened by the armoured glass screen between the officer and applicant. The Birmingham study found that, even in the interview cubicles, conversation was within easy earshot of those waiting in the queues, and again there was a bolted seat and armoured glass, with no additional seats for children or relatives.[51]

Experiments with mechanical ticket devices to eliminate queuing in stand-up lines have been tried in various offices, but there has not been general acceptance of this Swedish system.[52] Payment by Giro orders through the post has also eased queuing, but it is suggested that one further possibility in reducing the strain of waiting would be for the receptionist to hand out self-reporting checklists on resources and requirements to be filled in while claimants wait. Although this will be non-applicable to blind or illiterate claimants, it will speed the claiming process at the counter, ease the tension of waiting and also reduce the anxiety of shouting personal details through the armoured glass.

Other obstacles to comfort include the number of steps to be climbed to many offices and the lack of care taken to accommodate the elderly and those with disabilities. In the Birmingham study, only five out of twenty-two buildings had no steps to negotiate, and one modern office had approximately sixty steps up to the Supplementary Benefits section.[53] Locations in relation to bus and train facilities are also often poor, although a former difficulty of having insurance and assistance offices far apart from each other is slowly decreasing after the 1966 amalgamation. Nevertheless, the Birmingham study found that, because of differential zoning, 'a claimant might visit a [National Insurance] office which had a Supplementary Benefits section in the same building, but that might not cover his area. The Supplementary Benefits office might be up to four miles away.'[54]

Physical comfort for claimants may not be the most important issue in welfare administration, but, if the Departments are concerned to reduce tension and misunderstanding, one immediate answer is for them, not simply to 'brighten up' their offices, but to examine closely such factors as physical access, toilet and refreshment facilities and, most important, to ensure complete privacy during interview sessions.

The Treatment of Claimants

The major criticisms of the administrative process are perhaps inevitably centred on the related topics of the method of claiming and the treatment of claimants by administrative personnel while they are making the claim. Because welfare law has to deal with complex situations, it is necessarily somewhat technical, but this should not mean a cumbersome procedure of initial application. The S.B.C. has made considerable progress in making available application forms in post offices which are simply filled in, but claiming unemployment benefit can still take up to a week with treks from one office to another becoming almost a full-time employment in itself.[55] Unfortunately, not only is there the need for physical activity in making a claim, but often a need for considerable mental agility which is frequently beyond the grasp of claimants not used to thinking in abstract terms. The expectations of welfare administrators are often too high, and misunderstanding inevitably results. Audrey Harvey believes that in relation to welfare and housing agencies generally 'the individual, in the eyes of the State, has a bright trained mind. He also has great stamina and considerable leisure . . . he needs both if he is to get his information'.[56]

The tortuous language used in certain administrative forms has long been notorious; in one unemployment case, for example, the Chief National Insurance Commissioner, Sir Robert Micklethwait, commented that 'the claimant, if I may say so, is obviously a man of education and intelligence, but in my judgement the form is so misleading that it is well understandable that he was misled by it'.[57] The question of treatment of the claimant is a more controversial issue, in that opinions vary widely. From the studies done on welfare clients we know a considerable amount about client characteristics, but relatively little about how clients assess the welfare administration and its officials, how they use welfare schemes, or do not use them, and why, and what difference the schemes make to their lives. The real need is for a large-scale 'inside out' survey of clients' views, but not of course from an officially selected group contacted through the welfare agency, where it is all too easy to elicit the wary response that everything is all right.

From small-scale studies, we know that sometimes difficulties may be partly attributable to the expectations of the claimant approaching the system; for example, in one study, a number of 'potential claimants thought that if they were to apply for help they would be subjected to a humiliating interrogation and then in all probability refused'.[58] Such feelings of stigma were of course consciously engendered in the Poor Law system of badging or even branding and mutilating welfare recipients.[59] However, modern welfare systems have often only moved from physical to mental stigma. The present system, by assuming dishonesty on the part of welfare clients as opposed to the method of assessment by self-reporting for tax purposes, and by putting the claimant in the position of proving his statements, has in essence still a punitive intake system which uses the stigma attached to public declarations of need as a rationing device. Moves towards rights and entitlement, making 'need' the only criterion for eligibility, reforming the means test, and ensuring privacy for applicants, are all clearly attempts to remove such feelings of stigma.

Many studies also show that claimants frequently encounter difficulties attributable to the attitude of the administrator towards them, classically defined by a former officer of the NAB as 'mucking applicants about'.[60] Seven out of twenty-four cases to the Parliamentary Commissioner involving Supplementary Benefits have alleged rudeness and victimization.[61] As an example, in one survey of 116 fatherless families dependent on welfare, no fewer than three-quarters of the claimants had felt 'very embarrassed at the initial application for assistance',[62] and the author then went on to make a number of serious accusations about the conduct of social security officers, alleging that 'officers harried mothers, particularly in the under-class, by illegal methods, endeavouring to prevent relationships with men or to break up any which had started'.[63] And in another more recent survey on single mothers drawing benefit, an appalling picture of 'abuse, sexual insult, harassment, persistent and prying questioning, and administrative delays and errors' was revealed.[64] However, variations clearly exist in the experiences of differing 'types' of claimant; in one study of widows and the National Assistance Board, 'several who had gone there with reluctance had been pleasantly surprised by the consideration with which they were treated'.[65] Similar reactions came from a survey of 'fathers alone'—perhaps because fathers are not generally regarded as suspect cohabitees—but it is nonetheless clear that substantial criticisms remain.[66]

The attitudes of social security officers in general reflect the prevailing social views and norms. It may even be that choice of a career in the Civil Service also means the selection of those who could be described as particularly sedate; Professor Walker found, for example, that in contrast to those in other occupations, Executive and Clerical Officers placed 'security of job' as their first choice in a list of job characteristics.[67] Unfortunately, arbitrary decisions due to commonly held social and moral beliefs have always seemed to be intermingled with welfare adjudication, not just in Poor Law days where there were blatant decisions endangering the lives of claimants, but also in the present day. In one study of a California employment service agency it was found that a mutual agreement by the staff automatically disqualified for unemployment benefit all males with long hair and females with mini-skirts. The local supervisor justified the action by stating that few employers in his area would hire such people.[68] In a revealing article by a student who had worked as a temporary Clerical Assistant in an S.B.C. office, attitudes of 'we-they' were predominant amongst his colleagues. Some of them were particularly punitive towards coloured claimants and one told the writer with pride that his own mother would not apply for benefit because of the stigma associated with it. The conclusion of the article was that 'at all levels, the old Poor Law attitudes are still to be found. It is on the changing of attitudes rather than the mechanics of administration that D.H.S.S. staff training should now perhaps be concentrated'.[69]

However, regulatory factors, such as internal office and administrative relationships and goals, as well as anti-discrimination legislation, can of course have a short- and long-term effect in reducing this kind of behaviour.[70] Whatever the basis of these attitudes, their operation on the actions of administrators is undoubted; one former S.B.C. officer provides a classic illustration of the more extreme form of 'siege mentality' of which the S.B.C. is often accused:

> There seems to be a general belief that the Department is really a public piggy bank, and that if members of staff are shouted at, rattled, shaken or hit on the head, money will spill out . . . Abuse of the system is so widespread that the public purse is being regularly plundered by a growing army of professional poverty-pleaders.[71]

But in a similar way, the attitudes of claimants form an operative factor. In discussing the legacy and received folklore of the past, Professor Meade states that, in the minds of claimants, 'there still surrounds the Supplementary Benefit system an atmosphere of the old poor law, under which every kind of social stigma was deliberately attached to the workhouse in order to minimize reliance on that system of relief'.[72] Although there has been a conscious awareness of this 'stigma' problem for some time,[73] nevertheless the complex battery of forms and claims, appeal processes and eligibility requirements, with which the claimant has to deal unaided, often and not unnaturally leads to the assumption that this baffling system is part of a co-ordinated attempt to discourage claimants. In one CPAG survey of Supplementary Benefit Tribunal appellants, only four out of fifty thought they would ever make a future appeal to a tribunal. This 'deterrent' aspect was further noticeable in the fact that only three people in the sample had had previous experience of an appeal.[74]

On this basis, there would seem to be scant evidence of a new 'claimant class' or 'professional poverty pleaders' as feared by some S.B.C. officers. The mythology of such groups, however, leading to considerable resentment on the part of hard-pressed welfare officers, can be seen to have a considerable effect on attitudes not just towards claimants but to groups representing them.[75] The associated problem of low or non-take-up of benefits and rights has for some time been seen to be directly linked to 'lack of information and know-how . . . [and] the tangle of welfare provisions'.[76] It had been the original vision of the post-war system, as expressed by the then Minister of Pensions and National Insurance, Jim Griffiths, that local social security offices should be places 'where people will not be afraid to go, where they will be welcomed, and where they will not only get benefit but advice. I want to see them become not only social security offices, but citizens' advice bureaux where everyone can go as of right, to speak to someone who is there not to rob them but to help them'.[77] Unfortunately, and despite the change in names, the new forms of social assistance have not completely shaken off the old connotations. Low take-up will not simply be solved by minor placebos such as new wallpaper in social security offices or television advertising,[78] while claimants feel themselves reduced to a lower status in society.[79] The ramifications of such attitudes are of course complex, in that prior loss of rights in the private market due to poverty may be just as important as the acquisition of labels through contact with the welfare system. As Professor Pinker states, 'many of the clientele of social services come to the welfare agency already stigmatised'.[80]

The use of a large force of civil servants to administer the present social security system is clearly necessary. As Professor Robson has pointed out, this is 'not only because it is more efficient than the older methods which it has superseded, but also because it is a levelling, rationalising force'.[81] However, the dangers of bureaucracy with a potential administrative impersonality towards claimants is a real threat in a system largely dependent on personalized service. Planning has to take account of this human factor, but the problems of staff in dealing with claimants must not be forgotten. By the nature of its work, the welfare system has to deal with a high proportion of people under stress, some of whom are in urgent need of financial support. And yet it must adjudicate speedily on a large number of complex administrative and statutory rules. Ensuring that under these circumstances the welfare machine remains flexible and responsive to the needs of claimants, and also to the sometimes conflicting demands of the taxpaying public, is no easy matter.

Client and Community Involvement

In recent years, considerable emphasis has been placed on a 'consumer' approach to welfare, mainly in an attempt to keep the system alive to the needs of the people it helps. Much of the impetus has come from the American experience,[82] but a British attempt to involve and divine public opinion has long existed with the use of 'advisory committees', and earlier the Poor Law Boards of Guardians were in some measure a rudimentary attempt to obtain a 'lay' perspective on welfare problems. In fact, by the 1920s, the practice of Guardian hearing cases arising from their own wards had aroused justifiable criticism of the strong 'pauper vote' in local elections.[83] However, it must be noted that, although in many respects a similar phenomenon, this 'participatory' effort involves two distinct strands of thought—'public' participation and 'claimant' participation. The rationale for obtaining a claimant's view of the system was expressed in Barbara Wootton's critisicm of the traditional paternalistic approach:

> Everything is viewed from the administrative angle, through administrative spectacles—benevolently, no doubt, but always from outside, at second hand. Only those who supply the various services, never those for whose benefit they are supplied, are fit to judge their quality. Be quiet, dear, Daddy knows best.[84]

The theory that users of a welfare agency can give a unique insight into its effectiveness may be unimpeachable; but it has been notoriously difficult to put into practice.[85] The immediate avenues of protest through direct communication with the agency, or through indirect means such as enlisting the support of a Member of Parliament, are of course always open to the claimant. But such factors as inarticulateness, lack of free time, apathy or lack of basic information among welfare claimants may mean that such approaches are not used. As Audrey Harvey, a long-term advocate for the rights of the poor has stated, 'selectivity always tends to concentrate inferior services on the inarticulate'.[86] Such bodies as the Citizens' Advice Bureaux, the Citizens' Rights Office and other volunteer pressure groups and advice centres have played an increasing role in this area in recent years, but it is clear that a serious vacuum still exists.[87]

The use of advisory committees as an attempt to create new avenues of communication with Government services has its origin in 1909, as a means of giving the Board of Trade advice on labour exchange problems; the German system of advisory committees for social insurance was probably the model.[88] They were basically designed to gain the help of employers and trade unions, in making the new exchanges work as a hiring centre, but also investigated public criticisms and complaints.[89] Experience with these national committees suggested more localised contact was needed, and in 1917 local advisory committees were also set up,[90] which subsequently played a considerable part in the inter-war administration of the unemployment insurance system. Initially this was in the nature of advice on local employment and job placement matters, but gradually the committees took on other functions, such as the suggestion of suitable members for tribunal panels, and in the 1920s they in fact constituted a special process of appeal for the grant of uncovenanted and extended benefit.[91] But from the start the selection of personnel for the committees, always a matter for the Ministry, made it clear that they were a gauge of 'public' opinion rather than 'claimant' opinion. With the reorganisation of the unemployment benefits scheme in 1934, the two-tier approach of national and local committees was maintained, and in fact built upon. A new Unemployment Insurance Statutory Committee at the national level, with wide-ranging powers, was in *de facto* control of the insurance system under Part One of the Act,[92] and an Unemployment Assistance Board with controversially wide powers was created to take full control of the secondary assistance scheme.[93] Local advisory committees were continued in relation to the unemployment insurance scheme attached to the employment exchanges, and new advisory committees were set up to assist the work of the Unemployment Assistance Board at a local level, although, as one study put it, 'It should not be thought, however, that there was any realization in 1934 . . . of the precise functions which it would be appropriate for these committees to fulfil.'[94] This system underwent substantial alteration at the national level in the post-war legislation, in that the successor to the Unemployment Insurance Statutory Committee had greatly reduced powers, although, as Professors Griffith and Street have pointed out, 'it is important to remember that the [National Insurance Advisory] Committee is far more than a hearing body which merely weighs evidence and evaluates objections. . . It is . . . a policy recommending body'.[95] However, as a comparison, the Industrial Injuries Advisory Council has considerably more power and influence; in 1972, for instance, the National Insurance Advisory Committee with nine members met three times, whereas the Industrial Injuries Council with eighteen members met seventeen times and, for example, exercised their quasi-legislative function by adding brucellosis to the list of industrial diseases covered by the National Insurance (Industrial Injuries) Act 1965. The work of the War Pensions Committee, which is as an institution fortunately in a process of historical decline, is also much more directive.[96] But on the non-contributory side, as has been noted, the S.B.C. is not only the legislative successor to previous forms of assistance, but has also taken over a scarcely modified administrative machinery.[97] It is important to note that in both 1945 and 1966, when there were supposedly dramatic changes, the same people remained to serve as officials on the new governing authority. It is however fair to say that, through the process of attrition, members of the Supplementary Benefits Commission are now of a higher calibre than those of previous years, and certainly do not regard their membership as an honorary formality, but as one involving a considerable time commitment.

Local advisory committees continued in the social security system until 1971, having been amalgamated from both sectors of the system in 1966.[98] A sub-committee dealt specifically with Supplementary Benefit matters. Having largely rid themselves of their initial function of interviewing the allegedly 'workshy',[99] the main role of the committee had been in practice to suggest names for local tribunal panels, often suggesting themselves.[100] However, by the Social Security Act 1971, all such local committees were abolished,[101] principally for economy reasons, although the Secretary of State also suggested that in recent years his Department had 'literally not been able to find any work to justify their continued existence'.[102] It was claimed that the abolition of the committees, with a 1971 total of 4,000 members, would represent a saving of £130,000 a year.[103]

However, local employment committees attached to the Department of Employment, known as District Manpower Committees, will continue as required. In general, these function sporadically, although they often provide the exchanges with useful contacts in relation to job placement. It is thought that they may be a useful source of nominations for 'workpeople' representatives on tribunals in the future, now that the social security advisory committees have been disbanded. There were 141 of these in 1970. Generally they consist of about half the members drawn from Local Authorities, employers and trade unionists, with usually one member from the local Old Age Pension Association, and the rest drawn at random.[104]

The cut-back in such committees in recent years seems most regrettable in circumstances where both client and community participation might considerably improve the form and content of existing welfare services. At present, the only avenue for anything like this kind of involvement exists in the indirect, and not entirely satisfactory, use of wingmen in the tribunal process, and in the national advisory committees and Supplementary Benefits Commission, bodies whose membership is difficult to square with wide community representation and certainly not with any form of claimant viewpoint. Despite the difficulties, it would certainly seem profitable as a general principle to do more in this direction. As the sociologist Georg Simmel has stated, 'within the modern relatively democratic state, public assistance is perhaps the only branch of administration in which the interested parties have no participation'.[105]

NOTES

1. David C. Marsh, *The Future of the Welfare State* (1964), p. 81.

2. *Report of the Committee on Abuse of Social Security Benefits* (1973), H.M.S.O. Cmnd. 5228, p. 7. See also generally, D.H.S.S., 'Social Security in Britain' (1972), in *International Social Security Review* **3** (1972).

3. D.H.S.S., *Central Office at Newcastle upon Tyne* (D.H.S.S. Background Material No. 1, February 1972), p. 3.

4. D.H.S.S., *Annual Report 1974* (1975), H.M.S.O. Cmnd. 6150, p. 22.

5. *ibid.*, p. 14.

6. *ibid.*, p. 90. In 1972 the administrative cost was £160 millions; D.H.S.S., *Annual Report 1972* (1973), H.M.S.O. Cmnd. 5660.

7. Olive Stevenson, *Claimant or Client?* (1973), p. 60.

8. D.H.S.S., 'Social Security in Great Britain' (1972), p. 166.

9. Claimants' Union, *Handbook for Strikers* (1972), pp. 2–3. See generally the polemical account of the activities of the Newton Abbot C.U. in Bill Jordan, *Paupers, The Making of the New Claiming Class* (1973). Mr. Jordan believes that 'The Claimants Union is poten tially a mass movement of paupers anticipating the workhouse'; *ibid.*, p. 23. And although written by a University lecturer, the book's conspiracy theory includes not only Social Security officers and appeal tribunals, but also 'poverty technician-specialists' who write on problems of social administration.

10. Peter Archer, *Social Welfare and the Citizen* (1957), p. 11. See for a Poor Law-style investigation into means, E. Wight Bakke, 'An American's views on English Unemployment', *The Listener*, **XII** (12 September 1934), p. 423; see also the same author's wider survey in *Insurance or Dole?* (1935). Home visiting under the Unemployment Assistance Board set up in 1934 seems to have been done in a similar manner; see for the activities of the notorious 'temporary clerks' who actually did the visiting, William Robson, *Social Security* (1948), p. 165.

11. K. C. Davies, *Discretionary Justice* (1971), p. 4.

12. A number of Department of Employment officials interviewed by the author stated that the I.O.'s job was a 'safe' one where it was possible to put a 'weak' member of staff to keep him out of 'trouble' which might occur if he were on the placement side.

13. Victor George and Paul Wilding, *Motherless Families* (1972), p. 85. See also the anecdotal evidence of a claimant who was visited by the same officer for eight years before he casually told her of a potential claim for children's shoes, although he knew this was a continual worry; Peter Laurie, 'Whose Benefit?' *Sunday Times* (26 November 1972).

14. See s. 3(1) SB Act 1966, re-enacting s. 2(2) National Assistance Act 1948.

15. Karl de Schweinitz, *People and Process in Social Security* (1948), pp. 56–7.

16. For the former position, see Charles Reich, 'Midnight Welfare Searches and the Social Security Act', *Yale Law Journal* **72** (1963), p. 1347. For an example of 300 police 'turn ups' within two months in one section of Baltimore, all on the basis of unverified anonymous tips, see *Lankford* v. *Gelston* 364 F. 2d 197 (4th Cir. 1966).

17. The Insight column in the *Sunday Times*, 'The Secret Machinery of the Poverty Code', (8 August 1971).

18. Olive Stevenson, *Claimant or Client?* (1973), p. 36.

19. My italics. Olive Stevenson, *op. cit.*, p. 58.

20. Joel F. Handler and Ellen Jane Hollingsworth, 'The Administration of Social Services and the Structure of Dependency: The Views of AFDC Recipients', *Social Services Review* **43** (1969), p. 40. See also, Joel F. Handler, *The Coercive Social Worker* (1973).

21. Olive Stevenson, *op. cit.*, p. 28.

22. Gilbert Y. Steiner, *The State of the Welfare* (1971), p. 39.

23. See for a general critique, Adrian Sinfield, *Which Way for Social Work?* (1969).

24. Olive Stevenson, *op. cit.*, p. 88.

25. Richard Elman, *The Poorhouse State* (1966), p. 11.

26. *loc. cit.*

27. 'Mrs Parris Discovers', an editorial in *New Society* **24** (28 June 1973), p. 734.

28. See generally, *Report of the Committee on Abuse of Social Security Benefits* (1973).

29. Molly Meacher, *Scrounging on the Welfare* (1974), p. 11; p. 27.

30. See earlier on the 'lump' at pp. 15–16.

31. David Piachaud, Letter in *The Times* (2 April 1973) commenting on the Fisher Committee proposals. Frank Field also points out, to gain some perspective, that 'the amount of money lost through wrongful claims of all social security benefits is miniscule compared to the extent of unclaimed benefits'; 'The Lost Benefits' *New Society* **31** (1974), p. 790.

32. Eveline Burns, *Social Security and Public Policy* (1956), p. 58.

33. See generally, Joseph M. Becker, *The Problem of Abuse in Unemployment Benefits* (1953), pp. 255–66, 300–7.

34. Julian Fulbrook, *The Appellant and his Case* (1975), p. 13.

35. See on the 'modest training' of the past, H. V. Rhodes, *Setting Up a New Government Department* (1949); Robin Page, *The Benefits Racket* (1971), p. 44; and K. R. Stowe, 'Staff Training in the N.A.B.: Problems and Policies', *Public Administration* **39** (1961), p. 331.

36. Peter M. Blau, *The Dynamics of Bureaucracy* (1955), p. 23.

37. The high proportion of young unmarried females employed by the S.B.C. prompted the remark of one official that 'as soon as we see the ring on their finger we know they will be gone for good.' Wastage from the Civil Service is on the whole very low, but occurs particularly with newly married female officers dealing with social security matters; see R. G. S. Brown, *The Administrative Process in Britain* (1970), p. 295.

38. Anon., 'The Feeling of Poverty', *Poverty* **27** (1973), p. 19.

39. Olive Stevenson, *op. cit.*, pp. 22, 172.

40. Olive Stevenson, *op. cit.*, p. 180.

41. *loc. cit.*

42. The author heard the Chairman of one Supplementary Benefit Appeal Tribunal make this suggestion to a claimant, with the enthusiastic endorsement of both the tribunal clerk and Presenting Officer from the Department.

43. *Report of the Committee on Abuse of Social Security Benefits* (1973), p. 12.

44. G. L. Reid, 'The role of the employment service in redeployment', *British Journal of Industrial Relations* **9** (1971), p. 96.

45. See generally, for the new image, Department of Employment, *People and Jobs* (1971).

46. Michael Hill, *Policies for the Unemployed: Help or Coercion?* (1974), p. 10. See also Brian

Showler, 'Manpower Services and the Unemployed' *Poverty* **32** (1975), p. 25. At present there are few 'Job Centres' in existence, and the target date for new purpose-built centres in urban areas with population over 25,000 by 1980 is unlikely.

47. 'The Job Hunt', *New Society* (16 December 1971).

48. para. 2, *Explanatory Memorandum, Ministry of Social Security Bill* (1966), H.M.S.O. Cmnd. 2997.

49. For graphic accounts of instances of physical violence in the Cambridge S.B.C. office, see Robin Page, *The Benefits Racket* (1971).

50. Bob Pike, Alison Gardener and John Wilkinson, 'Social Security Revisited', *Social Work Today* **6** (1975), p. 76.

51. Bob Pike *et al.*, *op. cit.*, p. 77.

52. See for a Cambridge experiment, subsequently discontinued, Ken Judge, 'Turn-o-matic' *New Society* **23** (25 January 1973), p. 186.

53. Bob Pike *et al.*, *op cit.*, p. 76.

54. *ibid.*, p. 77.

55. See Jennifer M. Wilson, 'Keeping the Unemployed Employed', *New Statesman*, **80** (7 August 1970), p. 147.

56. Audrey Harvey, *Casualties of the Welfare State* (1960). p. 15.

57. The appeal was allowed, R(U) 3/70.

58. Frank Field and Margaret Grieve, *Abuse and the Abused* (1971), p. 3.

59. See later at p. 85.

60. Michael Hill, 'The Exercise of Discretion in the N.A.B.', *Public Administration* (1969), p. 82.

61. See generally, Martin Partington 'Supplementary Benefits and the Parliamentary Commissioner' in Michael Adler and Anthony Bradley (eds.) *Justice, Discretion and Poverty* (1976), p. 159.

62. Dennis Marsden, *Mothers Alone* (1969), p. 176.

63. *ibid.*, p. 192.

64. Jane Streather and Stuart Weir, *Social Insecurity: Single Mothers on Benefit* (1974), p. 11.

65. Peter Marris, *Widows and their Families* (1958), p. 122.

66. Victor George and Paul Wilding, *Motherless Families* (1972), p. 82. See for attitudes among welfare claimants, Virginia Bottomley, *Families with Low Income in London* (1971), p. 7; see for the experience of pensioners, Peter Townsend, *The Family Life of Old People* (1957), pp. 161–5.

67. See generally, Nigel Walker, *Morale in the Civil Service: a Study of the Desk Worker* (1961).

68. Joel F. Handler, *Reforming the Poor* (1972), p. 21.

69. Anon., 'Over the Counter', *New Society*, **30**, No. 633 (21 November 1974), p. 467.

70. See for a commentary on the 'distortion process' in arbitrary decisions, Jeffrey Jowell, 'The Legal Control of Administrative Discretion', *Public Law* (1973), p. 186, and also generally, Jeffrey Jowell, 'The Adminstrative Enforcement of Laws against Discrimination', *Public Law* (1965), p. 119. See also generally Peter M. Blau, *op. cit.*

71. Robin Page, *The Benefits Racket* (1971), pp. 40–4; a colourful portrait of the Cambridge S.B.C. office with numerous examples of alleged rampant abuse. See also the chapter on 'Conflict with Clients' in Peter M. Blau, *op cit.*, pp. 100–71.

72. J. E. Meade, *Poverty in the Welfare State* (1972), p. 294.

73. See the classic formulation of the concept by Erving Goffman, *Stigma* (1963); see also the discussion of the S.B.C.'s attempt to 'de-stigmatise', in Olive Stevenson, *op cit.*, p. 16.

74. Julian Fulbrook, *The Appellant and his Case: The Appellant's View of Supplementary Benefit Appeal Tribunals* (1975), p. 6.

75. See the letter from a Visiting Officer who complains of time-wasting appeals, and believes that there is such a person as 'the professional claimant usually in a high position in one of these associations [Check! in Liverpool and the Claimants Union], who is on the books merely to try and fool the social security or wring as much money as possible from everyone else's tax'; *New Society* **29** No 620 (22 August 1974), p. 501. A subsequent letter from the Director of Check! made clear that they have no 'membership' and that the organization, a legal and welfare rights centre, rarely represented a claimant more than once; *New Society*, **29**, No. 623 (12 September 1974), p. 691.

76. Richard Bryant and Jonathan Bradshaw, *Welfare Rights and Social Action, The York Experiment* (1972), p. 3; see also The National Innovations Centre, *Welfare Rights Stalls* (1972), and the 'mini-survey' in Tony Lynes, 'Broadcasting Benefits', *New Society* (24 December 1970)—'In most cases, the reason for not claiming benefit was simply ignorance'.

77. James Griffiths, M.P., *Hansard*, 418, H. C. Deb. (6 February 1946), col. 1751.

78. Although these may help. See for a Swedish example of a 'Social Directory' resembling a telephone directory, and listing all available services (' a catalogue of words from A to Z about social rights and benefits and a lot more besides') with an additional 'Miss County Council' to call for further information; John Veit Wilson, 'Through the Welfare Jungle', *New Society* (28 January 1971).

79. It should be noted, however, that 'many people at the bottom of society are less resentful of the system, and many nearer the top are more so, than their actual position appears to warrant'; W. G. Runciman, *Relative Deprivation and Social Justice* (1966), p. 72.

80. Robert Pinker, *Social Theory and Social Policy* (1971), p. 142.

81. William A. Robson, *The Governors and the Governed* (1964), p. 17.

82. See generally, Ben Whitaker, *Participation and Poverty* (1968); Charles A. Reich, 'Individual Rights and Social Welfare: The emerging Legal Issues', *Yale Law Journal* **74** (1965), p. 1245; Robert J. Levy, Thomas P. Lewis and Peter W. Martin, *Social Welfare and the Individual* (1971), p. 1525 *et seq.*

83. See generally, Alan Deacon and Eric Briggs, 'Local Democracy and Central Policy: The Issue of Pauper Votes in the 1920s', *Policy and Politics* **2** (1974), p. 374.

84. Barbara Wooton, 'Daddy Knows Best', *Twentieth Century* (1959), p. 256, quoted in Adrian Sinfield, *Which Way for Social Work* (1969), p. 5.

85. See for an incisive account of American failure, Peter Marris and Martin Rein, *Dilemmas of Social Reform* (1972); see also Richard A. Cloward, 'The War on Poverty, Are the Poor Left Out?, *The Nation* **201** (2 August 1965), p. 55. But see for an interesting and helpful British survey of sixty-one clients of the Family Welfare Association, John E. Mayer and Noel Timms, *The Client Speaks* (1970).

86. Audrey Harvey, 'Defrauding the Poor', *New Statesman* **75** (12 January 1968), p. 39—a comparison of Supplementary Benefit and Inland Revenue procedures.

87. See generally Brian Abel-Smith, Michael Zander and Rosalind Brooke, *Legal Problems and the Citizen* (1973). See also Rosalind Brooke, *Information and Advice Services* (1972) and the Legal Action Group, *Legal Advice Centres—an Explosion?* (1972).

88. Set up under s. 2(5) Labour Exchanges Act 1909. See for mention of the German advisory committees of 'Labour and capital' by the President of the Board of Trade, *Hansard* **4**, H.C. Deb. (19 May 1909). col. 504.

89. See John Barton Seymor, *The British Employment Exchange* (1928), p. 16.

90. By the Employment Exchange (Advisory Committee) Regs. (1971) S.R.&.O. 1917, p. 418. These committees later became known as local employment committees.

91. See generally, p. 155. This was in the role of an investigative committee for the 'workshy' or other 'difficult cases' referred to them by the employment exchanges.

92. Part I of the Unemployment Act 1934; see generally, p. 162.

93. See generally, p. 164.

94. R. V. Vernon and N. Mansergh, Advisory Bodies (1940), p. 315, a survey of their use in relation to Government Service from 1919–39, with the conclusion that 'the consideration of outside opinion is a means of effecting a continuous penetration of the machinery of government by the spirit of democracy and thereby making of it something more than a piece of machinery—a vital organism'; *ibid.* See also Harold Laski, *The Grammar of Politics* (1938), p. 383.

95. J. A. G. Griffith and Harry Street, *Principles of Administrative Law* (1967), p. 36. Members other than the chairman are drawn from groups representing employers, workers, the Friendly Societies, and, a recent addition, a member having special knowledge of the needs of the chronically sick and disabled; see para. 3, Schedule 15, SS Act 1975.

96. See for a general survey of war pensions in Britain and France, Seth Otuteye, 'Some Aspects of Social Security Law—A Comparison between English and French Legal Methods' (unpublished Cambridge Ph.D. thesis, 1971). See also Enid Harrison, 'The Work of the National Insurance Advisory Committee', *Public Administration* (1952), p. 149, and P.E.P., *Advisory Committees in British Government* (1960), p. 174.

97. 'In general [the Supplementary Benefits system] is run from the same buildings and by the same people who ran the Assistance Board, and the "A Code" (one of the departmental Bibles), although continually being amended by a never-ending casade of

amendments and amendments to amendments, is still largely the same National Assistance Code, with "N.A.B." written across the cover'; Robin Page, *op. cit.*, p. 58.

98. By s. 27(2) SB Act 1966: 'The persons from among whom members of such committees are selected shall include persons representing employers, persons representing employees, and persons having local knowledge and experience'. See also the Social Security (Local Advisory Committees) Regs. (1967) SI 1967 No. 190.

99. A case involving the interviewing function of the 'workshy' by a local advisory committee in July 1970 was taken up by the Parliamentary Commissioner; see Parliamentary Commissioner for Administration, C167/G, H.C. No. 178 (1972–1973), (1973), p. 29.

100. See Howard Glennerster, *National Assistance, Service or Charity?* (1962), p. 29.

101. s. 9, Social Security Act 1971.

102. *Hansard*, **814**, H. C. Deb. (29 March 1971), col. 1156. This was echoed to the author by one former secretary of a local advisory committee—'the time and expense was too much for the result obtained'. In future, nominations for members of tribunals will be, in official terms, acquired from people whom the D.H.S.S. regards as representative of the community.

103. *ibid.*, col. 1156.

104. E. N. Gladden, *British Public Service Administration* (1961), p. 146.

105. Quoted in Richard Elman, *The Poorhouse State* (1966), p. 210.

PART 2

The Historical Development

5

The Poor Law Origins of Relief for the Unemployed

Any proper understanding of the present British welfare system must be grounded in a knowledge of its historical roots in the old Poor Law, whose workings dominated British social history for 350 years. Recent scholarship is continually refining, and sometimes destroying, our notions of its legislative theory and practical application. However, the structures of Poor Law forms have so profoundly influenced both British social thought and administrative procedure that their stamp is readily apparent throughout our social welfare system. This chapter draws together some of the strands of the evolution of the Poor Law which have played a part in moulding the modern system of benefits for the unemployed.

From a British historical perspective, the term 'unemployment' seems to have been used only since the seventeenth century,[1] although its implications were clearly felt much earlier. However, it can be stated that, in its modern sense, there was no 'unemployment problem' in this country until the collapse of the feudal structure of society in the fourteenth century. For, as Professor de Schweinitz put it, 'under feudalism there could, at least in theory, be no uncared-for distress'.[2] Society was based on an agricultural economy where the men of the Manor worked huge unenclosed fields on a principle of strip allotments, with surrounding meadowlands left free for common pasture. Legal and social rights and duties were ascribed to each man through regulations settled by the village community.[3] Above this loose peasant democracy, the feudal power and legal rights of the Lord of the Manor were heavily superimposed, with serfs holding their tenure in return for fixed 'workdays' of cultivation on their Lord's demesne. But there were no wages, no movement of labour, and no difficult questions of the poor or the unemployed.

For notes see p. 110

From Chaucer and other medieval sources we know there were many wandering beggars, war cripples, village idiots and 'lewed knaves'. However, the medieval Church dealt with these on a basis of voluntary alms, in fulfilment of a religious duty to grant relief for the suffering of 'God's poor'.[4]

Many factors combined to overthrow this oppressive—and yet internally peaceful—economic and political system. Primitive technology in methods of cultivation and the rapid growth in the use of money led to the custom of commuting, for money rents, the forced personal services owed by the serf to the Lord of the Manor. Also, the immense growth of the wool trade, in exporting material for the Flemish and Italian looms, increased communal prosperity,[5] and villeins were able to shake off many of the practical obligations of servility. One major factor was the over-whelming eruption of the Black Death in 1348, which cut the population by nearly one half. Other contributing features may have been the effect of enclosures, a trend towards sheep farming, and inflation caused by the importation of Spanish gold and silver into Europe, although the precise reasons for the change to a new social order are still very much a matter of historical debate.

The feudal economy had relied fundamentally on the labour of numerous serfs; but, as Trevelyan comments, with the coming of plague, 'the decreased numbers and the increasing recalcitrance of the villagers . . . clogged the wheels of the old system'.[6] The burgeoning growth of commerce enticed men to the towns. And because of a dearth of hired labour following the onset of the plague wages were forced up in the need for employers to compete for a limited supply. Labourers were therefore given a new embryonic power to bargain for wages, in place of the old machinery of servile tenure. Villeins increasingly went on tour to search out the best terms and conditions of employment, although some evidently preferred to 'live by pillage and robbery rather than work and wages'.[7] In time this separation of labourers from the system of land tenure resulted in 'an army of able-bodied beggars'[8] who wandered the countryside in token pursuit of work. The feudal practice had been that lordless or landless men should be required to find a kinsman with whom to be domiciled; this quasi-legal requirement dated from the laws of King Athelstan.[9] The custom had grown up that a wanderer should be allowed the choice of a lord in the first instance. If he refused, then the folkmoot assigned him one without choice. But clearly this system was impotent in the existing circumstances of the fourteenth century.

However, when legislation was enacted, it was merely an attempt to reimpose the feudal order and not an attempt to gear the law to the changing social and economic conditions. From 1350, the various Statutes of Labourers empowered the justices, by authority of the Privy Council, to bind wandering labourers at their place of settlement.[10] Their wages and conditions of employment were then to be arbitrarily fixed at pre-plague rates. The 1350 Act described its subject-matter as 'sturdy beggars', who were legally defined as 'all persons able to labour and without other means of support'.[11] Honest citizens were commanded to have no pity on those who 'do refuse to labour, giving themselves only to idleness and vice . . . and so that they may be, through want, compelled to labour for their necessary living'.[12] However, the work incentive of want was obviously not thought sufficient to persuade men back to work at low rates at an often notional 'place of settlement'. Whipping, branding, multilation, imprisonment in solitary confinement, slavery and execution were also prescribed. One statute, for example, laid down that any man who ran away from his assigned master, and who was recovered alive, should be, at the discretion of the magistrate, 'burnt on the forehead with an iron formed to the letter "F" in token of his falsity'.[13] But however brutal their sanctions, these laws proved to be unsuccessful in suppressing the wandering labourers. Rural unrest between the 'sturdy beggars' and the feudal lords, often of a violent nature, raged up to Wat Tyler's rebellion of 1381, and beyond. The justices were naturally on the side of the feudal masters—when they were not identical with them. Riots and primitive collective action were frequent occurrences, and repeated bouts of the plague aided the cause, though not the membership, of such movements by maintaining a gross shortage of labour.

In the face of this relentless economic and social pressure, the laws were becoming futile. It was obviously not enough simply to threaten 'beggars' with dire sanctions. Professor Jennings put the point clearly, which in the fourteenth century was only dimly appreciated if at all, that 'something had to be done for those who could not possibly work, and work had to be found for those who were able to and willing to work but could find none'.[14] One change to the law made in 1388 allowed the justices to grant licences for able-bodied vagrants to beg their way across country to a specified destination in search of work. By this, the feudal imperative of identity with one Manor was relaxed, but only within strict limitations, and with considerable reluctance on the part of the employers and authorities.

The origins of British unemployment problems occurred with this transition from an exclusively agrarian society. Drastic change was necessarily forced on to a community, which was in the process of evolving from feudal customs of personal service to a money economy progressively based on industry and commerce. The only response forthcoming from a bewildered governing class was a harsh repression of the wandering beggars who were the immediate manifestation of the feudal breakdown. Given that widespread poverty was viewed by contemporary thinkers as a means of keeping the masses industrious, it was perhaps natural that society sought only to relieve poverty to the extent that this safeguarded public security.[15]

The Origins of the Poor Law

The care of the poor had traditionally been regarded as a matter for private Christian charity; injunctions in the early books of the Bible show how the Jewish people formulated duties towards their fellows, and the story of Ruth is an illustration of an early form of charity where reapers deliberately failed to glean all the harvest. Until the dissolution of the monasteries under Henry VIII, in the period 1536 to 1540,[16] the bulk of the Church's charity had been channelled through these institutions, imperfect and riddled with corruption as they were; medieval charity, as Professor Rimlinger points out, had an inbuilt tendency towards being indiscriminate in that its major motivation was the salvation of the giver and not the behaviour of the beneficiary.[17] A statutory alternative seemed to be the solution for the resultant vacuum, and in fact the earliest English law for the relief of the poor appears to have been a statute of Henty VIII in 1531, foreshadowing the legislation following the dissolution of the monasteries.[18] The 1531 statute was entitled 'How Aged and Impotent Persons compelled to live by alms shall be ordered', but an Act of 1536 went much further. Under its terms,

> Every preacher, parson, vicar and curate, as well as in their sermons, collections, bidding of the beads, as in the time of confession and making of wills, is to exhort, move, stir, and provoke people to be liberal for the relief of the impotent, and setting and keeping to work the said sturdy vagabonds.[19]

However, sanctions of an unpleasant nature were not immediately dispensed with. Under the Act, those who 'voluntarily' became sturdy beggars were to be whipped on their first offence against its provisions, to have their right ears cropped on the second offence, and 'if he again offend, to be sent to the next gaol till the next quarter sessions . . . and if convicted shall suffer execution as a felon'.[20] The Act was eventually repealed in 1547, but, according to the preamble of the new legislation, this was because its measures had not been properly carried out in the punishment of offenders, 'partly by foolish pity and mercy'.[21]

Further Acts concentrated on exhorting the Church to urge its members to give alms. An Act in 1563 allowed the Diocesan Bishops to utilize their own form of 'persuasion' if anyone refused to give the required amount by 'voluntary' charitable offering. Failing these exhortations from the Church, the justices were empowered to 'charitably and gently persuade and move the said obstinate persons to extend his or their charity towards the relief of the Poor'.[22] But in the final analysis force was the real persuader and sanction. Stubborn parishioners, refusing to pay their 'charitable' donations, could be imprisoned and, if necessary, subjected to brutality, although in general this was reserved for the 'sturdy vagabonds' themselves.[23]

The levy on parishioners, originating as a voluntary contribution, had thus become an embryo parish poor rate in the form of a land tax. Assessment was fixed by the churchwardens, and this mechanism laid the basis for the 1601 Poor Relief Act which revolutionized the existing English situation with a new formula whose shape remained for three centuries.[24] The Act is often referred to as the foundation of the Poor Law system, and indeed it is interesting to note some of the astonishingly similar wording contained in the 1930 Poor Law Act.

By 1601, the impracticality of excessive punishments had come to be recognized, although the problem of policing the bands of wanderers remained; Professor Tawney wrote that, in the sixteenth century, people lived 'in terror of the vagabond and the tramp'.[25] But clearly the whipping of beggars was by itself no solution to the ordering of labour and the relief of the poor. The constructive methods used by the 1601 Act were to levy a compulsory poor rate on the occupiers of property within each parish, and for justices to appoint a general 'Overseer' to take care of the poor with money from the poor rate fund. The concept was not simply to give immediate cash relief, as the Overseers were compelled by the Act to buy 'a convenient stock of flax, hemp, wool, thread, iron and other stuff to set the poor to work'. Although the 1601 legislation is generally taken to be a radical departure, the Act was in fact merely an embellishment and consolidation of other welfare statutes passed in the preceding decade.[26] What has made it a historical landmark is, as Professor de Schweinitz pointed out, that the Act is the final re-writing of the total law.[27]

In its theoretical form, the Act was highly progressive for its time. However, it would be entirely wrong to see it as the establishment of an embryonic welfare state. Professor Jordan's description of the Act as having 'a brilliantly conceived system of administration in which the remotest parish was linked with Westminster; and the whole realm was declared to be a single community of responsibility for the relief of poverty',[28] needs to be treated with caution. As Professor ten

Broek pointed out, in any legal sense, the 1601 statute 'is better characterized as rambling, imprecise and inartistic'.[29] Nevertheless, the Act did establish the firm theoretical principle of public responsibility for the maintenance of the poor. Unfortunately, neither the spirit nor the letter of the law was lived up to after a short period of forty years or so, and only then, as Miss Leonard showed, in certain areas of the country such as the eastern counties.[30]

But perhaps inevitably, given the circumstances of the times, the ideals of the 1601 Act were lost in the swirls of local corrpution, and also, perhaps more importantly, in the widespread apathy of the justices and overseers. Inactivity and neglect was the rule rather than the exception in most parishes. A pamphleteer of 1698 concentrated on the collection aspect of the relief machinery, and declared that 'in many places no such rates were made in twenty, thirty or forty years after; and when they were first made and in many years after, the money so risen, was inconsiderable to the present charge'.[31] Certain parishes became notorious for their apathy. North stated, some time in the reign of Charles II, that no poor rate had ever been levied in the parish of Stow-on-the-Wold,[32] and used many other examples to show the ineffectiveness of the poor relief system. As the Webbs put it, 'between the statute book and the actual administration of the parish officers there was normally only a casual connection'.[33] However, these years of inaction must be seen in the context of the turmoil of civil war and the swiftly changing political scene. When relative security was reinstated, the legislature turned again to the problems of the poor and the unemployed.

When a reappraisal was made in the early part of the eighteenth century, it was clear that one reform must be the drastic limitation of the powers of the magistrates. Widespread abuse sapped the totally inadequate sums raised through the poor rate, which although hit by inflation had in many parts of the country remained unaltered for nearly a century. Little was being done by the authorities to ensure that work was found in place of relief being given. A statute of 1723, commonly known as Sir Edward Knatchbull's Act, attempted a restriction of the powers of the magistrates. One important innovation was its authorisation of the setting up of 'workhouses' in an endeavour to fulfil the 1601 principle of 'setting the poor to work'. The Act also permitted the justices to build houses for the poor, almshouses, out of the poor rate rather than from sporadic charitable funds set up for the purpose. This not only provided employment through the building operations involved, but it was also an attempt to ensure that overseers housed itinerant vagrants. Other parts of the Act dealt with administrative reforms in the hope that poor relief when given would not be given with 'mischievous profusion'.[34] But this tinkering with the administrative machinery could not hope to remodel a system which would cope effectively with the massive numbers now applying for relief. Gregory King's *Tables* show that, at this time, over one million people—nearly one fifth of the entire population—were in occasional receipt of alms raised by the poor rate system.[35]

Certainly one cannot assume that parishes were properly administered after the Knatchbull Act. There was a total lack of uniformity in the relief given in differing parts of the country, and corruption was still rife. Critics at the time, similar to the welfare critics of the present day, seem to have concentrated on the liberality of the alms given. Richard Dunning, for example, declared in 1698 that the parish 'dole' for an unemployed man was often three times as much as a common labourer, having to maintain a wife and three children, could afford to expend upon themselves.[36]

The 1388 Act had first made the crucial delineation between the 'impotent' and the 'sturdy beggar'; the crippled, aged and the sick, as against the fit unemployed man looking for work. Under successive legislation, this distinction became more important, in that it determined the nature of the relief given. For the 'impotent', poor relief was technically (though not often in practice) granted automatically and without prior conditions. But the 'able-bodied', on the other hand, were to be 'set to work', and only given relief in extreme circumstances. As Professor Rimlinger has pointed out, the early Poor Law was essentially a manpower policy aiming to maintain work habits among marginal workers.[37] As such it was of course not always successful, and certainly was unsuitable for changing conditions when labour became scarce. It therefore became a fundamental principle of the Poor Law that the family of an able-bodied man could only be given relief on the condition that he enter the parish workhouse. The first of these institutions had been established in Bristol by one John Carey in 1697. His intention had been to encourage the unemployed man by providing institutional work, for which he was paid, until such time as he was able to find alternative suitable employment outside the workhouse; unfortunately, the scheme was perverted into a bureaucratic tyranny that still today evokes harsh memories.[38] In time, the basic Poor Law test of destitution for the able-bodied unemployed man was the offer of 'the House' or 'the journey up the Hill'. And developing from this was the concept of a 'labour test' given at the workhouse, but enabling the worker, if he passed the test, to live in his own home drawing 'out relief'. 'Out relief' was discretionary, and the granting of it was at first severely curtailed. The labour test varied with the taste of the parish overseer, and with a zealous local administration it could be gruelling. But in many areas it eventually became minimal and even fictional.

Gilbert's Act of 1782 attempted to provide some regulation for this proliferating system of 'out relief'.[39] It established a primary obligation on the justices, and through them on the parish administrators, to find employment for the able-bodied at normal wages. Failing this, relief was to be granted but only after a stringent labour test at the workhouse. But in the words of one nineteenth century commentator, with 'the double panic of famine and rebellion',[40] the labour test was conveniently forgotten at the parish level by the pressure of events. There was consequently an enormous increase in the numbers of those granted 'out-relief', which no doubt included many who were not legally entitled to relief. Writing at this time, one pamphleteer estimated that 'the Poor Rate of England amounts to near a million pounds per annum'.[41] Coupled with this enormous cost, however, was the fact that the direction of the system had altered radically. For example, although the extension of the workhouse system had been potentially valuable, its idealistic aims were now completely discarded; one commentator, writing of workhouses, thought that 'the truth is that these were erected more with a view of exciting terror than providing comforts for the poor'.[42]

The years between 1793 and 1815 constituted a period of almost continual war; and despite the phenomenal growth of industry there was nevertheless widespread distress. Wages were cut owing to an excess of available labour, and in this situation the workhouse and labour tests for 'out relief' were relaxed still further. Poor Law administrators faced with wide-spread poverty took to supplementing low wages out of the poor rates. This led employers, facing imminent bankruptcy, to slash their wages even more, as any payment they made would be topped up to what the Poor Law authorities thought was a subsistence level. Unfortunately, this supplementation usually occurred only after lengthy administrative delay, and the hardship forced upon labouring families was chronic.[43] In 1818, expenditure on the poor reached £8 millions—a quite staggering figure at the time. But it must be remembered that the Laws of Settlement and Removal made this burden of expenditure fall unevenly across the population. Of these years, the Hammonds asked, 'is such a decline in the standard of life recorded anywhere else in History?'[44]

The Laws of Settlement and Removal

These laws applied not, as it is commonly thought, simply to vagrants and criminals,[45] but, in the Webbs' phrase, 'to the entire body of the manual-working wage-earners of the kingdom'.[46] The whole evolution of a welfare system in Britain must therefore be seen against the background of a legally enforced place of settlement, and many of the residency regulations of the modern system can be traced to settlement case law. Although the laws had near universal application, the majority of cases not unnaturally involved wandering labourers and other 'sturdy beggars'. Under the laws, each parish was required to support its own poor. However acceptable this might be in a social situation of relative agrarian stability, its limitations were obvious with the coming of industry and the movement to the towns. In periods of economic boom, a worker would emigrate to the town; the benefit of his wages, however, would be lost to his home parish. When the inevitable slump came, the law compelled him to be 'removed' to his place of 'settlement'. The home parish in this way bore the high cost of his deportation and his poor relief during depressions, when it had not participated in the boom. As the poor rates were levied on the occupiers of property, the law meant in effect that, as Professor Jennings put it, 'the farmer, smallholder and landowner paid the rates which supported the workmen of the manufacturer'.[47]

The origin of the laws is obscure. It seems that the legal requirement that the poor should 'get them to the place where they were born and there remain' is far older than any legal system laid down by statute.[48] As Professor Marshall has pointed out, not just the laws of settlement but many Poor Law practices such as the 'badging' of the poor by insignia on the clothing, authorizing certificates for 'tramping' and the building of workhouses were the result of parochial experimentation and only after proving successful were they then incorporated into legislation.[49] However, it should be noted that not only economic factors of business cycles forced workers to return to be a charge on their home parishes. Unhealthy unsafe conditions and long hours in a factory might render him unfit for further work in the town. And on applying for relief there, he would be immediately removed, and so would become a permanent charge on his home parish.

Removal was normally a peaceful process, despite the hostility often shown to those returning to be a burden on the parish. However, an Act of 1530 provided authority for the justices to use force where a 'vagrant' proved reluctant on being asked to return to his home parish. This sanction was for 'beggars of both sexes, being whole and mighty in body and able to work . . . to be tied to the end of a cart naked, and to be beaten with whips through the town until the body be bloody, and then to go to the place of birth'.[50] The word 'beggar' was dropped in later statutes, so that eventually the law came to apply to all manual workers. And in a diluted form the laws continued into the twentieth century. Many theories have been put forward for the original statutory formulation of the laws; perhaps the most convincing is that the initial purpose was to suppress wandering monks, who had been dislodged following the dissolution of their monasteries.[51]

The operation of the laws of settlement and removal brought untold suffering. One Assistant Secretary of the Poor Law Commission said in 1834 that the laws had 'made of the parish of the settlement a prison and every other parish a hostile fortress'.[52] Quite literally, labourers and their families were left to starve on the highway. Not until they reached their home parish could they be assured of assistance. Although mitigated in later years, the excessive cruelty of the laws had been a subject of protest for centuries.[53] Indeed, one critic went so far as to say in 1606 that the law of settlement had been the principal cause for divine wrath and judgement on the City of London through the annual visitation of the plague.[54] With advancing age, the law became increasingly complex—and illogical. For example, illegitimate children took, not the placement of their mother or father, but of the parish in which they were born; inevitably, perhaps, parish relieving records are full of small sums given to pregnant women to move quickly to another parish.[55] Adam Smith was one of a number of critics of the legislation, propounding the view that 'to remove a man who has committed no misdemeanour from a parish where he chooses to reside, is an evident violation of natural liberty and justice'.[56]

It must also be realized that the law was not just a marginal part of the work of the courts. In 1735, William Hay, a zealous pamphleteer and advocate for reform in this field, stated in the House of Commons that 'it is notorious that half the business of every Quarter Sessions consists in deciding appeals on orders of removal'.[57] Commentators have described the laws of settlement as having been a 'lawyer's paradise', where half the sum collected for the parish was often claimed as the lawyer's fee.[58] The courts built up a large body of case-law on a myriad of esoteric points such as 'double derivative', 'the age of nurture', and 'settlement by estoppel'.[59] The laws were only finally removed by the 1948 National Assistance Act, and even in 1909, when the laws were thought by many to be obsolete, removals were still running at the rate of 12,000 a year.[60]

The Poor Law Commission Report of 1834

In the early decades of the nineteenth century, the Poor Law system was being run on virtually identical lines as when it originated in 1601; it was, as the Webbs put it, a welfare system in which 'relief of the poor [was] within a framework of repression'.[61] The system was also clearly failing to meet the needs of the poor. Few people regarded it as ideal, but no one method of overall reform had gained general acceptance. The crucial factor in bringing about change was the crippling cost of the poor rate. In rural areas this had grown out of all proportion, and many landowners were faced with imminent bankruptcy. And it was this impetus that brought about the setting up of a Royal Commission by the predominantly landowner-constituted Parliament of 1832. It was 'to make a diligent and full inquiry into the practical operation of the Laws for the Relief of the Poor in England and Wales and into the manner in which those laws are administered'.[62] The Commissioners in fact paid little attention to the relief of the sick and the aged and other 'impotent poor', but mainly concerned themselves with the relief of 'unemployed paupers'.[63] Their condemnation of the existing system was sweeping. Men were just not being given the work which was required by the Poor Law. Relief was, they thought, being frivolously handed out without any labour test whatsoever. And there were many recipients, according to the Commissioners, who were quite content to take the meagre allowance from the parish indefinitely, supplementing it with open begging on the streets, and never attempting to find a job. The inadequacy of the administrative machinery in terms of checks and controls also allowed the common practice of claimants moving from parish to parish to claim casual out-relief. Professor Marshall comments that it is 'not surprising that both parties [Poor Law official and recipient] prospered at the expense of the ratepayer'.[64]

The picture painted of the existing Poor Law, and in particular of children in the workhouses, was graphic.[65] It must be remembered that at this time they formed an integral part of the workforce, and it was normal practice for manufacturers to recruit workers from the large numbers of orphans or abandoned children in the workhouses; a twelve-hour day was common for pre-teenagers. One commentator in 1797 stated that child labourers were 'chiefly collected from the parish workhouse',[66] from where they were taken, as Sir Samuel Romilly put it during a debate in the House of Commons in 1807, 'in carts like so many Negro slaves'.[67]

The Commissioners discovered numerous instances of abuse, not only in the payment of out-relief, but in the administration of the workhouses and of the 'Roundsman' system.[68] For example, where the overseer paid a pauper's rent, the forerunner of the present rent addition in Supplementary Benefits, the practice had grown up to build houses with an intentional defect. This would not only ensure escape from the poor rate, as the house was only fit for paupers to live in, but also provided a secure income from rent paid from the parish poor fund.

One feature of the background to the 1834 Report was the 'Speenhamland Act'. The twenty years of war with France from 1793 to 1815 had produced grave effects on the social and economic development of Britain: owing to war prices and low wages, there was imminent danger in many rural areas of mass starvation. This was averted by a remedy which, however, was to bring even greater suffering. On 6 May 1795, the magistrates of Berkshire met at the Pelican Inn in Speenhamland near Newbury and, in the light of the existing circumstances among the poor in their county, collectively resolved to enforce a minimum wage. This was to be regulated according to the price of bread, and the remedy was indeed one that had been sanctioned both by ancient custom and by the existing law; a similar system was in use in Colchester as early as 1601.[69] However, it was clearly impossible for the magistrates to enforce the wage against the resistance of farmers in a period of violent price fluctuation; so, taking an expedient approach, they resolved to make wages paid by employers up to the minimum level by payment out of the parish poor rate.

When the Berkshire justices drew up and published their scale, it attracted widespread publicity and, as well as influencing overseers in their own country, the system in fact spread to many other areas, although why this was so is not readily discernible.[70] Eventually about half the parishes in rural England adopted the Speenhamland system by order of their own magistrates, and it appears that many felt they were legally bound to do so, mistaking the phrase 'Speenhamland Act' for Act of Parliament.[71]

In reality, the Speenhamland system relieved the landowner and farmer from the necessity of giving a living wage to his workers. The real burden of the poor rate levied as a consequence fell on the small independent parishioner who owned land but did not employ labourers. Simultaneously it compelled labourers to become paupers by definition even when they were in full-time employment, and as a by-product provided labourers with little material incentive to satisfy their employer's instructions.[72] Trevelyan comments that 'the moral effect was devastating on all concerned. The large farmers were confirmed in their selfish refusal to raise wages, the independent classes staggered under the burden of the poor rate, while idleness and crime increased among the pauperised labourers'.[73] Such a view has been questioned by recent commentators who believe that the system did not of itself produce the negative results attributed to it, nor was it of much help to anyone.[74] Nevertheless, whether from the Speenhamland system or as a result of other causal factors, it was not difficult for the Commissioners to find widespread wretchedness, particularly in rural areas. However, the concentration of their analysis followed public opinion and concerned itself principally with questions of abuse. It was not difficult to find. The Commissioners felt it their 'painful duty to report' that the Poor Law was being applied 'to purposes opposed to the letter and still more to the spirit of the Law'.[75]

The conclusion of the Report was that the disease to be eradicated was 'pauperism', defined as an unwarranted dependence on the poor rate for maintenance. Such a simplistic diagnosis naturally suggested its own remedy, and the remainder of the century passed, as Professor Mendelsohn puts it, in a futile attempt to 'discourage the poor from their poverty'.[76]

The 1834 Report was clearly geared to publicity. It exposed a great deal of corruption and scandalous misuse of funds, but there is evidence to suggest that its revelations were somewhat exaggerated to give greater effect. The Checklands write that the Commissioners 'expected to find certain evils rampant; they were fearful of an indigent and debauched working class'.[77] Professor Tawney described the 1834 Report as 'that brilliant, influential and wildly unhistorical report,'[78] and the leading economist of the time wrote that it 'contains a curious mixture of authentic, questionable and erroneous statements. The Commissioners, with very few exceptions appear to have set out with a determination to find nothing but abuses in the Old Poor Law, and have to make the most of them. . . Hence the exaggeration, one-sidedness and quackery so glaringly evident'.[79] Edwin Chadwick was undoubtedly the most influential person among the Commissioners, but whether he in fact wrote the Report is a matter of debate. He always claimed he did. Nassau Senior, the Oxford economist, wrote to the Government informing them that Chadwick had been 'the principal framer of the remedial measures,'[80] but he also wrote to a friend that 'three-fourths of it was written by me, and all that was not written by me was re-written by me'.[81]

As a document of contemporary social history the Report may be unreliable, but as a study of social philosophy on welfare matters the Report is without parallel. The stock twentieth century clichés on malingering and abuse seem often to have been derived from its pages. The Webbs summarized the internal atmosphere of the workhouses at that time—the 'home' then for an estimated one hundred thousand people—as 'a sink of corruption', in which every kind of unfortunate was indiscriminately mixed,[82] although recent research reveals that life within the pre-1834 mixed workhouses might not always have been as grim as supposed.[83] What was perhaps more serious than the lack of categorization according to need was the fact that, once inside the institution, every pressure prevented the inhabitants from ever leaving.[84]

With its massive evidence of abuse, the 1834 Report became a prodigious success in stirring public opinion. Drastic reform was demanded from every quarter. In consequence, Parliament quickly prepared and passed the Poor Law Amendment Act of 1834, which followed the Report's proposals in their entirety. In a Parliament largely composed of landowners who paid the poor rate, opposition was hardly to be expected, although, as Professor Bendix points out:

> The salient fact is that the system of poor relief which had led to untold abuses through the deliberate or unwitting connivance of entrepreneurs, farmers, Parish authorities, and others, as well as through the gradual demoralization of the labourers themselves, was now to be reformed solely by means of disciplines imposed upon the last.[85]

Foremost among the changes was the abolition of out-relief for the able-bodied, and the application of the 'workhouse test' in its full rigour. But the immediate abolition of out-relief was not a practical proposition since there were not enough workhouse places to accommodate the numbers. Given that an abrupt change might precipitate protest of a violent nature, the alternative taken was to give the new Poor Law Commission, set up as a central body to control the administration of the Poor Law, wide and sweeping powers of framing regulations for the granting of out-relief. Parishes were grouped by the Act into larger administrative units known as 'Unions' and it was hoped that this tighter administration would aid central control of the operation of the Poor Law. Permanent officials would still be appointed by the unions, but the Board had the power of recommending suitable candidates and could also remove unsuitable officials. Eventually, it was hoped, out-relief would be abolished, except for that given to the sick and the aged. And in an attempt to provide an incentive to those in the workhouse capable of work outside, conditions were to be made as spartan as possible. However, this action was to ignore the labour situation in the open market: under the Speenhamland system of giving relief in place of wage increases, even the fully employed had been brought into the category of pauper. Wages had become so low that the unemployed had no logical reason to accept offers of employment; and, as the Commissioners had no power to make employment prospects more attractive, their only control was to make the workhouse system as harsh and as uncomfortable as possible. But in their preoccupation with getting the malingerers and 'idle' unemployed out of the workhouse, the old, the young and the sick were trampled underfoot. As Trevelyan puts it, 'an operation was necessary to save society, but the knife was applied without anaesthetics'.[86]

Benthamite ideas pervaded the new administration. This was not altogether surprising in that Chadwick had been Bentham's literary secretary immediately prior to working on the Poor Law Commission. In this way the philosophical outlook of the new system was the opposite of the prevailing nineteenth century view of *laissez-faire*. It could perhaps be described as a combination of the elective and the bureaucratic approach to the social services. The three Commissioners in London laid down the precise guiding regulations, which were then administered, but with considerable flexibility and discretion, by locally elected Boards of Guardians. Both the centralized bureaucracy and the tempering democratically elected local boards had been Benthamite prescriptions; and Chadwick's biographer states of his subject that 'many details of the New Poor Law were taken from Bentham's unfinished but amazing Constitutional Code, whilst many of the arguments he [Chadwick] used in the Poor Law Commission Report had already been advanced by other writers'.[87] The three Poor Law Commissioners established by the 1834 Act owed no responsibility to Parliament. Their one required duty was to make an annual report, and beyond this they were left entirely free to frame regulations for the government of workhouses, to decide the nature and amount of poor relief, and to impose a uniform system of accounting and management.

The Implementation of the 1834 Act

The Commissioners' primary task, as they saw it, was to embark upon a merger of the existing parish structure of the Poor Law into Unions. This administrative unit disappeared in 1930, but for a century it dominated the whole system of British local government. The theory was, following Bentham's guidelines, to have the centre of the Union in a town, preferably a market town, and to organize boundaries so that a pauper could reasonably come into the town by available means of transport and return home, all in the same day; similar considerations of course still determine the siting of welfare offices to the present day. The Boards of Guardians were to be elected on a popular franchise, though with plural voting according to the ratable value of an elector's property. And for the first time in British local government voting was by written papers.

The 'Three Kings of Somerset House',[88] as the Commissioners were commonly called, soon earned the widespread hatred of the working population. Agitation against the new system was also widespread,[89] and Chadwick, the secretary to the Commissioners, came in for particular abuse. An extremely complex man, he became totally obsessed with the new system he had created and, although possessing considerable ability, his actions at Somerset House were quite outrageous. His defects of personality contributed in no small way to the New Poor Law's failure to grapple with the needs of the time. Disraeli described Chadwick in the House of Commons as 'a monster in human shape',[90] although other contemporary descriptions would have been less flattering. One Commissioner, the somewhat pompous country squire, Sir Thomas Frankland Lewis, resigned in despair over Chadwick's behaviour and told a House of Commons Select Committee that Chadwick was 'an able man, but I thought him as unscrupulous and as dangerous an officer as I ever saw within the walls of an office'.[91] Chadwick's actions certainly provide an illustrative case-study of the impact of personalities on administrative machinery, equal and sometimes more important than the formulation of procedural devices.

The working class in town and country regarded the new system as obnoxious and tyrannical; the Hammonds state that, during this era of the New Poor Law, they endured 'a low and grovelling mode of living'.[92] Even in the first year of its administration, one critic wrote giving thanks to Almighty God 'that in this country at least the hand of arbitrary power dare seldom enter this enchanted circle [of the Family], and tear asunder husband from wife, parent from children, brother from sister, as it does in the lands of Slavery. Yet our New Poor Laws, have aimed a deadly blow at this blessed security. . .'[93] Many people responded in emotional terms to the attack on workhouse management mounted by writers such as Disraeli and Dickens, but few acted. Numerous tracts written by evangelical clergymen on the iniquities of the New Poor Law were addressed to the nation and continual unrest led Chadwick to point out in a letter to Lord John Russell, in relation to the 1839 Constabulary Report, that a strong rural police force was essential for 'the suppression of tumults connected with the administration of relief'.[94] But the factor that brought about some early administrative change was a defect in the original 1834 structure. Whether or not all the criticisms of the system were entirely justified, the Commissioners had no one to defend their record in Parliament. Bagehot, using the example of the Commissioners as his chief illustration, stated in *The English Constitution* that 'the experiment of conducting the administration of a public department by an independent unsheltered authority has often been tried, and has always failed. Parliament always poked at it, till it made it impossible'.[95] Such advice was not heeded in the twentieth century when the Unemployment Assistance Board was set up outside the control of Parliament, although with a Minister theoretically answerable for its actions.[96] However, following the *Andover* case the Poor Law Commission was superseded by a Poor Law Board answerable and represented by a Minister in Parliament.[97]

The 1834 system, however, remained substantially unaltered until the 1930 Poor Law Act. Its structure has determined that of subsequent welfare machinery, and its importance cannot be minimized as the first national and centralized agency dealing with the welfare of the poor and needy. By 1930, the territorially unchanged Unions, which has been such a valuable innovation in the 1830s, had become hopelessly inadequate both in size and resources, but the Poor Law system had proved to be a useful mechanism for the implementation of central government policy. Many other social functions were tacked on to the system, many unrelated to the granting of poor relief. Thus in time the Boards of Guardians became responsible for hospitals and medical services, for the education of substantial numbers of children, and for the treatment of the blind and the mentally disturbed.[98] Other bodies were, however, also set up to deal with such services for the non-pauper community in many cases, and consequently there was a great deal of duplication and confusion. But, although the 'break up' of this system was advocated early in the twentieth century, its eventual dismemberment and limitation to a relief agency took much longer.

The C.O.S. and the Social Surveyors

The recurring theme of the Victorian era was the question of what action society should take about the relief of poverty. It was a theological argument as much as a political debate. The prevailing viewpoint grew out of the 'Classical' or 'Manchester' school of economic theory, which assumed that at some wage level jobs would be available for all. It followed, therefore, that it was a man's own fault if his laziness denied him a job. Poverty was, in the words of Charles Loch, the Secretary of the Charity Organisation Society, 'principally the result of a moral failure'.[99]

It was natural that the Poor Law mechanisms of the nineteenth century should be geared to this individualistic philosophy. The perspective of the 1834 Royal Commission set the theme for the rest of the century, and the continuing fear was that indiscriminate and universal charity would undermine the moral fibre of the individual in society, and increase his dependence on the Poor Law.

The Charity Organisation Society founded in 1869 was the characteristic product of its age, growing out of an earlier pressure group named the Society for the Prevention of Pauperism and Crime. Its avowed aim was to offer an alternative to socialism as a means of achieving a better society, and it capitalized on the prevailing social obligation that 'those who were, or wished to be, anybody' subscribed to a favourite charity.[100] Although principally a propagandist body, the C.O.S. pioneered the use of casework by professional social workers, and saw itself as a centralized co-ordinating agency for distributing charity in a 'proper' manner. Its principles included 'the promotion of habits of providence and self-reliance, and of those social and sanitary principles . . . essential to the well-being of the poor and of the community at large . . . the repression of mendicity and imposture, and the correction of the maladministration of charity'.[101]

The Reverend Dr. Thomas Chalmers, leader of the secession from the Kirk which formed the Free Church of Scotland, was the patron saint of the C.O.S. His formula for clearing up poverty of every description was 'the simple expedient of compelling pauperised city populations to stand on their own feet'.[102] While minister of St. John's, Glasgow, he persuaded the civic authorities to use his parish as a 'social laboratory' for a four year period, 1819–23. His experiment was to forbid all indiscriminate almsgiving, and then to institute a system of friendly visiting among the needy by a corps of voluntary workers, drawn mainly from his congregation. Relief in the form of money was given only in cases of extreme necessity. The result claimed by Chalmers was that suffering was much diminished.[103] Chalmers, it was said, had a 'rooted objection to all kinds of legal provision for the destitute',[104] and it was the stated aim of Charles Loch to reconstruct the C.O.S. on the Chalmers' pattern.[105]

But the grim reality of the Victorian poor, particularly in the urban situation, frequently swayed the emotions of the charitably disposed away from the stern 'common-sense' of the C.O.S. principles standing as they did for 'a scientific organisation of benevolence, designed to outwit the malingerer and the ne'er-do-well, while helping more adequately those whom it regarded as capable of being helped to help themselves'.[106] One man who came in for particularly shrill abuse was General William Booth of the Salvation Army.[107] His writing about 'Darkest England' and the 'submerged tenth' in immediate contrast to Henry Stanley's writings about 'Darkest Africa' brought a tremendous public reaction, but his moral fervour in performing 'social salvage' operations was ridiculed by the C.O.S. as being unscientific and leading to further dependency.[108] Even Dr. Barnardo, whose Homes for orphans and rejected children became a national institution, with their motto 'No destitute child ever refused admission', came in for one furious encounter with the C.O.S.[109]

The prevailing opinions of the time were perhaps best summed up by the apostle of Victorian virtues of individualism and hard work, Dr.

Samuel Smiles, in his book *Self Help*. Professor Briggs says of it that 'there are few books in history which have reflected the spirit of their age more faithfully and successfully'.[110]

One original motive of the C.O.S., as of the early Poor Law, had been to clear the streets of beggars. Henry Mayhew, a journalist, in a series in the *Morning Chronicle* had given readers a classic picture of life amongst the London poor in the 1840s, and of the professional 'cadgers' and imposters.[111] But it needed neither the pens of Dickens nor Mayhew to convince Londoners of the army of tramps abroad in the streets. They were accosted each day; Professor Mowat maintains that children exhibited by their parents to excite sympathy had their sores deliberately induced; filthy rags were donned for the day's 'work'; and 'begging had become a trade, and, in the importunities of the writers of begging letters it was growing into a profession'.[112]

The general and traditional reaction to such situations was to urge the repression of mendicity, rather than to inquire into the social causes involved. Nevertheless, in 1883, the publication of *The Bitter Cry of Outcast London*, a pamphlet describing the conditions of the poor, created an immense public debate. The pamphlet which sold for a penny was anonymous, and subsequent claims to authorship were disputed.[113] It contained no new ideas, and its descriptions were little different in detail from Mayhew's and others before. But, although following on dozens of similar surveys, it was, according to Professor Gilbert, 'perhaps the most influential single piece of writing about the poor that England has ever seen'.[114] The study itself was a primitive attempt at house-to-house classification, but it was the prose that principally caught the public imagination; it described 'men and women living in pestilential human rookeries . . . where tens of thousands are crowded together amidst horrors which call to mind what we have heard of the middle passage of the slave ship'.[115]

One response was interest in social problems which led to the foundation of University Settlements, notably Toynbee Hall, with immense social implications for the future.[116] Samuel Barnett's original idea was not an elaborate scheme for reform, but simply to urge students to live among his parishioners in the Stepney area, and then await developments. As Vicar of St. Judes' in Whitechapel, Canon Barnett firmly believed that 'the sense of sin has been the starting-point of progress'.[117] However, although the inculcation of a feeling of guilt among undergraduates about the plight of the poor was the aim, the development of University Settlements led not only to understanding but also to the collection of hard data on the precise circumstances of the underprivileged.[118]

This too was the great contribution of Charles Booth, often described as 'the father of scientific social surveys'. Although a Conservative in politics, a merchant, shipowner and typical Victorian industrial magnate in most respects, he produced a seventeen year-long study of the poor in London which changed the whole structure of the debate on poverty. No longer would it be sufficient to rely on emotional arguments; his legacy was that 'after his work had become generally known, no amendment of social policy was possible without a carefully tested appeal to experience and the evaluation of proposals in the light of the relevant evidence'.[119] Influenced by Mayhew's sketches and *The Bitter Cry*, Booth's original aim was to test the truth of their assertions.[120] His study was primarily a study of people and not one of poverty, 'but it soon developed that the poor formed a large proportion of the people'.[121] Published in seventeen volumes between 1889 and 1903, Booth's work in terms of social classification was clearly rudimentary,[122] but the investigative techniques involved represented a feat of pioneering work.

Booth's contribution was rather more to show the path of advance than to formulate or develop a conceptual science of sociology. Although employing statisticians and a considerable research team, Booth's focus was 'pragmatic—the problem of poverty in the midst of urban plenty—and his appraoch was essentially on the common-sense level'.[123] Booth's factual revelation of poverty had immense effect: the C.O.S. not unnaturally greeted its publication with some tepid reviews. The first of three in 1889, while acknowledging Booth's insistent claim to an 'individualistic' philosophy, commented that 'Mr. Booth's faith is not very robust'.[124] Booth's thinking was certainly at this point not so different from that of the C.O.S., but it was clear that his findings challenged many of their assumptions. In time his worry over the problem of poverty among the old, for example, led him to advocate the then revolutionary suggestion of an Old Age Pension of five shillings a week on reaching the age of 65.[125]

Friedrich Engels in his earlier study of the working class in England had relied largely on newspaper articles and official reports for his observations.[126] Writing in the *Hungry Forties* about conditions in Manchester, where he was agent for his father's business, his survey was of an impressionistic nature, and perhaps 'not wholly accurate although terrifying in its implications'.[127] The only real forerunner of Booth's survey had been the study of the poor made by Sir Frederick Eden at the end of the eighteenth century. In writing a history of the labouring classes in England, Eden's work was written before any census of the population, or even before the country had been properly surveyed. Nevertheless, Eden worked with investigators visiting selected county areas, even though his own stern philosophy on poverty tended to be uncannily vindicated in every situation.[128]

The great drawback of Eden's nation-wide approach was simply its size. Booth's work, although gigantic, had concentrated on the metropolis. His successors concentrated on even smaller areas. Seebohm Rowntree, the Quaker philanthropist and member of the cocoa manufacturing family, resolved to investigate his home city of York in an attempt to extend Booth's work,[129] and also to rebut the 'incendiary' comments being made at the time. Booth too had originally been motivated in 1886 by a need to disprove the discovery of the newly established Social Democratic Federation that a quarter of working-class wage levels were totally insufficient to keep men in health.[130]

Rowntree's house-to-house survey of York was a much more thorough investigation than Booth's study had been with its use of School Board Visitors.[131] With one paid investigator, Rowntree studied 11,560 families in two years' work. However, the surveys revealed comparable situations,[132] and it was clear that the facts of poverty in London were part of a nation-wide phenomenon. Indeed, some commentators suggested that conditions elsewhere in the North were even worse than those in London.[133] But the chief result of both Rowntree's and Booth's work was to place the debate on poverty on a new level. Commenting on Booth's survey, Beatrice Webb wrote that prior to this enquiry, neither the individualist nor the socialist could state with any approach to accuracy what exactly was the condition of the people in England. Hence the unreality of their controversy'.[134] The nineteenth century British Poor Law had been grounded in the Victorian view of economic logic. Professor Briggs has suggested that this logic was difficult if not impossible to sustain when the social surveyors such as Booth and Rowntree 'showed that a large number of poor people were poor through no fault of their own but because of tendencies within the market system'.[135]

Developments in the Poor Law 1834–1905

Although the passing of the 1834 Poor Law Amendment Act had been easily facilitated, hostile criticisms of the Poor Law Commissioners were made from the moment of their appointment. Chadwick and Senior has perhaps been successful in using 'the evidence collected by the Royal Commission selectively rather than analytically in order to stampede public opinion into backing the measures they put forward'.[136] But once on the statute book, it was not so easy to manipulate and control public attitudes to the workings of the new vast Poor Law machinery. Critical comments were made by many on the dangers of centralization and the non-accountability of the Commissioners to Parliament. The opinions of those enduring the stringent new system were less esoteric but just as clear, although the threat rather than the experience of the workhouse was the fear of most working people.[137]

Chadwick, 'the aggressive, ever-active disciple of Jeremy Bentham',[138] clearly intended to dominate the Poor Law Commissioners as their Secretary, but his brash tactlessness led to continual personality difficulties. He was, according to Professor Gilbert, 'perhaps the archetype, certainly one of the first, of the impatient, domineering, officious, administrative technicians, who appears to have been bred for the administration of public or private institutions of public welfare'.[139] Chadwick and his Benthamite associates had hoped that he might be appointed a Commissioner by the Government, but the authorities felt it prudent to make him Secretary at a much lower salary. According to the Webbs, he 'therefore started in a bad temper'.[140] However, Chadwick's actions were at times quite outrageous, and clearly contributed to the malfunctioning of the Poor Law Commission. Not content with spreading malicious rumours among his friends on the incompetence of the Commissioners, which had some basis in fact, he invariably went behind their backs to intervene directly with the Government.

Hampered by severe attacks which they were unable to answer in Parliament, the Commissioners eventually requested to be legislated out of existence. This was largely as a result of criticisms arising from the scandal of the Andover workhouse, where the diet was so meagre that the inmates had taken to chewing the putrefying marrow of the pig bones which they were set to crush. The Commissioners' request was agreed to, and in 1847 a Poor Law Board was set up with a President who had a seat in the Commons. The Board consisted of the President and four *ex officio* members of the Government, but in fact it never met and the Poor Law system grew to operate in an identical manner to every other Government Department. From 1871 the Board's functions were transferred to the Local Government Board.

A much more far-reaching change was made by the Local Government Act of 1894, which removed both the remnants of the property qualifications for prospective Poor Law guardians and plural voting in the exercise of the Poor Law Franchise. An earlier reduction of the qualifications in 1892 had led to socialists like George Lansbury and Will Crooks being elected on to the Poplar Board of Guardians as 'the first fruits of the reduced qualification for Guardians'[141] and to a change of ethos in the operation of the Poor Law in many areas. Lansbury's experience of the Poor Law machine was to lead to some of the merciless cross-examination inflicted by the Minority group in the 1905–9 Royal Commission on the officials who came before them. Following his first dramatic visit to a workhouse,[142] which influenced all his later feelings on the Poor Law, Lansbury's motto became 'Decent treatment and hang the rates'.[143] Such an attitude naturally brought him and his colleagues into direct collision with the C.O.S.[144] and eventually to a brief stay in Brixton gaol in 1921 over the issue of 'Poplarism'.[145]

The Setting up of the Poor Law Commission 1905–1909

The Webbs thought that the creation of the historic 1905 Royal Commission owed a great deal to the appointment of J. S. Davy as Chief Inspector of the Poor Law Division of the Local Government Board.[146] Davy appeared to Beatrice Webb to be 'an energetic man of affairs intent on reaction',[147] and he certainly expressed himself repeatedly as looking back 'with some wistful longing to the early days after the 1834 Act'.[148] Davy opened his evidence to the Royal Commission with his personal testimony to the 'Principles of 1834', stating that the unemployed person must 'stand by his accidents; he must suffer for the general good of the body politic; according to my view, what you have to consider is not this or that pauper, but the general good of the whole community'.[149] Davy was quite clear that what was needed was a revival of Chadwick's view of Poor Law administration. According to George Lansbury, one of the Commissioners, Davy was 'steeped in what he constantly described as the eternal principles laid down by the Poor Law Commissioners of 1834'.[150] But Davy's view was by no means an unusual perspective. One of the historians of the Poor Law writing in 1899 on the 1834 Commission took the view that 'the labours of the early reformers of Poor Law administration are regarded with reverence and admiration by every thoughtful student of social history'.[151]

Certainly the initial view of the six prominent members of the C.O.S. on the 1905 Royal Commission would have been to agree with Davy's opinions. Their secretary, by now Sir Charles Loch, held the uncompromising belief that any provision by the State 'excludes the motives for energy and endeavour that come from self-maintenance'.[152] The C.O.S. representatives were to form the nucleus of the fourteen members who signed the Majority Report,[153] and it was clear that they were determined to stamp their characteristic mark on the proceedings from the start. The Royal Commission became a mammoth project; the complete published report with appendices covers forty-seven volumes.

The effect of the Commission in the long term was revolutionary. Even in the short term it had dramatic results on the kind of approach made to the subject of poverty. Starting with a dogmatic determination to uphold the Poor Law 'Principles of 1834', the Majority changed their view sufficiently to be able to state in their final report that:

> It has been impressed upon us in the course of our enquiry that the name Poor Law has gathered about it associations of harshness and still more of hopelessness, which we fear might seriously obstruct the reforms which we desire to see initiated. We are aware that a mere change of name will not prevent the old associations from recurring, if it does not represent an essential change in the spirit of the work.[154]

Some commentators have asserted that the moving spirit which changed the whole course of the Royal Commission on the Poor Law was Beatrice Webb, backed by her indefatigable husband, whom she described as 'the predominant partner of the firm of Webb'.[155] Their biographer states somewhat glowingly that, compared to her fellow Commissioners, Beatrice 'in range and in scope of knowledge: in intellectual grasp and pounce: above all, in drive of will, surpassed every one of them'.[156] But, although the Minority Report became one of the most important social documents of its generation, it cannot be said that, in the words of one Fabian commentator, 'the Majority Report was never considered to be even a basis of discussion'.[157] Unfortunately, the only record of the internal workings of the Commission that we have is that of Beatrice Webb. In the absence of others, and in the brilliance of her own, our only perspective is through her eyes—'The Commission is harried and dominated by her; the necessary evidence is organised and prepared by her'.[158] Before a month has passed, Beatrice Webb was referring in her diary to 'my little teacup of a Royal Commission'[159] and believed the whole project to be 'in a rudderless condition, at the mercy of the little clique of officials'.[160]

Lord George Hamilton, a former Conservative Cabinet Minister, had been appointed to the chairmanship,[161] and was in effect the only non-expert on the Commission in relation to Poor Law affairs. For as well as the six C.O.S. members, the composition of the Commission also included four senior civil servants and five members of Boards of Guardians. Davy's plan for the Commission was soon overwhelmed. It was clear that the Commissioners were not the kind merely to question a few routine witnesses before publishing a report dictated to them by the Poor Law administrators. Although the C.O.S. showed their independence of the officials repeatedly during the Commission's hearings, this initial reverse was without doubt due to Beatrice Webb and her ceaseless flow of memoranda. Instead of a quick mundane report, the Commissioners embarked on a detailed survey of all the existing machinery to relieve poverty and not just in terms of financial cost but also in terms of humanity and efficiency.

Charles Booth, appointed a Commissioner, was forced to retire through ill-health in 1908, but his role for much of the proceedings was confined to writing memoranda from afar.[162] It is evident from their content how far the centre of debate in the Royal Commission had shifted during the early months, when it seemed that superficially 'the quarrels centred on the question of whether it was Beatrice or the chairman who was supposed to be running the Commission'.[163]

Although the Commission was perhaps Beatrice Webb's finest hour, some of the subsequent eulogy must be tempered. It is surely stretching the historical position to state, as Margaret Cole surprisingly does, that in 1909 'Beatrice Webb . . . was ready with the sensational Minority Report which was to demand social security years before Beveridge had even thought of the phrase'.[164] It is interesting to note that another diary version of the Commission never mentions Beatrice Webb as playing an active role, although this may have been coloured by other motives.[165] George Lansbury, one of the Minority and possessing a great deal of experience in Poor Law administration, certainly 'never believed that the famous Minority Report was an all-Webb production to which he had painfully put his proletarian pen'.[166] Although the precise effect of the Webbs' role is unclear, the resulting Report, split as it was, covered a tremendous breadth of issues with detailed investigation of the multiple ramifications of the Poor Law. It contained factual evidence which was sifted and built on for decades and, although the immediate legislative effect was limited,[167] the Webbs were quite right to note the decisive change which had been accomplished: 'for what we believe is the first time since 1834, a public enquiry into the Poor Law has ended without paying even lip-homage to the "Principles of 1834"'.[168]

The Implications of the Report

When the Poor Law Commission was appointed in 1905, the Poor Law was the sole statutory cash-paying social service in Britian. Its origins had certainly been in the suppression of vagrancy rather than in the relief of poverty, but by the twentieth century it provided the only means of assistance to a wide range of social casualties. These services had evolved or had been tacked on to the existing structure in a sporadic manner; they provided 'a leaky umbrella'[169] for a surprisingly diverse number of groups. As well as maternity cases and old people, the sick and apprentices undergoing training, the Poor Law also sought to cater—with the same clumsy devices—for the mentally defective, those adjudged to be 'workshy' and for able-bodied men who were temporarily unemployed. All these categories were dealt with through the diverging policies of the various Unions as interpreted by their untrained and occasionally unsuitable Relieving Officers.

The Webbs summarized the 'Principles of 1834' as the Principle of National Uniformity, the Principle of Less Eligibility (the 'root principle') and the 'Workhouse System'.[170] The evidence to the 1905–9 Royal Commission revealed, however, that these sacred principles had been steadily abandoned in practice. Using their discretionary powers, certain Boards of Guardians had attempted a rudimentary classification of 'paupers' with differing services according to their special needs. Even the C.O.S. members with their rigid views on indiscriminate charity could see the benefits of this process. But the difficulty was the lack of direction from the top in terms of policy and the subsequent overlapping and competition of services. Furthermore, it was possible to see this trend as part of a broader movement towards public services 'which were aiming, not at the prevention of pauperism, but at the prevention of the various types of destitution out of which pauperism arose'.[171]

The classic contribution of the Minority Report was to advocate the complete 'break-up' of the monolithic Poor Law structure into specialist agencies dealing with separate individual needs. The Minority Commissioners[172] recommended the distribution of Poor Law functions among the existing authorities which had grown up alongside the Poor Law system. This meant that the care of school-age children would be given to local education committees;[173] the care of the sick, disabled and the aged needing institutional treatment would be given to the Health committees; the care of mental defectives to Asylum committees; and the aged to whom pensions were awarded would be placed under the care of Pension committees. Finally, the able-bodied worker would be provided for by a scheme of unemployment insurance, though at the time it was believed that various economic measures taken by the Government could prevent undue market fluctuations which were thought by the Webbs to be the predominant cause of unemployment. In this way the Poor Law would have each of its functions peeled away until nothing but a small residue of final recourse remained.

Under the sheer bulk of the Final Report of the Royal Commission it was perhaps difficult for the general public to perceive the distinction between the Majority and Minority positions. Certainly the Majority viewpoint had veered sharply away from its original course. All members of the Commission 'revolted by the harshness [shown in the evidence], distracted by Mrs. Webb's creeping barrage of facts and figures . . . came to one unanimous decision: that the Poor Law should be abolished'.[174] The crucial distinction lay in the method of abolition. The Majority limited themselves to the hope that they could 'show the way to a system of help which will be better expressed by the title of Public Assistance than by that of Poor Law'.[175] The Minority, on the other hand, believed that 'the only effective substitute for deterrence is . . . the Principle of Prevention—prevention, that is, not merely of pauperism, but of the very occurrence of destitution'.[176] While the Majority Report wanted a thorough overhaul and a partial rebuilding of the Poor Law system, the Minority wanted to demolish it entirely and build afresh; it was not only a plan for the break-up of the Poor Law, but also a formula for political change with the lofty intention to 'ensure to the workers by hand and by brain steady progress in health and happiness, honesty and kindliness, culture and scientific knowledge, and the spirit of adventureship'.[177] With such aims it was little wonder that the Liberal Government of the time baulked at providing the means. The pigeon-holing of Royal Commission Reports is notoriously standard practice, but the Webbs were determined that their Minority Report was not simply going to be 'smothered in the heavy dust of Blue Books'.[178] It is quite clear that they had determined on the device of a Minority Report early on in the life of the Commission following the success of Tom Mann's Minority Report to the 1894 Royal Commission on Labour,[179] and the 'Minority' evidence to the Select Committee on the Aged Deserving Poor,[180] both drafted by Sidney Webb.[181] With the aid of the Fabian Society a cheap edition of the Minority Report was put out replete with annotations by the Webbs, and, when the Government were quite clearly uninterested in the immediate implications of the Minority Report, the Webbs then launched themselves furiously into a campaign under the banner of a National Committee for the Prevention of Destitution, backed by its journal *The Crusade*. At its height in January 1911, the campaign had enlisted over 20,000 members, and had a staff of 400 lecturers touring the country,[182] but the ceaseless agitation during the years 1909–12 had little or no effect on a Government preoccupied with other matters, possessed of its own separate ideology, and determined on thinking out its own social reforms.

In summary, the campaign for the break-up of the Poor Law was 'highly educational, but politically quite ineffective'.[183] Although a major factor involved was the Liberal Government's struggle with the House of Lords,[184] nevertheless there perhaps also existed the malicious desire to 'dish the Webbs'.[185] Some critics, such as Professor Mowat, have stated that the achievement of the Webbs' campaign was 'to alienate the government, bore the country and postpone reform'.[186] But this is to view the reforms which came with the inevitability of hindsight.

When the Royal Commission commenced its work in 1905, no one could have contemplated the repercussions it would have in the eventual break-up of the Poor Law edifice, which had been rooted in British life for centuries. The Minority Report proved to be seminal in the construction of the modern machinery of social services. As is often stated, turning points are a dubious concept in social policy, especially when they are Reports rather than Acts of Parliament. But perhaps the best test of the influence of the Webbs and the Minority Report was in the nature of the final Majority Report viewed in relation to the attitudes of its signatories four years earlier. The manifold subsequent repercussions of the 1909 Royal Commission meant in the last analysis, as Beatrice Webb put it, 'success to our cause, but not victory to ourselves'.[187]

NOTES

1. The Oxford English Dictionary records that it has been in common usage since c. 1895; but that the term 'unemployed' as 'not engaged in any occupation; idle; specially temporarily out of work' has been in use at least since Milton, *Paradise Lost* (1667).

2. Karl de Schweinitz, *England's Road to Social Security* (1943), p. 2.

3. See generally, C. S. and C. S. Orwin, *The Open Fields* (1967).

4. See for a study of the medieval Church's work in this field, Gilbert Slater, *Poverty and the State* (1930), p. 42 *et seq.*

5. See generally, Eileen Power, *The Wool Trade in English Medieval History* (1949).

6. Sir George Trevelyan, *English Social History* (1944), p. 9.

7. John Clarke, *Social Welfare* (1953), p. 18.

8. Sir Ivor Jennings, *The Poor Law Code* (1936), p. 15. One generally accepted theory is that of Miss Leonard, that 'the poor laws themselves were at least partly police measures and, until they were successfuly administered the country was repeatedly disturbed by rebellions and constantly plagued by vagrants': E. M. Leonard, *The Early History of English Poor Relief* (1900), p. vii.

9. Statute of AD 924.

10. 25 Edw. III, c. 2 (1350–1351), preceded by the Ordinance of Labourers, 23 Edward III, c. 1–8 (1349).

11. 23 Edward III, c. 7 (1350).

12. *ibid.*

13. 34 Edward III, c. 10 (1360). This should, however, be judged in the context of British social history, in that 'up to the middle of the sixteenth century many men were mutilated and some were hanged for little worse than idleness'; see generally Christopher Hibbert, *The Roots of Evil, A Social History of Crime and Punishment* (1963), p. 26.

14. Sir Ivor Jennings, *op. cit.*, p. 14.

15. See the famous comment by Arthur Young in *Eastern Tour* (1771), vol. IV, p. 361, that 'every one but an idiot knows that the lower classes must be kept poor or they will never be industrious'; quoted in E. S. Furniss, *The Position of the Labourer in a System of Nationalism* (1920), p. 118. See for similar viewpoints in Europe, L. Lallemand, *Histoire de la Charité* (1912), vol. IV, pp. 149–214.

16. See 31 Henry VIII, c. 13 (1539) and 27 Henry VIII, c. 28 (1535–1536).

17. Gaston V. Rimlinger, *Welfare Policy and Industrialization in Europe, America and Russia* (1971), p. 19.

18. Certain commentators—for example, Sir Frederick Eden, *The State of the Poor* (1797), vol. I, p. 63—state that 'the English Poor Law dates really not from Elizabeth but from 1391'. However, the 1391 statute referred merely to 'a convenient sum of money' which should be allocated annually 'to the poor parishioners'. The 1531 statute was the first attempt at *regulation* of poor relief.

19. 27 Henry VIII, c. 25 (1536).

20. *ibid.*

21. 1 Edward VI, c. 3 (1547).

22. 5 Elizabeth I, c. 3.

23. E. P. Cheyney, *A History of England* (1926), vol. II, p. 333.

24. 43 Elizabeth I, c. 2 (1601). It should be remembered, however, that the Elizabethan Poor Law in context was 'but the English phase of a general European movement of reform'; Sir William Ashley, *An Introdution to English Economic History and Theory, The Middle Ages* (1925), p. 350.

25. R. H. Tawney, *The Agrarian Problem in the Sixteenth Century* (1912), p. 268.

26. See in particular, 39 Elizabeth I, c. 3 and c. 4 (1597).

27. Karl de Schweinitz, *op. cit.*, p. 28.

28. W. K. Jordan, *Philanthropy in England 1480–1660* (1959), p. 126.

29. Jacobus ten Broek, *Family Law and the Poor* (1971), p. 9.

30. E. M. Leonard, *op. cit.*, p. 293.

31. *Bread for the Poor* (1698), reprinted in *A Collection of Pamphlets concerning the Poor* (1787), and quoted in Sir Frederick Eden, *op. cit.*, vol. I, p. 144.

32. North, *Discourse on the Pernicious Tendency of the Laws for the Maintenance and Settlement of the Poor* (1753). In fact the first payment at Stow-on-the-Wold seems to have been made only in 1689 at the personal instigation of Lord Atkins CB, a resident of the parish; Sir Frederick Eden, *op. cit.*, vol. II, p. 889.

33. Sidney and Beatrice Webb, *English Poor Law History* (1927), vol. I, p. 149.

34. 9 George I, c. 7 (1723).

35. Printed in Charles Davenant's *Works* (1771), vol. II, p. 184.

36. It is interesting to note, however, that Dunning's strongest objection was that 'Paupers seldom drink other than the strongest ale-house beer'; quoted in Trevelyan, *op. cit.*, p. 278.

37. Gaston V. Rimlinger, *op. cit.*, p. 5.

38. See generally, Norman Longmate, *The Workhouse* (1974).

39. 22 George III, c. 83 (1782). See generally, G. W. Oxley, *Poor Relief in England and Wales 1601–1834* (1974), pp. 61–78.

40. J. R. Pretyman, *Dispauperisation* (1878), p. 27.

41. James Puckle, *England's Path to Wealth and Honour*, quoted in Somer's *Tracts* (1814), vol. XI, pp. 371–86. See also for an attack on the administration, Joseph Townsend, *A Dissertation on the Poor Laws* (1786).

42. Thomas Rudge, *General View of the Agriculture of Gloucestershire* (1807), p. 348.

43. See generally, G. D. H. Cole, *A Short History of the British Working Class Movement 1789–1925* (1948), p. 52 *et seq.*

44. J. L. and Barbara Hammond, *The Village Labourer* (1912), p. 185.

45. See for a brief summary of the law on vagrants, chapter 5 in Philip O'Connor, *Vagrancy* (1963).

46. Sidney and Beatrice Webb, *op. cit.*, vol. I, p. 314.

47. Sir Ivor Jennings, *op. cit.*, *p.* 3.

48. See generally, George Coode, *Report on the Law of Settlement and Removal* (1851), H.C. No 675.

49. Dorothy Marshall, *The English Poor in the Eighteenth Century* (1926), p. 9, p. 104.

50. 22 Henry VIII, c. 12 (1530).

51. See Robert Pashley, *Pauperism and the Poor Laws* (1852), p. 184; and Gilbert Burnet, Bishop of Salisbury, *History of the Reformation of the Church of England* (1681), part II, book I, p. 83.

52. George Coode, *Report to the Poor Law Board* (1834), p. 188, quoted in de Schweinitz, *op. cit.*, p. 42.

53. For instance, it had been the subject of remonstrance by the Puritans from the early days of the reign of King James I; see generally, F. A. Inderwick, *The Interregnum 1648–1660* (1891).

54. Thomas Dekker, *Seven Deadly Sins of London* (1606).

55. Dorothy Marshall, *op. cit.*, pp. 211–13. The same was true of smallpox victims who, instead of being quarantined, were bribed or driven to move to spread the infection elsewhere; *ibid.*, p. 11.

56. Adam Smith, *The Wealth of Nations* (1776), vol. I, p. 194. As well as preventing the 'free circulation of labour', Adam Smith also believed that the Laws of Settlement contributed to corruption in the administration of the system, in that 'parish officers sometimes bribe their own poor to go clandestinely to another parish'; *ibid.*, pp. 170–1.

57. William Hay, *Collected Works* (1794), vol. I, p. 121. Hay was M.P. for Seaford in the period 1734 to 1755.

58. Brian Rodgers, *The Battle Against Poverty: From Pauperism to Human Rights* (1969), vol. I, pp. 16–17.

59. For an introduction to the subject, now fortunately one of legal history, see generally, A. F. Vulliamy, *The Law of Settlement and*

Removal of Paupers (1895); E. J. Lidbetter, *Settlement and Removal* (1932); Sir John Burrows, *Decisions in the Court of Kings' Bench upon Settlement Cases* (2 vols., 1786).

60. *Final Report of the Royal Commission on the Poor Laws* (1909) H.M.S.O. Cd. 4499, p. 402; see generally, *ibid.*, Chapter IX. See for an illustrative twentieth century case, the judgement of Lord Alverstone CJ, in *Great Yarmouth Union* v. *Bethnal Green Union* (1907) 71 J.P. 422.

61. Sidney and Beatrice Webb, *English Poor Law History* (1927), vol. I, p. 396.

62. *Report of the Royal Commission on the Poor Laws* (1834), xxvii, p. 5.

63. *ibid.*, p. 31.

64. Dorothy Marshall, *The English Poor in the Eighteenth Century* (1926), p. 65.

65. *Report of the Royal Commission on the Poor Laws* (1834); see generally, Appendix A, p. 1.

66. William Sabatier, *Treatise on Poverty, its Consequences and the Remedy* (1797), p. 103.

67. *Hansard*, **9**, H. C. Deb. (1807), p. 800.

68. A kind of rotational billeting of the poor with parishioners who could exact labour in return for maintenance; see Sidney and Beatrice Webb, *English Poor Law History* (1927), vol. I, p. 190.

69. Mark Newman, 'Speenhamland in Berkshire', in E. W. Martin (ed.), *Comparative Development in Social Welfare* (1972), p. 89.

70. See generally, G. W. Oxley, *Poor Relief in England and Wales 1601–1834* (1974), p. 112.

71. Trevelyan, *op. cit.*, p. 468.

72. Karl Polanyi, *The Great Transformation* (1944), p. 79.

73. Trevelyan, *op. cit.*, pp. 469–470.

74. Jeffrey Galper, 'The Speenhamland Scales: Political, Social or Economic Disaster?', *The Social Service Review* **43** (1970), p. 54. See also Mark Newman, *op. cit.*, p. 85 *et seq.*, who calls the Speenhamland system a 'token'.

75. *Report of the Royal Commission on the Poor Laws* (1834), p. 8.

76. Ronald Mendelsohn, *Social Security in the British Commonwealth* (1954), p. 23.

77. S. G. and E. O. A. Checkland (ed., with Introduction), *The Poor Law Report of 1834* (1974), pp. 29–30.

78. R. H. Tawney, *Religion and the Rise of Capitalism* (1926), p. 242.

79. J. R. McCulloch, *The Literature of Political Economy* (1845), p. 83.

80. *A History of the English Poor Law* (1899), quoted in Sir Thomas Mackay, vol. III, p. 55.

81. Nassau Senior (ed. M. C. M. Simpson), *Correspondence with Alexis de Tocqueville from 1834 to 1859* (1872), p. 213.

82. Sidney and Beatrice Webb, *op. cit.*, p. 249.

83. See James S. Taylor, 'The Unreformed Workhouse 1776–1834' in E. W. M. Martin (ed.), *op. cit.*, p. 57 *et seq.*

84. Cases of life-long condemnation to a workhouse still emerge occasionally in the newspapers. The author was recently shown the records of inmates in a former Canterbury workhouse, which has now been turned into a well-equipped hospital and day-care centre for the elderly, who came as abandoned children and never left.

85. Reinhard Bendix, *Work and Authority in Industry* (1956), p. 98.

86. Trevelyan, *op. cit.*, p. 538.

87. Maurice Marston, *Sir Edwin Chadwick* (1925), p. 22. See also Jeremy Bentham, *Constitutional Code for the Use of all Nations professing Liberal Opinions* (1830).

88. Or alternatively, the 'Three Bashaws'; G. D. H. Cole, *Chartist Portraits* (1941), p. 94.

89. See generally, Nicholas C. Edsall, *The Anti-Poor Law Movement 1834–1844* (1971), a survey of the widespread opposition to the New Poor Law, particularly in the North. See also Asa Briggs, *Chartist Studies* (1962)—one of the 'dynamics of Chartism' was 'hatred of the New Poor Law'; *ibid.*, p. 139.

90. Sir William Monypenny, *The Life of Benjamin Disraeli* (1929), p. 374. Disraeli was an ardent critic of the divisive effects of the Poor Law on society; see particularly the famous passage on the 'Two Nations between whom there is no intercourse and no sympathy; who are ignorant of each other's habits, thoughts, and feelings, as if they were dwellers in different zones, or inhabitants of different planets . . . THE RICH AND THE POOR'; Benjamin Disraeli, *Sybil* (1845), pp. 76–7. See also Charles Dickens, *Oliver Twist*, serialized in 1837 and 1838.

91. Evidence in the House of Commons *Committee on the Andover Workhouse* (1846), Parliamentary Papers 663, Part II, Question 22.

92. J. L. and B. L. Hammond, *The Bleak Age* (1947), p. 52.

93. William Howitt, *The Rural Life of England* (1838,) vol. II, p. 131.

94. Quoted in S. E. Finer, *Sir Edwin Chadwick* (1952), p. 126.

95. Walter Bagehot, *The English Constitution* (1867), p. 189.

96. See later discussion at p. .164

97. The *Andover* case was an investigation into conditions at the Andover Union's workhouse, which revealed appalling conditions; see generally, *Report of the Committee on the Andover Workhouse* (1846), See also later discussion on p. 104.

98. For a general survey of the late nineteenth and early twentieth century Poor Law functions, see T. W. Fowle, *The Poor Law* (1890).

99. Quoted in C. L. Mowat, *The Charity Organisation Society 1869–1913* (1961), p. 68.

100. David Owen, *English Philanthropy 1660–1960* (1965), p. 165.

101. Charity Organisation Society *5th Annual Report* (1875), pp. 5–6, quoted in C. L. Mowat, *op. cit.*, p. 26. The C.O.S., as well as spreading to the U.S.A., the former British Empire and to Europe, has how evolved into the Family Welfare Association. The Charity Organisation *Review* has been the quarterly *Social Work* since 1939.

102. David Owen, *op. cit.*, p. 225.

103. See John Lewis Gillin, *Poverty and Dependency* (1921); and *Dr Chalmers and the Poor Law* (1911), a republication of Chalmers' evidence to the Select Committee of the House of Commons on the Poor Laws in 1817 and a selection of his other articles.

104. Mrs. George Kerr, Secretary of the C.O.S. in Edinburgh, in the Preface to *Dr Chalmers and the Poor Laws* (1911), p. 2. See also N. Masterman (ed.), *Chalmers on Charity* (1900).

105. Charles Stewart Loch, *Charity and Social Life* (1910), p. 345.

106. G. D. H. Cole in A. F. C. Bourdillon (ed.), *Voluntary Social Services* (1945), p. 19.

107. The open-handed undiscriminating charity of the Salvation Army, according to one prominent C.O.S. member, 'cut at the root of all the teachings and endeavours of twenty years'; Helen Bosanquet, *Social Work in London* (1914), p. 341.

108. General William Booth, *In Darkest England and the Way Out* (1890), p. 14: 'The foul and fetid breath of our slums is almost as poisonous as that of the African Swamp'. See for a C.O.S. critique, Bernard Bosanquet, '*In Darkest England' On the Wrong Track* (1891).

109. Over a polemical book by a C.O.S. member, George Reynolds, *Dr Barnardo's Homes, Startling Revelations* (1877). Barnardo was completely cleared of any fraud in a subsequent arbitration of the dispute, and the undignified assault on him temporarily damaged the C.O.S. reputation. See generally, A. E. Williams, *Barnardo of Stepney, The Father of Nobody's Children* (1943).

110. Asa Briggs in the Introduction to the Centenary edition of Samuel Smiles, *Self Help* (1859) p. 7.

111. Henry Mayhew, *London Labour and the London Poor* (1851).

112. C. L. Mowat, *op. cit.*, p. 6. See also for a general description of the ploys utilized, E. P. Thompson, *The Making of the English Working Class* (1963), pp. 265–6.

113. The Rev. Andrew Mearns is quoted in *Contemporary Review* **XLIV** (December 1883) as the sole author, but this was contested by William Preston, a journalist, who was thought by Mearns to have been an 'assistant' who 'merely compiled the text'. See the Introduction by Antony S. Wohl to the 1970 edition of *The Bitter Cry of Outcast London* (1883, 1970), p. 14. The British Museum catalogue and Halkett and Laing, *Dictionary of Anonymous and Pseudonymous English Literature* ascribe it to Preston. See also P. d'Arcy Jones, *The Christian Socialist Revival 1877–1914* (1968), p. 414.

114. Bentley B. Gilbert, *The Evolution of National Insurance in Great Britain* (1966), p. 28.

115. Andrew Mearns, *The Bitter Cry of Outcast London* (1883, 1970), p. 75. Any profits which arose from the sale of the pamphlet were 'devoted to the aggressive work of the London Congregational Union'.

116. Among the resident workers in later years were Lord Beveridge (first Director of Labour Exchanges, etc.); Sir Hubert Llewellyn Smith (architect with Beveridge of the 1911 unemployment insurance scheme); Albert Mansbridge (founder and first General Secretary of the Workers' Educational Association); Professor R. H. Tawney (the first W.E.A. tutor); and Clement Attlee.

117. J. A. R. Pimlott, *Toynbee Hall* (1935), p. 1. Beveridge once described Toynbee Hall as 'a school of humanity in Whitechapel for those who had done Literae Humaniores in Oxford'; Beveridge, *Voluntary Action* (1948), p. 130. See also M. D. Stocks, *Fifty Years in Every Street* (1945), on the Manchester University Settlement. There are now over one thousand University Settlements in various parts of the world. See also W. Reason, *University and Social Settlements* (1898) and

A. F. Young and E. T. Ashton, *British Social Work in the Nineteenth Century* (1956), pp. 223–34.

118. For example, Beveridge's famous book on unemployment relied extensively on his researches in East London while sub-warden and resident of Toynbee Hall from 1903–7; *Unemployment, A Problem of Industry* (1909). Eleanor Rathbone's advocacy of family allowances also came out of her experience in the Manchester University Settlement; *The Disinherited Family* (1924).

119. T. S. and M. B. Simey, *Charles Booth, Social Scientist* (1960), pp. 265–6.

120. Mary Booth, *Charles Booth, A Memoir* (1918), p. 15.

121. Karl de Schweinitz, *England's Road to Social Security* (1943), p. 178.

122. Class A, 'the lowest of occasional labourers, loafers and semi-criminals', up to Class H, 'the upper middle-class'; Charles Booth, *Life and Labour of the People of London* (1889–1903), vol. 1, p. 33. Ruth Glass wryly comments that Booth 'has always been more admired than read', 'Urban Sociology in Great Britain', *Current Sociology* **4** (1955), p. 46. See also Sir Hubert Llewellyn Smith, 'The New Survey of Life and Labour in London', *Journal of the Royal Statistical Society* **92** (1929), part 4, p. 536.

123. Harold W. Pfautz, *Charles Booth on the City* (1967), p. 6.

124. *Charity Organisation Review*, **V** (July 1889), p. 279. An unsigned review (usually signifying the work of the editor, Charles Loch) which expressed the hope in its final sentence that, in future volumes, Mr. Booth would 'lead the hunt against the inspectors and other myrmidions of State socialism'; *ibid.*, p. 282.

125. In Charles Booth, *Pauperism, A Picture* (1892). For a C.O.S. attack on this, see Helen Bosanquet, *The Strength of the People* (1902) which has as its basic theme that the elderly should rely not on pensions but on their families' earning power. Beatrice Webb (who was a cousin of Booth's wife, and served as an investigator into 'sweating' for the Survey in Bishopsgate) states that Booth was persuaded into his views on old age pensions by Canon Barnett; Beatrice Webb, *My Apprenticeship* (1926), p. 208.

126. Mainly cuttings from the *Northern Star;* Friedrich Engels, *The Condition of the Working Class in England* (1845, 1958 transl., 2nd ed., 1971).

127. David Owen, *op. cit.*, p. 135.

128. See, for example, Sir Frederick Eden's account of the sturdy independence of farm labourers in Radnorshire; Sir Frederick Eden, *The State of the Poor* (1797, republished 1928), p. 374.

129. 'Well, one knows there is a great deal of poverty in the East End of London, but I wonder whethere there is in provincial cities. Why not investigate York?', in a letter quoted by Asa Briggs, *Social Thought and Social Action: A Study of Seebohm Rowntree* (1954), p. 17.

130. He later found himself confirming the S.D.F. conclusions; Simeys, *op. cit.*, pp. 69–70. See also H. M. Hyndman, *The Record of an Adventurous Life* (1911), p. 331; the autobiography of the Marxist stockbroker who formed the S.D.F. in 1884.

131. Booth based his survey on the census returns of 1881, but, taking a hint from Joseph Chamberlain who had used the same method when preparing for slum clearance in Birmingham, he depended largely on interviews with 250 school attendance officers.

132. Letter from Charles Booth quoted in B. Seebohm Rowntree, *Poverty: A Study of Town Life* (1901), p. 355.

133. T. H. Escott, *England: Its People, Policy and Pursuits* (1885), pp. 128–9; the views of a journalist writing on conditions in Liverpool and Manchester.

134. Beatrice Webb, *op. cit.*, p. 343.

135. Asa Briggs, 'The Welfare State in Historical Perspective', in S. P. Aiyar, *Perspectives on the Welfare State* (1966), p. 35.

136. Michael Rose, *The English Poor Law* (1971), p. 76, quoting Nassau Senior's *Diary* for April/May 1834 at pp. 88–90.

137. It has been estimated that only 10–20 per cent of 'paupers' in the mid-nineteenth century ever saw the inside of a workhouse; Rose, *op. cit.*, p. 160.

138. J. T. Ward, *The Factory System* (1970), p. 182.

139. Bentley B. Gilbert, *The Evolution of National Insurance in Great Britain* (1966), p. 17.

140. Sidney and Beatrice Webb, *English Poor Law History* (1929), Part II, vol. II, p. 108. His sense of grievance was perhaps understandable in the light of the Government's reasons. In a wounding letter, Lord Althorp explained the view of the Cabinet: 'I must frankly admit that your station in society was not such as would have made it fit that you should be appointed one of the

commissioners'. From the Chadwick papers, quoted in R. A. Lewis, *Edwin Chadwick and the Public Health Movement* (1952); see David Roberts, *Victorian Origins of the British Welfare State* (1960), p. 146.

141. George Haw, *From Workhouse to Westminster* (1907), p. 105—the biography of Will Crooks M.P., who had lived in the workhouse as a child.

142. Graphically described in George Lansbury, *My Life* (1928), pp. 135–6.

143. George Lansbury, *op. cit.*, p. 133.

144. Lansbury consistently described the C.O.S. as 'hypocritical, heartless and brutal, and urged kind-hearted people, whatever they did with their money, at least never to give it to the C.O.S.'; Raymond Postgate, *The Life of George Lansbury* (1951), p. 39.

145. See 'Poplarism' in Raymond Postgate, *op. cit.*, and the pamphlet *Guilty and Proud of It! Poplar's Answer* (1921), in part quoted in Rose, *op. cit.*, p. 300. See generally, B. Keith-Lucas, 'Poplarism', *Public Law* (1962), pp. 52–80.

146. There is considerable dispute over this view. Professor McBriar states that, despite the various theories, 'there still remains some mystery about the reasons for setting up the Commission at that particular time'; A. M. McBriar, *Fabian Socialism and English Politics 1884–1918* (1962), p. 263. See the discussion on this point in J. C. Brown, 'Ideas concerning Social Policy and their influence on Legislation in Britain 1902–11', (unpublished London Ph.D. thesis, 1964), pp. 190–2. See for the Fabian view, Edward R. Pease, *The History of the Fabian Society* (1925), p. 212.

147. Beatrice Webb, *Our Partnership* (1948), p. 317.

148. Harold E. Raynes, *Social Security in Britain* (1960), p. 175.

149. *Report of the Royal Commission on the Poor Laws* (1909), Cd–4499, Appendix Vol. 1. Minutes of Evidence, Question 3219.

150. George Lansbury, *op. cit.*, p. 165.

151. Sir Thomas Mackay, *A History of the English Poor Law* (1899), vol. III, p. vi.

152. C. S. Loch, *Charity and Social Life* (1910), p. 368. Loch's obituary in *The Times* (25 January 1923) states: 'He made the C.O.S.: he was the C.O.S.'

153. These included Sir Charles Loch, Mrs. Helen Bosanquet, Octavia Hill and T. Hancock Nunn, all prominent writers on the subject of pauperism. From near the outset, the Majority represented, however, 'united opposition to Minority proposals rather than absolute unanimity of signatories'; John H. Muirhead, *By What Authority* (1909), quoted in E. F. Stevenson, *Unemployment Relief, the Basic Problem* (1934), p. 207.

154. *Report of the Royal Commission on the Poor Laws* (1909), Cd–4499, Majority Report, Part IV, p. 96.

155. Beatrice Webb, *My Apprenticeship* (1926), p. 343.

156. Mary Agnes Hamilton, *Sidney and Beatrice Webb* (1933), p. 189.

157. Joan Simeon Clarke in Margaret Cole (ed.), *The Webbs and Their Work* (1949), p. 102.

158. Raymond Postgate, *op. cit.*, p. 88.

159. Beatrice Webb, *Our Partnership* (1948), (ed. Barbara Drake and Margaret Cole) p. 324.

160. Beatrice Webb, *op. cit.*, p. 328.

161. 'An attractive grand seigneur', Beatrice Webb, *op. cit.*, p. 321. Hamilton said of the Royal Commission in his memoirs, however, that it 'was by far the heaviest business in which I was ever engaged'; Lord George Hamilton, *Parliamentary Reminiscences and Reflections* (1922), p. 329.

162. Collected into Charles Booth, *Poor Law Reform* (1911).

163. Kitty Muggeridge and Ruth Adam, *Beatrice Webb* (1967), p. 181.

164. Margaret Cole, *The Life of G. D. H. Cole* (1971), p. 45.

165. The diary of the C.O.S. activist, Miss Octavia Hill, quoted extensively in E. Moberly Bell, *Octavia Hill* (1942). Nor is Mrs. Webb mentioned anywhere in Lord George Hamilton's tedious autobiography, although it should be noted that the Royal Commission receives scant attention; Lord George Hamilton, *op. cit.*, pp. 237, 328–30.

166. Raymond Postage, op. cit., p. 88. Lansbury is referred to patronizingly in Beatrice Webb's *Diary* as 'the working man on the Commission' (2 December 1905).

167. The 1908 Old Age Pensions Act, with tax-levied payments free of the Poor Law stigma, was passed before the Royal Commission report was finalized.

168. Sidney and Beatrice Webb, *The Break-Up of the Poor Law: Part One of the Minority Report* (1909), Introduction, p. ix.

169. Joan Simeon Clarke in Margaret Cole, *The Webbs and Their Work* (1949), p. 107.

170. Sidney and Beatrice Webb, *English*

Poor Law Policy (1910), p. 11 ('root principle' —*ibid*., p. 260.

171. Sidney and Beatrice Webb, *English Poor Law History* (1929), Part II, vol. I, p. 470.

172. Beatrice Webb, George Lansbury, Francis Chandler (Secretary of the Carpenters Union) and H. Russell Wakefield (the Chairman of the Central Board for the Unemployed in London).

173. There were, for instance, 24,000 children still maintained in workhouses and workhouse infirmaries on 1 January 1911; see generally, Tom Percival, *Poor Law Children* (1912), p. 24.

174. Raymond Postgate, *op. cit*., p. 91.

175. *Report of the Royal Commission on the Poor Laws* (1909), Cd–4499, Majority Report, Part IV, p. 96.

176. Sidney and Beatrice Webb, *English Poor Law Policy* (1910), p. 315.

177. Beatrice Webb, *Our Partnership* (1948), p. 477.

178. Joan Simeon Clarke in Margaret Cole (ed.), *op. cit*., p. 103.

179. *Fifth and Final Report of the Royal Commission on Labour* (1894), C–7421, p. 127.

180. *Select Committee on the Aged Deserving Poor* (1899), House of Commons 296.

181. Margaret Cole, *Beatrice Webb* (1945), p. 95.

182. Margaret Cole, *op. cit*., p. 104.

183. Raymond Postgate, *op. cit*., p. 92.

184. See generally, Roy Jenkins, *Mr Balfour's Poodle* (1954), a study of the controversy of the House of Lords' claim to a veto on legislation. Eric Hobsbawm comments that 'Lloyd George's "People's Budget" coming within a few months of the Minority Report, robbed the agitation of [the Webbs] of nine-tenths of its immediate public appeal'; 'Fabianism and the Fabians 1884–1914', (unpublished Cambridge Ph.D. thesis, 1949) p. 143.

185. A statement of John Burns reported back to the Webbs; Beatrice Webb, *Our Partnership* (1948), p. 475.

186. C. L. Mowat, *The Charity Organisation Society* (1961), p. 163.

187. Beatrice Webb, *op. cit*., p. 426.

6

The Origins of Unemployment Insurance

The origins of National Insurance in Britain were bound up with a changing view of the nature of poverty, and the reaction of society to its problems. Throughout the centuries of the Poor Law, charitable impulses stemming from a felt moral duty had been the impetus for giving aid for the poor. Even in the nineteenth century, despite the growth of the administrative machinery of the State, charity was recognized by economists and Poor Law administrators to be a crucial, and integral, supplement.[1]

The apparatus of the State had been kept to the minimum through the conscious application of principles involved in the doctrine of *laissez-faire*. Their extension into the 'Principles of 1834' had, as the Webbs put it, assumed the 'non-responsibility of the community for anything beyond keeping the destitute applicant alive'.[2] It was the fear of pauperism and dependence which dominated the Victorian debate on the poor, not the fear of poverty itself. The extent to which this feeling went can be seen in the ceaseless propaganda of the C.O.S., the main opposition to the reforms of 'New Liberalism' in the field of Unemployment Insurance both during and after their inception. In 1923, the Chairman of a Denison House[3] committee could write that:

> Till within the last quarter of a century dependence on the State has been a disappearing factor, but now it has reappeared in all its force. It is a chronic disease, for the same cases come back again and again for public assistance. It is hereditary in certain families from generation to generation, and it is contagious.[4]

The altered political climate which saw the passage of the 1911 National Insurance Act was perhaps not so much due to a revision of such views on poverty, but more to a growing consciousness amongst the poor that they had the capacity to alter their situation.[5] This was not due to an

For notes see p. 141

immediate reaction through the ballot box, but it induced a feeling that 'a system of public relief deliberately made hideous for its recipients could not long outlast the grant of universal franchise'.[6]

In Victorian Britain, pauperism meant more than poverty: it implied a moral failure. But there were a growing number of commentators who did not accept the personal accountability of individuals to be the sole or even the major determining factor of poverty. From the statistical surveys of Booth and Rowntree, wider economic and social forces could be seen to be at work, which would not be controlled merely by a 'regimentation', in the nineteenth century terminology, of the 'workshy', the 'weary willies' and the 'unemployables'. The C.O.S. statistical tables caught the mood, even if the Movement's stern philosophy went unaltered; in 1886 they changed from classifying the 'undeserving' to calling them 'those not likely to benefit', and in 1888 came the more neutral 'not assisted'.[7]

The change away from a rigid view of individual responsibility found many expressions. Perhaps the outlook on the able-bodied, but unemployed, working man was the slowest to alter. The aged and the young and the sick were more easily accommodated as particularly vulnerable members of the community. But it had taken British and other Western societies a considerable period of time 'to grasp the truth that under modern industrial conditions great numbers of working men out of work are not personally blameworthy for their misfortunes'.[8] In the light of earlier economic theories, the answer to questions of unemployment had been simple. The assumption was made that the unemployed man was 'bad' in moral terms and that he therefore 'deserved' the workhouse test. The history of the Poor Laws makes it quite plain that 'until the twentieth century punishment had always been the basic official response to mendicancy and poverty'.[9] But when the new assumption was made that poverty might be in part due to social causes, then a re-appraisal took place. Helping to speed the change was the undoubted unease felt by many who feared that unoccupied and idle men might turn to revolutionary outlets for their frustrations.

David Lloyd George, the guiding influence in the passage of the 1911 National Insurance Act, believed it would 'do more to hinder or assuage human misery than any Bill carried by the Legislature since the abolition of the Corn Laws' in that it would strike hard at two of 'the three principal causes of poverty and destitution in the homes of the industrial population of the country . . . ill-health, unemployment and drink'.[10]

Of considerable importance was the factual recognition of 'unemployment', whose introduction as a term of art made headway only in the latter part of the nineteenth century following its use by Alfred Marshall.[11] And it was only with 'the greatest reluctance and then in qualified terms' that the C.O.S., in the words of one historian, would 'admit unemployment as a fact'.[12] However, it was becoming steadily clearer that the old policies of repression had failed, in that 'no amount of the moral medicine would do much good' to unemployment in large cities caused by genuine economic factors.[13] What was 'modern' about unemployment was 'the recognition of the fact rather than the fact itself'.[14] Charles Loch could carry on using the word unemployment in quotation marks,[15] but the real question that had to be faced was, now that unemployment had secured recognition as an economic problem, what new remedies could be formulated to cope with its deleterious social effects?

The Unemployed Workmen Act 1905

The social mechanisms designed to relieve poverty caused by unemployment before the introduction of National Insurance in 1911 were extremely varied; perhaps their one similarity was that they were all inadequate to meet the problem. As well as Poor Law relief, both indoor and outdoor, the remedial measures involved a mixture of relief works (both with and without Exchequer grants); trade union insurance—largely confined to craftsmen; systematic short-time working; institutional training for both disabled and fit men; Land Settlement and afforestation; road construction and land drainage; some training schemes run by employers; a few Juvenile Unemployment centres run from charity; and an embryonic form of State subsidies to Industry. Emigration was a drastic but well-utilized solution. However, the most direct method of specific relief for the unemployed was private charity, particularly in the form of the disposal of voluntary funds through *ad hoc* local committees.[16]

In each recurring crisis of unemployment from 1862 onwards to 1911, Mansion House Relief Funds were opened under the auspices of the Lord Mayor of London, and countless similar appeals were made elsewhere.[17] The disposition of such sums was a matter of great variety: 'sometimes it was merely scrambled for; thrown to anyone who, at first glance, did not look too respectable. Sometimes it was doled out in more orderly ways'.[18] It was understandable that in this situation the C.O.S. should put itself forward as a centralized agency for distributing charity, co-ordinating the efforts of the myriad funds and relief projects in the hands of enthusiastic amateurs. The opportunities for abuse were manifold. In 1882 the C.O.S. Inquiries Section made reports on over

2,000 individual 'imposters' utilizing the funds of charities.[19] But in the evolving economic circumstances, the moral aims of the C.O.S. were clearly unrealistic. It was no longer possible to talk of poverty as not being in any way connected with material needs but solely with 'a poverty and degradation of life, an habitual reliance on others, due to want of self-control and foresight, and of the goodness that underlies these things'.[20] The C.O.S. in fact declined rapidly after 1909, with Charles Loch retiring in 1912, but in 1911 a Fabian critic was well able to substantiate her claim that the C.O.S. was 'almost grotesquely out of accord with the facts of everyday experience'.[21]

The beginning of the end of 'voluntaryism' as an approach to unemployment can be clearly traced from the Unemployed Workmen Act of 1905. Following a special Unemployed Fund for London in the winter of 1904–5, it was generally agreed that some regularization had to be made of the local relief committees. Allegations had been made of corruption and waste, which were substantiated in some instances. Many such complaints had been made before. The Mansion House Relief Fund of 1886 had been particularly notorious in leading to the misapplication of funds and an extensive trafficking of relief tickets.[22] Adding to these administrative difficulties was the fact that, in the aftermath of the Boer Wars, many local Boards of Guardians had been inundated with requests for help by soldiers who had returned home to find themselves unemployed. A number of local initiatives were taken, and in 1903 the Local Government Board had expressly to inform the York Board of Guardians that they had no powers to continue finding work for the unemployed. Their sole duty, stressed, the Local Government Board, was to concern themselves with the relief of destitution.[23] Plainly this sort of attitude could do nothing for a worsening situation, and Walter Long, the President of the Board of Trade, called a conference of Metropolitan Guardians in October 1904 to discuss a scheme for dealing with the unemployed. From these proposals grew the 1905 Act, whose aim, according to Beveridge, was 'not to do any new thing, but to do slightly better what had been done before'.[24] However, its importance as a landmark lay, as Professor Bruce points out, not in its effect but rather in the hesitant steps it had taken towards a unified and national approach to the problems of unemployment.[25]

The Act authorized the setting up of Distress Committees by each major local authority, although this depended entirely on their own initiative as the Act was in no way compulsory. The principal aim was to supervise the administration of all relief work and other unofficial activities for the aid of the unemployed. The Act was not a great success, and Professor Gilbert believes that the most which can be said about it is that 'it showed what was *not* possible in the way of help for the jobless'.[26] However, this very failure may, he thinks, have had important repercussions, for 'it turned serious social thinkers—most important among them, Sidney Webb and William Beveridge—to the search for other alternatives to the Poor Law'.[27]

Beveridge himself, who served as a member of the Central Body for the Unemployed which supervised the work of the London committees set up under the Act, thought that the system had 'done a little to co-ordinate existing agencies and improve in minor points the administration of special relief. It has not had any appreciable impression upon the problem. Its main service has been to demonstrate beyond question its own essential inadequacy'.[28] When the legislation was announced it was expressly stated by the Government that it would provisionally last for three years pending the Report of the Royal Commission on the Poor Laws, but despite this temporary nature it was subjected to considerable criticism. The President of the T.U.C. in 1905, for example, referred to it as an 'abortion born of political expediency and desperation'.[29] And the Webbs thought that the entire machinery for 'Relief Works for the Unemployed represents only a counsel of despair, in a community knowing no better alternative'.[30]

Labour Exchanges

During the nineteenth century there had been many experiments in co-operative farming and labour colonies, sometimes merely to provide employment but usually with a moral aim in mind. Canon Barnett, George Lansbury and many others of a radical disposition saw this 'Back to the Land' ideal of farm colonies as a dynamic answer to the problems of listless men in the cities.[31] Their ideas were in logical descent from the radical utopian tradition of Chartism and Owenism with their possible memories of the Levellers and Diggers of the seventeenth century.[32] The Salvation Army, founded in Britain in 1878, had long advocated land colonization as a remedy for unemployment, and General William Booth himself saw the extension of this idea into emigration and colonization overseas as an answer to what he called 'the surplus problem'.[33]

Although they were both on the Central Body for the Unemployed in London, Beveridge was somewhat sceptical of his colleague George Lansbury's views on land colonies.[34] But Beveridge had his own pet scheme—the setting up of a national system of Labour Exchanges. A fluent speaker of German,[35] Beveridge had paid a personal visit to Germany in August 1907 to investigate for himself the workings of employment exchanges. A public 'registry' had been established in

Stuttgart as early as 1865.[36] It was as a direct result of Beveridge's leaders in the *Morning Post*,[37] and his personal advocacy of the new procedure to the Royal Commission on the Poor Laws, that the idea took root in Britain, culminating in the introduction of exchanges in 1910. Beveridge's self-confessed 'fetish of National Labour Exchanges'[38] had grown directly from his theories and practice with the temporary work of the Central Body for the Unemployed in London. As well as being the first witness before the Royal Commission on questions relating to unemployment, Beveridge spent an influential weekend with the Webbs at George Bernard Shaw's home in Ayot St Lawrence, where he 'converted them to labour exchanges'.[39]

The result was that both the Majority and Minority Reports came out firmly in favour of them being set up. The Majority stated that 'in the forefront of our proposals we place labour exchanges',[40] while the Minority felt that their idea of a national system of exchanges, 'though in itself not an adequate remedy, is the foundation of all our proposals. It is in our view an indispensable condition of real reform.'[41] The basic function of the labour exchange idea was as 'a placing and educative agency'.[42] The British concept can be traced in the special provision made for merchant seamen under the Merchant Shipping Acts designed to do away with the evils of 'crimping'. Under this authority, special employment officers were appointed in all major ports to supervise the proper allocation of berths to seamen desiring a passage.[43]

Following on the experience of the seamen's exchanges, the Labour Bureaux (London) Act of 1902 enabled the council of any metropolitan borough to maintain a labour bureau by deductions from the general rates. But since the Act was optional, few boroughs took up their potential powers. Of equal importance were the pioneering voluntary schemes in existence, and the Movement led by Mrs. Ogilvie Gordon from 1904 for the setting up by Local Education committees of 'Educational Information and Employment Bureaux' which became the forerunners of the modern Youth Employment Service.[44] The first voluntary Labour Exchange for adults had been set up by Nathaniel Cohen at Egham in 1885.[45]

Owing to the personal intervention of the new President of the Board of Trade, Winston Churchill—and after numerous previous offers from the Board of Trade—Beveridge accepted a permanent job in 1908 as the first Director of Labour Exchanges. His first responsibility was to pilot legislation through Parliament to create a national system of exchanges.[46] Beveridge himself believed that Churchill's presence in the Board of Trade at that particular moment was a striking illustration 'of how much the personality of the Minister in a few critical months may change the course of social legislation'.[47] The same comment could perhaps be applied to Beveridge's own unique contribution to the course of subsequent social legislation.

Churchill was alleged to have stated on becoming President of the Board of Trade that 'there is nothing to do here. Lloyd George has taken all the plums,'[48] but it is clear that he had an awareness of the problems of unemployment from the start of his appointment.[49] Enthusiastically backing Beveridge, and with the weighty opinion of the Royal Commission Reports swaying public opinion, the Labour Exchanges Act of 1909 went through both Houses of Parliament without division or amendment. Six clauses long, the Act when passed empowered the Board of Trade to set up exchanges where necessary and to make any regulations for their management. A special fund was set up to provide loans to men having to travel to find work, a new dimension to the old Poor Law licensing system.

Sixty-one new exchanges opened on 1 February 1910, including nineteen 'registries' which were taken over from the Central Body for the Unemployed in London.[50] From the start, Beveridge ensured through administrative regulations that an effort was made to observe strict neutrality in industrial disputes.[51] Exchanges were to be closed to any employers seeking black-leg labour in strike situations. The full co-operation of the trade unions was also secured in that workers were permitted to refuse any job offer made which might result in their being paid less than the going union rate, without jeopardizing the possibility of the Exchange giving them further notifications of jobs.

The new Labour Exchanges, as Professor Gilbert states, 'created, to be sure, not a single extra job, but they made it possible for the workman to offer himself for employment anywhere in the country',[52] in an attempt to make more routinized and efficient the age-old system of 'tramping' from town to town seeking employment.[53] As a method for obtaining work used mainly by travelling artisans since its adoption by craftsmen such as the Devon wool-combers at the start of the eighteenth century, the practice of 'tramping' had rarely lived up to the theory. For the skilled or craft worker of the nineteenth century, who was a member of a trade union, tramping had developed into a complex system of relief at 'lodge houses', whose administrative details of registration and insurance procedures helped shape the later system of National Insurance.[54]

Churchill's oft-repeated boast was that 'one hundred new Labour Exchanges would be less costly and more valuable to the nation than one new battleship'.[55] However, Beveridge all along had seen the new system as a means to a further end; that of unemployment insurance. By 1906, he had come to view exchanges as 'one of the most thoroughgoing and indispensable measures of reform falling within the practical politics of this century',[56] although it was clear that, at that time, Beveridge's interest mainly centred on the effect of labour exchanges on problems of de-casualization, particularly amongst dockers, of whom he had made a special study while at Toynbee Hall. However, one year later, Beveridge thought the principle of exchanges was of 'universal application'.[57] And it was evident that he was thinking of their potential role in operating a stage scheme of insurance benefit for the unemployed. As Beveridge put it some years later, employment exchanges were established with the dual purpose of trying to 'diminish unemployment by reducing the time taken by workmen in looking for work and to supply the machinery for compulsory unemployment insurance'.[58]

The German Influence

The National Insurance Act of 1911 was not the first piece of legislation for compulsory insurance in Britain.[59] But in the political climate of the time it was a monumental step forward. To Beveridge, 'the project seemed then, and was, a daring adventure'.[60]

A National Insurance League had in fact been formed as early as 1882 to propagate the ideas of Canon Blackley,[61] who had written an article in 1878 advocating National Insurance for sickness and old age.[62] But Canon Blackley had no belief in a compulsory insurance system, although he advocated a state-run scheme. His opponents might agree to some form of insurance, but the view of one critic was that 'nothing in the nature of insurance warranted its removal from the healthy influence of private enterprise'.[63] However, the argument which subsequently developed was not on the nature of insurance but on the nature of the need in the community which could be aided by a community insurance scheme.

The announcement that advanced research had been done on the possible introduction of social insurance, made in Lloyd George's speech introducing the 'People's Budget'[64] of 1909, was a considerable surprise. It was followed by the further announcement, made one month later by the President of the Board of Trade, Winston Churchill, that the scheme would include compulsory unemployment insurance for certain selected trades.[65] Lloyd George had become personally committed to a project of social insurance following a tour of Germany with Young Liberals in August 1908, where he 'had been much impressed with the best side of everything which had been shown him'.[66] But the German models he had seen did not include a *compulsory* unemployment benefit scheme. The only model here was a law of the canton of St Gall in Switzerland in 1894. The scheme lasted for a trial period of two years and was speedily abandoned after a referendum in which there was near unanimity in the view that it had been a complete failure. No premiums had been required of employers and on investigation the project was found to have been 'badly conceived and badly executed'.[67]

Lloyd George himself was certain that his inspiration came from Germany. Describing himself as 'an ardent advocate of compulsory State Insurance against social and industrial vicissitudes',[68] he wrote of the

> success attained by Germany, the pioneer of National Insurance . . . which is now triumphant, unquestioned alike by employers and employed. It was from Germany that we who were privileged to be associated with the application of the principle to the United Kingdom found our first inspiration, and it is with her experience before us that we feel confident of the future.[69]

However, apart from the German legislation, there was considerable precedent for health insurance in the varied benefits developed by the friendly societies and the trade unions in Britain. Many craft trade unions also paid benefits during periods of unemployment, although the individual sums were usually small. In 1908, for example, trade union membership stood at 2,357,381 and £1,254,000 had been paid out in unemployment benefits—about ten shillings per head per annum.[70]

The Minority Report of the Royal Commission on the Poor Laws favoured the introduction of social insurance by a state scheme of subsidies to this already existing system of trade union insurance. This was along the lines of the Ghent system, whereby union benefit funds had been supplemented largely to avoid the expense and administrative problems of a Government-run scheme. In Ghent the scheme had meant only limited coverage as a minority of wage-earners were trade union members, but Sidney Webb's views were manifestly coloured by his vision of 100 per cent trade unionism. Certainly the Minority Report's scheme would not have alleviated the position of the great majority of claimants to the Distress Committees under the Unemployed Workmen Act, as they were not members of the trade unions.[71]

Lloyd George believed that the Liberal Government of the time was 'carried forward on a tide of social pity that was only waiting for a chance of expression',[72] But how far he can be said to have owed the details of the legislation to German impetus is disputed. Certainly the origins of Bismarck's social policy were not in 'social pity'. And to talk of Bismarck creating a 'welfare state' system is, according to Professor Asa Briggs, 'very misleading. Bismarck's legislation rested on a basic conservatism . . . and was sustained by a bureaucracy which had no counterpart in Britain except in Chadwick's imagination'.[73] The German intention was rather more to assuage socialist feelings than to nurture 'social pity'. More than anything, Bismarck feared 'class war' and wanted to keep it at bay. He felt that the movement of the masses towards socialism 'will cease as soon as working-men see that the government and legislative bodies are earnestly concerned for their welfare'.[74] The Imperial message of 17 November 1881, which announced a bill of social insurance for health, was even more explicit: 'the cure of social ills must be sought not exclusively in the repression of Social Democrat excesses, but simultaneously in the positive advancement of the welfare of the working classes'.[75]

A similar view could perhaps be detected in Liberal motivations for the introduction of social legislation, although this was vigorously denied by Lloyd George, albeit in a not particularly convincing manner:

> I am told I have tried to bribe the working classes. If I set out to bribe the working classes I should know how to do it, but in future when I try to take the next measure that calls upon the working classes for a fair share of contribution I shall know that the people who are always flaunting the honesty of their opinions are the first to join with the extremist Socialist in the land to embarrass and hinder me on the way.[76]

Lloyd George was, of course, fully capable of such deviousness. One biographer comments that his political morality 'judged by conventional standards . . . was not wholly admirable'.[77] To his civil service advisers on the National Insurance Act, Lloyd George appeared to believe that he was 'doing the work of the Man of Nazareth, whatever his somewhat reluctant colleagues might feel about his particular way of doing it'.[78] Nonetheless it was largely due to Lloyd George's personal drive and initiative that the National Insurance Bill reached the statute book.

William Braithwaite, Lloyd George's adviser on the sickness benefit side of the 1911 Act, made it clear in his memoirs that his aspect of the scheme owed a great deal to German influence. He himself visited Germany on a number of occasions to 'plough through' the legislation, and then to report personally to Lloyd George.[79] However, Beveridge, one of the architects of the unemployment insurance aspects of the 1911 Act, stated bluntly in his memoirs that 'compulsory insurance against unemployment owed nothing to any working model in Germany or elsewhere', but that it was solely the product of hard work in the Board of Trade.[80]

Certainly the unemployment side of the Act was without real

precedent in its narrow sense. However, all available analogies were utilized. Beveridge himself freely admitted that 'the idea of collecting contributions by stamping of cards carried by the workman, till then unknown in Britain, was copied from Germany',[81] but he stated later on that it was 'the one feature of the scheme which, if we were starting again, I should most like to reconsider'.[82] However, the major part of the work involved, in particular the contribution requirements, disqualification provisions and the appeal machinery, were 'the original fruit of hard thinking'.[83]

The Board of Trade Team

Unemployment insurance, Part Two of the National Insurance Act of 1911 represented 'perhaps the boldest experiment in social legislation of the entire period of the New Liberalism'.[84] It developed in large part from the nucleus of civil servants working in the Board of Trade from 1909 onwards. There was in fact no logic in putting both labour exchanges and unemployment insurance under the Board of Trade other than an understandable desire to short-circuit the actions of John Burns at the Local Government Board, and also because of the ambitions and personalities of the successive Presidents of the Board of Trade, Lloyd George and Churchill.[85]

Churchill made his outlook on unemployment clear in a speech in October 1908, when he stated in Dundee that:

> I do not agree with those who say that every man must look after himself, and that the intervention by the State in such matters as I have referred to will be fatal to his self-reliance, his foresight and his thrift . . . If terror be an incentive to thrift, surely the penalties of the system which we have abandoned ought to have stimulated thrift as much as anything could have been stimulated in this world.[86]

This was a far cry from the views of many of his contemporaries, and certainly a long way from the old dogmas of the past. For example, Sir Thomas Mackay, the Poor Law historian, had thought that 'the object of modern statesmanship should be, not to plunge forward into the unlimited slough of social legislation'.[87] Mackay's tirade against any form of socialism, using 'proof' from history of its catastrophic consequences, was perhaps only equalled by Hilaire Belloc's book *The Servile State*, published in 1912 with the National Insurance Act firmly in mind as the first step in society's downward fall.[88]

Churchill was aided in his scheme to establish unemployment

insurance by two able lieutenants, both products of Toynbee Hall, William Beveridge and Hubert Llewellyn Smith; one American commentator states that 'it is probably not far from the truth to say that the Bill was a Toynbee Hall product'.[89] Although Beveridge was primarily responsible for the work of the new Labour Exchanges and was junior to Llewellyn Smith, the Permanent Under-Secretary, their work on the legislation and the stream of memoranda to Churchill and the Government was essentially a team effort. Llewellyn Smith had been the youngest member of Charles Booth's survey team in 1888 and was later to be the Director of the follow-up New Survey of London Life and Labour in 1928.[90] He was, in the words of one biographer, 'essentially the "professional", a bureaucrat of the highest calibre',[91] and as such initiated Beveridge into the art of dealing adroitly with Parliamentary questions and in effecting the speedy passage of legislation.[92] It may be that Llewellyn Smith kept strictly to a backstage role, as Braithwaite, who liaised with the Board of Trade on Part One of the Act, thought Beveridge 'was in charge of the Unemployment scheme, which was running concurrently' with the Sickness benefit scheme.[93]

Churchill's malicious remark many years later in a 1943 broadcast to the effect that 'my friend Sir William Beveridge' had been an expert on labour exchanges but had only been marginally concerned with the 1911 Act was totally unjustified. Lady Beveridge's comment that her husband in fact 'took the brunt of the work of preparing the legislative measures for establishing unemployment insurance' was perhaps overstressed in the need for justification.[94] On the other hand, Llewellyn Smith's biographer believes that the Permanent Under-Secretary was 'primarily responsible for the inception of unemployment benefit'.[95] However, Churchill's successor as President of the Board of Trade, Sidney Buxton, in writing a note of congratulation to Beveridge on the passage of the 1911 Act stated that 'to you and to H. Smith, the country owes a deep debt of gratitude for the inception of the measure, for working it out, for its successful modification and for its successful passage through Parliament'.[96]

Both Beveridge and Llewellyn Smith had had a 'youthful alliance with the Webbs', although Beveridge felt somewhat cynically at the time that it 'had achieved its purpose when it landed labour exchanges and me in the Board of Trade'.[97] Although Beveridge never broke off the contact, and indeed later took up the Directorship of the Webbs' favourite project, the London School of Economics, at their express request, Llewellyn Smith took a very different view, seeing it as his role to ease his Minister, Churchill, away from the grasp of the Webbs.[98]

The principal reason for this parting of the ways was the Webbs' continuing advocacy of the Ghent system of insurance and also their belief that the 1911 Act was an attempt to 'dish' their broad schemes for the break-up of the Poor Law and the setting up of community social services.[99] The socialist view of the final version of the Act was understandably diffident. Caught in a classic dilemma, on the one hand they welcomed the help it would give working people, but they also regarded it as a palliative which would prevent further reform on the subject for some time.[100] Keir Hardie, the founder of the Independent Labour Party in 1893 and the so-called Member for the Unemployed,[101] took the second view:

> No, say the Liberals, but we will give you an Insurance Bill. We shall not uproot the cause of poverty, but we will give you a porous plaster to cover the disease that poverty causes.[102]

The Ghent scheme had been established in 1901 and was completely reorganized in 1904. The trade unions were able under its provisions to increase the unemployment and other benefits which they were already paying by a supplement received from the Municipality. The ratio of this contribution was settled by a Managing Committee at the end of each month, but it could not go beyond the sum assessed and paid in trade union benefit. Similar schemes had been adopted by most Belgian towns, and there was normally a sixty-day maximum benefit period.[103] The ethos of the scheme was expressly stated to be 'help thyself, and the municipality will help thee'.[104]

Beveridge, who had personally investigated the Ghent scheme on commission from the Board of Trade in November 1907, had come to the conclusion that this system of subsidizing trade unions would not work in the British context, because it 'would not cover the people most in need of insurance'.[105] Unlike the Webbs, it was not part of Beveridge's political philosophy to see an expanded role for trade unions within British society. The parting of the ways was further advanced by disagreement on the nature of the Labour Exchanges. Whereas the Webbs wanted compulsory exchanges and voluntary trade union insurance, Beveridge desired, and got, voluntary exchanges—which he hoped would assist in winning the confidence of both employers and workers—but a compulsory state scheme of insurance. However, the success of the now institutional and ubiquitous 'Labour Exchange' was not immediate.[106] At first many employers stood aloof, which, thought one commentator a decade after their introduction, was in part 'due to mere inertia, ignorance of the part the Exchanges are designed to play, and a hereditary distrust of socialistic enterprise by the State. This distrust has undoubtedly been strengthened by vicious, exaggerated, and sometimes entirely false charges brought by a section of the press'.[107] Fortunately, this phase passed and employment exchanges have entered fully into the everyday consciousness of British life, although their coverage of vacancies is by no means universal, and the Service as a whole has recently been criticized for ignoring the needs of the low skilled.[108]

Beveridge's long-term aim was explicit. He wrote that 'in the scheme of 1911, labour exchanges and unemployment insurance went together as two halves of a single programme. The exchanges were to abolish the hawking of labour, so as to reduce unemployment to its minimum; insurance was to maintain men in the intervals of unemployment that remained'.[109] His view on how this system could be brought about was entirely pragmatic. Exchanges, he felt, could only operate effectively within the framework of willing co-operation by both sides of industry; and in the prevailing industrial and social climate this meant a voluntary scheme. But on the insurance aspect he was clearly undeterred by the experience of the St Gall experiment, whose scheme was doomed, many commentators believed, simply because it was compulsory. One such writer believed that the scheme in effect failed in advance because 'it is not generally desirable to exercise coercion in social matters unless there is an obvious necessity or very clear and great advantages'.[110] Beveridge, however, felt there was such a necessity, and that there were also clear advantages.

The Passage of the Act

One romantic picture of the 1911 National Insurance Act was that Part Two was very much 'an unsolicited and spontaneous venture on the part of the Board of Trade . . . Mr Lloyd George used all his fighting powers to carry the unpopular National Insurance Bill and . . . the tentative Unemployment Insurance scheme crept on to the Statute Book under the shelter of its more conspicuous twin'.[111] Certainly the Lloyd George slogan 'ninepence for fourpence' was arresting, perhaps irresistible, and his demagogic speeches all around the country were tremendously effective. However, those concerned with Part One of the Act saw their section as 'almost an improvisation',[112] although the struggle to get the legislation past 'a reluctant Cabinet, a suspicious trade union and socialist front, a rapacious Industrial Assurance world and a venomous Press'[113] was extremely fierce.

In contrast, Part Two of the Act dealing with the unemployment insurance scheme had 'a surprisingly easy passage', partly due to the fact that no one seriously opposed the measure in principle, and perhaps also because, as Beveridge put it, 'no one outside the Board of Trade knew enough to criticize it in detail'.[114] Certainly Beveridge and

Llewellyn Smith had prepared the ground with consummate artistry. Their tactics included switching their main Parliamentary speakers, Sidney Buxton the President of the Board and Sir John Simon the Solicitor-General, at appropriate points. The first was used when broad statements of principle could muddy certain controversial clauses, and the second was used to enunciate clearly the advantageous sections.[115] It led to the passage of their Part of the Bill through the Committee and Report stages with 'almost ridiculous ease in six days'.[116]

The basic provisions of the 1911 Act's unemployment sections covered seven trades, with a workforce of about 2¼ million workers. Eighty per cent of these workers had not been previously insured under trade union unemployment insurance schemes.[117] The trades were building, construction of works, shipbuilding, engineering, construction of vehicles, iron-founding, and certain kinds of sawmilling.[118] All were regarded as particularly prone to fluctuations of a seasonal or cyclical nature, and this was perhaps the most significant long-term feature of the British system. The 1911 formulation led to an 'organisation of social insurance [which] does not, and cannot, meet the whole need. It is a remedy for fluctuations in employment, not for unemployment.'[119] This concept was built-in, so that the insured worker needed to contribute for twenty-six weeks before he could claim benefit. Similarly, the maximum benefit he could obtain was limited to one week for each five weeks of fully paid contributions, or a fifteen weeks maximum in any twelve month period. The original scheme allowed for six 'waiting days' or one calendar week before any benefit was paid after a claim was lodged.

To pay insurance benefit to these groups of workers when unemployed, as a legal right, was clearly a tremendous advance on the existing methods of Poor Relief, paltry relief works or sporadic outbreaks of charity. It is interesting to note, in contrast to the modern situation, that a follow-up study in 1913 showed insurance benefits to be adequate to the extent that there was little need for recourse by recipients to the Poor Law or to private charity.[120] However, the scheme was clearly only a partial answer. The insistence on maintaining the view of unemployment which saw it as a transitory phenomenon was the most potent cause of the post-war difficulties with the unemployment insurance scheme which followed in the Depression.

To produce the original benefit of seven shillings per week,[121] the worker and his employer each paid a weekly contribution of 2½ pence. The Government then added a subsidy which brought the total contribution up to 6⅔ pence, of which a net 6 pence went into the insurance fund. The scheme designed by the Board of Trade assumed an average unemployment rate of about 8.46 per cent in the insured categories. Of vital significance for the future were the sectors of industry left out of the original scheme; Professor Gilbert comments that

> In effect the planners of the world's first compulsory state unemployment insurance programme loaded their actuarial calculations and narrowed their risk in every possible way. Deliberately they did not choose for insurance a representative sample of British industrial society and while this sensible policy protected a highly experimental programme, it also made the programme less useful as a guide in the years ahead.[122]

Lloyd George himself recognized that the 1911 Act was 'purely a relief scheme for unemployment which is due to fluctuations of trade'.[123] In following this limited aim, the crucial decision was made not to build up a permanent reserve, but simply to create a revolving fund to be supported by current premiums and to be depleted by current benefits. In effect, the men at work were sustaining those who were temporarily unemployed; such a simple device could not be expected to withstand the shocks of mass unemployment when the original scheme was distorted by the haphazard addition of other trade categories whose unemployment was altogether of a different kind.

Statistics and the Contribution of the Trade Unions

One real difficulty in the economic analysis of the precise nature of unemployment was the unavailability of hard data on past levels of unemployment. Sketchy records had been laboriously compiled from such sources as the trade union tramping records or the Poor Law figures on the numbers of paupers relieved, but these were vague shadows of reality. This was especially so of the Poor Law records, not only because 'parish relief or the hated Workhouse after 1834 was the last resort of despair', but also because 'the very notion of regularity of employment—at one place of work over a number of years for regular hours and at a standard wage—[was] an anachronistic notion, imposed by twentieth century experience upon nineteenth century realities'.[124]

The introduction of employment exchanges had been a significant aid in the collection of data. Without them, the search for work was a matter of total chance,[125] and the unemployed worker could only 'tramp from one firm to another, in the attempt to discover, by actual application to one after another, which of them wants another hand'.[126] It was true also that the introduction of the Government's employment exchanges had been in part to discourage the exploitation of workers by various ravenous private labour agencies.[127] But added to these possibilities of guiding men into available vacancies was the first real opportunity to collect adequate figures on the unemployed, and this was used to the full. In fact A. J. Mundella, a former President of the Board of Trade, had inaugurated a bureau for the collection and publication of statistics in 1886.[128] This had been converted in 1892 into a small Department of Labour with its own *Gazette*, still today an indispensable source of official labour statistics. Unfortunately, the Department in its early years had to rely largely on figures gleaned from among trade union members, which gave an unreliable view of the overall position, but which was nevertheless helpful in forging strong links between the Board of Trade and the trade unions. The 1911 Act was the start of much more reliable figures, and also had a secondary effect on economic theories. As. G. D. H. Cole pointed out, 'the older economists used even sometimes to deny that "involuntary unemployment" could exist at all, because they said, everyone could find some competitive capitalist willing to employ him if he would only accept a low enough wage'.[129] But even if that proposition had in fact ever been historically accurate, its unreal nature was demonstrated clearly by a breakdown of the new collected figures on unemployment.

The 1911 National Insurance Act owed a considerable debt to the trade union movement which had pioneered the way in so many respects, although it should be noted that trade union insurance never covered more than a small fraction of workers—in 1891, for instance, less than 5 per cent.[130] Their rules and practices were freely copied by Beveridge and Llewellyn Smith in framing the official schemes.[131] For example, trade union rulebooks had long contained a 'waiting period' during which the worker could draw no benefit. This was partly to test the veracity of the claim, and partly to offset the administrative difficulties involved in paying out small claims when a worker succeeded in finding a job almost immediately. Most rulebooks back-dated the benefit after this period to the commencement of unemployment,[132] and the 1911 Act followed suit with the refund scheme. Again the trade union rulebooks contained a maximum period of benefit in relation to contributions, based more on common-sense than actuarial considerations, so as not to exhaust their limited funds. Interestingly enough, the old rulebooks contain relatively little mention of disqualification clauses, and these were usually of a very general nature, though customary practices grew up to make them in certain cases more specific.[133] Generally, there seems to have been little experience of 'malingering' or benefit fraud under the union schemes, perhaps because of the personal involvement of the member in his union's activities.[134] The impersonality of the State scheme may have encouraged such activities partly because of the feeling of alienation which it clearly gives to many.[135]

Relations with the trade unions were carefully cultivated by the Board of Trade in this period and, in regard to the 1911 Act, Llewellyn Smith was determined 'from the outset . . . to design the unemployment insurance scheme to placate trade union opinion'.[136] It may well be that 'National Insurance was the Liberal response to the threat of socialism',[137] but the trade unions were willing advisers to the architects of the 1911 Act at the Board of Trade.

The Disqualification Clauses

The contribution aspect of the 1911 unemployment scheme involved an arithmetical calculation. But the co-existing disqualification conditions were based on subjective judgements of human behaviour. It was these 'longstop' exclusion clauses which were so difficult to formulate.

Beatrice Webb took the somewhat jaundiced view that Lloyd George and his civil service advisers had 'taken every item that could be popular with anyone, mixed them together and produced a Bill which takes some twenty millions from the propertied class to be handed over to the wage-earners *sans phrase* to be spent by them, as they think fit, in times of sickness or unemployment'.[138] Her husband was firm in his support of the Bill when it appeared, but Mrs. Webb feared 'the growth of malingering and the right to money independently of the obligation to good conduct'.[139] This fear of malingering, on occasions approaching mild hysteria, had of course long been a British trait. The C.O.S. had carried out effective propaganda on the subject for many years and it was the mainspring of the 'Principles of 1834'. In 1871, for example, one-third of all the cases referred to the C.O.S. committees were adjudged to be 'undeserving', largely because of 'such misconduct as makes it impossible to render effectual assistance'.[140] In the eyes of the C.O.S., misconduct meant drink, habitual laziness and the omnibus epithet 'vice'. Their individualistic philosophy naturally inclined the C.O.S. members to view any state-run scheme with misgivings, but their greatest fear was of dependence by the poor on the welfare machine. In their opinion, the casual introduction of unemployment insurance without proper safeguards would lead to a position where there would be many content to make 'a living by looking for work and successfully failing to find it'.[141]

Many of those who feared the growth of malingering were interestingly among the 'respectable' trade union and working-class ranks. John Burns, the near-revolutionary co-leader of the dockers with Ben Tillet, who subsequently turned into an obsequious Liberal Cabinet Minister, summed up their position, stating that:

> In spite of what some advocates of work for the unemployed may say, I contend, as a socialist . . . that until the differentiation of the labourer from the loafer takes place, the unemployed question can never be properly discussed and dealt with. Till the tramp, thief, the ne'er-do-well, however pitiable he may be, is dealt with distinctly from the genuine worker, no permanent benefit will result to any one of them.[142]

Charles Loch, the Secretary of the C.O.S., had taken the firm view that 'want of employment in nine cases out of ten in which the plea is used, is not the cause of distress. It is, as often as not, drink.'[143] The C.O.S. assumed from the first that even the most carefully administered aid would be wasted on the mass of those in poverty, who were in the main those of pathologically weak character who had been further corrupted by indiscriminate charity. The philosophy implied a Calvinistic theory of the elect and the damned, and any kind of welfare scheme which did not trouble to differentiate between the deserving and the undeserving poor was not only wrong, but was in effect perpetuating the dependence of those who had already been corrupted. The C.O.S. stance was certainly consistent: they 'fought every attempt to weaken the poor law, and when they were proposed, the society would oppose old age pensions, unemployment insurance and health insurance'.[144]

A more moderate view taken by some critics of the 1911 Act was to welcome the introduction of unemployment insurance, but to think that it alone would 'not solve the problem of the loafer, the disabled and the inefficient idle'.[145] There was certainly a basis of fact for the fear that the unemployed were idle and listless, but this stemmed from a much more fundamental problem than the deleterious effects of relief. In Seebohm Rowntree's 1910 study of unemployment in York,[146] a tiny proportion of men were adjudged to be 'workshy',[147] with the comment that 'among a number of casual workers a process of gradual deterioration is going on'.[148] However, the crucial factor here was that the casual worker,

> especially if not very successful in securing jobs, is generally underfed. This does not necessarily mean that he is hungry—any more than a horse fed on green meat is hungry—but he is physically unfitted to undertake hard work for a sustained period. Add to this physical disability, the mental despondency due to continued failure to find employment, and the deteriorating influence of the environment in which he and his fellows, as a rule, are obliged to live—an influence which there is no physical vigour to resist—and you have a perfect machine for the manufacture of 'unemployables'.[149]

Whatever the rational view of such a situation might be, however, the emotional response of many reared in the C.O.S. philosophy overpowered such considerations as Rowntree had advanced for 'the deadly effieiency of this machine for unemployables'.[150] They preferred the descriptions used by Rowntree's investigators—'born tired', 'shiftless and loafer', 'gaol bird' and 'drinker and wastrel'—and all the moral connotations attached to such images. The embedded legacy of Samuel Smiles that 'Heaven helps those who help themselves' led them to believe with him that

> The spirit of self-help is the root of genuine growth in the individual; and, exhibited in the lives of many, it constitutes the true source of national vigour and strength . . . Whatever is done *for* men or classes . . . takes away the stimulus and necessity of doing for themselves; and where men are subjected to over-guidance and over-government, the inevitable tendency is to render them comparatively helpless.[151]

The reformers of the Poor Law Commission in 1834 had believed that 'industrious and self-respecting persons could always earn a living'.[152] Indeed, Nassau Senior, the Oxford economist and co-architect of the 1834 Report, believed that the unemployed positively enjoyed their condition in that 'nothing is so much disliked as steady regular labour'.[153] In 1911 this perspective had been clearly modified, but Samuel Smiles' fear of 'over-government' still remained. As Lloyd George put it, the Act was to substitute 'for tardy relief provision made in anticipation of need, no more costly, but infinitely more effective and more kindly in its operation than distress funds or the Poor Law'. However, Lloyd George knew his audience, and he made it quite clear that in his view society had not progressed to the point where the Government could enact legislation 'to reach the lowest deeps, to grasp the utterly incapable, the loafer, or the wastrel, and set him too, on the firm ground of self-respecting manhood fit to withstand all the shocks of adversity, but we may claim to have established barriers to prevent men falling into that abyss of human despair'.[154]

Lloyd George's strong moral presuppositions, reflective certainly of public opinion, were built into the new scheme of unemployment insurance, but not without a struggle. The Board of Trade team were agreed on the contribution criteria, which were the initial threshold to separate the deserving from the undeserving. The principle was simple —if the casual worker in the insured trade categories had not paid the requisite number of contributions, he was automatically excluded from benefit. Llewellyn Smith, however, with his Quaker background, insisted that there had to be a secondary stage whereby a demand could be made of good conduct. Beatrice Webb took the same view, writing in her diary that,

> If their schemes can be carried out we should not much object. Both [unemployment and health insurance] have good consequences. But we still doubt their practicality, and some of the necessary conditions strike us as very unsatisfactory. The *unconditionality* of all payments under unemployment insurance schemes constitutes a grave defect. The State gets nothing for its money in the way of conduct, and it may even encourage malingerers.[155]

Llewellyn Smith was determined to remedy such a defect. He 'always insisted that workers within a given trade, who lost employment through their own misconduct—laziness, drunkenness, or carelessness—should be ineligible for unemployment insurance'.[156] In Llewellyn Smith's address to the British Association for the Advancement of Science in 1910, there is a remarkable statement of his personal beliefs on the way the insurance scheme for unemployment benefits should operate. He thought that

> most people would agree that the personal risk of losing employment through bad work, irregular attendance, or drunken habits is one which it is absolutely necessary to leave attached in all its forces to the individual workman. For the community to guarantee employment to all irrespective of personal effort or efficiency would necessarily impair the national character and lower the national standard.[157]

He believed that armed with the 'double weapon of a maximum limit to benefit and of a minimum contribution, the operation of the scheme itself would automatically exclude the loafer'.[158] But this by itself was not enough. For him personally it was 'absolutely necessary in the public interest'[159] to exclude any claims arising from personal misbehaviour, and he set in train the drafting of clauses which would disqualify an applicant for benefit who lost his employment through 'misconduct' or who left 'without just cause'.[160] However, this was not without immediate protest from his political superior, Winston Churchill, who wrote in a lengthy memorandum to his permanent officials that

> I do not feel convinced that we are entitled to refuse benefit to a qualified man who loses his employment through drunkenness. He has paid his contributions; he has insured himself against the fact of unemployment, and I think it arguable that his foresight should be rewarded irrespective of his dismissal, whether he lost his

> situation through his own habits of intemperance or through his employer's habits of intemperance. I do not like mixing up moralities and mathematics.[161]

The final sentence was characteristic. In advocating the passage of the 1911 Act, Churchill had used the phrase 'bringing in the magic of averages to the aid of the millions'.[162] Following the General Election of December 1910, he was promoted to the Home Office. Churchill's removal to other spheres enabled Llewellyn Smith to carry on with his own ideas. The eventual inclusion of the disqualification clauses perhaps shows that Churchill's successor as President of the Board of Trade, Sidney Buxton, proved to be easier to handle.

The Appeal Machinery

In many respects, the 1911 National Insurance Act was 'the prototype of all later social insurance statutes',[163] both in Britain and in many other countries who copied, and still copy, its provisions. One of its most distinctive features, as the scheme was launched on 15 January 1913, was the appeal mechanism allowing a second opinion on disqualification from benefit as adjudged by the local officer of the Labour Exchange.

The original motivation for setting up this appeal structure was the potential burden on the Board of Trade, and its President accountable in Parliament, of the numerous complaints which might flood in from disappointed claimants. It was a means of giving an effective avenue of complaint to an independent arbitrator outside the executive arm of the Government. The basic scheme seems to have been an entirely original idea thought up by Llewellyn Smith, whose civil service mentality wished to save the Board of Trade the time and bother involved in answering 'trivial questions'.[164]

The 1911 arrangement was to have a special officer attached to each Labour Exchange to deal with questions relating to disqualification from benefit. The claimant who was not satisfied by the officer's decision had a right of appeal to a locally constituted 'Court of Referees' whose composition was 'one or more members chosen to represent employers, with an equal number chosen to represent workmen, and a chairman appointed by the Board of Trade'.[165] A further appeal could be made from the decision of the Court of Referees to an 'Umpire', 'whose decision [was] final and conclusive'.[166] Originally the Umpire also decided 'insurance questions' as to which groups of workers came under the scheme. But this duty was transferred in 1920 to the internal administration of the Ministry of Labour, and is now part of the function of the Department of Health and Social Security.

The meshing of the insurance scheme into the Labour Exchanges was vital. As Beveridge had foreseen, they were 'necessary to administer insurance, they are necessary for their own sake, and they are necessary to prevent insurance itself from having harmful effects in immobilizing labour'.[167] The hope was that, before long, so much of the marketing of labour would be done through the Government exchanges as to make it unnecessary to test the reality of unemployment by any form of inspectorate, but merely to insist on the formal requirement of signing on at the Exchange's register for work.[168]

Many critics believed that the introduction of unemployment insurance had 'had reactions in encouraging laziness and in rendering labour less mobile',[169] but these were unproven defects and had to be offset against the proven and real advantages of exchanges shown right from their inception. As Beveridge believed, they had challenged the Poor Law system by opening up 'a way of "dispauperisation" more humane, less costly and more effective than that of the "workhouse test"—the way of making the finding of work easy instead of merely making relief hard'.[170] This constructive approach with its concentration on job-finding has been the great contribution of the Exchanges. And although the 'relief' function in administering unemployment insurance benefits has been an integral part of the work of Exchanges, many who work in them have hopes that, now this has been hived off, the poor public image of the placings bureau section of the Exchanges' work will be considerably enhanced.[171]

The disqualification appeal machinery grew out of the Poor Law experience and Victorian attitudes. Although partly motivated by the fear of malingering,[172] there was also a growing and genuine desire to see introduced a fair means of redress. Certain experiences with Poor Law Relieving Officers encouraged the use of an independent mechanism of second resort, and the sincere spirit in which this move was made can perhaps best be seen in the sporting metaphors used to name the newly formed Courts of Referees and Umpires. An additional precedent seems to have been the appeal to the local pensions committees under the Old Age Pensions Act 1908, followed by the further possibility of an appeal to the Local Government Board.[173]

But the question arises, why not utilize the courts as a means of independent arbitration? The tribunal mechanism set up was after all using legal tools to come to a decision on statutory rules. The answer seems to lie in the hideous difficulties of the courts at the time in connection with the Workmen's Compensation Acts. The statute of 1897 had laid down a limited cover to certain specially dangerous industries.[174]

But in 1906 the scheme was made general. The legal liability imposed upon employers was to pay compensation for injury arising out of and in the course of employment to a worker *automatically*. The scheme had considerable merits over the pre-existing legal position, but the compensation given was small[175] and was expressed as a fraction of the worker's weekly wage. Normally the courts judged this fraction to be considerably less than half. Sometimes the amount was derisory. If the accident proved fatal, a lump sum payment was made; and workers could also be paid a lump sum when a claim was disputed. The ensuing litigation at the county court level was fierce and bitter, with the unions backing their members in conflict with employers who were in turn backed by the insurance companies. It was made clear in the Parliamentary debates when the Act was passed that the prudent employer would voluntarily wish to insure privately against potential liability; but this tacit understanding which introduced Insurance Companies into the fray, concerned with their profits rather than with the maiming of workers, if anything exacerbated the existing problems.

Numerous cases were appealed to the House of Lords, and as a result the courts became clogged with cases and appeals. Extra-judicial complaints were voluminous, particularly to the Board of Trade who had the oversight of the legislation, and it is certain that, as Professor Wedderburn states, 'the complaints against the conduct of cases and decisions in court . . . [led] to the new social security system being administered by tribunals firmly set apart from the ordinary courts'.[176] This new scheme of universal insurance against injury at work was of course the direct result of the later 1942 *Beveridge Report*, and in it Beveridge is scathing in his criticism of the old system.[177] There is also reason to think that in 1911 his personal experience of the law during pupillage for the Bar had led him to doubt both the efficacy of the courts and their impartiality in industrial matters.[178] But such an attitude was also typical of many administrators of the time, and not just in Britain. As Professor Nonet has stated, in relation to Workmen's Compensation in California,

> The architects of the welfare state had a characteristically narrow and negative conception of the role of law in government. To them, law evoked a system of rigid constraints that paralyzed initiative and prevented effective action to solve the problems of society.[179]

The machinery worked out by Beveridge and Llewellyn Smith has been the basis of the ensuing legislation on unemployment benefit, with remarkably few changes. Perhaps of all their innovations, the establishment of the tribunal as a device for British administrative justice has had the most far-reaching consequences. But in so far as the Liberal Government's social legislation 'out-trumped the Labour Party', it was the work of personally committed but apolitical civil servants at the Board of Trade that was to a large measure responsible.

NOTES

1. Henry Sidgwick, *Principles of Political Economy* (1887), p. 536.
2. Sidney and Beatrice Webb, *English Poor Law Policy* (1910), p. 270.
3. Denison House, the headquarters of the C.O.S. and late of the Family Welfare Association.
4. Geoffrey Drage, in the *Quarterly Review*, July 1923, contained in Drage, *Public Assistance* (1930), p. 30.
5. One of the first working men in Parliament, Will Crooks, gained his seat at a by-election in Woolwich in 1903 by defeating the Tory/C.O.S. candidate, Geoffrey Drage. Crooks was Mayor of Poplar in 1901 and a close collaborator of Lansbury.
6. Bentley B. Gilbert, *The Evolution of National Insurance in Great Britain* (1966), p. 15.
7. C. L. Mowat, *The Charity Organisation Society* (1961), p. 36.
8. Editorial in the American newspaper *The Independent*, 19 March 1908, quoted in Daniel Nelson, *Unemployment Insurance, The American Experience 1915–1935* (1969), p. 3.
9. Philip O'Connor, *Vagrancy* (1963), p. 40.
10. David Lloyd-George, in a speech at Whitefield's Tabernacle on 14 October 1911, quoted in David Lloyd-George, *The People's Insurance* (1912), p. 189.
11. Alfred Marshall, *Official Papers* (1888, ed. J. M. Keynes, 1926), p. 5. Contained in the *Oxford English Dictionary* at the same time; see earlier at p. 110.
12. David Owen, *English Philanthropy 1660–1960* (1965), p. 242.
13. Ronald C. Davison, *The Unemployed, Old Policies and New* (1929), p. 10.
14. Gilbert Slater, *Poverty and the State* (1930), p. 333.
15. As he did habitually in his C.O.S. Annual Reports until the turn of the century.
16. See generally, Ronald C. Davison, *op. cit.*, and particularly José Harris, *Unemployment and Politics* (1973).
17. Harold E. Raynes, *Social Security in Britain* (1957), p. 169.
18. Ronald C. Davison, *op. cit.*, p. 14.
19. C. L. Mowat, *op. cit.*, p. 48.
20. *C.O.S. 18th Annual Report* (1886), p. 2.
21. Emily C. Townshend, *The Case against the C.O.S.* (1911), p. 5.
22. See the note by Samuel Barnett, writing for the C.O.S. before he broke with them over the issue of Old Age Pensions; *Charity Organisation Review* (1886), vol. II, pp. 99–100.
23. John Clarke, *Social Welfare* (1953), p. 79.
24. William Beveridge, *Unemployment, A Problem of Industry* (1909), p. 165.
25. Maurice Bruce, *The Coming of the Welfare State* (1961), p. 188.
26. Bentley B. Gilbert, *British Social Policy 1914–1939* (1970), p. 52.
27. Bentley B. Gilbert, *The Evolution of National Insurance in Great Britain* (1966), p. 238.
28. Beveridge, *op. cit.*, p. 191.
29. James Sexton, *Report of the Hanley T.U.C.* (1905), pp. 48–9, quoted in José Harris, *op. cit.*, p. 165.
30. Minority Report of the *Royal Commission on the Poor Laws* (1909), Cd–4499, p. 1203.
31. See Raymond Postgate, *The Life of George Lansbury* (1951), and the biography of Joseph Fels, the American soap millionaire and Lansbury's financial backer; Mary Fels, *Joseph Fels: His Life Work* (1920). Fels was particularly interested in the projects at Laindon Farm and Hollesley Bay. See also James F. Muirhead, *Land and Unemployment* (1935) for an elucidation of the views of Henry George's advocacy of making land into common property, *Poverty and Progress* (1880).
32. See for a general survey, W. H. G. Armytage, *Heavens Below, Utopian Experiments in England 1560–1960* (1961), pp. 77–358. See also J. W. Scott, *Self-Subsistence for the Unemployed* (1935).
33. William Booth, *The Surplus* (1908), p. 5 *et seq.* and also his *The Vagrant and the Unemployable* (1909).

34. Beveridge, *Power and Influence* (1953), p. 60. Beveridge recalled on the fiftieth anniversary of employment exchanges that he and Lansbury 'were the two wild young men of the C.U.B., he urging "back to the land" and I urging Labour Exchanges'; Beveridge, 'The Birth of Labour Exchanges', *Min. Labour* **14**, no. 1 (January 1960), p. 2. See also his views on 'back to the land' 56 years earlier; W. H. Beveridge, 'The Preservation of Efficiency', *Toynbee Record*, **XVII** (December 1904), p. 43.

35. Beveridge had a German governess as a child while his parents were in India.

36. Other pioneering ventures were set up in Cologne in 1874 and Berlin in 1883; Lord Askwith, *Industrial Problems and Disputes* (1920), p. 273. See also David Schloss, *Report* on the German experience (1904), Cd–2304.

37. 1905–1908. Beveridge explored the issues of employment exchanges and unemployment insurance from July 1907 onwards as well as strongly advocating the introduction of Old Age Pensions in 1908. See also W. H. Beveridge, 'Public Labour Exchanges in Germany', *Economic Journal*, **18** No. 69, (1908), pp. 1–18.

38. Beveridge, *The London School of Economics and its Problems 1919–37* (1960), p. 110.

39. Beveridge, *Power and Influence* (1953), p. 64.

40. Majority Report of the *Royal Commission on the Poor Laws* (1909), Cd–4499, p. 630.

41. Minority Report of the *Royal Commission on the Poor Laws* (1909), Cd–4499, p. 1180.

42. Sir Thomas Chegwidden and G. Myrddin-Evans, *The Employment Exchange Service of Great Britain* (1934), p. 3.

43. Sir Thomas Chegwidden and G. Myrddin-Evans, *op. cit.*, p. 67.

44. James Leicester and James Farndale, *Trends in the Services for Youth* (1967), p. 556. The Cambridge branch of the C.O.S. opened the first such 'Registry' for young people in 1907. See also Frederick Keeling, *The Labour Exchange in relation to Boy and Girl Labour* (1910), and Arthur Greenwood, *Juvenile Labour Exchanges and Aftercare* (1911).

45. Beveridge, *Voluntary Action* (1948), p. 224. See also for earlier experimentation, W. H. Beveridge, 'A Seventeenth Century Labour Exchange', *Economic Journal*, **24** (1914), pp. 371–6, 635–6.

46. He wrote triumphantly in his daily letter to his mother: 'It gets me into the State machine exactly where I want to be'; Beveridge, *Power and Influence* (1953), p. 68.

47. Sir William Beveridge, *The Past and Present of Unemployment Insurance* (1930), p. 4.

48. Askwith, *op. cit.*, p. 272.

49. See the public letter on unemployment entitled 'The Untrodden Field of Politics'; *The Nation*, (7 March 1908). Beatrice Webb claimed that Sidney had in fact written it for Churchill's use, but there is no doubt that it expressed Churchill's feelings at the time; Beatrice Webb, *Our Partnership* (1948), p. 404.

50. Sir Thomas Chegwidden and G. Myrddin-Evans, *op. cit.*, p. 70.

51. See for Beveridge's views on 'strict neutrality' his evidence to the *Royal Commission on the Poor Laws*, Minutes of Evidence (1910), H.M.S.O. Cd 5066, Question 77832, paras. 52–76.

52. Bentley B. Gilbert, *The Evolution of National Insurance in Great Britain* (1966), p. 264.

53. See for studies on this system, E. J. Hobsbawm, *Labouring Men* (1964). See also P. H. J. M. Gosden, *The Friendly Societies in England 1815–1875* (1961), pp. 76–7 and Appendix A; and A. Aspinall, *The Early English Trade Unions* (1949), p. 93.

54. For example, rule 25 of the London Tin-Plate Workers in 1853 stated that: 'The Secretary shall attend the call of any tramp coming to town who can produce a card signed by the secretary of any similar society and is in want of employment; he shall be allowed the sum of 3s., two nights' lodgings and one pint of ale. The secretary to be allowed one pint of ale for attending to receive each tramp or member'; Archibald T. Kidd, *History of the Tin Plate Workers* (and Sheet Metal Workers and Brazier's Societies) (1949), p. 101. The 1860 rulebook, after allegations of drunkenness, changed the allowance of ale to payment in cash for the services of the secretary. The national Tin-Plate Workers' Union, in common with many other craft unions, was formed in 1862 with the primary aim of acting as a clearing-house for tramping craftsmen in the trade; *ibid.*, p. 93.

55. Quoted by Ronald C. Davidson, *The Unemployed, Old Policies and New* (1929), p. 68.

56. William Beveridge, 'Labour Bureaux', *Economic Journal*, **XVI**, No. 63 (September 1906), p. 437.

57. William Beveridge, 'Labour Exchanges

and the Unemployed', *Economic Journal*, **XVII**, No. 65 (March 1907), p. 76.

58. Sir William Beveridge to a *Committee of Enquiry on Unemployment Insurance* (1921), Cmd 1140, p .180. Their report states bluntly that Employment Exchanges 'were founded, not solely or even mainly as placing agencies, but in order to prepare a machinery for the administration of unemployment insurance', *Final Report* (1920), Cmd 1054, p. 10.

59. Eden describes Acts of Parliament making insurance against sickness and attached risks compulsory upon coalheavers in London in 1757, and upon shippers and keelmen employed in the coal trade on the River Wear in the 1790s. Both involved compulsory deductions from earnings; Sir Frederick Eden, *The State of the Poor* (1797, reprint 1928), vol. I, p. 605.

60. Sir William Beveridge, *The Past and Present of Unemployment Insurance* (1930), p. 3.

61. See M. J. J. Blackley, *Collected Essays* (1882).

62. M. J. J. Blackley, 'National Insurance', *Nineteenth Century*, (November 1878), reprinted in M. J. J. Blackley, *Thrift and National Insurance as a Security against Pauperism* (1906), p. 44 *et seq.* But see also Bentham's proposal for state-subsidized annuities which could be realized in times of distress, one hundred years before national insurance, in his *Abstract or Compressed View of a Tract intituled Circulating Annuities* (1880) in W. Stark, *Jeremy Bentham's Economic Writings* (1952), vol. II, pp. 49–50.

63. Thomas Mackay, *Working-class Insurance* (1890), p. v. Interestingly the author confines his arguments to the 'three risks against which working people wish to insure, *sickness, old age, death*'; *ibid.*, p. 1.

64. As it became known later in the fierce and protracted argument with the House of Lords; *Hansard*, **4**, H. C. Deb. (29 April 1909), cols. 488–9.

65. *Hansard*, **4**, H. C. Deb. (19 May 1909), col. 507.

66. William J. Braithwaite, *Lloyd George's Ambulance Wagon* (1957), p. 71. This account is the 'inside' story of the passage of the 1911 Act told in the memoirs of Lloyd George's special adviser on the sickness benefit aspect of the Act. See also T. R. Marr, *The Example of Germany* (1904).

67. I. G. Gibbon, 'Unemployment Insurance' (1911), p. 34; a Ph.D. thesis surveying a number of European systems. See also the description of the St Gall experiment in the Board of Trade submission to the *Royal Commision on the Poor Laws* (1909), Cd–4499, vol. ix, Appendix XXI (K). The St Gall *Report on the Second Year* of the scheme sadly relates that: 'It must also be stated that in the second, as in the first year, a large number of men drew the full *maximum* of unemployment pay, and then at once left St Gall'; quoted in David Schloss, *Insurance against Unemployment* (1909), p. 18.

68. David Lloyd George, in 'Introduction' to L. G. Chiozza Money, *Insurance versus Poverty* (1912), p. ix.

69. *loc. cit.*, p. viii.

70. See generally, the Yellow Book on *Trade Union Unemployment Benefits* (1911), Cd–5703.

71. Sir William Beveridge, *The Past and Present of Unemployment Insurance* (1930), p. 3.

72. David Lloyd George, *The People's Insurance* (1911), p. 152.

73. Asa Briggs, 'The Welfare State in Historical Perspective' in S. P. Aiyar, *Perspectives on the Welfare State* (1966), p. 30.

74. A remark made in 1884 and quoted in W. H. Dawson, *Bismarck and State Socialism* (1890), p. 35.

75. Quoted in W. H. Dawson, *Social Insurance in Germany 1883–1911* (1912), p. 16.

76. David Lloyd George, *The People's Insurance* (1912), p. 205.

77. C. L. Mowat, *Lloyd George* (1964), p. 60.

78. Sir Henry Bunbury in Introduction to William J. Braithwaite, *op. cit.*, p. 22.

79. William J. Braithwaite, *op. cit.*, p. 153.

80. Beveridge, *Power and Influence* (1953), p. 80.

81. Sir William Beveridge, *The Past and Present of Unemployment Insurance* (1930), p. 11.

82. Sir William Beveridge, *Planning Under Socialism* (1936), p. 84.

83. Sir William Beveridge, *The Past and Present of Unemployment Insurance* (1930), p. 11.

84. Bentley B. Gilbert, *British Social Policy 1914–39* (1970), p. 52.

85. See generally, J. A. M. Caldwell, 'The Genesis of the Ministry of Labour', *Public Administration*, **37** (1959), pp. 371–82.

86. Quoted in Winston Churchill, *Liberalism and the Social Problem* (1909), pp. 208–9.

87. Thomas Mackay, *The English Poor* (1889), p. 194.

88. Hilaire Belloc, *The Servile State* (1912).

89. Helen F. Hohman, *The Development of Social Insurance and Minimum Wage Legislation in Great Britain* (1933), p. 217.

90. See generally, Sir Hubert Llewellyn Smith, 'The New Survey of London Life and Labour', *Journal of the Royal Statistical Society*, **92**, Part 4 (1929), p. 530.

91. Roger Davidson, 'Sir Hubert Llewellyn Smith and Labour Policy 1886–1916' (unpublished Cambridge Ph.D. thesis, 1971) p. 254.

92. Beveridge, *Power and Influence* (1953), p. 83.

93. William J. Braithwaite, *op. cit.*, p. 93. Indeed one of Braithwaite's mentions of Hubert Llewellyn Smith is the somewhat unflattering remark that 'he had to put his hat on with a shoe horn'; *ibid.*, p. 103.

94. Janet Beveridge, *Beveridge and his Plan* (1954), p. 63.

95. Roger Davidson, *op. cit.*, p. 301.

96. Quoted in Janet Beveridge, *op. cit.*, p. 80.

97. Beveridge, *Power and Influence* (1953), p. 85.

98. Bentley B. Gilbert, 'Winston Churchill versus the Webbs', *American Historical Review* **LXXI** (1966), p. 851. See also Roger Davidson, *op. cit.*, p. 254.

99. Lloyd George's personal assistant, C. F. G. Masterman, walked up to George Lansbury at the time of the 1911 Act and said grinning, 'We have spiked your guns, eh?'; quoted in Raymond Postgate, *op. cit.*, p. 112.

100. See generally, Arthur Marwick, 'The Labour Party and the Welfare State in Britain 1900–1948', *American Historical Review* **73** (1967), p. 380. See also Kenneth D. Brown, *Labour and Unemployment 1900–1914* (1971).

101. Hardie's maiden speech was a plea for public provision for the unemployed; *Hansard*, **8**, H. C. Deb. (February 1893), cols. 724–32.

102. Emrys Hughes, *Keir Hardie* (1956), p. 200. Lansbury (and Philip Snowden) voted against the Bill, and Ramsay MacDonald who, like the rest of the Parliamentary Labour Party, voted for the measure, condemned it as 'superficial'; *Hansard*, **26**, H. C. Deb. (29 May 1911), col. 724. See also J. Ramsay MacDonald, *The New Unemployed Bill of the Labour Party* (1909).

103. See generally, David Schloss, *Insurance against Unemployment* (1909); the report by the same author, (1904), Cd–2304; and Joseph L. Cohen, *Insurance against Unemployment* (1921), Part II.

104. Quoted from a report issued by the Ghent municipality in I. G. Gibbon, *Unemployment Insurance* (1911), p. 82. Dr. Gibbon's text includes correspondence with the originator of the Ghent scheme, Louis Varlez.

105. Beveridge, *Power and Influence* (1953), p. 371.

106. The name was in fact changed to Employment Exchange in official terminology as long ago as 1916 on the setting up of the then Ministry of Labour.

107. Felix Morley, *Unemployment Relief in Great Britain* (1924), p. 108.

108. See Michael Hill, *Policies for the Unemployed: Help or Coercion?* (1974), p. 10.

109. Sir William Beveridge, *The Past and Present of Unemployment Insurance* (1930), p. 24 f.

110. I. G. Gibbon, *op. cit.*, p. 238.

111. Ronald C. Davison, *The Unemployed, Old Policies and New* (1929), p. 74.

112. Sir Henry Bunbury in the Introduction to William J. Braithwaite, *op. cit.*, p. 40.

113. R. M. Titmuss in the Commentary on William J. Braithwaite, *op. cit.*, p. 43.

114. Sir William Beveridge, *The Past and Present of Unemployment Insurance* (1930), p. 11. See also the comment in Lloyd George's famous Budget Speech that, given the climate of opinion, even the Tory Opposition would have made provision 'in some shape or other for those who are out of work through no fault of their own'; *Hansard*, **4**, H. C. Deb. (29 April 1909), col. 482.

115. Beveridge, *Power and Influence* (1953), p. 88.

116. Beveridge, *ibid.*

117. John Barton Seymour, *The British Employment Exchange* (1928), p. 16.

118. The effect of the Act was to create certain anomalies in particular industries by its rigid categorization of 'insured trades'. For example, members of the Tin-Plate Workers' Union who worked directly on building ships came under the compulsory provisions, whereas those members whose sole occupation it was to make ship lamps were held not to be in 'insured' employment; Archibald T. Kidd, *History of the Tin Plate Workers* (1949), p. 214.

119. E. F. Stevenson, *Unemployment Relief, The Basic Problem* (1934), p. 188.

120. Board of Trade, *First Report of the Proceedings of the Board of Trade under Part II of the National Insurance Act 1911*, (1913), H.M.S.O., Cd 6965.

121. Six shillings per week benefit in the building categories.

122. Bentley B. Gilbert, *British Social Policy 1914–1939* (1970), p. 53.

123. David Lloyd George, *The People's Insurance* (1912), p. 30.

124. E. P. Thompson, *The Making of the English Working Class* (1963), pp. 248–9.

125. See the graphic description of a search for a cooper's job by Will Crooks in George Haw, *From Workhouse to Westminster* (1907), pp. 53–4.

126. Minority Report of the *Royal Commision on the Poor Laws* (1909), Cd–4499, p. 1125.

127. This was a reason for their introduction which appealed to many, including George Lansbury; Raymond Postgate, *op. cit.*, p. 112.

128. When Robert Owen had proposed in 1816 that there should be a Department of State which 'shall collect and publish each quarter the condition of labour, unemployment and wages in each district', he had been branded a political lunatic; see Joseph McCabe, *Robert Owen* (1920), p. 38.

129. G. D. H. Cole, *Fabian Socialism* (1943), p. 76.

130. B. R. Mitchell and Phyllis Deane, *Abstract of British Historical Statistics* (1971), p. 60.

131. See the exhaustive compilation prepared by Beveridge, *Tables showing the Rules and Expenditure of Trade Unions in Respect of Unemployed Benefits* (1911), Cd–5703.

132. See, for example, rule 26 of the Sheet Metal Workers' Union rulebook (1973 amended edition). Most of these sections in union rulebooks have not changed since Victorian times. A valuable collection is contained in the Squire Law Library, Cambridge.

133. The present TGWU rules on sickness benefit state, for example, that, after nine months' membership and having made over thirty-nine contributions, benefit will be paid after a visit from a sick steward, unless the sickness was 'occasioned by drunkenness, disorderly or improper conduct or through the member exposing himself to unnecessary risks', *TGWU Rules* (1962 and subsequent amendments) p. 65. Interestingly the comparable provisions on women members refer more delicately to 'intemperance or misconduct or neglect of the ordinary rules of life', *ibid.*, p. 68.

134. It is a truism that financial mishaps occur in unions not because of conscious embezzlement or fraud but because of overwork and incompetent book-keeping. Unions are naturally loath to take up legal action even when improper conduct has been discovered; a rare but famous exception was *Hornby* v. *Close* (1867) L.R. 2 QB 153.

135. F. J. Maclean, *The Human Side of Insurance* (1931) excludes discussion of National Insurance as 'besides being a vast and highly specialised development of the insurance movement, it is comparatively an impersonal affair', p. v.

136. Roger Davidson, *op. cit.*, p. 272.

137. Bentley B. Gilbert, *The Evolution of National Insurance in Great Britain* (1966), p. 448.

138. Beatrice Webb, *Our Partnership* (1948), p. 473.

139. *ibid.*, p. 474.

140. C. L. Mowat, *The Charity Organisation Society* (1961), p. 36.

141. Washington Gladden, quoted in John Lewis Gillin, *Poverty and Dependency* (1921), p. 20.

142. Quoted in Joseph L. Cohen, *op. cit.*, p. 28.

143. Quoted in St John Ervine, *God's Soldier: General William Booth* (1934), p. 708.

144. Bentley B. Gilbert, *The Evolution of National Insurance in Great Britain* (1966), p. 52.

145. John Lewis Gillin, *op. cit.*, p. 489.

146. B. Seebohm Rowntree (and Bruno Lasker), *Unemployment, A Social Study* (1911) covering the entire City, with a population of 82,000, by the use of three investigators in three days from 7–10 June 1910.

147. A chapter heading in Rowntree's book.

148. *ibid.*, p. 174.

149. *ibid.*, pp. 174–5.

150. *loc. cit.*,

151. Samuel Smiles, *Self Help* (1859), p. 35.

152. E. F. Stevenson, *op. cit.*, p. 13.

153. Nassau Senior, *Political Economy* (1850, 6th ed., 1872), pp. 207–8.

154. David Lloyd George in the 'Introduction' to A. S. Comyns Carr, Stuart

Garnett and J. H. Taylor, *National Insurance* (1912), p. iii

155. Beatrice Webb, *op. cit.*, p. 430.

156. Bentley B. Gilbert, *op. cit.*, pp. 270–1, based on Hubert Llewellyn Smith, 'Memorandum on a Scheme for Unemployment Insurance, April 1909, p. 3, in the Beveridge Papers.

157. Sir Hubert Llewellyn Smith, Presidential address to the Economic Science and Statistics Section of the British Association for the Advancement of Science, 'Economic Security and Unemployment Insurance', *Economic Journal*, **XX**, No. 80, p. 513.

158. *ibid.*, p. 527.

159. *loc. cit.*

160. *loc. cit.* These phrases became s.87 in the 1911 National Insurance Act, foreshadowing s.13 of the 1946 Act, s.22 of the 1965 Act, and now s.20 of the Social Security Act 1975.

161. Winston Churchill to Sir Hubert Llewellyn Smith, 'Notes on Malingering' 6 June 1909 in the Beveridge Papers, quoted by Bentley B. Gilbert, *op. cit.*, pp. 271–2.

162. *Hansard*, **26**, H. C. Deb. (25 May 1911), col. 509. Seemingly inspired by the last chapter of Beveridge's *Unemployment, A Problem of Industry* (1909) — 'The Averaging of Work and Earnings'.

163. Douglas Potter and D. H. Stansfield, *National Insurance* (1949), p. 3.

164. Beveridge, *Power and Influence* (1953), p. 83.

165. s. 90(1) National Insurance Act 1911.

166. s. 88(1)(a) National Insurance Act 1911.

167. Sir William Beveridge, *Planning Under Socialism* (1936), p. 84.

168. Sir William Beveridge, *The Past and Present of Unemployment Insurance* (1930), p. 24f.

169. Geo. W. Mullins, *Unemployment, the Gateway to a New Life* (1926), p. 121; the intriguing views of a 'practical Birmingham businessman'.

170. William Beveridge, *Unemployment, A Problem of Industry* (1909), p. 216.

171. Various interviews with Exchange officials. See *People and Jobs* (H.M.S.O. 1971), and Brian Showler, *Onto a Comprehensive Employment Service* (1973).

172. That 'abuse' and the Poor Law were synonymous in many people's eyes can be seen from the following passage by one of the Historians of the Poor Law — 'there presents itself to our minds the whole history of the Poor Law, and the hideous abuses which resulted from too great a facility of relief. . .'; T. Mackay, *Public Relief of the Poor* (1901).

173. See Brian Abel-Smith and Robert Stevens, *Lawyers and the Courts* (1970), p. 8.

174. See for a full discussion, David G. Hanes, *The First British Workmen's Compensation Act* (1968), and the earlier classic study, A. T. Wilson and H. Levy, *Workmen's Compensation* (1939).

175. Always below 50 per cent of the damages, as the principle of the Act was to apportion blame between employer and employee.

176. K. W. Wedderburn, *The Worker and the Law* (1971), p. 288. See generally, Walter F. Dodd, *Administration of Workmen's Compensation* (1936).

177. See, for example, para. 80, *Social Insurance and Allied Services*, (1942), H.M.S.O. Cmd 6404.

178. Beveridge's pupil master, Loehnis, appeared as counsel in *Howden* v. *Yorkshire Miners* (1905) A.C. 256. See Beveridge's comments as to the bias of the judge at first instance and the activities of the colliery company who 'were almost openly financing the nominal plaintiff'; Beveridge, *Power and Influence* (1953), p. 11.

179. Philippe Nonet, *Administrative Justice* (1969), p. 3.

7

The Inter-War Period and the Beveridge Watershed

Although utilizing the experience of the mutual benefit funds of the trade unions, and borrowing some modifications from continental programmes, the introduction of compulsory unemployment insurance in 1911 was nevertheless a clear break with the past. As an instrument of social policy, to deal with poverty caused by unemployment, it attempted to circumvent the stigma of charity by providing a legal arrangement between equals involving joint contributions. What was most remarkable about the National Insurance Act was, however, as Professor Titmuss has pointed out, 'its originality in the circumstances of 1911'.[1] For its framers had no accumulation of tested experience to guide them, and the ground-plan laid down in 1911 was the result of shrewd thinking and careful administrative preparation.

The tripartite contractual relationship between insured worker, employer and the State was a wholly new phenomenon. The arrangement showed a peculiarly British approach to the allocation of responsibility as between notionally equal partners, with the Government standing as guarantor of the overall terms; an approach, however, which has influenced the organization of many schemes in other countries.[2] There was also initially the hope that this contractual element would prevent it from 'becoming the plaything of party politics',[3] in that Governments would think twice before cutting or raising benefits in the interests of either economy or electoral advantage. However, the crass application of the 1911 principles, in themselves valuable and even daring, to the fluctuating economic circumstances following the First World War, led to disaster for the insurance system and near bankruptcy for the nation. And such difficulties unavoidably kept the whole question of unemployment insurance and benefits at the centre of the political stage throughout the Inter-War period.

Some of the problems were caused by a misunderstanding of the

For notes see p. 183

basic concept of social insurance. Firstly, as the Webbs pointed out, using fire insurance as an illustration, 'insurance does not prevent!'[4] No insurance scheme could have guarded effectively against the onset of mass unemployment on an unprecedented scale, and, added to the fall in the value of money, such difficulties necessitated the constant revision of benefit and contribution requirements. As a mechanism, unemployment insurance was an administrative device to cope with the social problems arising out of economic circumstances, not a tool of economic regulation.[5]

A second misconception was the trite equation of the principles of unemployment insurance with the principles of commercial insurance: a misunderstanding which confuses numerous contemporary writers. It was quite clear that insurance companies operating for profit could not insure against the kind of unemployment experienced in the Depression as, in a classic understatement, 'it would not prove a profitable activity'.[6] Furthermore, the state scheme, in being a compulsory levy, lacked the element of personal thrift which enhances the status of private insurance. Nonetheless, this did not stop people 'dazzled by the magic word "insurance" from asserting that they had a right to their benefits because they had paid for them'.[7] This recognition of a 'right' to adequate maintenance was of itself no bad thing, but the expectations it aroused led in the event to an ill-considered patchwork of temporary measures to be added to the 1911 Act which grossly distorted its original intentions, but also proved to be unable to meet the demands of the post-war slump. In the years up to the 1920 legislation, this administrative improvisation, as Professor Gilbert has shown, destroyed the 'assumption that unemployment insurance was basically state-aided self-insurance'.[8] And by 1930, Beveridge could complain that his original scheme had now become 'a general system of out-door relief to the able-bodied, administered by a national in place of a local authority, and financed mainly by a tax on employment'.[9]

Following the holocaust of the First World War, both politicians and the nation as a whole came to think of unemployment insurance as no longer merely an 'insurance' scheme, but as 'a government guarantee of maintenance for the working man, to which the recipient of benefit happened also to make contributions'.[10] Such a view is, however, perhaps over-simplified. Certainly the embryonic Labour Party made repeated demands for a 'Right to Work', and, when the Liberal Government had first announced their intention to introduce unemployment insurance in the King's Speech at the opening of Parliament in 1911, a number of Labour members put forward an amendment to 'humbly regret that no promise has been made of a Bill establishing the right to work by placing upon the State the responsibility of directly providing employment or maintenance for the genuine unemployed'.[11] But the general view which came to adopt in practice the slogan 'Work or Maintenance' was probably attributable more to paralysis in the face of the economic and social situation than to any clearly defined ideological belief.

The 1911 unemployment insurance scheme worked well in the short period between its creation and the onset of the First World War. Its compulsory contribution aspect proved to be administratively practicable and caused few problems; and on the benefits' side, the Director of Labour Exchanges, William Beveridge, was able to report after the scheme's first full year in operation that 'no insoluble difficulties have presented themselves as regards the definition and test of unemployment'.[12] Given normal conditions, it seemed perfectly feasible to Beveridge to expand the insurance scheme to cover other groups and categories of workers. However, the expansion, when it came in the war years, was hurried and ill-prepared.

By the National Insurance (Part II) (Munitions Workers) Act 1916, the immediate extension of the scheme by departmental order was made possible to any trade or branch of an industry in which substantial amounts of munitions work were being carried on. Furthermore, this extension was also possible to all other parts of industry where any 'work for war purposes' was in operation.[13] As practically no enterprise in the country was without war work of some kind this clause allowed virtually limitless expansion. But even under the first head the numbers of insured contributors were doubled; one estimate was that the Act immediately added 1½ to 2 million workers to the scheme, bringing the total to over 3½ million.[14] An important additional change made at this time was the creation of a new Ministry of Labour, to which the responsibility for both unemployment insurance and emememployment exchanges was transferred on 1 January 1917.[15]

However, the crucial problems arose at the cessation of hostilities. Although there was a weak attempt to keep unemployment benefits notionally on the basis of insurance, the abnormal levels of unemployment immediately following the Armistice made this practically, if not politically, impossible. Faced with the large numbers of unemployed men just discharged from the armed forces, the Government put forward in November 1918 a temporary 'out-of-work donation' scheme. This was to run parallel with the insurance scheme and was confined to ex-servicemen who as yet had not been able to work up a full insurance contribution record. One important feature that it introduced for the first time was the principle of a payment to the unemployed worker of a separate allowance for dependent children. However, it had also established the precedent of adequate maintenance, from which it became more and more impossible to retreat. With the Victorian Poor Law as a relief mechanism, the electoral wishes of its clients had been effectively stifled by disenfranchisement.[16] But following the abolition of pauper disqualification in 1918,[17] and with a large part of the electorate affected by unemployment, a Government dependent on their votes could only react with an attempt to assuage their immediate needs. The process escalated as, according to Professor Gilbert,

> The relaxation of any rule, passed in haste by a frightened Parliament, came immediately to be regarded as a vested right by the working class, leading to further relaxations. Actuarial safeguards disappeared and unemployment insurance became simply an awkward and expensive agency for the payment of general welfare benefits basically financed by ordinary taxation.[18]

However, although pure theory no doubt demanded a clear separation of the insurance fund from general relief, the overwhelming impact of the post-war slump and the human suffering it entailed meant that the Government had no practical alternative. When the Prime Minister himself had outlined the task ahead as being 'to make Britain a fit country for heroes to live in',[19] there could be no political possibility of placing the returning heroes into the care of the Poor Law authorities.

The Unemployment Insurance Act 1920

Beveridge felt that the 'donation' schemes for ex-servicemen were the principal reason for the collapse of the original 1911 scheme in that they 'let loose a flood of criticism and damaged the whole principle of insurance'.[20] Many of the criticisms centred on widespread accusations of fraud, and a committee was appointed by the Minister of Labour to investigate them. Set up in May 1919 under the chairmanship of Lord Aberconway, the committee's report stated that they had found 'no grounds for supposing that there had been extensive fraudulent abuse of the donation scheme'; but the evidence given to the committee provides an illustration of the rumours and gossip which formed the prevalent mythology at the time.[21] It was from this period that the term 'dole' came into general use, first in relation to the donation scheme, and then more generally to unemployment benefits; it was a term to which Beveridge much objected, with its connotations of unearned largesse.[22]

The assumption had been made with the 1911 scheme that, if a worker could not find employment within his permitted period of benefit, then there was something wrong with his 'employability'. And if he were not prepared to take up employment, it followed that he had no moral claim to be an insured worker in the first place. His position ought necessarily to be 'under the Poor Law, among the unemployables and down-and-outs whom society had somehow to salve its conscience by keeping barely alive'.[23] Such a view was demonstrably untenable in the catastrophic social and economic situation following the war. Similarly, the 'tiding over' view of unemployment insurance for a limited period to help the worker over a temporary difficulty could not answer the persistent problems of mass unemployment on a nation-wide scale.

The Government did not plan for overall compulsory unemployment insurance but was 'driven to it at the end of 1920 by the fear of what would happen when the unemployment donation ended'.[24] Having made the original concession to out-of-work servicemen in 1918, there could be no going back. The 1920 Act was therefore the product of a series of prior expedients, although a firm recommendation for a general insurance scheme to cover the whole field of employment had been made by a Government committee set up under the Ministry of Reconstruction to advise on post-war problems. A sub-committee, under the chairmanship of the ubiquitous Beveridge, felt that a general scheme would be 'in spite of its magnitude . . . likely to prove less controversial than any attempt to single out particular trades, while it makes certain, as no partial scheme would, of really covering all the ground and excluding the necessity for hastily improvised supplementary schemes'.[25] But, despite, these almost prophetic words, no immediate action was taken to set up the new machinery for such a scheme, although the Government announced soon afterwards that they were 'pressing forward with a scheme for general contributory insurance'.[26] In the meantime they extended the out-of-work donation scheme to cover all *civilian* workers without a full contribution record, although it was stressed that this was only for a temporary period of six months. But the Government, having established a precedent, were forced to renew this arrangement for another six months until 24 November 1919. And when this temporary scheme expired, the Government felt itself compelled to reiterate their announcement of universal unemployment insurance to take its place, although little work had in fact been done on the formulation of such a policy.

The overall scheme, when it came with the 1920 Unemployment Insurance Act, was prepared in quite different circumstances to those of the original legislation of 1911. The apparatus which was to be used to counteract the effects of massive unemployment for the next twenty years was hastily and incompetently put together. Although in large part a word-for-word textual copy of much of the 1911 Act, it extended the principle of insurance into uncharted areas with a totally inadequate supply of information. No one could perhaps have foreseen the length and bitterness of the trade depression in which the scheme was to operate, but certain basic assumptions were made which proved wildly inaccurate. For example, coal-mining, which with over one million workers formed nearly one-tenth of the working population, was estimated by the Government actuary to have an average unemployment rate in the foreseeable future of only 1.5 per cent.[27] Some of the reasons for the inaccuracy of forecast were due to the paucity of official statistics, despite seven years' experience with unemployment insurance and nine years with employment exchanges, but much more was due to the hurried and ramshackle construction of the new administrative system. It was clear that, as the role of unemployment insurance widened to include less secure risks, so the possibility of conflict with strict actuarial principles became that much greater.

The provisions of the 1920 Act brought into unemployment insurance all workers under a contract of employment, including apprentices, with the exception of those employed in agriculture and related farming industries, private domestic service, or those employed in non-manual labour remunerated at over £250 per annum—the so-called 'black-coated' workers. The reason for the exclusion of these classes, which gave the scheme an additional in-built risk, seems to have been partly to appease the land-owning and servant-employing section of the community, who had objected so vehemently to 'licking stamps for Lloyd George' in relation to the National Health Insurance scheme. One structural change was that the period of 'waiting days' was cut from six to three, although Beveridge had shown that in the circumstances of 1912 this had relieved the Fund of half the cost in benefit payments;[28] but beyond this, little change was made to the existing framework. However, the number of workers covered by insurance jumped from 2½ million to over 11 million.[29] More ominously, the figures of those registered as unemployed were 500,000 in November 1920 when the Act came into force,[30] but six months later this had risen to over 2 million unemployed and over 1 million on short time working.[31] Unemployment through the winter of 1921 remained above 1½ million with many men now entering their second year without work. It was clearly not a temporary cyclical slump of the sort for which the 1911 Act had been designed; between 1921 and 1931 the percentage of those unemployed was to oscillate between 8.6 per cent and 23 per cent, with far higher rates in the depressed regional areas.[32]

The Fear of Revolution

It was to be expected that a major factor in the situation of rising unemployment was its impact on the temper of ex-servicemen. Having returned from the trenches, many of them had no possibility of civilian employment, or if they had returned to their old jobs, the mounting crisis threw them on to the 'dole' or at best on to short time working. Behind the desperate haste to produce the overall insurance scheme was to be found 'the fear of popular violence if something were not done to provide economic security for the British working man'.[33] Professor Gilbert's study of Cabinet records of the period shows the extent to which this fear prevailed in pressing the Government towards an overall compulsory insurance scheme. In particular, the reports of the Director of Intelligence to the Home Office, Basil Thomson, which went straight to the Cabinet, showed a high degree of alarmism:

> As seems inevitable under conditions of widespread distress and discontent, the Communists are gaining converts: the facts relating to unemployment are indisputable and they form a powerful weapon for attacking the Capitalist system; the workless are only too ready to believe that their lot could not be worse under a different form of government and might conceivably be better. The right to work is one which is difficult to deny and Soviet Russia is held up as a Utopia where work is not only a right but a duty. Class hatred is increasing . . . [34]

The writer of these reports was in fact forced to retire under threat of loss of pension in the same year, but his reports clearly had a considerable effect on the thinking of the Government.[35] Although undoubtedly overdrawn, the comparison with the Russian situation was not as wild as it might seem. As an example of the interest shown in Russian affairs at the time, it is instructive to note that, at a special meeting privately called by George Lansbury at the Albert Hall to welcome the revolutionary overthrow of the Czar, over 5,000 people had to be turned away for lack of space.[36] And a number of contemporary commentators were prepared to state that the growth of unemployment insurance and benefits was a major factor in warding off the potential threat of class warfare—for example, Alban Gordon believed that:

> Although the Unemployment Insurance scheme receives more criticism than Health Insurance, it is, nevertheless, probably owing solely to its existence in the years 1920–23 that revolution in this country has been averted and there is no doubt whatever that had the Government of the day attempted to face the unemployment of 1922 with the machinery of 1909 a definite uprising would have taken place.[37]

Such a view is of course necessarily hypothetical. In a complex social and political situation it would be naïve to pinpoint an unemployment insurance statute as a safety valve for the supposedly revolutionary fervour of a widely disparate mass of unemployed men. Particularly so, when the insurance scheme applied to only a minority of those out of work. Nevertheless, whatever the real dangers, it is clear that the Government at the time firmly agreed with the proposition that 'a mass of hungry men and women is the natural bed for revolution',[38] and the Webbs themselves believed that any social reform in this period was partly attributable to 'the incessant reports of the Secret Service Departments which filled the Minister's minds week by week with all sorts of tales of subversive agitation . . . agitation which is always so easy to discover, and which it is almost impossible for a secret agent not to magnify both the extent and the importance'.[39] If the inception of unemployment insurance was brought about through the exercise of altruism, then its extension can be said to have been brought about in large measure through fear of the alternatives.

Uncovenanted Benefits

Behind the appalling figures of unemployment in the early 1920s was a chronic dislocation in the structure of British industry. The frictional or cyclical unemployment, which Beveridge had talked about in his first edition of *Unemployment, A Problem of Industry*,[40] and for which the 1911 Act had been designed, had now been replaced by a permanent breakdown in a large number of industries. There was little chance of an unemployed worker gaining the necessary contribution record if his trade had ceased to exist or had contracted beyond repair.

The sudden onset of the 1921 slump resulted therefore in a massive increase of workers who, although technically insurable, had not had sufficient time to pay the full number of contributions in order to claim benefit. An Insurance Act of 1920[41] had attempted to alleviate their plight by reducing the statutory requirements for new entrants who could qualify for benefit after only four contributions. But this was coupled with a maximum of only eight weeks' benefit in the following twelve months and proved useless in the face of growing unemployment. The Government, forced to choose between putting ex-servicemen and civilian war-workers on to the Poor Law or extending the out-of-work donations yet again, felt they had no option but to carry on with the temporary arrangements despite the setting up of the new overall scheme which was supposed to have catered for everyone. Meanwhile, the cost of the donation scheme was becoming enormous,[42] and, as the 'temporary' scheme continued under various terminological descriptions as an almost permanent feature of the period, the basic insurance scheme was rapidly becoming redundant.

The Government's response to these circumstances was to invent a system of 'extended' benefit grafted on to the unemployment insurance system. But despite the change in name, this was in reality simply a continuance of the out-of-work donation scheme. To accomplish the 'reform', the first Unemployment Act of 1921 introduced the possibility of payment of benefits in advance of achieving the required contribution record, although special conditions were laid down for their receipt. The most important condition required the claimant to prove that he was 'genuinely seeking whole-time employment but unable to obtain such employment',[43] with the onus of proof on the claimant if called before the Local Employment Committees or appealing to the Court of Referees. But having established the precedent of paying benefits above an applicant's contribution record, it was a simple step for the Government in the second Act of the same year to pay these 'uncovenanted benefits' simply on the basis of need. The political pressures seemed too great to do anything else, and Professor Gilbert states that 'the question of whether the money might be better spent some other way was not considered . . . Unemployed workmen would have to be supported if England were to avoid revolution, and unemployment insurance was assigned to do the job'.[44]

The reason for the overburdening of the Unemployment Insurance Fund in the following decade is not obscure. It was used repeatedly as a 'temporary' means of escape from a desperate situation. Confronted with unemployment entirely different in both quality and quantity from anything that could be anticipated, each successive Government attempted to stretch the principle of limited liability to cover what they imagined to be a short-term emergency. However, it was this principle of limitation on which the stability of unemployment insurance depended and, having 'stripped the insurance scheme of its proper scientific cover, there ensued a desperate search for shreds and patches of clothing with which to hide its nakedness'.[45] With the lowering and then partial abandonment of entry requirements, the core of the insurance system of a fixed ratio between contributions and subsequent benefits was destroyed. And in a desperate attempt to keep the scheme in equilibrium in such circumstances, Beveridge felt that the 'custom of passing two or three Unemployment Insurance Acts each year' had been established and that 'everything that could be called system disappeared'.[46]

The welter of legislation which followed up to 1934 amply displays the chaos.[47] Over thirty amending Acts were passed in this period putting contributions' and benefits' periods and rates up and down, with many of the Acts contradicting earlier legislation in an infinitely complex and tangled web. But they all clearly bear the stamp of being in 'the nature of emergency readjustments'.[48] Any analysis of this confusion must point to the fact that the retention of any 'insurance' principle relating to unemployment relief was in large part an illusion. The original scheme had revolved around the concept of short-term breaks from a regular routine of work, but in a study of British unemployment and unemployment insurance in this period, an American observer thought that 'insurance' had become 'a dignified name for a form of poor relief. Why not admit that England never has had insurance?'[49] However, the crucial social fact to remember in this situation is that, when the Unemployment Insurance Acts increased or decreased the number of those entitled to uncovenanted benefits, so the number who were compelled to seek the much less generous relief given by the residual Poor Law authorities varied.

One amendment to the insurance system in this period, however, remained. Following the example of the out-of-work donation schemes, dependants' benefits were introduced by the Unemployed Workers' Dependants (Temporary Provisions) Act 1921. This was an interim measure which included wives as well as children for a six months period, but it remained to become an integral part of the modern social security system.

Whatever the actuarial and theoretical difficulties with the extended schemes, the limited aid given to the families of the unemployed through its agency must not be minimized. As a direct result of this aid, a prominent research group stated in 1923:

> The widespread physical distress, which was the normal accompaniment of unemployment in previous depressions, has been prevented . . . In the past two winters, with unemployment far more extensive and severe than in any other pre-war depression, this physical distress is not noticeable.[50]

Breakdown

The principal element in the unemployment history of this period was the struggle, as Professor Robson puts it, to 'maintain the "insurance" basis of the [unemployment] scheme in the face of liabilities far greater than any which could be met by "actuarial" means'.[51] With the advent of a Labour Government in January 1924, one might have supposed that dramatic changes would have been made to the direction of British industry, but Ramsay MacDonald was hampered by the need to rely on the support of the Liberals. The new Minister of Labour, Tom Shaw, attempted to make uncovenanted benefits indefinite in length as a temporary relief measure, but this move was frustrated by the Liberals.[52] The response of the incoming Baldwin administration was to appoint an 'Unemployment Insurance Committee' under the chairmanship of a Law Lord, the Blanesburgh Committee. It took two years to report, and its main conclusions were that 'persons with so poor a record of unemployment (as having done less than 15 weeks' work in 52 weeks) [can] scarcely claim still to be in the insured field; that there is grave doubt as to the genuineness of their search for work; and that the exclusion of such individuals is only fair to the general body of insured contributors'.[53] But such a view ignored the fact that men were helpless to find employment and gain a contribution record in the existing economic climate. Their remedy for a complex problem was simply a 'Back to the Poor Law' statement, although added to their list of recommendations was the seemingly contradictory plan for standard insurance benefit unlimited in duration. Professor Gilbert states that 'any assessment of the committee's work must conclude that its effect on the insurance programme was almost entirely bad'.[54]

However, the Government felt unable to adopt all the Blanesburgh proposals but, by the Unemployment Insurance Act 1927, introduced a scheme of 'transitional benefits' which ran parallel to standard insurance benefits. The distinction was that the applicant for 'transitional benefits', who had not the full contribution record to apply for standard benefit, was required to show that he was 'genuinely seeking work but unable to obtain *suitable* employment' (my italics); if he fulfilled this requirement, then benefit was unlimited in duration.[55] In an unguarded statement at the time, Beveridge said that with this Act 'the ten-year chaos since 1918 may be said to have ended'.[56] But despite all the insuperable difficulties ahead, as the country moved into the Depression of 1929–31, the Blanesburgh Committee had made one important affirmation in that 'it has been recognised by all who have appeared before us, and we ourselves share the view, that an unemployment insurance scheme must now be regarded as a permanent feature of our code of social legislation'.[57] For it was clear that the introduction of National Insurance had changed the terms of the debate on unemployment. Until this period, it could be said of unemployment that 'relief works, chiefly with pick and shovel, were the usual British response to this complex of needs'.[58] It was true that the Poor Law had always stood as the last long-stop before destitution, but it was now no longer possible to fall back, as a first answer to the problem, on a succession of meaningless relief work schemes. The proceedings of the Blanesburgh Committee show clearly that the lesson had been learned, and that such relief measures were indeed 'wasteful, inefficient, and [had] a deteriorating effect on all concerned'.[59]

But what was the answer to the mounting difficulties of the situation? With the return of a Labour Government in 1929, and following the report of a committee under the chairmanship of an eminent socialist barrister, Sir Harold Morris Q.C., the 1930 Unemployment Insurance Act repealed the one legal device for policing the payment of transitional benefits set up in the 1927 Act—that of 'genuinely seeking work'. Instead, an applicant would be disqualified from receipt of benefit for up to six weeks if he failed to accept a vacant and suitable job of which he had been notified in writing by an Employment Exchange.[60] The immediate effect of this measure was, as it was intended to be, to reduce substantially the number of men subsisting on Poor Law relief, as they now became eligible once again for transitional benefits.[61]

The Labour Government also appointed J. H. Thomas as the Cabinet Minister responsible for dealing with unemployment, but the figures increased dramatically in spite of his efforts. In December 1929, the unemployed numbered 1,300,000, which was the approximate average for each of the previous seven years. But a year later this figure had almost doubled to 2,400,000 or about 19.6 per cent of all insured persons.[62] The trend was naturally paralleled in the growth of the Unemployment Insurance Fund, which included transitional benefit payments, and was by March 1930 £75 millions—amounting to a debt of £36 millions.[63]

Groping for a means to cope with this explosion, the Government appointed a Royal Commission on Unemployment Insurance under the chairmanship of Mr. Justice Holman Gregory.[64] It was required to make recommendations for the insurance scheme 'by which it may be made solvent, and the arrangements which should be made outside the scheme for the unemployed who are capable of and available for work'.[65] But the Royal Commission was repeatedly overtaken by events in the two years of its work. A first interim Report in 1931 recommended a test of need on all those drawing transitional benefits,[66] and this suggestion was promptly endorsed by a special Committee on National Expenditure set up under the chairmanship of George May, the Secretary of the Prudential Assurance Company, which was appointed in March 1931.[67] But the May Committee went further in producing a chilling forecast that the budget deficit for the current fiscal year would be £120 millions, of which the amount attributable to the Insurance Fund deficit would be £105 millions. However, this was a controversial estimate, and one view was that the Report had been 'unduly alarmist in tone and [had] grossly exaggerated the real dangers of the situation'.[68] The May Committee recommended drastic and urgent economies in all government departments, but in particular it urged a saving of £66 millions on unemployment benefits. However, when this programme was put to the Cabinet, Professor Gilbert states that 'the final agony of the Labour Government began. Suddenly the gap appeared between social justice and fiscal responsibility. What the Government could afford according to accepted economic tenets and what the working population needed in order to keep alive could not be reconciled in financial terms.'[69]

Faced with the stubborn refusal of the majority of his Cabinet to make cuts in unemployment benefits,[70] MacDonald reviewed the political situation and decided to break with the party he had helped build and form a National Government. Although the relief of the unemployed through the transitional benefits scheme was at the centre of the projected budget deficit in 1931, it is now clear that there were many other political and economic factors which contributed as much to the crisis.[71] But through the failure of successive administrations to cope both with the rise of unemployment and with its proper relief, and their continued tinkering with the makeshift 1920 insurance system, some kind of crisis seemed inevitable. The insurance principle had been 'smothered in a patchwork of emergency measures, until contributions, benefits and the permitted limits of a vast insolvency [had] all become quite arbitrary'.[72] Drastic measures needed to be taken to restore the insurance scheme to solvency, but, even more important, a new formula had to be devised to give effective relief to the unemployed men and their families at the mercy of the worst economic depression ever experienced.[73]

The 1934 'Double-Decker' Scheme

Recovery from these catastrophic difficulties came slowly. The immediate reaction of the National Government to the May Committee's recommendations was to abolish transitional benefits under the insurance scheme and to substitute in their place a system of 'transitional payments' administered by Public Assistance Committees. These committees were drawn from the local authorities, and were modelled on the Poor Law, but they were financed separately by the Treasury. As this was part of the Government's economy legislation, the sieving device was to be a strict Household Means Test adapted from the Poor Law, although standards throughout the country varied considerably. In this way, the long-term unemployed were again saved from immediate resort to the Poor Law, although it was a commonplace in this period that, as Professor Pigou put it, 'the curve of pauperism . . .

[followed] about a year behind the curve of unemployment'.[74] For six years following October 1931, less than half the unemployed qualified for insurance benefit, and public opinion increasingly reacted against treating all the off-insurance unemployed as 'able-bodied paupers' under the Poor Law.[75]

The weaknesses of the Poor Law in coping with such a situation were evident. Although modernized to a degree, it was difficult to rid the structure of its centuries-old legacy of parochialism which made the system into what one writer described as 'an anarchy of local autonomy . . . [with] each parish anxious to do as little as possible for its own poor, and nothing for any stranger'.[76] The handicap of the insurance system had been that 'no plan had been adopted for those who were not only unemployed but had exhausted their benefits'.[77] Yet the only alternative to destitution was the offer of the Poor Law, even though it was generally known to be ineffective and ponderous, still using antiquated administrative machinery established a century before.[78] This reluctance of Governments to cast the unemployed into the hands of the Poor Law authorities was partly due to the knowledge of its occasionally extravagant use of central funds without central control, but also because they knew the Poor Law to be, without exaggeration, 'a system whose name stinks in the nostrils even of those compelled to seek its aid'.[79] Given that those who might have to be transferred from the 'transitional' quasi-insurance scheme to the Poor Law were electors, Governments were clearly anxious to make alternative arrangements if possible. With this in mind, it is perhaps reasonable to conclude without cynicism that, in the words of Aneurin Bevan, a number of 'the social reforms of the twentieth century are a consequence of the democratic power of the masses and not of increased enlightenment'.[80]

Some considerable effort had, however, been expended on the Poor Law to bring it into line with modern conditions. In 1926, the existing ninety-nine Acts of Parliament which formed the statutory provisions for dealing with the poor were 'operated on by the parliamentary draughtsmen'.[81] However, these statutes were not the sole statement of the law, for since 1834 there had been wide powers to make Orders. So in 1927 this huge conglomeration of delegated legislation was consolidated into one Public Assistance Order and a subsidiary Relief Regulation Order, which together with the 1927 Poor Law Act, consisting of 244 sections, was a distillation of the previously existing jumble. But perhaps the most vital changes were effected by Neville Chamberlain's Local Government Act 1929, which abolished the long-established Boards of Guardians as an agency for distributing relief. Their functions were turned over to county and county borough authorities, so that in contrast to 643 Unions there were now 145 urban and rural administrative units dealing with the Poor Law under firm central control. At the same time, Poor Law Relieving Officers had their title changed to Public Assistance Officers, which of itself was a significant change of emphasis.[82] The Poor Law continued, but its established functions were close to being broken up.

The system of 'transitional payments' through the specially constituted Public Assistance Committees under the economy legislation of 1931 was an interim scheme. But it had established a precedent of central administrative control, and also 'implied in effect, the recognition of a national responsibility for the long-term unemployed'.[83] This responsibility was recognized by the Royal Commission on Unemployment Insurance which finally reported in 1932.[84] The majority felt that a self-supporting scheme of insurance could no longer include any benefits for the long-term unemployed who must be separately provided for. The minority, however, disagreed vehemently with this 'proposal that the unemployed should be divided into two classes—one to receive insurance benefit at the Employment Exchanges as of right, the other to apply to the Local Authorities on the grounds of need'.[85] But although the majority view was approximately that followed by the Government in their subsequent legislation, it is wrong to consider that the Royal Commission had much effect on their thinking, as some commentators believe. Although the Commission was appointed in the full glare of publicity, by the time its report emerged in October 1932 it had largely been forgotten in the turmoil of events, and many of its findings had been utilized by the May Committee. The Government had by this stage worked out its own plan, part of which was attributable to a desire to create a strong administrative structure for any new system of relief. For although the transitional payments scheme had operated reasonably smoothly, some trouble had been experienced with a number of Public Assistance Committees, resulting finally in the suspension of two of them.[86] Their work had then been carried out by the Ministry of Labour, and the satisfactory nature of this operation may have been a major factor in the formulation of the Government scheme.

The Unemployment Insurance Bill, as proposed by the Government in 1933, was basically an attempt to take the whole topic of unemployment 'out of politics'. Its structure revolved around a total segregation of the unemployed into two categories: the insured, and those who no longer had a contribution record or who had never had one but were nonetheless fit for work. Two bodies, the Unemployment Insurance Statutory Committee and the Unemployment Assistance Board, were to supervise the implementation of the Act completely outside ministerial control. By this means Neville Chamberlain thought that it would be possible to 'avoid the danger of the relief being put up to auction by the [political] parties'.[87] But in this aim of taking unemployment 'out of politics' the Government were to be sorely disappointed, although the Act at last marked the clear recognition that the pretence of insurance, which had soured the official scheme and had also proved inadequate for those who had no contributions, had to be ended; 20 per cent of the men on transitional benefits also received Poor Law relief.[88]

The Unemployment Insurance Statutory Committee

The top deck of the new 'double-decker' scheme, Part I of the 1934 Unemployment Act, was principally under the direction of the Unemployment Insurance Statutory Committee (the U.I.S.C.). Although in form a consultative and advisory body, it was charged with the task of overseeing the solvency of the Unemployment Insurance Fund, which by June 1934, when the Committee started its work, was in debt by £105 millions. To enable it to perform this task the U.I.S.C. had 'the use of financial powers uncontrolled by any Minister and [was] not itself responsible to Parliament',[89] in that it could recommend to the Ministry of Labour any changes it regarded as necessary in the rates of benefits and contributions, and also in the regulations which guarded the Insurance Fund. Previously this had been the sole responsibility of the Treasury, in conjunction with the Ministry of Labour.

The U.I.S.C. consisted of a part-time Chairman and four to six part-time members appointed by the Minister of Labour for a term of five years at a time. The Government chose Beveridge to be the new Chairman with considerable powers over the administration of the new system in that all the recommendations of the committee were automatically accepted. As Beveridge had been instrumental in setting up the original insurance scheme, and had made several attempts in the First World War to extend the scheme, the Government could not have found anyone with more experience of the system, although Aneurin Bevan claimed at the time of his appointment that 'whereas hitherto laws had been made by Act of Parliament, now in regard to unemployment insurance they were being made by Sir William Beveridge'.[90] In the circumstances this was perhaps no bad thing. The Committee, as Beveridge saw it, was in effect a standing Royal Commission on Unemployment Insurance, but also with the exceptional power of being able to put their proposals into effect immediately.[91]

The balance of the U.I.S.C. was that of three representatives from the employers and three from the trade unions, with Beveridge as Chairman. Members of Parliament were expressly disbarred from serving.[92] On the whole the work of the U.I.S.C. was remarkably successful. Although 'by the year 1931 the original carefully constructed scheme was hardly recognisable through the tangled maze of opportunist legislation',[93] the agencies of the 1934 Act had, according to a PEP Report, 're-affirmed, if not the principles, the practice of 1911'.[94] By 1939, the U.I.S.C. had reduced the Unemployment Insurance Fund debt from £105 millions to £77 millions, with a balance of £57 millions—in fact 'the growing surplus in the unemployment insurance fund was nearly as embarrassing politically as had been the deficit in the previous decade'.[95]

Little change was made by the Committee to the existing insurance framework—except to change the waiting days period back from six days to three days once again—but amongst subsequent changes was the setting up of a special unemployment insurance scheme for agricultural workers in 1936, with both contributions and benefits very much lower than those for the general scheme;[96] and an extension of the general scheme to cover domestic servants in 1937.[97] This brought into the system all but a small section of the employed population. Generally, the insurance scheme 'progressed favourably'[98] between 1934 and 1946. But this must be seen in the context of steadily falling unemployment from 1932 onwards,[99] and also in the light of the sharp cleavage of the unemployed in 1934, which left only the short-term unemployed in the care of the insurance scheme. This differentiation had been made with the express aim of 'maintaining the insurance principle', and it certainly relieved the insurance scheme of a heavy burden of 'difficult cases'; for example, it is clear from an analysis of the applicants to the Unemployment Assistance Board that their average age was far higher than of those claiming unemployment insurance.[100] The nature of unemployment had not changed dramatically, but rather the burden of it had shifted away from the insurance scheme.

The 1934 Act was a major reconstruction but, as the economic crisis had aggravated the defects of the patchwork schemes, so the ebbing away of mass unemployment allowed the insurance section of the new framework to operate smoothly. The calculations of the Government in 1934 were based on the sheer magnitude of the 'off-insurance' problems they had to face, and Sir Ronald Davison thought that they 'would never have committed themselves to so drastic a transformation, if they had known that the number of the off-insurance unemployed would, in a year or so, be reduced by 40%, and highly localised at that'.[101] But at that stage no one could dare hope that the relief problems which had proved so unsurmountable for the last decade could ever be overcome. Nevertheless, although the insurance principle was to be saved, almost overnight, by Part I of the 1934 Act, Part II was not such a success, and particularly not so in the short term.

The Unemployment Assistance Board

The Unemployment Assistance Board under the 1934 Act was set up to make provision for the long-term unemployed. This included all those on transitional payments under the Public Assistance committees and also those who had had to fall back on the Poor Law but were fit to work. Its internal operating procedures and regulations controlling the amount of relief granted were taken directly from those governing the Poor Law system. Relief given by the U.A.B. was by means of a household means test, which became a matter of considerable personal and political bitterness. Six hundred thousand unemployed men on transitional payments were taken over by the Board on 7 January 1935, and this amounted with their dependants to responsibility for approximately $2\frac{1}{2}$ million people.[102] Added to this figure was an indeterminate number of those who were adjudged to be the 'able-bodied unemployed' on 1 April 1937, with the intention of eventually leaving only a small number of claimants, mainly 'vagrants', on the Poor Law.[103]

The opposition to the setting up of the Board was intense. In all, the House of Commons spent twenty-seven days in debate on the Act, the longest period on any legislation since the First World War.[104] Particularly bitter was the onslaught launched on the new proposals by the Labour Party under its leader, George Lansbury, who, taking a lead from the Minority Report to the Royal Commission on Unemployment Insurance, strongly criticized the creation of two classes in the ranks of the unemployed: the insured and the 'less eligible'. But more disgraceful in their eyes was that an individual objecting to harsh treatment could not raise his case in Parliament through his M.P., as the U.A.B. was, like the U.I.S.C., entirely unaccountable to Parliament and under no Minister's responsibility; in this respect, both the Board and the Statutory Committee were 'neo-Chadwickian' in nature.[105] The Act's opponents believed this to cut across the fundamental British political principle that, in the words of Professor Laski, 'after forming a Government, the most essential function of the House of Commons . . . is the ventilation of grievance'.[106] The precedent which was pointed to as an illustration of the chaos caused by the denial of this principle was the setting up of the Poor Law Board following the 1834 Poor Law Amendment Act, but the lesson that its downfall was caused mainly by its non-accountability in Parliament had not been learned, or went unheeded.[107] Aneurin Bevan, Lansbury's P.P.S. and one of the strongest opponents of the measure, argued that it was legislation 'to take poverty out of politics and to make the poor dumb . . . The only way for a man to protest will be to throw a brick through the window . . . You want to suffocate the unemployed man's cries in a maze of bureaucracy'.[108]

But despite attacks of this nature, the Government continued with its attempt to insulate the operation of the U.A.B. from political pressure in every possible way. The Board's six permanent members were to be paid from the Consolidated Fund and were to hold office indefinitely. They were given wide powers to give assistance according to need to any able-bodied person between the ages of 16 and 65,[109] and the Board was also empowered to set up work and training schemes as it saw fit.[110] Through a widely spread net of local offices, the U.A.B. quickly became, according to Professor Gilbert, 'virtually a centralised Poor Law for all working people in the country'.[111] And, despite widespread political criticism, a P.E.P. broadsheet published soon after the passage of the Act was able to state that 'the general consensus of opinion was that the new scale and means test were reasonable and adequate'.[112] Perhaps the words had been written in advance of the commencement of operations, for in the event this forecast of opinion proved wildly inaccurate.

The U.A.B. recruited 6,000 officials from government departments and local authorities, and centred them in twenty-eight districts; few had previous experience of relief or social work.[113] Local office accommodation was found, often with the help of local advisory committees set up under the Act, which proved to be of 'essential importance as the means of securing protection and popular goodwill for the Board's administration in the localities'.[114] The Board also set up a new system of 138 appeal tribunals along the lines of the National Insurance Courts of Referees, with a part-time chairman and two wingmen.[115] But there were important distinctions in their constitution and procedure, which in the case of U.A.B. tribunals were weighted heavily in favour of the Board. This was done deliberately, and was thought explainable by one critic in the context of

> Hunger marches, riots and sustained political acrimony . . . The facts clearly suggest that those responsible for the [1934 Act] were determined that the appeal tribunals should not be free to weaken the Board's policy in any way and accordingly the tribunals were made an integral part of the Board.[116]

Weighting was achieved by, among other things, having one wingman 'appointed by the Board to represent the Board',[117] who served frequently in comparison with the other wingman who was drawn in rotation from a sizeable panel to represent workpeople. The Chairman was also appointed directly by the Minister and the clerk was originally a senior officer of the Board who sat in on the decision-making process of the tribunal after the appellant had withdrawn.[118] Some kind of appeal process was perhaps inevitable in the new system, as those who had formerly been on transitional payments had become accustomed to making appeals to the Courts of Referees, and also to the Public Assistance Committees in the years 1931–5. But the 'independence' of the new tribunals was clearly spurious for reasons of policy, and the initial weighting of the tribunals was to have important consequences later when the Board moved from an agency dealing solely with crisis unemployment situations to one handling the general relief system of National Assistance, now known as Supplementary Benefits.

The institution of a separate system for the long-term unemployed was justified by the Government in the circumstances of mass unemployment. But the creation of the U.A.B. beyond ministerial and parliamentary control drew repeated criticism, based on the constitutional theory of Ministerial Responsibility.[119] The American observer of the workings of the U.A.B., Professor Millett, commented that it was

> surprising that so little comment has been made on this unprecedented departure from the accepted principle of no taxation without representation, and on the handing over of the control of the expenditure of vast sums of public money to a non-elective bureaucratic authority, operating a machine manned by thousands of enthusiastic officials working empirically on social problems of which not a few had had no previous experience.[120]

In these circumstances, it was not surprising that the scheme had a rebound effect. First, the U.A.B. not having any possibility of Parliamentary control was also unable to defend itself against Parliamentary attackers, so that, according to Professor Jennings, 'the chief result of "taking unemployment benefits assistance out of politics" was that the Board had no means of defending itself against attacks . . . It is an advantage to be openly attacked. For attack implies defence'.[121] Secondly, the start of the scheme saw absolute administrative chaos. Throughout the country there were innumerable complaints, demonstrations and disruptions. The U.A.B. 'having worked coolly and objectively on the task, freed from ignorant parliamentary pressure . . . brought forward proposals which—almost unintentionally, perhaps—meant a cut in benefits for a large number of applicants'.[122] The simple fact was that payments under the U.A.B. rules were smaller than under the Public Assistance Committees' rates, and the income of many claimants was drastically cut. The difference was largely because of the huge regional disparities in the Public Assistance rates, which could not easily be amalgamated into a national standard rate. A storm of protest followed, the Minister of Labour was shouted down in the House of Commons, and, ironically, 'at no time in the recently completed century of its existence had the new Poor Law been so popular'.[123] The Government were forced to intervene, and announced immediately that the U.A.B. rules would be suspended in cases where Public Assistance relief would have been more generous. By the Unemployment Assistance (Temporary Provisions) Act 1935—the so-called 'Standstill Act'—relieving officers were allowed to use the U.A.B. scale or the Public Assistance scale, whichever was more generous to the applicant.

A revised code of regulations was also drafted and introduced in 1936. It was described by one critic as 'the negation of a code' or 'a code of exceptional circumstances'[124] in that it contained abundant possibility for discretionary payment above the standard scale, but it was naturally well received by the unemployed. This was the first full consolidation of existing practice and formed the basis for the later regulations and the internal administrative codes instructing officers on their precise application to individual circumstances. The difficulties over the Board died away quickly, partly because unemployment was steadily dropping, but also because the U.A.B. used its discretion to the full in an attempt to steer well clear of further controversy. Nevertheless, it would not be true to say that the unemployment problem was disappearing. Although the figures were falling, serious regional and local problems remained,[125] and these coupled with chronically low rates of pay persisted until the war years. George Orwell in his study of Lancashire reviewed a local census at this time, which showed that 40,000 cotton mill workers were receiving less in pay than the U.A.B. scale rate for the area.[126] However, although the start of the Board's work had been catastrophic, it was nevertheless crucially important as representing one further step away from the Poor Law and the Principles of 1834. Its setting up had perhaps been, in the words of a P.E.P. Broadsheet, 'due to other considerations than the needs of the people chiefly concerned—the off-insurance class who are in poverty. Politics and Treasury finance smothered the truth of social issues',[127] but nevertheless the Board survived to evolve into a national agency of vital importance to the welfare of the poor.

The Means Test

The principle that state-provided security for the needy should be unpleasant is the most venerable of administrative devices in that historically, as Professor Burns has pointed out, 'public welfare systems which stand between the incomeless individual and starvation have always given assistance as grudgingly and unpleasantly as possible'.[128] No survey of this era can be complete without a study of the household means test which, although not a new mechanism in that it was an inheritance from the Poor Law, became notorious in the Inter-War period through its use in relation to the various categories of extended benefits and under the U.A.B. Closely related to the means test was the 'Genuinely Seeking Work' clause, already referred to, which was a further attempt to divide the 'deserving' from the 'undeserving' unemployed.

The household means test was an administrative device for enforcing family contributions towards the relief of those receiving benefits. It clearly inferred the financial interdependence of relatives living under the same roof, although this was not necessarily the case in many working-class homes.[129] In the 1601 Poor Law Act, this responsibility for relatives stretched from grandparents to grandchildren living under the same roof, and included relationships by marriage, but in the 1930s this had become limited in practice to close relations, although no definition of 'household' was given in the Acts or public regulations.[130] Under the nineteenth century Poor Law, the threat of the 'House' was widely used to induce relatives to support their elderly relatives, but following the introduction of old age pensions this was rarely at issue. The present practice is for the S.B.C. to make a standard assumption on the amount which non-dependent relatives should contribute to the household budget. There is no doubt that, in its extreme form, the principle caused grave hardship, and often had the effect of splitting up families who could no longer afford to live together. One famous study of the unemployed found ample evidence that children were forced to leave home to avoid the imposition of the test on their parents[131]—it was a principle which, in the words of one critic at the time, Aneurin Bevan, 'eats like an acid into the homes of the poor. In the small rooms and around the meagre tables of the poor hells of personal acrimony and wounded vanities arise'.[132] Eleanor Rathbone, in her studies of 'the disinherited family' and the need for the introduction of family allowances, thought that 'unless the enquiries made to verify statements of income are so thorough as to be unpleasantly inquisitorial, the restriction is easily eroded and the temptation to evasion put in the way of people of narrow means turns the process into a veritable school of lying and destructor of self-respect'.[133] The general effect of the household means test was often to encourage 'a kind of cleverness' in that people 'felt they had to "beat the State" and hence the whole spirit of the administration with all its conflicts grew up'.[134] During the inter-war period, Poor Law and U.A.B. regulations suggested the investigation of all recipients' homes once every four weeks, but this procedure led inevitably to counter-strategies.[135] For example, the communist-led National Unemployed Workers' Movement devised schemes of switching working sons and daughters around in their beds with the children of neighbouring relatives, to avoid the incidence of the means test.[136] The N.U.W.M., which became the leading champion of the unemployed at this time, was, according to George Orwell, 'a revolutionary organisation intended to hold the unemployed together, stop them blacklegging during strikes and give them legal aid against the Means Test'.[137] But little was needed to stir the emotions of those who had been means-tested into a hatred of the system. By its use in the 1930s, the household means test had become, according to Professor Robson, 'the most hated expression in the entire vocabulary of social administration'.[138]

Appeals could be made to the U.A.B.'s tribunals, but to the unemployed these often seemed 'distant and potentially alien . . . to eyes dimmed by helplessness'.[139] One commentator claimed that unemployed claimants were 'hauled' before the Courts of Referees

> to find themselves subjected to a rapid fire of questions from the chairman . . . in an effort to trap him into a contradiction of some previous statement, and if, under this third-degree method, he became confused and was unable to remember important points in connection with his search for work, he would be as good as called a liar and charged with malingering.[140]

Whatever the precise nature of these encounters with tribunals, and a number of surviving accounts of their proceedings are highly tendentious, it is clear from the classic studies made by E. Wight Bakke of unemployment in this period that, subjectively, many claimants felt that they had been

> suddenly thrown into another class, a less eligible and less secure class. As one engineer said to me, 'It gives you the idea that you aren't so good as some and that's a sad thing to happen, mate. You tell yourself that there are plenty of chaps in the same fix, but all the same it's small comfort. But thinking doesn't alter your being on the Means Test. It's a real shock.'[141]

Perhaps it is difficult to recall the agonies which the household means test involved during the 1930s and the scale of unemployment suffered,[142] or to understand fully how much they moulded the feelings and fears of working-class people towards the relief agencies of the State. The direct operation of the test was, as G. K. Chesterton pointed out, 'a definite deliberate campaign to make the poor poorer . . . People who are already clinging with their teeth and finger-nails to the edge of the chasm are to be formally and legally kicked into the chasm'.[143] It must be remembered that some of the unemployed had by 1937 been out of work for fifteen years with an occasional break of a few days to do a labouring job.

In contrast to the above views, some commentators have suggested that what gave the means test its notoriety during the 1930s was its application and not its form. Simply as a diagnosis of a man's capacity and personal circumstances there was 'no reason for such a policy to be rejected as harsh or retrograde or wrong in principle'.[144] But in practice such a distinction was meaningless to those subjected to the test. And it is clear that the hatred and suspicion felt by many forms a legacy which must represent a substantial factor in any discussion of social policy today.

Towards a New System

The principle of insurance in unemployment relief had gone through many difficulties by the time of its reconstitution in 1934. The persistence of high unemployment had necessitated a waiver of contributions and benefits requirements, but with the immediate pre-War years of the late 1930s, the insurance scheme settled back into its original role as a provider for cyclical and short-term unemployment. However, the 1934 legislation had legally confirmed a previously existing state in making a sharp distinction between those covered by insurance and the less fortunate long-term unemployed. The insecurity which this caused and the suspicion which it engendered in this 'less eligible' class led to the immediate crisis over the introduction of the U.A.B. scale rates. But this controversy died down quickly following the 'Standstill Act' and the implementation of a more generous relief policy in 1936. The U.A.B. was also careful to differentiate itself in both style and procedure from the Poor Law, and the effect of the 1934 Act was to create, as Professor Marshall puts it, 'a new Limbo . . . in between the Heaven of insurance benefits and the Hell of poor relief'.[145] However, this new 'Limbo' quickly transformed itself from being simply an unemployment relief agency to one of national welfare provision in a series of administrative 'take-overs'. With the outbreak of War in 1939 the Government empowered the U.A.B. to include in its work any 'persons who are in distress as the result of circumstances caused by the war',[146] and this was extended by regulation to cover civil defence workers suffering from injury, and then to all adult civilians injured in an air raid. Further additions followed through the operations of Orders passed under the 1939 Act. And by the 'P.R.D.' scheme (Prevention and Relief of Wartime Distress), the Board was able to give assistance on the basis of need to a whole range of war casualties from Government evacuees and foreign refugees to the dependants of interned aliens. The experiences of the War had proved the efficiency of the Board's administration and 'as a swift-working, well-organised, centrally controlled body' it became 'the obvious choice when the Government [was] looking for an agency to administer or enquire into the need for payments to fresh groups of citizens'.[147]

Gradually the U.A.B. turned to swallowing up some of the existing functions of the residual Poor Law, and in Part II of the Old Age and Widows' Pension Act 1940 it took over the administration of all supplementary pensions given to those over 60 in receipt of Old Age or Widows' Pensions.[148] With this fundamental change in its functions, the Government decided to alter the name of the Board simply to 'Assistance Board' as being more descriptive of its new role. The Board had truly become 'a maid of all work'.[149] But the most dramatic change in the system was perhaps due to the Blitz, for, as one historian wryly observes, 'the Luftwaffe did not distinguish between the deserving and the undeserving'.[150] In these circumstances, and with the need to keep civilian morale high, relief for the homeless and unemployed had to be generous, and so, by the Determination of Needs Act 1941, the household means test was narrowed into unimportance.[151] This had happened at the insistence of the Labour Party, now joined in the Coalition Government to fight the war,[152] and it marked the end of an era.

The Beveridge Report

With the onset of the Second World War, Sir William Beveridge, now Master of University College, Oxford, volunteered his services to the Government and was duly appointed to his former department, the Ministry of Labour. However, his personality was not in tune with that of the Minister, Ernest Bevin,[153] and arrangements were made to pass Beveridge on to consider questions of reconstruction following the war, under the oversight of Arthur Greenwood—'largely to keep him quiet'.[154] Beveridge's main task was to chair an Inter-Departmental Committee on Social Insurance and Allied Services, which was appointed in June 1941. The propulsion for setting up the Committee seems to have come from a deputation of the T.U.C. General Council, who had put forward to the Government a number of detailed criticisms concerning health insurance and workmen's compensation.

Apart from Beveridge, there were eleven other members of the Committee, appointed from all the Government departments which had an interest in insurance matters. Oral evidence was taken in fortnightly sessions during the first half of 1942, in which witnesses 'were able at all times to talk frankly and fruitfully off the record'.[155] With his knowledge of the original 1911 unemployment insurance structure and his subsequent experience with the Unemployment Insurance Statutory Committee, Beveridge had been 'allotted a most congenial task'.[156] He set about it with obvious enthusiasm. On publication in December 1942, the 'Beveridge Report', as it became known,[157] was an instantaneous best-seller with enormous world press coverage, temporarily overshadowing the war news. Although the work of a committee, the Report appeared over the name of Beveridge only, to preserve civil service anonymity. Much of the initial impact of the Report was due to the astute propaganda campaign of Brendan Bracken, the Minister of Information, but in the grim circumstances of the war the immense public reaction was understandable in that Beveridge's Plan was 'an eloquent cry to end poverty, disease, and unemployment, and purported to supply the means of doing so'.[158]

Beveridge himself, in an eve-of-publication broadcast, described the Report as 'a completion of what was begun a little more than thirty years ago when Mr Lloyd George introduced National Health Insurance and Mr Winston Churchill introduced Unemployment Insurance'.[159] But it was clear that, although the proposals involved an extension of existing mechanisms, the Beveridge scheme propounded a new comprehensive approach to social security. In fact, Beveridge had put forward just such a design eighteen years earlier, in a pamphlet entitled *Insurance For All and Everything*,[160] which included his ideas for replacing workmen's compensation with contributory insurance. Some modifications and extensions were made to this earlier scheme in the light of civil service advice and professional estimates of the finance involved, but there was surprisingly little structural change. Beveridge summarized his recommendations in the following terms:

> The main feature of my Plan for Social Security is a unified comprehensive scheme of social insurance to be administered by one Department, to provide cash benefits adequate in amount and in time without a means test, at a flat rate of benefit in return for a flat rate of contributions. With this goes a comprehensive health service and a system of children's allowances.[161]

The explanation for the astonishing impact of the Beveridge Report must be that with the harsh memories of the 1930s still fresh in the minds of many, and with the immediate privations and fears of the war, the Report answered a deep-felt need. The inter-war years had been marked by a feeling of helplessness in the face of continued unemployment and its attack on 'want . . . one of the five giants on the road of reconstruction'[162] struck a note of reassurance and security for the years after the war. One estimate of poverty in the 1930s had suggested that approximately 4 million families lived 'from hand-to-mouth', with half of this number continually living in debt.[163] The recollection of such difficulties made certain a large and receptive audience for the new proposals. The Ministry of Information, appreciating this interest, furthered it by conducting a vigorous campaign of education. This included a special Beveridge-written synopsis of the Report sent to all servicemen in an effort to boost morale, and a series of lectures through the scheme for Adult Education in H.M. Forces.

But having created intense public interest, the Government suddenly back-pedalled, even to the extent of withdrawing copies of the Report sent to the troops, though these were still freely available to civilians. This astonishing move was expressly commanded by the Prime Minister, who in a memorandum to the Cabinet stated that it was 'because I do not wish to deceive the people by false hopes and airy visions of Utopia and Eldorado'.[164] Churchill followed this up with a broadcast in which he belittled Beveridge's role in the origins of unemployment insurance, by attributing its formulation to Llewellyn Smith and himself.[165] When, on Churchill's instructions, a Labour Party amendment calling for the immediate implementation of the Beveridge scheme was firmly voted down by the Government,[166] one Labour M.P. prophetically informed Beveridge that 'this makes the return of the Labour Party to power at the next election an absolute certainty'.[167] Despite the enthusiastic interest displayed for the Beveridge scheme, the Government repeatedly stonewalled any attempt at putting any part of the scheme into effect in the immediate future, showing towards it, according to Beveridge, 'an attitude of marked reserve and to its author an attitude which developed from ignoring him into boycott'.[168] Following the example of the Webbs three decades earlier, and in an attempt to mobilize public support, Beveridge became President of the Social Security League, an organization formed in October 1943 to campaign for the Plan, lecturing extensively on the proposals.[169]

Although some of the difficulties may have been due to Beveridge's personality traits and the hostility these sometimes aroused,[170] it is clear that 'the handling of the whole affair was incredibly inept'.[171] The expectations of the country had been aroused and yet little seemed to be happening to follow up the Beveridge proposals, except for endless assurances that they were being 'considered'. However, the collective war effort had shown the effectiveness of mutual security and the pooling of national resources,[172] so that in time, Professor Marshall believed, 'the idea of the Welfare State came to be identified with the war aims of a nation fighting for its life'.[173] The Beveridge Plan, although placed on cold storage by the Government, had aroused such strong interest that its eventual implementation could only be delayed and not stifled.

The Plan

Beveridge's scheme was based on an analysis of the existing welfare mechanisms. This system was, he believed, 'a complex of disconnected administrative organs, proceeding on different principles, doing invaluable service but at a cost in money and trouble and anomalous treatment of identical problems for which there is no justification'.[174] The remedy he proposed was one of unification, but also of extension and innovation. However, Professor Lafitte believes that 'Beveridge did little more than apply the principles of the Lloyd George system as thoroughly and widely as they could be stretched.[175] Although this is largely true, it must not be allowed to detract from the important introductions such as family allowances and industrial injuries insurance.[176] And in relation to the latter he had, from his early days as a law student, been aware of what Professor Robson described as 'the fantastic manner in which the legal decisions on Workmen's Compensation proliferated year by year'.[177]

However, the consolidation of the existing welfare system was no easy task. The confusions and uncertainties of the years since 1911 had left a 'tangled maze of legislation and administration'[178] in the insurance services, and there was also the older legacy of the Poor Law rules. Beveridge felt that a complete overhaul had to be made in that 'a revolutionary moment in the world's history is a time for revolutions, not for patching'.[179] His subsequent proposals centred on six fundamental principles: 'flat-rate of subsistence benefit; flat-rate of contribution; unification of administrative responsibility; adequacy of benefit; comprehensiveness; and classification'.[180] Beveridge believed that, with the application of these principles to the existing mechanisms, it would be possible to achieve his central aim for reconstruction after the war, which he defined as 'the abolition of want after this war'.[181]

In formulating his views, Beveridge had made an extensive analysis of the pre-war literature on poverty. His conclusion was that the effects of unemployment were crucial in that

> Of all the want shown by the surveys, from three-quarters to five-sixths, according to the precise standards chosen for want, was due to interruption or loss of earning power. Practically the whole of the remaining one-quarter to one-sixth was due to failure to relate income during earning to the size of the family.[182]

The case for family allowances in the light of this was, he believed, irrefutable. In her thirty years' campaign for family allowances in Britain, Eleanor Rathbone had repeatedly stated that 'by far the greatest cause of primary poverty is the failure of the wage system to adapt itself to the needs of the variously sized households actually dependent on the wage-earner'.[183] It therefore followed in her argument that, in relation to social security, benefits should be adjusted 'to the real needs of real human beings instead of being, like wages, based on a fiction'.[184] The introduction of dependants' allowances with the out-of-donation schemes and subsequently to the unemployment insurance scheme went some way towards meeting this argument, although the allowances were low. In effect, the Beveridge proposals meant the extension of this system to the entire working population and not just to those who were unemployed, with the addition that benefits should be adequate and not based on 'fiction'.

But perhaps the most important conclusions Beveridge drew from the existing literature concerned the 'scientific' assessment of a notional 'poverty line'. His own calculations as to the level of subsistence need were drawn up with the help of a small sub-committee of experts, which included Seebohm Rowntree. Rowntree had pioneered the concept of 'primary poverty' caused by the utter insufficiency of family income,[185] and his second survey of York, made in 1936, was carefully studied by Beveridge along with the earlier work, *The Human Need of Labour*.[186] Another of the sub-committee members, the statistician A. L. Bowley, had also made an attempt to fix a 'poverty line', although he admitted it to be 'arbitrary'. However, Professor Bowley thought it was at least 'intelligible' and believed that 'the actual standard of living obtained at its level can be judged by anyone who has personal knowledge of how the poorer working-class live'.[187] Such optimism, that a static inflexible line could be calculated, has come under increasing criticism,[188] but it played an important part in Beveridge's thinking and in the subsequent fixing of benefit rates.

In the light of Beveridge's career it was not surprising that he showed such faith in the 'insurance principle' with regard to unemployment insurance, and it must be noted in assessing the Report that it was, as Professor Bruce points out, 'almost a private, and certainly a very personal document'.[189] Beveridge remained convinced that welfare benefits should be raised by the contribution method rather than by general taxation,[190] although he frequently acknowledged in his writings that this was a highly regressive form of personal taxation. But despite his advocacy of insurance, it was clearly impossible 'to preserve the contributory principle without also preserving a dual system'.[191] For despite the universality of the new insurance scheme, there would be necessarily a limitation on unemployment benefits in relation to contributions, and a secondary mechanism of social assistance would be needed. Beveridge could see that 'Assistance is an indispensable supplement to social insurance, however the scope of the latter may be widened'.[192] Nevertheless, although he was forced to retain an Assistance scheme below unemployment insurance for those who, for one reason or another, did not have a sufficient contribution record, he believed this would be a 'residual' service. For the Beveridge structure was 'first and foremost a plan of how social insurance should be organised, with National Assistance and voluntary insurance as subsidiary methods, for maintenance of income'.[193]

Beveridge proposed that Assistance should be given on the basis of proved need in the light of individual circumstances, but he had clearly learned, in Professor Marshall's words, that 'nothing in the history of social policy, except perhaps the old mixed workhouse, [had] inspired such hatred and detestation as [the] household means test'.[194] The humiliating inquisition of the U.A.B., and its insistence on the pooling of household finances, was not to be revived. Indeed Beveridge himself went so far as to state that to reduce the income of an unemployed person, 'either directly or by application of a means test, because the unemployment . . . has lasted for a certain period, is wrong in principle'.[195] But he tempered this view with the belief that there was a danger in providing adequate benefits which were completely indefinite in length, in that 'men, as creatures who adapt themselves to circumstances, may settle down to them'.[196] The answer to this problem, Beveridge thought, was outside the scope of social security and could only be solved by the maintenance of full employment, to which issue he devoted his later private study.[197] But, in narrowing the size of the mesh and widening the scope of insurance, Beveridge believed that large numbers of beneficiaries would be prevented from falling through on to what has repeatedly been described as 'the safety net of assistance'.[198]

Implementation

Despite Beveridge's campaign, the putting into effect of the Report awaited the end of the war and the advent of a Labour Government.[199] In many respects the legislation modelled on Beveridge's proposals was in the nature of an administrative reorganization, reshaping 'the incoherence of the administrative structure' which existed at the time.[200] The 1946 National Insurance Act, dealing with unemployment benefit, merged the existing insurance scheme into a general system covering sickness, old age and widowhood; a separate Act dealt with industrial injuries insurance which replaced the system of Workmen's

Compensation. Out of the total of 32 millions who were insured, 19¼ million were covered for unemployment insurance benefits. However, little change was made to the structure of the existing unemployment insurance scheme,[201] and indeed it has been said of the post-war 'setting up' of the Welfare State that, 'if each of the measures which brought about these developments is examined it is not always easy to see precisely where the changes lay or what is new in them'.[202] This is certainly true of unemployment insurance, where the process was largely one of 'tidying up' and merging with the new general structure. One important change, however, was the abolition of the Unemployment Insurance Statutory Committee. In its place was put a National Insurance Advisory Committee of nine members, but the role of the new committee was entirely different in that direct policy and financial control of the Insurance Fund passed to the new Ministry of National Insurance. Although possessing none of the powers of its predecessor, which were formidable by virtue of the circumstances, the Advisory Committee has nonetheless performed a useful if peripheral function: 'when regulations are needed . . . the Committee . . . is consulted while the proposals are still in draft and many changes have been made as the result of their advice'.[203] The administrative consolidation of insurance took place in July 1948,[204] although little change, except in nomenclature, took place in the unemployment benefit section. 'Courts of Referees' became 'National Insurance Local Appeal Tribunals', and the 'Umpires' became the 'Commissioners', but otherwise the system went on much as before.[205]

In contrast, the change from the remnants of the Poor Law to the new system of National Assistance in 1948 was hailed as a major breakthrough. In the Parliamentary debates, Aneurin Bevan called National Assistance 'the coping-stone to the structure of social services in Great Britain', and stated that the occasion 'marked the end of a whole period of social history'.[206] In paying a tribute to the work of the Webbs in this eventual break-up of the Poor Law, Bevan quoted a passage of theirs on the operation of the Workhouse system and followed with the comment: 'these are not things we are immediately leaving behind . . . but this is the sort of thing on which we are finally turning our backs'.[207] The euphoria of the moment was perhaps summed up for many of her colleagues by Bessie Braddock, who, in saying that she was 'glad [to] have lived to see this day',[208] made the revealing statement that 'I think of what we are repealing more than of what we are proposing'.[209]

However, despite the ambitious statement at the commencement of the 1948 Act that 'the existing Poor Law shall cease to have effect',[210] one member in a maiden speech made the sceptical observation that,

> If this Bill is successful in removing that stigma [of the Poor Law] from the minds of the poor, then it will indeed go down in History as a great measure. But if the stigma is to go . . . it will need a different attitude of mind on the part of the administrators.[211]

And perhaps it could also have been added, it would need a different *kind* of administration. For despite the trumpetings, the Act is, on examination, a consolidation of the regulations of the Assistance Board as grafted on to the 1934 U.A.B. system, and not the setting up of a new and wholly different service.[212] Many of the underlying principles could be clearly seen as derivative from the Poor Law, and this was hardly surprising since the new system was, like its predecessors, providing cash benefits to people satisfying a means test. Perhaps the single significant statutory change was that this means test was henceforth to be mainly a 'personal' and not a 'household' test, although this change had been largely accomplished in practice by regulations in 1941.[213] It is interesting to note, for example, that the six members of the old Assistance Board were, without change, set up as the National Assistance Board when the Act came into force on 3 July 1948.[214]

The setting up of the post-war Welfare State was, as the Prime Minister remarked in the debate on the National Insurance Bill, 'founded on the Beveridge Report'.[215] But it is important to realize that, apart from the 1945 Family Allowances Act, the other Acts were in large measure not original, but simply extensions of an accumulated collection of administrative remedies for various types of social problems. The fact that the unemployment insurance and assistance systems went on much as before is a critical factor in an assessment of their present-day administration. However, in a number of important respects, the post-war legislation differed from the Beveridge Plan; particularly with regard to benefit rates, much of the subsequent criticism of social security must be levelled not at Beveridge but at succeeding Governments for not adhering to his guidelines. For example, flat-rate unemployment insurance rates have been consistently below National Assistance/Supplementary Benefit levels when the rent addition is taken into account, and perhaps most importantly for the unemployed, Beveridge's proposal that insurance benefits should continue as long as need lasted, subject only to attendance at a training centre and the usual statutory controls, has never been implemented.[216]

Subsequent Developments

The Beveridge watershed was by no means an uncontroversial change,[217] and, although it established in large part the existing British system of social security, there have been many subsequent criticisms of its principles, yet relatively few legislative changes of its structure. Some commentators have gone as far as to say that the Beveridge system was 'obsolescent from the day it was established',[218] in that the social conditions it set out to guard against were those of the inter-war period and not those of the present day. The circumstances of the 1920s and 1930s had created a general belief in the adequate maintenance of the unemployed and had partially destroyed the Victorian dogma of the moral culpability of the unemployed.[219] It had also taught the futility of meeting mass unemployment with threadbare insurance schemes. But, in looking back on this experience, it is clear that Beveridge felt impelled to formulate a new scheme of income maintenance which would guarantee 'bread for everyone before cake for anybody'.[220] This concept of a minimum subsistence income for all beneficiaries was basic to the Beveridge scheme; but, as well as increasing doubt as to the 'scientific' value of the standard set, there has been growing criticism of the subsistence principle itself.

Unquestionably, the views held on this issue depend largely on the political orientation of the individual critic. Social security questions cannot be considered in a vacuum, and attitudes towards the reform or continuance of the present structure are formulated within the context of a whole perspective on the nature of poverty and society.[221] One Conservative politician, for example, wrote that to continue applying the Beveridge principles in modern circumstances would be 'to swallow the drug after the disease has gone. For primary poverty has now almost disappeared. Full employment has lifted the mass of our working population to a level of affluence unprecedented in our social history'.[222] Such assumptions of prosperity are perhaps questionable,[223] in concrete as well as in relative terms, but clearly those with similar views see the simple Beveridge system of universal and low benefits as inappropriate for the affluent society. On the other hand, the flat-rate contribution system which existed until 1975, had come under attack by the opposite political wing. One Marxist critic described its operation in the post-war period as 'a strait-jacket on the whole system'[224] in its discrimination against the low-paid worker paying for a standard rate of stamp.

Some of these criticisms have been partly assuaged by the one major change in the Beveridge formula. Following the introduction of graduated pensions in 1961, in an attempt to restore a deficit on the flat-rate insurance scheme,[225] earnings-related benefits were introduced in 1966 for the other insurance schemes.[226] However, one basic difference was that it was not possible to contract out of the 1966 scheme. In relation to unemployment, the earnings-related benefits are payable for spells of unemployment up to six months' duration, and commence from the thirteenth day of unemployment. Contributions are similarly related to earnings, although they are not on a scale which could seriously be regarded as redistributive of income. The justification for earnings-related benefits, it has been said, is that recognition is given to the fact that 'need' is 'in some degree geared to a person's salary and way of life, and that those with higher incomes can afford larger contributions, which may benefit not only themselves, but also lower-paid workers'.[227] Certainly higher-paid workers are less likely to draw benefits, although the drop in income for the long-term unemployed from earnings-related benefits down to drawing Supplementary Benefits alone has considerable social effects.[228]

Part of the reluctance concerning the introduction of earnings-related insurance schemes may have been caused by the administrative complexity which was thought to be involved, although this has not proved an insuperable task in practice. There had been few advocates for earnings-related benefits at the time of the setting up of the 1946 scheme,[229] and indeed the prevailing opinion seemed to be expressed by Professor Robson, when he stated that 'such systems are out of place in a scheme designed to establish a national minimum standard of living below which no one should fall . . . It is soundly democratic to have flat rates paid by everybody and payable to everybody on an equal footing'.[230] However, such a view does not take account of existing inequalities in society, which a flat-rate scheme can do nothing to change. In a much-quoted statement, Professor Tirmuss summed up the difficulties entailed in a simplistic view of 'flat-rate democracy':

> Many of us must also now admit that we put too much faith in the 1940s in the concept of universality as applied to social security. Mistakenly, it was linked with economic egalitarianism. Those who have benefited most are those who have needed it least.[231]

Unfortunately, this statement has been taken, in some circles, to mean that selectivity in the form of private enterprise welfare is therefore the solution, and that the existing Welfare State should be gradually dismantled. The view is taken from a belief that, to quote a Conservative M.P. and former Poor Law historian, through the operation of the Welfare State,

> the moral fibre of our people has been weakened. A state which does for its citizens what they can do for themselves is an evil state; and a state which removes all choice and responsibility for its people and makes them like broiler hens will create the irresponsible society. In such an irresponsible society no one cares, no one saves, no one bothers—why should they when the state spends its energies taking money from the energetic, successful and thrifty to give to the idle, the failures and the feckless?[232]

However, as has been pointed out by Professor Abel-Smith, a demand for more 'choice' can be met by extensions within the existing welfare structure and not just by a return 'to the market and the means test'.[233] In fact it is not true to say that Beveridge rigidly believed in the flat-rate schemes, as he felt that private voluntary insurance could be utilized by higher-paid workers and those in the professions to gain higher benefits for themselves above the minimum.[234] But although there has been a tremendous post-war development in private and occupational welfare schemes—notably in pensions, superannuation and sickness benefits[235]—voluntary insurance has not been utilized in relation to unemployment on any scale in Britain, and certainly not on the scale of the Supplemental Unemployment Benefits schemes in the United States.[236]

Wider criticisms, however, have been made of the whole 'insurance' principle in relation to social security. This debate is partly clouded by the tendency of a number of critics to equate social insurance with the terms of commercial insurance,[237] which often leads to the encouragement of what has been called the 'public burden' view of the social services. It is clear that solvency or insolvency are difficult terms to use in connection with a public welfare system, which, even if notionally based on a direct relationship between contributions and benefits, is nonetheless dependent in some degree on general taxation levy. The use of an 'insurance' technique can, according to Professor George, 'be explained on historical and social psychological reasons, but it has no actuarial foundation'.[238] In the wider context, social security is clearly a transfer payment in terms of economic analysis, but it is interesting that, highly regressive though they have been, the cost of insurance contributions are rarely complained of by workers. However, the myth of a contributory insurance system entirely divorced from the tax system clearly has its political usefulness, and the reluctance to abandon insurance analogies is understandable. It would mean 'giving up a nice, simple automatic test, and facing the central and perplexing issue of social policy'.[239] For it is arguable that the acceptance of an 'insurance principle' in relation to unemployment insurance in 1911 made the new social policy respectable, and perhaps continues in part to make it so. By its operation, the principle had 'removed, or at least mitigated, the notion that the "left-out millions" were actually getting something for nothing'.[240] However, in the sense that the retention of the insurance principle can no longer be linked with the financial stability of the scheme, a number of writers have urged that it is positively misleading 'to create the illusion that in some sense insurance benefits have to be paid for while other types of benefits do not'.[241]

Moreover, the concentration on this insurance myth has led to an artificial distinction between types of benefits, which is in some respects harmful to the administrative functioning of the system, and possibly harmful to public attitudes towards the recipients of certain kinds of relief. In this it has 'helped to maintain the flavour of inferiority and shame'[242] which still clings to 'assistance' forms of benefit paid out of general taxation. The attempt to rid the system of this tendency was the clear intention behind the 1966 change from National Assistance to Supplementary Benefits, and the carrying out of Beveridge's proposal that there should be a Ministry of Social Security administering all cash-benefits given by the State.[243] It was an endeavour, in the words of the Government's Explanatory Memorandum, 'to eliminate those features of the existing scheme which are misunderstood or disliked, while preserving the humanity and efficiency of its administration'.[244]

However, despite these aims, it must be noted that in legal and administrative terms the 1966 Act was a mild measure introducing some procedural reforms and structural consolidation, but doing little to reform the existing system beyond changing the name of the 'assistance' service. The innovations were in the express provision of a specific *entitlement* to supplementary benefits; the introduction of a long-term addition for certain groups which has since 1973 been included in the basic scale rate for all but the unemployed, and the simplification of procedures for claiming benefits. In fact, the title 'Supplementary' was somewhat misleading in that it could only be properly applied to the secondary 'topping up' function of the assistance scheme, which, however, has played an increasing role in the overall welfare system because of the erosion of flat-rate insurance benefits through inflation and the failure of successive Governments to raise them to Beveridge standards. This was coupled with a substantial increase in the scale-rates of Supplementary Benefits, and a campaign to improve the take-up of benefits. The Labour Government believed that these changes of 'the National Assistance Board, and the deletion of the word "assistance" from the dictionary of social security . . . had remarkable success'.[245] But if this could be described as a success, it was one of remarkably short duration and, in the total context of welfare, Professor Atkinson thinks that, if because of the changes 'people are better informed about their entitlement to assistance, then there are still a good many who are reluctant to apply'.[246]

The Beveridge reforms were clearly formulated in the light of the overwhelming social and economic problems of the inter-war period. But in many respects they represented a modified continuance of the pre-war system, which had grown up without coherent overall structure. Although the post-war legislation centralized the administration of social security, a policy which was furthered with the setting up of the

Ministry of Social Security, nevertheless the legacy of old structures remains. Certain crucial questions have been left unanswered, although it is now being recognized that a number of basic divisions in the present system, such as that between 'insurance' and 'assistance', are devoid of real meaning, and that 'many of the old antitheses are largely imaginary'.[247] And although no one could have forecast the pattern of post-war society, it is apparent that new problems and complexities have arisen which require a different approach in social security. In many respects, as Professor George points out, 'the Beveridge revolution spent itself with the rise in national prosperity. Social insurance benefits must [now] not only guarantee a minimum subsistence living but a decent standard of living above the minimum'.[248]

Certainly the hope that National Assistance would be a residual service without 'an active future'[249] has not been realized. And although 'poverty' is clearly a relative term, its discovery as a widespread phenomenon, in a number of surveys which have demonstrated the non-take-up of existing benefits or certain 'gaps' in the insurance system, is disturbing in the context of a society with a great deal of overall prosperity.[250] But there are those who believe that talk of 'gaps' 'sounds like an unfortunate throwback to Beveridge's now discarded principle of the national minimum at subsistence level' and that we have moved beyond such a simple system into an era where both insurance and Supplementary Benefits are 'integral parts of a single system of social security'.[251] However, it is clear that this theoretical unity of the two streams of income maintenance has not been achieved either in the administrative system or in its adjudicatory practice, and certainly not in the minds of welfare beneficiaries. However, although the 'insurance principle' may be an actuarial myth and theoretically illogical, there is little doubt that in practical terms, both in 1948 and at present, it 'has come to stay . . . and logic was never a characteristic of the British social services'.[252]

NOTES

1. R. M. Titmuss in his *Commentary* to William J. Braithwaite, *Lloyd George's Ambulance Wagon* (1957), p. 43.

2. For the impact of the ideas of the 1911 programme on some other social security systems, see Domenico Gagliardo, *American Social Insurance* (1949) p. 234 *et seq.*; 'Enquête par l'Institut scientifique de recherches économiques et sociales', *Le Chômage en France* (1938), p. 202 *et seq.*

3. T. H. Marshall, *Social Policy* (1970), p. 48.

4. Sidney and Beatrice Webb, *The Prevention of Destitution* (1911), p. 160.

5. As to how much the economic crisis of 1931 was partially caused by the over. loading of the unemployment insurance scheme, see Robert Skidelsky, *Politicians and the Slump* (1967), p. 365.

6. Joseph L. Cohen, *Insurance against Unemployment* (1921), p. 75.

7. T. H. Marshall, *op. cit.*, p. 50.

8. Bentley B. Gilbert, *Britain Since 1918* (1967), p. 29.

9. Sir William Beveridge, *Unemployment, A Problem of Industry* (1930 ed.), pp. 288–9.

10. Bentley B. Gilbert, *op. cit.*, p. 30.

11. Moved by James O'Grady, the M.P. for Leeds; *Hansard*, **21**, H. C. Deb. (10 February 1911), col. 586. See generally on the Right to Work Bill, Kenneth D. Brown, *Labour and Unemployment 1900–1914* (1971), pp. 68–130.

12. Report in July 1913 by the Director of Labour Exchanges, *Report on Labour Exchanges and Unemployment Insurance* (1913), H.M.S.O. Cd–6965, p. 46. Part of the reason for this success was due to a concentrated follow-up programme of educating the country after the Act became law. For example, a team of lecturers toured the country explaining the provisions of the Act. Clement Attlee was one of them; Roy Jenkins, *Mr Attlee* (1948), pp. 61–2.

13. s. 2(1) National Insurance (Part II) (Munitions Workers) Act 1916.

14. Sir Thomas Chegwidden and G. Myrddin Evans, *The Employment Exchange Service of Great Britain* (1934), p. 71.

15. ss. 1 and 2, New Ministers and Secretaries Act 1916.

16. See for a discussion, W. H. Beveridge, 'The Question of Disenfranchisement', *Toynbee Record*, **XVII,** No. 6 (March 1905), p. 100.

17. s. 9(1) Representation of the People Act 1918. Perhaps nearly as significant was the change in s.4 which allowed the wives of the unemployed to vote, if they were women over the age of 30.

18. Bentley B. Gilbert, *British Social Policy 1914–1939* (1970), p. 51.

19. David Lloyd George, speaking at Wolverhampton on 23 November 1918, reported in *The Times*, (25 November 1918).

20. Sir William Beveridge, *The Past and Present of Unemployment Insurance* (1930), p. 16.

21. *Committee of Inquiry* under Lord Aberconway, *Final Report* (1919), H.M.S.O. Cmd. 305, plus Appendices.

22. Sir William Beveridge, *Unemployment. A Problem of Induslry* (1909), p. 274,

23. G. D. H. and M. I. Cole, *The Condition of Britain* (1937), p. 193.

24. Bentley B. Gilbert, *op, cit.*, p. 56.

25. *Civil War Workers Committee*, Sub-committee Second Interim Report (1918), H.M.S.O. Cd–9192, p. 659.

26. Coupled with the announcement of a civilian out-of-work donation scheme, *The Times*, (13 November 1918). See generally, C. L. Mowat, *Britain between the Wars* (1955).

27. The maximum estimate was that unemployment could never go above 5.2 per cent; Sir Alfred Watson 'Report by the Government Actuary on the Financial Provisions of the Bill', *Journal of the Institute of Actuaries* (April 1920) p. 72.

28. *Report on Labour Exchanges and Unemployment Insurance* (1913), p. 41.

29. *Report of the Ministry of Labour on National Unemployment Insurance* (1923), H.M. S.O. Cmd. 2481, p. 5.

30. The Act became law on 9 August 1920 and its main provisions went into effect on 8 November 1920.

31. Sir Thomas Chegwidden and G. Myrddin-Evans, *op. cit.*, p. 92.

32. See generally, Eveline M. Burns, *British Unemployment Programs 1920–1938* (1941) and B. R. Mitchell and Phyllis Deane, *Abstract of British Historical Statistics* (1962), p. 400.

33. Bentley B. Gilbert, *op. cit.*, p. 66.

34. Cabinet Minute, 27 January 1921, quoted in Bentley B. Gilbert, *ibid.*

35. Basil Thomson was Director of Intelligence at the Home Office from 1919 to 1921. A son of the Archbishop of York he eventually retired from the public scene as a result of his arrest in Hyde Park in 1925 for consorting with a prostitute and was later convicted for violation of public decency.

36. Raymond Postgate, *The Life of George Lansbury* (1951),, p. 154. See also for another illustration of revolutionary zeal, the storming by a mob of a Board of Guardians office, where the police were pelted with stones and 'struck with banner poles of the demonstrators, who carried red flags'; quoted from Cabinet papers by Eric Briggs and Alan Deacon, 'The Creation of the Unemployment Assistance Board', *Policy and Politics* **2** (1973), p. 46.

37. Alban Gordon, *Social Insurance* (1924), pp. 30–1.

38. John Clarke, *Social Administration* (1935), p. 754.

39. Sidney and Beatrice Webb, *English Poor Law History* (1929), vol. III, pp. 910, 912.

40. First published 1909, a compilation of Beveridge's research at Toynbee Hall, his freelance work for the Board of Trade and his evidence to the Royal Commision on the Poor Laws.

41. The Unemployment Insurance (Temporary Provisions Amendment) Act 1920.

42. The cost between November 1918 and November 1919 was £39 millions for ex-service donations and £21 millions for civilian donations; John Clarke, *op. cit.*, p. 631.

43. s. 3(3)(b) Unemployment Insurance Act 1921. This was changed significantly in s. 3(1)(iv) of the 1924 Act in that the unemployed worker had to show that he was 'genuinely seeking work but was unable to obtain *suitable* employment' (my italics). Cf. the present s. 20(1)(c) Social Security Act 1975 — a six weeks disqualification if 'he has neglected to avail himself of a *reasonable* opportunity of *suitable* employment' (my italics).

44. Bentley B. Gilbert, *op. cit.*, p. 86.

45. Ronald C. Davison, *What's Wrong with Unemployment Insurance* (1930), p. 5.

46. Sir William Beveridge, *The Past and Present of Unemployment Insurance* (1930), p. 18.

47. There were fifteen Acts of Parliament alone from 1920–6. See for a thorough survey of the piecemeal changes, John Clarke, *op. cit.* (1935 ed.), pp. 630–714.

48. Ronald C. Davison, *British Unemployment Policy* (1938), p. 9.

49. E. Wight Bakke, *Insurance or Dole?* (1935), p. 106.

50. *The Third Winter of Unemployment* (1923), a report by J. J. Astor, A. L. Bowley, Henry Clay, Robert Grant, W. T. Layton, P. J. Pybus, B. Seebohm Rowntree, George Schuster and F. D. Stuart, p. 69.

51. William Robson (ed.), *Social Security* (1943), p. 26.

52. *Hansard*, **175**, H.C. Deb. (8 June 1924), cols. 2296–2320.

53. *Report of the Unemployment Insurance Committee* (1927), (Non-parliamentary papers).

54. Bentley B. Gilbert, *op. cit.*, p. 91.

55. s. 5(1)(b) Unemployment Insurance Act 1927. This was the considerable modification of the 1921 clause; see earlier at p. 155.

56. Sir William Beveridge, *The Past and Present of Unemployment Insurance* (1930), p. 20. Repeated in the 1930 edition of *Unemployment, A Problem of Industry*, p. 276.

57. *Report of the Unemployment Insurance Committee* (1927), p. 49.

58. Ronald C. Davison, *op. cit.*, p. 114.

59. Alban Gordon, *op. cit.*, p. 80.

60. s. 4, Unemployment Insurance Act 1930. See also Sir Frank Tillyard, *Unemployment Insurance in Great Britain* (1949), pp. 92–8, and 'Unemployment Insurance Bill', *Explanatory Memorandum*, (1929), H.M. S.O. Cmd. 3430.

61. Between March and June 1930, the number of heads of families receiving poor relief dropped from 92,000 to 43,000; Eveline M. Burns, *op. cit.*, p. 53.

62. B. R. Mitchell and Phyllis Deane *op. cit.*, p. 400.

63. See generally, Guy Routh, *Occupation and Pay in Great Britain 1906–1960* (1965), p. 109 *et seq.*, and Eveline M. Burns, *loc. cit.*

64. See Robert Skidelsky, *Politicians and the Slump* (1967), pp. 233, 263.

65. *First Report of the Royal Commission on Unemployment Insurance* (1931), H.M.S.O. Cmd. 3872.

66. *ibid.*, para. 99.

67. It reported in August 1931; *Committee on National Expenditure* (1931), H.M.S.O. Cmd. 3920, para. 380.

68. G. D. H. Cole, *The Intelligent Man's Guide through World Chaos* (1932), p. 98.

69. Bentley B. Gilbert, *op. cit.*, p. 168.

70. Though they were quite willing to make cuts in other areas.

71. See generally, Robert Skidelsky *op. cit.*

72. Ronald C. Davison, *What's Wrong with Unemployment Insurance* (1930), p. 60.

73. See for the comparative situation in the United States, the analysis by Irving Bernstein, *The Lean Years 1920–33* (1960), and for a novelist's impression, John Steinbeck, *The Grapes of Wrath* (1939).

74. A. C. Pigou, *The Economics of Welfare* (1932), p. 524.

75. François Lafitte, *Britain's Way to Social Security* (1945), p. 15.

76. Isabel Grubb, *Quakerism and Industry before 1800* (1929), p. 133.

77. Grace Abbott, *From Relief to Social Security* (1941), p. 258.

78. See generally, C. H. Exley, *The Guide to Poor Relief* (1932).

79. Alban Gordon *op. cit.*, p. 66.

80. Aneurin Bevan, *In Place of Fear* (1952), p. 5.

81. Sir Ivor Jennings, *The Poor Law Code* (1936), p. 7 — 'Their language varied from the Elizabethan to the Johnsonian, and from the sonority of the eighteenth century to the terseness of the twentieth'; *ibid.*

82. Brian Rodgers, *The Battle Against Poverty* (1969),vol. II, p. 13.

83. Maurice Bruce, *The Rise of the Welfare State* (1973), p. 26.

84. *Final Report of the Royal Commission on Unemployment Insurance* (1932), H.M.S.O. Cmd. 4185.

85. *Minority Report of the Royal Commission on Unemployment Insurance* (1932), p. 375.

86. Ronald C. Davison, *British Unemployment Policy* (1938), pp. 22–5.

87. Keith Feiling, *The Life of Neville Chamberlain* (1946), p. 230.

88. Appendices to Minutes of Evidence, *Royal Commission on Unemployment Insurance* (1931), Part V, H.M.S.O. Cmd. 4185, p. 283. The number who 'needed' the relief, but who did not apply for it, was presumably much higher; see the 'remarkable discovery of secret need' when pensioners were granted their supplementary allowances through the Assistance Board in 1940 rather than through the Poor Law; R. M. Titmuss, *Problem of Social Policy* (1950), p. 516.

89. Sir William Beveridge, *The Unemployment Insurance Statutory Committee* (1937), p. 5.

90. Lord Beveridge, *Power and Influence* (1953), p. 225.

91. *loc. cit*,

92. Beveridge retired from the chairmanship of the committee when he stood as a Liberal at the Berwick-upon-Tweed by-election and was elected to the House of Commons.

93. Political and Economic Planning Report, *The British Social Services* (1937), p. 115.

94. *ibid.*, p. 117.

95. Bentley B. Gilbert, *op. cit.*, p. 179.

96. Unemployment Insurance (Agriculture) Act 1936.

97. Unemployment Insurance (Insurable Employments) Regs. (1937) S.R.&O. 1937 No. 1207.

98. David C. Marsh, *National Insurance and Assistance in Great Britain* (1950), p. 46.

99. Guy Routh, *op. cit.*, p. 127.

100. Harold E. Raynes, *Social Security in Britain* (1957), p. 200.

101. Ronald C. Davison, *op. cit.*, p. 45.

102. *First Annual Report of the Unemployment Assistance Board* (1936), H.M.S.O. Cmd. 5177, p. 7.

103. Polly Hill, *The Unemployment Services* (1940), pp. 72–7.

104. See in particular, *Hansard*, **296**, H.C. Deb. (17–19 December 1934), cols. 829–927, 967–1088 and 1163–1284.

105. Brian Rodgers, *op. cit.*, vol. II, p. 22.

106. Harold Laski, *Parliamentary Government in England* (1938), p. 147.

107. David Roberts, *Victorian Origins of the Welfare State* (1960), p. 109.

108. Quoted in Michael Foot, *Aneurin Bevan* (1963), vol. I, p. 161.

109. The 1936 amending Act extended coverage down to 14 years, the then school-leaving age.

110. See generally, John D. Millett, *The Unemployment Assistance Board* (1940), a brilliant survey which Professor Millett entitled 'A case study in Administrative Autonomy

111. Bentley B. Gilbert, *op. cit.*, p. 181.

112. Political and Economic Planning *Broadsheet No. 47*, 'Inquest on the Unemployment Act', (26 March 1935), p. 4.

113. *First Annual Report of the Unemployment Assistance Board* (1936), p. 8.

114. R. V. Vernon and N. Mansergh, *Advisory Bodies* (1940), p. 315.

115. s. 39 and the 7th Schedule, 1934 Unemployment Act.

116. George Lach, 'Assistance Board Appeal Tribunals' in R. S. W. Pollard, *Administrative Tribunals at Work* (1950), p. 55.

117. s. 9(4) Unemployment Act 1934.

118. *First Annual Report of the Unemployment Assistance Board* (1936), p. 50.

119. See generally for a definition, H. R. G. Greaves, *The British Constitution* (1955), p. 176.

120. John D. Millett, *op. cit.*, p. 296.

121. Sir Ivor Jennings, *Cabinet Government* (1969), pp. 82, 374.

122. Michael Foot, *op. cit.*, p. 167.

123. Bentley B. Gilbert, *op. cit.*, p. 184.

124. Ronald C. Davison, *op. cit.*, p. 75.

125. For example, unemployment in Ebbw Vale was still over 50 per cent Michael Foot, *loc. cit.*; see also Hilda Jennings, *Brynmawr, A study of a distressed area* (1934); and G. D. H. Cole and Raymond Postgate, *The Common People* (1938) pp. 596–600.

126. George Orwell, *The Road to Wigan Pier* (1937), p. 67n.

127. Political and Economic Planning *Broadsheet No. 47* (1935), p. 8.

128. Eveline M. Burns, *Towards Social Security* (1936), p. 139.

129. See for a classic American legal analysis of the means test, Jacobus ten Broek and R. B. Wilson, 'Public Assistance and Social Insurance — A Normative Evaluation', *U.C.L.A. Law Review* **1** (1954), p. 237, pp. 264–7. See for a general British survey, P. Ford, *Incomes, Means Test and Personal Responsibility* (1939).

130. See for the Poor Law practice, C. H. Exley, *The Guide to the Law and Administration of the Needs Test* (1933). The relevant section in the 1934 Unemployment Act is s. 52.

131. Pilgrim Trust Report, *Men Without Work* (1938), p. 144. See also H. W. Singer, *Unemployment and the Unemployed* (1940) based on his experience as a researcher for the Pilgrim Trust survey.

132. Michael Foot, *op. cit.*, p. 161. Bevan himself had had the experience of seeing his 'dole' cut off because of his younger sister Arianwen's earnings as a stenographer when she returned from College; *ibid.*, p. 45.

133. Eleanor Rathbone, *Family Allowances* (1949), p. 230.

134. Alan Bullock, *The Life and Times of Ernest Bevin* (1960), vol. II, p. 241.

135. See for the constant battle of wits as seen by two disillusioned U.A.B. investigators, Edward Warburton and Carl Butler, *Disallowed: The Tragedy of the Means Test* (1935).

136. Tony Gould and Joe Kenyon, *Stories from the Dole Queue* (1972), p. 173.

137. George Orwell, *op. cit.*, p. 84. See generally, the chapter on 'Unemployment', pp. 76–91.

138. W. A. Robson (ed.), *Social Security* (1943), p. 14.

139. H. L. Beales and R. S. Lambert, *Memoirs of the Unemployed* (1934), p. 48. A collection of essays collected by the B.B.C.

140. Wal Hannington, *Ten Lean Years* (1940), p. 15. A chapter on 'Administrative Injustices' contains a very bitter account of suicides and wrecked families; *ibid.*, p. 245 *et seq.*

141. E. Wight Bakke, *Insurance or Dole?* (1935), p. 191. See generally, *ibid.*, pp. 188–96; *The Unemployed Man* (1933); and 'An American's views on English Unemployment', *The Listener*, **XII**, No. 296 (12 September 1934), p. 423.

142. See the portrait of Jarrow in Ellen Wilkinson, *The Town that was Murdered* (1939).

143. Quoted in Wal Hannington, *The Problem of the Distressed Areas* (1937), p. 48. A Marxist survey with poignant photographs of dole queues, and a chapter on unemployment 'creating a potential breeding-ground for Facism'; *ibid.*, p. 249 *et seq.*

144. Ronald C. Davison, *What's Wrong with Unemployment Insurance* (1930), p. 36.

145. T. H. Marshall, *Social Policy* (1970), p. 65.

146. s. 1, Unemployment Assistance (Emergency Powers) Act 1939.

147. Joan Simeon Clarke, 'The Assistance Board' in William Robson (ed.), *Social Security* (1943), p. 138.

148. The dependants of the supplementary pensioners were taken over by the Board in 1943.

149. David C. Marsh, *National Insurance and Assistance in Great Britain* (1950), p. 51.

150. Michael Rose, *The English Poor Law* (1971), p. 322.

151. 'The resources of members of the household, other than the applicant, the husband or wife of the applicant, and any member of the household dependent on the applicant, shall not be regarded as resources of the applicant'; para. 1, Schedule I, Determination of Needs Act 1941.

152. R. M. Titmuss, *Problems of Social Policy* (1950), p. 89.

153. Alan Bullock, *The Life and Times of Ernest Bevin* (1960), vol. II, p. 225. Bevin thought Beveridge 'a difficult colleague' and 'a prima donna'. For this side of Beveridge, in evidence when he was Director of the L.S.E., see C. H. Rolph, *Kingsley Martin* (1973), pp. 136–8.

154. Brian Rodgers, *The Battle Against Poverty* (1969), vol. II, p. 33.

155. Lord Beveridge, *Power and Influence* (1953), p. 300.

156. Maurice Bruce, *The Coming of the Welfare State* (1968), p. 305.

157. *Report of a Committee on Social Insurance and Allied Services* (1942) ('The Beveridge Report'), H. M. S. O. Cmd. 6404.

158. Pauline Gregg, *The Welfare State* (1967), p. 19.

159. Sir William Beveridge, *The Pillars of Security* (1943), p. 57.

160. Sir William Beveridge, *Insurance For All and Everything* (1924), *Daily News* pamphlet.

161. Sir William Beveridge in a speech at Caxton Hall, 3 March 1943; reprinted in *The Pillars of Security* (1943), p. 142.

162. The Beveridge Report, *op. cit.*, para. 7.

163. John Hilton, *Rich Man, Poor Man* (1944), p. 42.

164. Cabinet minute, quoted in Winston Churchill, *The Second World War* (1948–54), vol. IV, p. 861. Apart from this minute, Churchill seems to have omitted any direct mention of the Beveridge Report from his Memoirs. He was not alone in his antipathy to Beveridge and his scheme: Ernest Bevin (who voted against the implementation of Beveridge) is supposed to have growlingly remarked that 'man cannot live by Beveridge alone'.

165. In an election broadcast of 1945, Churchill even went so far as to state that Beveridge was returning in 1942 to a field from which he had long been absent. This grossly ill-informed comment also seemed to suggest that Churchill had spent the intervening years deeply involved in social reform; Janet Beveridge, *Beveridge and his Plan* (1954), p. 221.

166. By 336 votes to 119 votes, *Hansard*, **386**, H. C. Deb. (18 February 1943), col. 2054. The amendment was moved by James Griffiths, the M. P. for Llanelli and the first Minister of National Insurance following the war: 'Our people have memories of what happened at the end of last war, memories of the period of depression, memories of the unemployment, frustration, poverty and distress into which large masses of our people were thrown. In public, and much more in private, at the fireside, men and women are asking: "After this, what? After victory, what ? A return to the old days?"'; *ibid.*, col. 1965.

167. James Griffiths; quoted in Janet Beveridge, *op. cit.*, p. 146. See generally James Griffiths, *Pages from Memory* (1969) for an account of Griffiths' own experience of unemployment before entering the House of Commons.

168. Lord Beveridge, *Power and Influence* (1953) p. 323. Chapter XV of Beveridge's autobiography is entitled 'Beveridge Boom and Boycott'.

169. Ironically, when invited to lecture in the United States, Beveridge sailed on the Queen Mary in the company of the Prime Minister who was somewhat cool towards him, if not disparaging. Churchill's strange behaviour towards Beveridge is commented on by his personal doctor, Lord Moran, who was also aboard; Lord Moran, *Winston Churchill, The Struggle for Survival* (1966) p. 94. The atmosphere of the trip was not helped by the dangers of a war-time Atlantic crossing, nor by the bed-bugs in the Beveridges' cabin; Janet Beveridge, *op. cit.*, p. 215.

170. Clement Attlee formed the impression that Beveridge thought the war should stand still until his Plan was implemented; Francis Williams, *A Prime Minister Remembers*,(1961), p. 57.

171. Maurice Bruce, *op. cit.*, p. 310.

172. R. M. Titmuss, *Problems of Social Policy* (in the series *The History of the Second World War*) (1950), p. 507.

173. T. H. Marshall, *Social Policy* (1965), p. 75.

174. The Beveridge Report, *op. cit.*, para. 3.

175. François Lafitte, 'The Future of Social Security', *Social and Economic Administration* (1967), vol. I, p. 7.

176. Beveridge had been strongly influenced by Eleanor Rathbone's study of family allowances — he stated that his conversion had been 'immediate and total'. Sir William Beveridge in an Epilogue to Eleanor Rathbone, *Family Allowances* (1949), p. 270.

177. William Robson, *Social Security* (1943), p. 15; see also David G. Hanes, *The First British Workmen's Compensation Act* (1968); and see also the discussion on pp. 185–6.

178. David C. Marsh, *Social Administration* (1965), p. 56.

179. The Beveridge Report, *op. cit.*, para. 7.

180. *ibid.*, para. 17. By classification, Beveridge meant that social insurance must take account of the different ways of life of differing sections of the community — for example, 'those rendering vital unpaid service as housewives' had to be treated in different respects, Beveridge thought, to working women in industry; *ibid.*, para. 309. A census of 1931 quoted by Beveridge showed that seven out of eight housewives made marriage their sole occupation. Cf. the very different position outlined in Viola Klein, *Britain's Married Women Workers* (1965).

181. *ibid.*, para. 14.

182. *ibid.*, para. 11.

183. Eleanor Rathbone. *The Disinherited Family* (1924), p. 27. Her initial perspective on the subject had been formed while in

residence at the Manchester University Settlement; see M. D. Stocks, *Fifty Years in Every Street* (1945), p. 35.

184. Eleanor Rathbone, *Family Allowances* (1949), p. 50, a revision of *The Disinherited Family* (1924). See generally, Mary Stocks, *Eleanor Rathbone* (1949).

185. B. Seebohm Rowntree, *Poverty, A Study of Town Life* (1902) p. 86. 'Secondary poverty', in Rowntree's definition, was caused by the misuse of what could have been an adequate income for proper physical existence if spent in a disciplined manner. For an interesting survey of 'secondary poverty', sponsored by the Rowntree Trust, see F. Zweig, *Labour, Life and Poverty* (1948).

186. *Poverty and Progress* (1941); *The Human Need of Labour* (1918). The comparisons of the 1936 study with the earlier York survey of 1899 were in many respects striking. In 1899, one in six of the population had been adjudged to be in 'primary poverty'; in 1936, this was one in fifteen. But Rowntree also noted that ideas of what constituted poverty had changed profoundly — 'There is no doubt that in 1899 investigators would not have regarded as "obvious want and squalor" conditions which would have been so regarded in 1936, and on the other hand a large proportion of families living below the 1936 poverty line would not in 1899 have been regarded as "showing signs of poverty"'; *ibid.*, p. 461. *The Human Need of Labour* (1918) was also the source of Eleanor Rathbone's figures; *Family Allowances* (1949), p. 17.

187. A. L. Bowley and Margaret Hogg, *Has Poverty Diminished?* (1925), p. 14. See also the earlier study, A. L. Bowley and A. R. Burnett-Hurst, *Livelihood and Poverty* (1915).

188. See in particular, Brian Abel-Smith and Peter Townsend, *The Poor and the Poorest* (1965), p. 63; Tony Lynes, *National Assistance and National Prosperity* (1961), p. 9.

189. Maurice Bruce, *op. cit.*, pp. 16–17.

190. The Beveridge Report, *op. cit.*, paras. 272–6.

191. Polly Hill, *The Unemployment Services* (1940), p. 16. In fact the system up until 1948 was a 'triple' system: unemployment insurance, assistance board benefits and public assistance.

192. The Beveridge Report, *op. cit.*, para. 302.

193. *ibid.*, para. 265.

194. T. H. Marshall, *Social Policy* (1970), p. 65.

195. The Beveridge Report, *op. cit.*, para. 130.

196. *loc. cit.*

197. Sir William Beveridge, *Full Employment in a Free Society* (1944). The money was provided anonymously by three friends; although a private report it took the form of a Government sponsored Report.

198. See for example, Alan T. Peacock, *The Economics of National Insurance* (1952), p. 19 *et seq.*

199. The Family Allowances Act 1945 was, however, passed during the final stages of the Coalition/Conservative administration of that year. Allowances were payable for each child in a family except for the first, although at a considerably lower rate than that recommended by Beveridge.

200. E. N. Gladden, *British Public Service Administration* (1961), p. 134.

201. 'Waiting days' were held at three, with a refund after twelve days' unemployment. Maximum benefit was 180 days, but with the possiblity of an extra 130 'added days' at the discretion of the Employment Exchange, and even then the possibility of an appearance before the appeal tribunal and on their recommendation a further period of benefit. These extensions were little used; see generally, Clara D. Rackham, 'Unemployment Insurance' in William Robson (ed.), *Social Security* (1948).

202. Joan L. M. Eyden in David C Marsh, *Social Administration* (1965), p. 37.

203. Sir Geoffrey King, *The Ministry of Pensions and National Insurance* (1958), pp. 12–13.

204. See for a description by the first Director of Establishments and Organisation of this administrative 'miracle'; H. V. Rhodes, *Setting up a New Government Department* (1949).

205. For the vigorous debate on whether it should be social insurance or national insurance, see *The Economist*, (18 January 1944). The relationship of 'social' to 'socialist' was thought too close.

206. *Hansard*, **444**, H. C. Deb. (24 November 1947), col. 1603 *et seq.*

207. *ibid.*, col. 1614.

208. *ibid.*, col. 1636.

209. *ibid.*, col. 1631.

210. s. 1, National Assistance Act 1948.

211. Albert Evans, M.P., *Hansard, op. cit.*, col. 1675.

212. See generally, R. D. Steele, *The National Assistance Act 1948* (1949).

213. A number of commentators state that this 'household' aspect has been entirely abolished, e. g. A. B. Atkinson, *Poverty in Britain and the Reform of Social Security* (1969), p. 23. But this is not so in relation to rent assessments of 'non-dependent relatives'; see *Supplementary Benefits Handbook* (1971) para. 38. See also Julian Fulbrook, *Tribune* **36**, No. 35, (1 September 1972) p. 1.

214. Howard Glennerster, *National Assistance, Service or Charity?* (1962), p. 6.

215. Clement Attlee, *Hansard*, **418**, H.C. Deb. (7 February 1946), col. 1896.

216. See for a discussion of this important distinction between 'Beveridge as implemented and Beveridge as intended', Brian Abel-Smith, 'Beveridge — Another Viewpoint'. *New Society* **1**, No. 22, 28 February 1963), p. 9.

217. See for one contemporary criticism, H. W. Singer, *Can We Afford Beveridge?* (1943).

218. François Lafitte, 'The Future of Social Security', *Social and Economic Administration* **I** (1967), p. 7.

219. For a discussion of the effects of the inter-war years on social thinking, see W. G. Runciman, *Relative Deprivation and Social Justice* (1966), p. 82.

220. Speech on 10 March 1943, reprinted in Sir William Beveridge, *The Pillars of Security* (1943), p. 178.

221. See Tony Lynes, 'Social Security Research', in Michael Young, *Forecasting and the Social Sciences* (1968), p. 136.

222. Charles Curran, M. P., *Crossbow* (Autumn 1960), quoted in T. H. Marshall, *Class, Citizenship and Social Development* (1964), pp. 264–265.

223. See for a survey, Adrian Sinfield, 'Poverty Rediscovered', *Race* **X** (1968), p. 202; Brian Abel-Smith and Peter Townsend, *op. cit.*; and for a graphic portrait of life among the dossers and in the 'spikes', see Jeremy Sandford, *Down and Out in Britain* (1971).

224. J. C. Kincaid, *Poverty and Equality in Britain* (1973), p. 30.

225. The Insurance Fund was £14 millions overdrawn in 1958 and a Government Report believed that 'within the next decade this deficiency [would] reach £260 millions a year', *Provision for Old Age* (1958), H.M.S.O. Cmnd. 538, p. 7.

226. National Insurance Act 1966.

227. Olga Aikin and Judy Reid, *Employment, Welfare and Safety at Work* (1971), p. 238. See, for example, 'A letter of complaint to Mr Heath and his ministers', *The Times* (30 May 1972) — an anonymous article by 'Hugh Barry', formerly a company managing director earning £5,000 a year, who was at that time 'living on the dole'.

229. See, however, Arthur Lewis, M.P., *Hansard*, **418**, H. C. Deb. (6 February 1946), col. 1806.

230. William Robson, *op. cit.*, p. 291.

231. R. M. Titmuss, *Essays on 'The Welfare State'* (1969), p. 229.

232. Rhodes Boyson, *Down With the Poor* (1971), p. 5.

233. Brian Abel-Smith, *Labour's Social Plans* (1966), p. 16.

234. The Beveridge Report, *op. cit.*, paras. 302–8.

235. See generally, Alex Rubner, *Fringe Benefits, The Golden Chains* (1962).

236. See generally, Joseph M. Becker, *Guaranteed Income for the Unemployed: The Story of SUB* (1968). SUB was first negotiated by the United Auto Workers in 1955 to stimulate management to provide steady full-time employment. In fact the model for the American schemes was a Rowntree Co. plan whereby redundant workers were able to claim supplementary unemployment benefits up to 50 per cent of their average weekly earnings, plus 10 per cent for a dependent wife, plus 5 per cent for each dependent child under 16; see generally, B. Seebohm Rowntree, *The Human Factor in Business* (1938).

237. See, for example, Peter Laurie 'Whose Benefit?', *Sunday Times*, (26 November 1972): 'But National Insurance is only nominally "insurance", since inflation threw the whole operation out of gear some time ago. The trouble is that yesterday's premiums were not large enough to finance today's inflated benefits'. One businessman commentator described unemployment insurance 'premiums' as being 'much more like taxes in aid of the unemployed, than premiums to secure an insurance'; Geo. W. Mullins, *Unemployment, The Gateway to a New Life* (1926), p. 121.

238. Victor George, *Social Security, Beveridge and After* (1968), p. 45.

239. Richard Hohaus, 'Equity, Adequacy and Related Factors in Old Age Security', *The Record* (American Institute of Actuaries) (June 1938), p. 13, quoted in R. M. Titmuss, *Commentary* on William J. Braithwaite, *Lloyd George's Ambulance Wagon* (1957), p. 56.

240. Maurice Bruce, *op. cit.*, p. 22.

241. Alan T. Peacock, *The Economics of National Insurance* (1952), pp. 103–4.

242. T. H. Marshall, *Social Policy* (1970), p. 48.

243. The Ministry of Social Security Act 1966; The Beveridge Report, *op. cit.*, para. 44.

244. Ministry of Pensions and National Insurance, *Explanatory Memorandum to the Ministry of Social Security Bill* (1966), para. 1.

245. Douglas Houghton, *Paying for the Social Services* (1967), p. 12.

246. A. B. Atkinson, *Poverty in Britain and the Reform of Social Security* (1969), p. 77.

247. T. H. Marshall, *Social Policy* (1970), p. 97.

248. Victor George, *op. cit.*, p. 38.

249. Thomas Steele, Parliamentary Secretary to the Ministry of National Insurance, *Hansard*, **448**, H. C. Deb. (5 March 1944), col. 71.

250. The first study to show the seriousness of non-take-up was that of Dorothy Cole and J. E. G. Utting, *The Economic Circumstances of Old People* (1962). Their findings were substantially confirmed by the Ministry of Pensions and National Insurance in 1965, *Financial and Other Circumstances of Retirement Pensioners* (1966).

251. T. H. Marshall in a letter to *New Society* **10**, No. 265, (26 October 1967), p. 603.

252. Clara D. Rackham in William Robson, *Social Security* (1948), p. 137

PART 3

The Tribunal Process

8

The Social Security Tribunals

The growth of social security and the acceptance of the principles of a twentieth century 'Welfare State' have led to a considerable expansion in personal liberty and security. But as a result of the growth of state activity needed to sustain such a welfare machinery, there has been a corresponding increase in problems concerning the protection of individual rights. Each measure widening the scope of Government action has necessarily brought with it the potential threat of an abuse of power, or, as in the words of Professor Wade, 'a new source of social friction'.[1] It is clear that where welfare programmes have direct power over income levels, such as the Supplementary Benefits Commission does over approximately one in thirteen of the population, considerable care must be taken to regulate and control the use of that power. The scale of expenditure on social security as a proportion of the economy also underlines the need for effective administration and control; one estimate is that social security payments alone represent 10.5 per cent of Gross National Product.[2]

The possibility of recourse to some form of judicial institution for the redress of grievances has become a fundamental tenet of British constitutional theory. In fact at the time of the 1601 Poor Law Act there was a well-established right of appeal to the justices from a decision of the overseers, and many claimants petitioned directly to the justices before a decision had been made.[3] By an Act of 1722 this appeal right was statutorily modified so that no Poor Law recipient could petition the justices until he had been refused benefit by the overseers. Similarly, there was a right of appeal to Quarter Sessions on an order of removal; however, this was usually exercised by parish officials on an adverse decision by the justices, rather than by paupers who were seldom able to stand the expense of an appeal.[4]

As has been discussed, such a right of appeal on the determination

For notes see p. 205

of social security claims was granted in this century by the setting up of a system of specialist tribunals. The historical reasons for preferring such bodies, rather than leaving disputes to be settled in the ordinary way by the courts, critically affect their present character.[5] However, just as important as the aim of redressing grievances was the additional purpose, of those framing the 1911 National Insurance appeal structure, to provide an orderly procedure for settling disputes rather than have claimants make their protests in an informal and possibly disruptive manner. The balancing of these two objectives remains the principal feature of the present tribunal process.

The advantages of tribunals as opposed to courts for the determination of claims were characterized by the 1957 Franks Committee Report as being 'cheapness, accessibility, freedom from technicality, expedition and expert knowledge of their subject'.[6] To attribute such high standards to the practical adjudication of all tribunals is perhaps to overstate the case, and there has been an unfortunate tendency in administrative texts merely to repeat the received wisdom of former inquiries without thorough investigation of the realities of adjudication in social security tribunals.

It is important to realize that the three types of tribunal at present utilized in relation to social security—in the contributory sector Local Appeal Tribunals and the National Insurance Commissioners, and on the non-contributory side the Supplementary Benefit Appeal Tribunal —are only part of a wider system of tribunals. The use of 'system' is perhaps a misnomer, certainly if this is misunderstood to mean a structure in the sense of German or French administrative courts. In recent years tribunals have proliferated often without any regard to overall planning; their categorization has also become a difficult matter, although it is possible to discern a grouping of 'social administration tribunals connected with personal welfare'.[7] The Council on Tribunals has repeatedly lamented this disorganized growth, stating that 'legislation about tribunals tends to be shaped by the short term exigencies of political and administrative convenience rather than by any coherent long term policy'.[8] Considerable disparities of role and composition exist between these differing types of tribunal, and the statement of general principles applicable to all situations has become exceedingly difficult, and in some instances unhelpful; in Appendix C of its Annual Report, the Council on Tribunals lists at present over 2,000 tribunals operating in Britain.[9] Moreover, much legal energy has been dissipated on theoretical disputation which could have more usefully been devoted to a study of the realities of the tribunal process, in what happens at hearings, who serves on tribunals, and what relationship is maintained with the agency and its officials under review.

What must now be undisputed, despite the sterile controversies of the past, is that tribunals are judicial bodies, even though they are not courts of record, and that they are bound by the rules of natural justice. For by the use of their powers of judicial review, the judges have repeatedly attempted to ensure that 'administrative justice' is not inferior to justice administered in the courts. The effectiveness of such a policy depends of course on the number of petitions for review which reach the courts. One feature of the present system is that, through a combination of factors, petitions to the High Court are only made in certain areas of tribunal jurisdiction. For example, there have been many applications on questions of industrial injury benefit, whereas only a handful of cases in relation to Supplementary Benefits jurisdiction. Indeed, the distinction between courts and tribunals has become an increasingly difficult one to perceive; Professors Abel-Smith and Stevens believe that 'such differences as there are between them are not in any sense fundamental but at most differences in degree. Tribunals tend to include a much wider range of skills than on the bench; and the most significant hallmark of policy-oriented tribunals is specialisation'.[10] The distinction of having non-lawyer opinion included among the decision-makers is, however, breaking down in the use of lay members in both the Restrictive Practices and the Industrial Relations Court, although the latter has now been disbanded. In fact the distinction was perhaps only ever superficially correct, in that the British system has long utilized the services of juries and lay magistrates in the administration of justice. The study by Professors Abel-Smith and Stevens concludes that, 'properly understood, tribunals are a more modern form of Court'.[11] Such a view has been criticized in a recent study, where Dr. Farmer argues in a somewhat sophisticated way that many tribunals of the 'policy-oriented' variety should be more properly treated as part of the administration and not as part of, or complementary to, the judicial system.[12] Dr. Farmer then lists what he regards as six major attributes of tribunals, but the shading of concepts and multiple exceptions which he makes, suggests that such an analysis is meaningless. Certainly transport licensing bodies can no longer be truly thought of as tribunals, but this would not appear to be a rationale for reversing the Franks Committee's general recommendation that tribunals should not be allowed to stay as 'appendages' to the Government Department under review.[13]

To restrict 'Lawyer's law' in these circumstances to the adjudication of the courts is to narrow considerably the impact of law on the regulation of society. Although initially social and political pressures limited the role of lawyers in the area of tribunals, it is now clear that, as Sir Carleton Allen stated in 1959, it has become

> impossible any longer to think of 'the administration of justice' as being merely the justice dispensed by courts of law, as so many of us were brought up to believe. To be ignorant of our extensive and extending supplementary justice is to be unaware of half the legal issues which are affecting the rights and liberties of innumerable lieges every day.[14]

Unfortunately, much Administrative Law analysis still concentrates on the judicial control of tribunals, which is a comparatively rare phenomenon, rather than on the actual practice of tribunals.

Although tribunals now cater for a wide variety of issues, it is clear that the main impetus for their growth in the twentieth century has come from their use in questions of social security, and in particular from their use in relation to unemployment benefits. Even today, it can be stated that 'social legislation, broadly so called, is the preponderant subject-matter of British administrative law'.[15] As an editorial in the *Law Society's Gazette*, discussing the Franks Report, pointed out, 'it was as a result of the creation of the Welfare State, [that] what had previously been an unobtrusive and rarely used piece of machinery [became] an ubiquitous and immensely influential means of settling conflicts between government departments and private individuals'.[16] But because of the piecemeal growth of social security, differing tribunals have been set up to cater for differing categories of claimants. Until 1966, for example, this included a distinction between National Insurance unemployment and sickness benefit appeals in one structure, and an identical but parallel structure for National Insurance industrial injuries benefit appeals, both set up following the post-Beveridge reforms. The present position in relation to unemployment benefits is that of a dual appeal system. One branch, dealing with National Insurance claims, consists of three stages, known collectively as 'the statutory authorities': an initial determination by an Insurance Officer; an appeal to a Local Appeal Tribunal; and a further appeal to the National Insurance Commissioners. Running alongside this structure is that of Supplementary Benefits, which consists of an initial determination by a local officer of the Supplementary Benefits Commission, with an appeal to a Supplementary Benefit Appeal Tribunal.

Although the two aspects of contributory and non-contributory income maintenance frequently overlap, as we have seen, this dual system is a legacy of the historical development of British social security. Perhaps largely because this area has been so little examined, there have been few advocates for unifying these two similar systems. The Franks Committee examined two proposals for amalgamation of the then three social security tribunals, put to it in evidence by Professor Robson and the Society of Labour Lawyers, but the Committee concluded that their functions were not 'sufficiently cognate to permit of complete integration'.[17] A recent and extensive study uncritically follows the Franks' view, making the strange and false statement that all the two tribunals 'have in common is that both are to do with the payment of money'.[18] This of course ignores the crucial inter-relationship of disqualification under s. 20 Social Security Act 1975, the trade dispute disqualification in Supplementary Benefit jurisdiction which goes on appeal to the Local Appeal Tribunal rather than to the Supplementary Benefit Appeal Tribunal, and the fact that both tribunals decide cohabitation cases, often with divergent results. Professor Robson's proposal had been that the National Insurance Local Appeal Tribunal might form a nucleus for all adjudication on money claims by individuals against social service authorities, in that these cases were 'concerned with more or less similar or related phenomena concerning industrial conditions, the domestic or personal circumstances of the applicant, and his personal conduct'.[19] It is argued here that, subject to certain safeguards, Professor Robson's suggestion deserves further attention; indeed, the beneficial effect of amalgamating the two kinds of National Insurance Tribunals in 1966 would seem to suggest advantages in a rationalization of the existing tribunals into a single local social security tribunal structure. For this reason, the discussion of issues in the present adjudicatory structure which follows will attempt to compare the two systems of tribunals at present dealing with social security appeals.[20] In this way it is hoped to focus on important distinctions between the way the tribunals operate, and to compare the efficiency and fairness of their adjudication.

Any discussion of the appeal process in social security adjudication must be based on the recognition that only a small fraction of claimants ever use the appeal machinery. As Professor de Smith pointed out, administrative review must be 'inevitably sporadic and peripheral' in that all administration would be brought to a standstill if every act or decision were 'reviewable on unrestricted grounds by an independent judicial body'.[21] In fact there are no legal limitations on appeals in social security matters, apart from time limits, and no mechanism to deter vexatious or frivolous appeals, but many other factors operate to deter appeals, as will be discussed later. From decisions of Insurance Officers, on all insurance benefit claims, approximately 0.22 per cent of cases are appealed to the Local Appeal Tribunal,[22] and in relation to Supplementary Benefits an appeal from initial determination by the

S.B.C., which reached the stage of a hearing before the Supplementary Benefit Appeal Tribunal, was made in approximately 0.5 per cent of cases.[23] Because few appeals are made in insurance cases to the National Insurance Commissioners, and an application for review to the High Court from the Supplementary Benefit Appeal Tribunal is an extreme rarity, these local tribunals enjoy a high degree of finality.

However, the internal administrative review procedure of a welfare agency may have a considerable effect on the number of appeals made which are brought to a full hearing. In a significant study, by Robert Coleman, of all appeals made on S.B.C. decisions in a twelve-month period, it was found that as many as one-third of all appeals were in fact resolved by an administrative process rather than through a hearing before a tribunal. This internal review mechanism was set in motion by the lodging of an appeal and involved an urgent home visit under the personal supervision of the area office manager, discussions between officers at both local and regional levels, a paper review of the case at both levels, and even the forwarding of papers to headquarters if the appeal concerned an important question of policy.[24] This considerable power of 'superseding' or 'revising' a claim once an appeal is lodged is not used to the same extent in insurance cases, although the theoretical powers of review are wide;[25] any decision given by the Insurance Officer, Local Appeal Tribunal or Commissioner may be reviewed if circumstances alter or if the initial decision is found to have been based on a mistake. This is, however, subject to a further appeal by the claimant on the new determination.[26]

The effect of such provisions on the rights of claimants, who are generally not properly advised, is however a potentially dangerous use of internal administrative procedure to circumvent the appeal process. The Coleman study showed that 11 per cent of Supplementary Benefit appellants abandon their appeals before hearing, even though no adjustment is made, and the reasons for this are unclear in the absence of a more detailed survey. Some critics have suggested that in some reviewed cases claimants may have been 'bought off' with the offer of an increase in benefit, which may be lower than their full entitlement. As Tony Lynes points out, in these circumstances the claimant can in theory appeal against the decision, 'but in the vast majority of cases, the appellant gratefully accepts whatever he is offered'.[27] However, it would seem that this situation occurs only rarely, and usually through arithmetical incompetence rather than intentional guile.[28] But the importance of this internal administrative process cannot be underestimated when it is realized that more Supplementary Benefit cases are altered administratively than by a subsequent and successful tribunal appeal.[29] The Coleman study points out that, for advisers of claimants, the real purpose of an appeal may be to secure an administrative review by regional officers, who will often have more knowledge of the regulations applicable, and will normally feel more able to alter a decision than do the local officers who initially made it.

Although the National Insurance Commissioners fulfil an important role in the adjudicatory structure of unemployment insurance claims, much of the following discussion will concentrate on social security adjudication at the local tribunal level. In numerical terms, the importance of this 'grass roots' approach can be seen by the fact that approximately 5 per cent of unemployment insurance appeal cases are appealed beyond the local tribunal level.[30] Nevertheless, the effectiveness of a second stage of appeal is an important distinctive feature between the National Insurance and Supplementary Benefit systems, and the possible extension of this second appeal to all social security jurisdiction is discussed later.[31]

The number of local tribunals dealing with social security varies according to need, but in 1974 there were 189 Local Appeal Tribunals[32] and 120 Supplementary Benefit Appeal Tribunals.[33] Figures show that in 1974 the Local Appeal Tribunals dealt with 28,510 cases, of which 15,769 were on claims for unemployment benefits,[34] and that in 1974 the Supplementary Benefits Appeal Tribunals dealt with 25,611 Supplementary Benefit appeals.[35] There has been a variation in the figures over time; for example, the Local Appeal Tribunals dealt with 16,871 unemployment appeals in 1964, which rose to 21,087 in 1967 and back to 15,769 in 1974,[36] and similarly Supplementary Benefit appeals ranged from 9,703 in 1964 to 33,735 in 1972 and back to 25,611 in 1974.[37] Appeals to the National Insurance Commissioners numbered 913 in 1964, reaching a high point in 1970 with 1,096 appeals and falling back to 837 in 1974.[38]

Discretion or Legalism?

The most prevailing myth of the British welfare system, and in particular of Supplementary Benefit adjudication, is that of 'discretion' as a contrast to legal rigidity. The term 'discretion' covers a variety of practices, but its classical use was in the form stated by the 1932 Donoughmore Committee on Ministers' Powers. Their belief was that there was an essential distinction between a judicial and a quasi-judicial function, which lay in the element of discretion which they thought resided only in the latter situation. A more modern version is that by Lord Collison in an Introduction to the *Supplementary Benefits*

Handbook, where he states that

> The distinctive feature of the Supplementary Benefits scheme is its discretionary element, those powers vested in the Commission which enable it to consider the claims of individual circumstances. By definition no one can claim as of 'right' that a particular discretionary power should be exercised in his favour. But for the individual claimant the existence of these discretionary powers may be more valuable than a precisely prescribed right because they give the scheme a flexibility of response to varying situations of human need.[39]

Such a statement is questionable on two main grounds. First, it cannot be maintained that 'discretion' in the practical application of S.B.C. jurisdiction denotes freedom from technical rules. In reality, 'discretion' in its pure form is rarely if ever exercised by individual officers on the basis of isolated judgment, but only through the application of internal regulations which are every bit as legalistic as the statutory rules laid down in the Supplementary Benefits Act. Certainly the legal framework in which the S.B.C. operates allows for flexibility of decision by the administrators in individual cases, but the entangling web of internal S.B.C. rules imposes a straitjacket on its application in practice. As Norman Lewis points, out, 'much of the individualised justice that both the Supplementary Benefit Act and official literature speak of is a chimera'.[40] This is not to say that flexibility is never exercised,[41] but to put it in its practical context, the A Code has become in effect a code of legal principles for the regulation of Supplementary Benefits, but without the protection of being open to public and parliamentary debate. The continued secrecy of the rules is justified by the S.B.C. on the flimsy grounds that they would be 'largely unintelligible to the lay reader'.[42] Such an attitude seems not only strange in a situation where lawyers, whose expertise presumably lies in the field of deciphering complex regulations, are taking an increasing interest, but, it is suggested, untenable in an area of crucial jurisdiction to a great number of people. Its unacceptability as a rational basis for continued secrecy is perhaps best illustrated by a comparison of the educational background of lawyers and other advisers active in the field, with that of S.B.C. officers who are presumably thought to find the A Code intelligible.

The second questionable proposition is the implicit assumption that there exists a clear divide between the 'discretion' of the British S.B.C. officer on the one hand and the judicial process on the other. This was the view taken by Professor Titmuss in an important article where he ridicules the American system of welfare itemization and points out the dangers of excessive rigidity.[43] Certainly some aspects of the New York system to which Professor Tirmuss took exception sound somewhat ludicrous when committed to paper—such as the number of can-openers and toilet-tissue holders regarded as standard for a welfare family—but the article conveniently ignores the detailed checklist of standard clothes, underwear and bedding requirements which S.B.C. officers utilize in assessing British welfare claims. In the American system all such checklists and general rules have become public documents after lengthy litigation, and occasionally outright theft, by legal services lawyers in the 1960s, whereas in Britain the internal rules are furtively hidden behind the Official Secrets Act. As Professor Jowell shows in his analysis of administrative discretion, an American 'up front' approach has considerable advantage in terms of administrative efficiency where claims become routinized, and also allows welfare rights organizations, legal advisers and claimants to help speed the process by putting in the appropriate claim.[44]

A further advantage to the administrative machinery is that clearly-stated public rules can have considerable benefits in predicting and planning a department's work, and also in reducing anxiety on the part of low-level officials where clear guidelines can serve as a 'shield'.[45] However, a move towards codification and certainty should not be regarded as a panacea for all evils, nor as a tool for the total elimination of any discretion on the part of officers. As Richard Wilding, a former Assistant Secretary in the Supplementary Benefits Division of the D.H.S.S. has pointed out, using Professor Titmuss's example, if 'it were a rule that everybody should possess a serviceable toothbrush, there would still be room for argument about whether the old toothbrush was worn out'. However, such a change would seem to be a helpful shift in terms of ensuring that poor people have toothbrushes at all, although Mr. Wilding believes it to transfer the exercise of discretion 'to a narrower and less fruitful area'.[46] At this point there is perhaps a clear division between the attitudes of social workers as opposed to lawyers. Mr. Wilding sees publication of the A Code as 'inevitably' leading to 'confrontations', which he obviously wishes to avoid,[47] whereas conflict from a lawyer's perspective is often seen as essential to the orderly resolution of social problems through the adversarial system. However, there is a more important reason for the publication of the A Code. Olive Stevenson, the former Social Work Adviser to the S.B.C., considers that 'publication of codes as such, seems . . . a somewhat trivial point from which to attack this problem [of knowledge of Supplementary Benefits]: manuals of instruction are by definition unsuitable for general consumption'.[48] Such an attitude ignores the reality that claimants at present are not getting their full entitlement in large part because they or their advisers are unable to consult the regulations on which benefit decisions are made. The *Supplementary Benefits Handbook* is an advance on the previous situation, but it is still couched in general terms and its language is at times obfuscatory. The important issue is that continued secrecy of the codes means that large numbers of families must live in poverty below the official standards; this may mean that the discretion of S.B.C. officials will be less 'fruitful' for a few families fortunate enough to receive individual attention, but it should not obscure the needs of a wide sector of claimants who are manifestly not receiving their full entitlement.

Professor Titmuss also ignored two built-in advantages of the New York system: firstly its effectiveness in a situation of high drug dependency where unallocated benefits disappear into narcotics purchase,[49] and secondly its equalizing strength as a standard of life below which no one should be allowed to fall in a civilized society, even if this does mean itemization 'from scrub brushes to panties'.

One non-legal commentator, Olive Stephenson, has stated that 'administrative discretion exists in a state of permanent and not unhealthy tension with its opposite, precisely prescribed rules'.[50] Such comments are unexceptional in jurisprudential terms, so long as they do not suggest that judges in the High Court or administrative judges in tribunals mechanically weigh precedents devoid of any flexibility or external consideration. For anyone with a proper acquaintance with the courts, such a view of the judicial process is clearly mistaken; yet it is often used as a false antithesis for the exercise of administrative 'discretion'. Additionally, there is unfortunately a tendency to leave undifferentiated the role of lawyers in the High Court as opposed to that in the lower courts; as Richard White has pointed out, Professor Titmuss's model is solely applicable to the High Court and does not take into account the much more appropriate analogy of practice in magistrates' courts, where 'argument about "what the law is" is very small, and . . . where there is any discussion about the law at all it is usually concerned not with the gaps in the law but with the application of reasonably settled norms to particular circumstances'.[51] Sentencing policy is perhaps the major example of almost total discretionary power being vested in a judge, but, as a recent survey of the judicial function of the House of Lords shows, 'there is no such thing as depersonalised adjudication, particularly in the Anglo-Saxon legal system which gives so much scope to its judges to indulge in individual pyrotechnics'.[52] Conversely, it would be mistaken to suppose that administrative discretion is uncontrolled, or indeed that it would be desirable if it were so: as William O. Douglas pointed out in a famous remark, 'absolute discretion, like corruption, marks the beginning of the end of liberty'.[53]

The study by Professor K. C. Davis of discretionary justice shows clearly the gradation there is in all legal and administrative decision-making between precise rules and unfettered discretion. It is his contention that

> the greatest and most frequent injustice occurs at the discretion end of the scale, where rules and principles provide little or no guidance, where emotions of deciding officers may affect what they do, where political or other favouritism may influence decisions, and where the imperfections of human nature are often reflected in the choices made.[54]

Professor Davis's plea is for more open and aware regulation of discretionary powers, which can then be easily altered—the supreme advantage of administrative over statutory rules—to suit changing circumstances. Recently, the Chairman of the S.B.C. has outlined what he sees as a fundamental choice for the British system: 'it can *either* go for more discretion, more flexibility, a labour-intensive service and "creative justice" for individual claimants, *or* it can go for more uniformity, more clearly understood civil rights, fewer civil servants, and "proportional justice" for larger categories of claimants'.[55] As he points out, the 'poverty lobby' is sometimes contradictory in its demands, and unsure which alternative should be the long-term strategy of the system. It will be clear that the author's preference is for the second alternative, but there must be an awareness of what this entails in terms of effective training, rule modification and sufficient benefit levels. Certainly the rigidity of hidebound rules is a vice to be guarded against in any jurisdiction, but in British welfare adjudication it is argued that the avoidance of rigidity should not be used as a pretext for continuing an amateurish system in which the rules are highly technical, and yet claimants are not properly informed of their rights under them.

NOTES

1. H. W. R. Wade, *Administrative Law* (1961), p. 196.
2. Peter Laurie, 'Whose Benefit?', *Sunday Times* (26 November 1972).
3. Brian Rodgers, *The Battle Against Poverty: From Pauperism to Human Rights* (1969), p. 14.
4. See Dorothy Marshall, *The English Poor in the Eighteenth Century* (1926), pp. 89, 169. For an early British experiment with a tribunal set up under an Elizabethan statute to deal with commercial arbitration, which consisted of six lawyers and eight 'grave and discreet merchants', see C. T. Carr, *Concerning English Administrative Law* (1941), p. 95.
5. See generally, the discussion at p. 140.
6. *Report of the Committee on Administrative Tribunals and Enquiries* (1957), H.M.S.O. Cmnd. 218, p. 9 (hereafter referred to as 'Franks Committee Report'). These words are almost an exact echo of the earlier

Donoughmore Committee Report; *Committee on Ministers' Powers* (1932), H.M.S.O. Cmd 4060, p. 97.

7. R. E. Wraith and P. G. Hutchesson, *Administrative Tribunals* (1973), p. 45.

8. *Report of the Council on Tribunals for 1969–1970* (1970), p. 10.

9. See for the best statements on general administrative law principles, J. A. G. Griffith and Harry Street, *Principles of Administrative Law* (1973, 5th ed.), and H. W. R. Wade, *Administrative Law* (1971, 3rd ed.).

10. Brian Abel-Smith and Robert Stevens, *In Search of Justice* (1968), p. 224.

11. *ibid.*, p. 228.

12. J. A. Farmer, *Tribunals and Government* (1974), pp. 3–4, 184.

13. *ibid.*, p. 191.

14. C. K. Allen, *Courts and Judgements* (1959) p. 25. As has been stated by Professor Wade, administrative tribunals are in substance courts of law, but 'they are "administrative" because the reasons for preferring them to the ordinary courts of law are administrative reasons'; H. W. R. Wade, *op. cit.*, p. 197.

15. Bernard Schwartz and H. W. R. Wade, *Legal Control of Government* (1972), p. 42.

16. Quoted in the *First Report of the Council on Tribunals* (1960), p. 1. It should be noted that some tribunals, such as rent tribunals and the industrial tribunals, determine disputes between individuals. For the use of tribunals prior to the twentieth century, see the study by D. M. Gordon, 'Administrative Tribunals and the Courts', *Law Quarterly Review* **49** (1933), p. 94 *et seq.*, and p. 419 *et seq.*

17. *Franks Committee Report* (1957), p. 33.

18. R. E. Wraith and P. G. Hutchesson, *op. cit.* p. 291.

19. Professor W. A. Robson, *Minutes of Evidence to the Franks Committee* (1957), p. 488. See for the recommendation of the Society of Labour Lawyers, *ibid.*, p. 516; and for the views of one of their witnesses in an expanded form, Gordon Borrie, *Justice and the Administration* (1957), p. 13.

20. It should be noted that, though unemployment questions provide the majority of appeals in both Local Appeal Tribunals and Supplementary Benefit Tribunals, a number of other important issues are also determined by the tribunals; for example, industrial injury benefit, sickness benefit, family allowances, maternity benefits, widows' benefits, guardian's allowance retirement pensions, death grants and children's special allowance by the Local Appeal Tribunal, and payments under the Family Income Supplement scheme in the Supplementary Benefit Appeal Tribunal.

21. S. A. de Smith, *Judicial Review of Administrative Action* (1974), p. 3.

22. The figures given for 1972 were 15,302,000 cases decided by the Insurance Officers, and 34,419 appealed to the Local Appeal Tribunals. A further breakdown into categories shows that of 3,360,000 claims for unemployment insurance benefit, 20,608 were appealed giving a higher percentage of 0.61 per cent; D.H.S.S. *Annual Report 1972* (1973), H.M.S.O. Cmnd. 5352, pp. 111, 126. However, these figures cannot be considered to give a completely accurate picture, in that a number of factors, such as repeating claims, may very well distort the true position. Appeals to the second stage of appeal before the National Insurance Commisioners are of course even fewer, averaging around 1,500 cases per annum; *ibid.*, p. 127.

23. The figures for 1972 were 33,735 appeal hearings out of a total of 6,901,000 claims for Supplementary Benefits; *ibid.*, pp. 111, 128. There seems to have been a discernible upward trend in the figures over the last five years, but the percentage of claims appealed is still extremely small. The number of supplementary allowance claims out of the total of Supplementary Benefit claims was 6,584,000, and it is generally assumed that the 317,000 supplementary pension claims are largely non-contentious. This assumption, however, has not been verified in any proper study.

24. See generally, R. J. Coleman, *Supplementary Benefits and the Administrative Review of Administrative Action* (1970). The wide powers for this pre-hearing process derive from s. 17(1) (d) SB Act 1966.

25. Under s. 104, SS Act 1975.

26. s. 104(4) SS Act 1975.

27. For example, Tony Lynes, *Welfare Rights* (1969), p. 7.

28. The S.B.C. invariably deny any wrongful intention; see Melvin Herman, *Administrative Justice and Supplementary Benefits* (1972), p. 31.

29. R. J. Coleman, *op. cit.*, p. 10.

30. The figures for 1972 were 1,001

unemployment benefit cases appealed to the Commissioners from 20,608; D.H.S.S., *Annual Report 1972* (1973) pp. 126–7. The overall percentage of appeals to the Commissioners was approximately 6 per cent for all National Insurance benefits, but it should be noted that the rate of appeal for industrial injury cases approached 25 per cent.

31. See p. 293 *et seq.*

32. D.H.S.S., *Annual Report 1974* (1975), H.M.S.O. Cmnd. 6150, p. 101. In 1972, regional figures were 26 in Scotland and 167 in England and Wales; D.H.S.S., *Annual Report 1972* (1973), p. 126.

33. Figures in 1972 were 18 in Scotland, 102 in England and Wales. This number has been reduced from the 151 tribunals existing in 1970; *Annual Report of the Council on Tribunals for 1971–1972* (1972), p. 33.

34. 5,148 appeals were on claims for sickness benefits, and 1,823 on claims for industrial injury benefits; D.H.S.S., *Annual Report 1974* (1975), p. 101.

35. D.H.S.S., *Social Security Statistics 1974* (1975), p. 146. There were 1,635 F.I.S. appeals; *ibid.*, p. 142.

36. See Table 1.20 in D.H.S.S., *Social Security Statistics 1974* (1975), p. 19.

37. See Table 34.20, *ibid.*,

38. See Table 1.20, *ibid.*. This Table also contains percentage success rates for insurance appeals.

39. *Supplementary Benefits Handbook* (1972), p. 1.

40. Norman Lewis, 'Discretionary Justice and the Supplementary Benefits System', in Michael Adler and Anthony Bradley (eds), *Justice, Discretion and Poverty* (1976), p. 77.

41. See, for example, the study of its important use as an internal administrative review of appeals before hearing, R. J. Coleman, *op. cit.*

42. *Supplementary Benefits Handbook* (1972), p. 3.

43. Richard M. Titmuss, 'Welfare "Rights", Law and Discretion', *Political Quarterly* **42** (1971), p. 113. See also Richard M. Titmuss, *Social Policy* (1974), pp. 85–6.

44. Jeffrey Jowell, 'The Legal Control of Administrative Discretion', *Public Law*, (1973), p. 178.

45. *ibid.*, p. 190.

46. Richard Wilding, 'Discretionary Benefits', in Michael Adler and Anthony Bradley (eds.), *op. cit.*, p. 62.

47. *loc. cit.*

48. Olive Stevenson, *Claimant or Client?* (1973), p. 50.

49. See for a brilliant fictional account of New York's welfare system from the viewpoint of a benevolent caseworker, Julius Horwitz, *The Inhabitants* (1960). See also Richard Elman, *The Poorhouse State* (1966).

50. Olive Stevenson, *op. cit.*, p. 40.

51. Richard White in Pauline Morris, Richard White and Philip Lewis, *Social Needs and Legal Action* (1973), p. 24.

52. Louis Blom-Cooper and Gavin Drury, *Final Appeal* (1972), p. 152. See also for an American analysis, Richard Wasserstrom, *The Judicial Decision* (1961).

53. Douglas J. dissenting in *New York* v. *United States* 342 U.S. 882, 884 (1951). See also the speech of Lord Halsbury in *Sharp* v. *Wakefield* [1891] A.C. 173.

54. K. C. Davis, *Discretionary Justice* (1971), p. v.

55. David Donnison, 'Dear David Bull. . .' *Social Work Today* **6** (1975), p. 662.

9

Tribunal Participants

The standard pattern of a chairman and two wingmen for social security tribunals was established by the 1911 National Insurance structure. (The number three seems to have acquired almost mystical proportions in many kinds of judicial forums as a number best representing a check on individual bias and idiosyncracy.) As has been noted, the Local Appeal Tribunal was originally known as the Court of Referees, and the appeal system set up to adjudicate on unemployment assistance in 1934 used its structure as a model. The new Assistance Tribunal, however, was qualitatively different because of policy decisions taken to control the process by which U.A.B. tribunal members were to be selected, and to ensure a considerable role for Board officials appearing before and staffing the U.A.B. tribunals; such historical factors still play a part in the modern character of their successors, the Supplementary Benefit Appeal Tribunals.

The fundamental question as to whether social security tribunals should be an integral part of the administrative machinery dealing with benefits, or a separate and independent 'court', has never been fully resolved in practical terms. Evidence to the Franks Committee by the Government Departments involved was that 'tribunals in the social service field should be regarded as adjuncts to the administration of the services themselves'.[1] However, the Committee rejected this assumption and declared that, as a general principle, 'tribunals should properly be regarded as machinery provided by Parliament for adjudication rather than as part of the machinery of administration'.[2] It is this same question concerning independence from the administrative machine that is the dominant theme of much of the present criticism levelled at the social security tribunals, both by academic writers and by the claimants themselves.

For notes see p. 245

The Chairman

It has been repeatedly asserted that the great benefit of a tribunal is its informality. However, as the Franks Committee pointed out, 'informality without procedure may be positively inimical to right adjudication'.[3] One witness before the Franks Committee, Jeremy Seabrook, stated that in his experience 'the informal atmosphere of most tribunals . . . does not seem to put Parties and Witnesses any more at ease in most cases than in ordinary Law Courts. It has the disadvantage of allowing the procedure sometimes to become muddled.'[4] The chief responsibility for the required blend of formal procedure and informal atmosphere, which the Franks Committee recommended, clearly lies with the chairman of the appeal tribunal. While the role of chairman is important in the work of any small committee, in relation to the working of tribunals it is crucial. In general, the chairman will be more familiar with the rules and legislation involved, if only because he sits more frequently than his wingmen; but it must also be noted that, in both Supplementary Benefit and Local Appeal Tribunal adjudication, he is primarily responsible for the conduct of business. The duty is an onerous one, and necessitates what Professor Robson characterized in a now familiar phrase as 'the judicial mind'.[5] The first Report of the Council on Tribunals pointed out that a tribunal chairman

> must see to it that the proceedings are conducted with scrupulous fairness to all parties and that the proper balance is struck between formality and informality. In particular he must make sure at the outset that the parties fully understand the issue, especially when they are not legally represented; and he must ensure that they have an opportunity to present their cases adequately. This demands much knowledge and tact as well as patience and courtesy, particularly since many of those who appear before tribunals may be overawed or flustered by their surrounding.[6]

Nevertheless, the precise manner in which he discharges this duty is left to the individual chairman to determine. In general, it can be stated that the adjudicatory process of most local tribunals takes the form of an uneasy synthesis between the adversary and the inquisitorial approach to justice. Although the distinction between these two legal formulae is often somewhat artificial, Professor Sawer has summed it up as follows:

> In the ideal type of inquisitory tribunal, the judge supervises and even himself carries out much of the process of calling evidence, and examining and cross-examining witnesses; he takes the

> initiative in establishing what happened. A basic theory of this type is characteristic of most systems which have been influenced by Roman and Canon law. In the adversary system, the main responsibility for calling, adducing, and testing evidence is with the parties; the judge has no independent power of calling evidence, interferes little with the conduct of the parties or their representatives when handling evidence except by way of excluding inadmissible material, and regards his task as judging on the basis of what he is told, not on a basis of the 'actual' facts.[7]

Much of the debate on which kind of procedure should be followed in tribunals has represented an unfortunate extension of the arguments as to whether 'administrative justice' really existed, and a further attempt to make a distinction between a judicial and a so-called 'quasi-judicial' function. The Donoughmore Committee in 1932 had, for example, stated that any form of French *droit administratif* tribunal procedure was 'wholly inapplicable in the United Kingdom'.[8] And Lord Hewart's famous outburst, which had led to the setting up of the Committee, portrayed administrative regulation and all forms of tribunals as a conspiracy against the Rule of Law in the courts.[9] This was derived directly from Dicey's concept of the Rule of Law, and, as Professor Wade puts it, Dicey's views 'for long threw a somewhat chilly shadow over administrative law'.[10] The resultant controversy centred academic discussion on the constitutional aspects of tribunals, rather than on their administrative form and procedure. As Professor de Smith stated,

> Years that might have seen a growth of intensive research into the manifold problems presented by the developing law of public administration (or administrative law) were largely dominated by impassioned but mainly sterile controversies concerning the constitutional propriety of administrative tribunals and delegated legislation.[11]

This legacy has not only ensured a dearth of knowledge and information about what actually happens at tribunals, but has also meant that a number of central issues in tribunal adjudication have never been settled. As one critic accurately states, the chairman of a social security tribunal generally 'conducts the proceedings according to his personal whims and fancies'.[12] In the light of this considerable power, it is clearly necessary to examine not only the role and function of this most dominant of tribunal members, but also to look at how he is appointed.

The selection of chairmen of social security tribunals is chiefly regulated by a confidential document circulated in the Department of

Health and Social Security, and entitled *Code for Tribunals and Committees*. Its provisions contain the basic distinction between the two tribunals, in that the chief qualification of a chairman of a Local Appeal Tribunal is that he be a qualified lawyer. The *Code* states that a non-legal appointment cannot be considered 'without the prior authority of Headquarters';[13] this is also the position with chairmen of Rent Tribunals where there is similarly no statutory requirement for a lawyer to be appointed, although invariably one is.[14] The Local Appeal Tribunal chairman must also 'have a knowledge of industrial and working class conditions [and] he must be a person who can be relied upon to show independence and impartiality'.[15] In many instances, unfortunately, the first requirement of knowledge of social and industrial questions seems to be a platitude, although by the nature of the job chairmen quickly pick up expertise on, and the jargon of, industrial matters. Other qualifications are that the appointee is over 35 and under 65, and that he has no close political affiliations. The latter point is particularly stressed as a ground for disqualification in the standard form letter of appointment to new chairman: 'All appointments are made subject to the condition that the holder will submit his resignation to the Lord Chancellor if he is adopted as a prospective candidate for Parliament, or is nominated as a candidate in a Parliamentary election, or becomes a political or election agent, or chairman of a party constituency association'.[16] Before appointment by the Lord Chancellor (the Lord President of the Court of Session in Scotland), the prospective Local Appeal Tribunal chairman is vetted at an interview with a senior official from the Department, usually the Assistant Regional Controller. The evidence submitted to the Franks Committee by the Ministry of Pensions and National Insurance was that at that time chairmen of local tribunals were appointed by the Minister after consultation with the Lord Chancellor, and discussion with such officials as the Registrar of the County Court.[17] The Franks Committee recommendation was that this should be significantly changed to appointment by the Lord Chancellor in consultation with the Minister and local court officials; this is the present procedure.[18]

According to one Local Appeal Tribunal chairman, Professor Street, 'the impression is given to the interviewee that others are being considered and that the views of local citizens in public life will be sought'.[19] However, another chairman interviewed by the author received the different impression that 'they were searching for a replacement for ——, and offered the job to me'. Professor Street maintains that since the Franks Report 'the Lord Chancellor's department is obviously taking much more care about appointments than was previously taken'.[20] It is of course essential that all such appointments be considered thoughtfully, rather than the overworked Lord Chancellor's office merely rubber-stamping Departmental choices.[21] An appointment is made notionally to a panel of persons from which chairmen are selected, but in most areas vacancies seem to be filled as they occur. The Lord Chancellor's office in fact compiles an ongoing list of people suitable for appointment to a wide variety of public offices, and suggestions are periodically solicited from bodies such as the Inns of Court, the Confederation of British Industry and the Trades Union Congress, and from individuals in a position to recognize available talent such as town clerks, Registrars of County Courts and clerks to local magistrates. Because of the preponderance of men in the legal profession it is not surprising that they form a majority of chairmen, but it is startling to find that there are only six women chairing Local Appeal Tribunals out of a total of 275 chairmen. This compares with thirty-seven women out of 240 chairmen of Supplementary Benefit Appeal Tribunals.[22]

One increasing trend is for 'pluralities' in that chairmen of one type of tribunal are often suggested for appointment to others; Local Appeal Tribunal chairmen, for example, are likely to serve on Industrial Tribunals because of their experience with industrial problems, and Professor Street is a prime example of a legal academic chairing a number of tribunals. This is possibly a useful move towards rationalization, but may also be an indication of a limited pool of officially recognized talent. The Council on Tribunals has long recommended the 'need to avoid an undue proliferation of tribunals by, wherever possible, organizing them into fewer and stronger units',[23] and one way towards this may be overlapping chairmanships. A sub-committee report of *Justice* recommended in 1972 the 'creation of career chairmen' moving from one sort of tribunal to another and then to the Bench,[24] and this might be helpful in gaining both quality chairmanship at lower levels of adjudication and also provide training for future judges in areas of social and industrial matters not normally gained from a mainstream legal practice.[25] Recent anecdotal evidence seems to suggest that some barristers also prefer to hold a number of part-time tribunal chairmanships rather than continuing private practice in the courts,[26] and this could certainly be extended to women lawyers taking sabbatical leave from full-time work to raise a family.

The Memorandum of Conditions of Service sent to new chairmen has always been substantially the same for chairmen of both tribunals,[27] and stipulates initial appointment for three years, with renewal at the discretion of the Lord Chancellor. All chairmen are expected to retire at the now standard judicial retirement age of 72.[28] The chairman's tenure of office can be terminated at any time by one month's written notice on either side, and the Lord Chancellor can also summarily terminate the appointment, if 'the holder becomes unfit to perform the duties of the office by reason of inability, misconduct, or any other cause, or there is a likelihood that public confidence in his impartiality will be impaired'.[29] The Attorney-General stated in a written answer in 1973 that there had been three such dismissals of National Insurance chairmen since 1946. There had been no dismissals of Supplementary Benefit chairmen.[30] However, non-renewal of appointment in some circumstances is a polite form of dismissal.[31] In one case, G. K. Haggen, the Dean of the Faculty of Law at Leeds University, was not re-appointed because, according to Lord Simonds, the Lord Chancellor, he 'time after time disregarded' the precedents of the National Insurance Commissioners.[32] During a debate on the case in the House of Lords, initiated by Lord Chorley, it was revealed that at that time there had been twenty-three previous instances where the Minister had refused a re-appointment, although no explanation had ever been given to the chairmen involved. One curious sidelight on the affair was that Professor Haggen had been visited three years earlier by the manager of the local National Insurance office and the Regional Insurance Officer to be warned that he was 'out of step'; Lord Chorley rightly characterized this as 'a complete infraction of the principle of judicial independence'.[33]

It is difficult to see precisely what channels of information are used to determine a chairman's re-appointment or dismissal. The Council on Tribunals do not attempt this kind of surveilliance, although the National Insurance Commissioners will on rare occasions pass information to the Lord Chancellor's office on a particular case which has been badly mishandled. Clerks and Presenting Officers are therefore the only real avenues of assessment, but it is clear from conversation with them that only outrageous conduct would compel them to make a report to their superiors in any but very general terms.

Although the chairman is authorized to act anywhere in the country, he is ordinarily assigned to one tribunal. Once appointed he is sent eighteen bound volumes containing the relevant statutes, statutory instruments and a digest of the National Insurance Commissioners decisions, but beyond this his training is accomplished by immediate practice in tribunal work or possibly a few opportunities to sit in on the work of the previous tribunal chairman. A short confidential Memorandum is sent by the Department, but this goes little beyond quoting generalized sections of the Franks Committee Report on tribunal procedure, and also giving some additional information on tribunals generally.[34] Unfortunately, little is done to help chairmen keep up-to-date with National Insurance precedents other than the annual publication of reported decisions; Professor Street reports the frustration of such buried precedent when

> Twice, early in 1974, an insurance officer appearing before me cited highly relevant unreported decisions of whose existence I was totally, and excusably, unaware. It is particularly disconcerting for a chairman to have his tribunal's decision reversed by the Commissioner because it conflicted with an unreported previous decision of the Commissioner of which both he and the Insurance Officer were unaware, and still worse to learn that the unreported decision had been considered in an unreported judgement of the Divisional Court of the Queen's Bench Division.[35]

The appointment of chairmen for the Supplementary Benefit Appeal Tribunals is, if anything, even more nebulous. The same internal *Code for Tribunals and Committees* applies to Supplementary Benefit chairmen, and their chief qualification under it appears to be, in the words of one commentator, 'rather vaguely laid out as a person who can be relied upon to treat applicants with sympathy and consideration and give them full opportunity to state their case'.[36] It is interesting to find in contrast that the U.A.B. looked for chairmen with 'knowledge of local conditions, good local standing, and ability to conduct the proceedings with thoroughness, impartiality and despatch'.[37] However, whereas Local Appeal Tribunal chairmen have rarely been involved in tribunal work before their appointment, it is the general practice to promote a regular 'Minister's member' on the Supplementary Benefit Appeal Tribunal to the chairmanship when a vacancy occurs. Indeed, if one is not promoted, then under the *Code*, 'the reasons for not promoting him must be stated in a report to Headquarters'.[38] As Ross Flockhart points out, this means that the composition of tribunals is in effect two members appointed directly by the Minister as against one Trades Council member.[39]

The roles of the Lord Chancellor (the Lord President of the Court of Session in Scotland) and the Department are reversed in the selection of a Supplementary Benefit chairman, in that chairmen are selected by the Secretary of State from a panel notionally appointed by the Lord Chancellor; before the Franks Committee Report such appointments were made by the Minister responsible without express need for consultation with anyone.[40] However, insofar as the promotion of a 'Minister's member' is automatic—the occasional exceptions to this are when the regular 'Minister's members' are elderly or clearly unsuitable—it is clear that still, as Professor Herman states, 'the present structure places primary responsibility for the selection of members and chairmen and their promotion in the hands of the same Department which appoints the [Supplementary Benefits] Commission whose decisions are the subject of the tribunal's work'.[41] The exact process of initial nomination, being neither specified in legislation or regulation, is generally through the typically British process of the 'suggestion of names by interested parties'.

The Franks Committee was convinced that 'objectivity in the treatment of cases and the proper sifting of facts are most often best secured by having a legally qualified chairman'.[42] In Local Appeal Tribunals this practice has been customary since 1946, and from the start of the appeal structure the great majority of chairmen have been lawyers. The exceptions which existed after the Second World War seem mainly to have been former chairmen of the Courts of Referees,[43] and the last chairman of a Local Appeal Tribunal without legal training retired in 1971. But although most of the original chairmen of the U.A.B. Appeal Tribunals in 1934 were solicitors,[44] the reverse process seems to have occurred in the secondary branch, as now few chairmen of Supplementary Benefit Appeal Tribunals possess legal qualifications. Very little was in fact known about the background and experience of Supplementary Benefit Appeal Tribunal chairmen and members until a recent study by Ruth Lister of those working in the London tribunals. Partly this has been because observers, other than representatives of appellants, have only been officially permitted to attend Supplementary Benefit Appeal Tribunal hearings since July 1971, but also because the area has been sadly neglected in serious academic discussions. An unpublished paper in 1968 by an American lawyer estimated, largely by guesswork, that one-third of Supplementary Benefit chairmen had legal qualifications, although an earlier study thought it was about one in eight.[45] In fact, the official figures are much lower, in that only 6 per cent of all Supplementary Benefit chairmen have legal training of any kind; this compares with 28 per cent of N.A.B. chairmen in 1956.[46] However, it is not entirely clear whether this means qualification as a barrister or solicitor, possession of a law degree, or merely experience as a lay magistrate. In Ruth Lister's study, one London chairman interviewed was a lawyer and two were magistrates; one Minister's member and, interestingly, two nominated workpeople's representatives were lawyers.[47]

The T.U.C. General Council in evidence to the Franks Committee urged that non-lawyers should be eligible for appointment to the Local Appeal Tribunals,[48] but the post-war policy seems to have been to appoint non-lawyers only in certain large cities, if at all, so that legally qualified chairmen would always be available to hear industrial injury cases.[49]

The argument for lawyers as chairmen of tribunals is not of course to suggest that they have a monopoly of expertise in this area, nor that they are possessed of superior skill or wisdom, but that, put at its lowest, their training and work should have prepared them to sort evidence and understand basic rules of fair procedure. Many criticisms can be made of 'legalism' producing excessive delay, cost, complication or unintelligibility, but this vice need not necessarily be an automatic concommitant of having legally qualified chairmen, although it has long been fashionable to assume so. As Professor Wade has remarked, the need for lawyers to play a part in the tribunal process lies in 'the universality of certain principles which have been brought to a high pitch of refinement in our traditional courts of law, which are recognised as being indispensable to justice, but which have not yet won complete recognition in the world of administration'.[50]

A political scientist has stated the case even higher, believing that 'lawyers, by virtue of their training, are able to keep a firm control of the shape of proceedings, while not allowing them to become unduly formal . . . he will be better able to see that cases are conducted with fairness, clarity and dispatch'.[51] When asked, the Supplementary Benefit Appeal Tribunal members in Ruth Lister's London study gave little support to a proposal for legally qualified chairmen; Minister's members and chairmen were particularly opposed, believing it to be unnecessary and irrelevant. However, observation of the tribunals at work supported a number of swingeing criticisms made by two lawyers in the sample of general disorder due to excessive informality and poor control by chairmen;[52] such chaos would seem directly attributable to lack of legal or, in fact, any other training in how to conduct business in an orderly judicial manner. A recent study by Professor Bell, sponsored by the D.H.S.S., of Northern Region Supplementary Benefit Appeal Tribunals also found a general lack of enthusiasm among chairmen and members for a legally qualified chairman. But as a result of observations, Professor Bell, herself a social scientist, states that 'the superior quality of the legal chairmen stood out from amongst their colleagues', and urges as a matter of priority that all Supplementary Benefit chairmen possess legal qualifications.[53] However, some commentators have recently suggested that non-lawyers could be appointed chairmen of tribunals if they had received requisite legal training;[54] such a point would seem to be unexceptionable, although there would necessarily be debate on how much training is required for a 'layman' to become sufficiently a 'lawyer' so as to appreciate the issues involved in impartial adjudication.

An additional factor in demanding legal qualifications is that this generally implies a knowledge of the rules of Evidence, and in particular an awareness of the need to control open bias and prejudicial remarks;

this is of particular importance when chairmen need to know at what point to restrain the remarks of Presenting Officers, as will be discussed later. However, there unfortunately exists evidence that chairmen of Supplementary Benefit Appeal Tribunals themselves indulge on occasion in unnecessarily hostile or even openly racist comments; such conduct would be an extreme rarity with a legally qualified chairman in a Local Appeal Tribunal. For example, Ruth Lister quotes one Supplementary Benefit chairman who seems to have stepped straight out of the Victorian era: 'there are two classes of claimants: the genuine who are generally elderly and hard up and who don't know their rights and the professional appellant who is in and out of work, always appealing and who is very well informed'.[55] Such a view, even when given in private, would hardly seem to accord with Lord Thankerton's famous statement that someone exercising 'quasi-judicial' functions 'must come to his adjudication with an independent mind, without any inclination or bias towards one side or the other in the dispute'.[56] Three tribunal members in the London study expressed concern over colour prejudice on the part of other members, largely in terms of remarks that immigrants came over just to claim benefit. Such a sentiment was in fact expressed to the interviewer by a tribunal member in the study.[57] In another study of actual conduct at Supplementary Benefit hearings, Professor Herman reported that when tribunal members considered their decisions it was 'not uncommon for them to attribute unemployment of immigrants to presumed deficiencies in their character'.[58] And in one Supplementary Benefit hearing observed by the author

> an Indian shopkeeper who knew little English had sent his son, a trainee accountant, to appear on his behalf; the son was met by a belligerent request to hand over a letter authorising him to represent his father and identifying him as the son. When the clerk pointed out tactfully that this was not required under the regulations the chairman added gratuitously that: 'The problem with you Indians is that you all look alike'.[59]

One interesting point is that legal qualifications seem to be reflected in the fees paid to chairmen of tribunals, although these of course bear little relation to any potential loss of earnings.[60] The great majority of members of three sorts of tribunals in one study stated that they would do the work even without payment, although practising lawyers were less willing than the other members.[61] However, Professor Bell's study of Supplementary Benefit members suggests that some members are concerned over the lack of remuneration, and she recommends the payment of adequate fees and expenses so as to attract members of higher calibre.[62] Payment of fees is still made to chairmen and members of social security tribunals by the Department whose decisions are under review, although the amount is fixed by the Lord Chancellor's office and the Civil Service Department in consultation with bodies such as the T.U.C. This 'appendage' factor does not necessarily imply conflict of interest, but it is unsatisfactory and could be easily changed to payment from a more independent source in the local judicial structure.

Perhaps the best answer to the charge which is frequently made that the appointment of legal chairmen leads to excessive formality can be gained by observing the actions of some non-lawyer chairmen in the work of tribunals. One explanation may be that legal chairmen seem generally to be more confident of themselves, allowing them to be flexible as the need arises. Certainly the ritualistic behaviour of some non-legal chairmen which can be observed is extraordinary. Repeatedly in the literature there are comments to the effect that, as in one recent study, there are strong arguments for legally qualified chairmen in Local Appeal Tribunals because 'it is often necessary to apply statute law or case law to complex situations; to control proceedings at a hearing in a 'court-like' manner, even if not according to court rules; and to see, as far as possible, that unrepresented appellants are not at a disadvantage'.[63] This is then followed by the illogical and perplexing statement that these attributes are not necessary in Supplementary Benefit Appeal Tribunals because they 'often have more of the character of social case-work conferences'.

Admittedly, industrial injuries adjudication involves some complex statutory and case law problems, but that cannot affect the procedural advantages of having a legally qualified chairman, which are valid for any form of tribunal hearing. The myth of Supplementary Benefit adjudication being similar to social work discussions clearly arose from the 'charity' background of the earlier Poor Law, but arguably the myth has been perpetuated by ignorance of what is really happening in Supplementary Benefit Appeal Tribunals. Professor Street, for example, seems equivocal about the issue: at one point he confirms the Franks Committee view that there is 'no real affinity between the two' tribunals, and that Supplementary Benefit Appeal Tribunals 'are not so much tribunals as an extension of social case work'.[64] Only one year later, Professor Street is excoriating the Court of Appeal for refusing to take jurisdiction on a clearly erroneous legal decision in a Supplementary Benefit Appeal Tribunal, and is calling on the House of Lords or Parliament to ensure adequate judicial review, stating that 'present arrangments for ensuring that uniform and legally correct decisions are made on claims for supplementary benefits are not adequate'.[65]

Those who have observed both sets of tribunals in action can confirm that the strong arguments for legal chairmen in Local Appeal Tribunals apply with equal force to Supplementary Benefit Appeal Tribunals. However, in making comparisons, it is important not to overplay the advantages of Local Appeal Tribunals. For example, one recent commentator in his desire to point out the 'grossly inadequate' nature of Supplementary Benefits adjudication, particularly in relation to unqualified chairmen, is perhaps insufficiently realistic about the nature of Local Appeal Tribunals in making his comparison.[66] The importance of Professor Bell's recent D.H.S.S. sponsored study of Northern Region Supplementary Benefit Appeal Tribunals is that it provides some empirical evidence which, while not exactly comparable, nevertheless can be used in conjunction with her previous research on Local Appeal Tribunals to assess the differences and similarities between the two structures. The general conclusion of the study is that many problems are common to both tribunals, although often occurring in a 'more acute form' in Supplementary Benefit Appeal Tribunals; Professor Bell's principal remedy is that there should only be legally qualified chairmen, preferably with joint appointments to cover both the Local Appeal Tribunal and the Supplementary Benefit Appeal Tribunal in the same locality, with the 'ultimate objective' to combine the tribunals.[67]

One campaign undertaken by the Council on Tribunals has been to propound the value of regular conferences of chairmen of social security tribunals, along the lines of sentencing and policy conferences of judges or magistrates.[68] The U.A.B. organized regional conferences for tribunal chairmen, but for very different reasons. They were addressed by senior officials of the Board in an attempt to ensure the implementation of administrative policy.[69] The Council on Tribunals has finally succeeded in part, as is shown by the announcement in the 1971–2 Report that steps had been taken by the Lord Chancellor's office to secure meetings for the chairmen of Supplementary Benefit Appeal Tribunals, organized by senior chairmen.[70] This was apparently initially opposed by the D.H.S.S., ostensibly because it might reduce the free exercise of 'discretion'.[71] In view of the fact that Insurance Officers have regular meetings and briefings on new policies and decisions, organized by the Chief Insurance Officer, it is to be hoped that conferences will soon be arranged for the chairmen of Local Appeal Tribunals as well, with a further extension to conferences for all social security tribunal members.

However, these conferences cannot, it is suggested, be regarded as a substitute for proper training for all tribunal chairmen and members by an independent source outside the Departments under review. In Professor Bell's study of Northern Region tribunal members, there was overwhelming support for chairmen's conferences, and considerable enthusiasm for training for all members; however, this was not true in Ruth Lister's London study, where 'it was argued that [tribunal adjudication] was a matter of commonsense; that experience of people was more important than training and that they could rely on the guidance of the clerk and presenting officer'.[72] Such a view is clearly contrary to the whole spirit of impartial and effective tribunal adjudication. In the light of such views it is vital to institute immediately both conferences and non-partisan training. Training should mean not only observation of existing bad habits at hearings, but lectures, group discussions and 'sensitivity training' to the issues involved. As well as a speaker to put the view of the Department, it would also be helpful to invite, for example, a representative from the Claimants Union, who would provide an interesting touchstone for discussion on bias and preconceived ideas. If some form of Presidential system on a national or regional basis were extended to the social security tribunals, then it is suggested that all training should flow from this supervision, or from the Chief National Insurance Commissioner.

At present Supplementary Benefit members are not even given a written guide to their duties as are Local Appeal Tribunal members, although it is suggested that these are not sufficiently specific or practical in scope.[73] Picking up such important duties 'on the job' will necessarily continue existing practices, and there will also be little self-critical evaluation of the nature of tribunal adjudication by chairmen and members. Training for magistrates has been compulsory since 1966, taking place before the new justice sits at sessions, and then another phase following some experience. This is backed up by review conferences and circulated documents on new issues and sentencing policies, and the entire system would form a useful model to adapt for social security tribunal members as a whole.

The Wingmen

In a similar manner to the appointment of chairmen, the process of finding suitable tribunal wingmen to serve on social security tribunals is neither specified in legislation nor by regulation. It is important to note at once the distinction between the personnel serving on each tribunal. In Local Appeal Tribunals, one wingman is drawn from a panel representing employers and self-employed persons, and the other from a panel representing the employed.[74] In Supplementary Benefit Appeal Tribunals, however, one wingman is directly appointed by the Secretary of State and is somewhat anachronistically known as the 'Minister's member', although to call him an 'independent' member is inaccurate, and the term 'other' member is hardly a description.[75] Originally, the function of the Minister's member in U.A.B. Tribunals was 'to represent the Board'.[76] After the 1948 National Assistance Act, appointment was retained by the Minister, but there was no specific requirement that he represent the new Board in any direct sense.[77] In fact, before 1948, it had been customary to appoint serving Ministry officials, or retired Ministry officials, as the Minister's member, and even after 1948 this was still permitted and 'may have occurred', although there are insufficient data on the point.[78] Officials from unrelated, and occasionally related, Civil Service Departments have been appointed to tribunals on retirement; but in recent years this practice too has come to be regarded as unacceptable, although apparently at least one retired N.A.B. official was appointed and still serves as a chairman of a Supplementary Benefit Appeal Tribunal.[79]

The second wingman is appointed also by the Secretary of State but, in the words of the Act, 'from among persons appearing to the Minister to represent workpeople'.[80] The practice of the U.A.B., following that of the Ministry of Labour with Local Employment Committees, had been to invite a number of nominations for trade union representatives and then to select one so as to ensure that members 'could in the main be trusted to see that the unemployed did not get more benefit than was strictly necessary. The Local Committees were doing most admirable and conscientious work.'[81] In fact, the zeal of such Committees under a special 'Tightening Up' Committee in 1925 was such that the Ministry was forced to restrain them.[82] The three members of the U.A.B. Appeal Tribunal were chosen in exactly the same manner as those of the Local Employment Committees in the previous decade, and the formal system is little altered today. It is clear, therefore, that the Department of Health and Social Security has direct control over all the names placed on the Supplementary Benefit Appeal Tribunal panels as well as over the appointment of the Supplementary Benefits chairman. With the Local Appeal Tribunals, too, the D.H.S.S. in conjunction with the Department of Employment appoints the tribunal wingmen and plays a considerable part in the selection of chairmen.

The Franks Committee strongly recommended that the Council on Tribunals should be responsible as an independent agency for all tribunal members, but this proposal has never been taken up, partly because the Council on Tribunals was largely concerned at first with Committees of Inquiry, but also because it has always been understaffed and has been seen by successive Governments as a purely advisory body. However, although this considerable power of the Department under review was used purposively in the operation of the

U.A.B. tribunals,[83] it is modern practice for the Department to accept relatively automatically the nominations from the local Trades Council for vacancies on 'workpeople' panels for both Local Appeal Tribunals and Supplementary Benefit Appeal Tribunals. Yet nominees are normally visited by the manager of the local D.H.S.S. office or a deputy in order 'to acquaint him with the duties expected of him and to check that he is neither blind nor deaf'.[84] Some form of evaluation is no doubt made unofficially at this time. Howard Elcock believes the test to be whether the nominee is 'sufficiently educated, intelligent and honest' to serve,[85] but in most cases the interview is no more than confirmation of a willingness to serve rather than an assessment of ability. Nevertheless, the interviews by a Departmental official and the unfettered power of appointment of the Department under review by the tribunals would seem open to criticism, even if bias only amounts, as has been alleged, to the confirmation of workpeople's representatives 'who can be counted on not to rock the boat too much'.[86] Such docile attitudes are in fact probably less due to the selection policy of the Department, but rather to the fact that names put forward by Local Trades Councils are generally not of full-time officials, particularly for Supplementary Benefit Appeal Tribunals; more usually they are senior, often retired members of branch and district committees who are not overworked with more immediate union business.

Panels for Local Appeal Tribunals generally consist of eight to twelve persons, and are reconstituted every three years. Generally the existing panel members continue to serve until they wish to resign. However, if a wingman fails to attend when summoned on three successive occasions, without giving a reasonable explanation to the clerk, he will be pointedly asked if he wishes to continue on the panel.[87] The workpeople panel for Supplementary Benefit Appeal Tribunals normally consists of four to six members, and there are usually two or three 'Minister's members' assigned to each tribunal; these wingmen are also re-appointed at three yearly intervals.[88] Nominations for the Local Appeal Tribunal panel representing employers and the self-employed generally come through the local Chamber of Commerce, in much the same way as nominations for the workpeople panel come from the local Trades Council. The use of the word 'employer' is perhaps inappropriate, as this panel is normally made up of middle-range executives, and in particular personnel managers. However, in relation to this panel and also to the nomination of 'Minister's members' for the Supplementary Benefit Appeal Tribunal, a wide and amorphous collection of organizations and persons are also invited to submit names. These sources are contained in a list of approved organizations compiled by the National Insurance Advisory Committee, and nominations are generally gleaned from individuals in groups such as Citizens Advice Bureaux, voluntary social service organizations, businessmen's groups, sporting clubs, churches, and local D.H.S.S. offices; quite often people seem to suggest themselves. When approaches were made to Local Advisory Committees before 1971, this mechanism of self-suggestion was standard practice. A small survey of members of Supplementary Benefit Appeal Tribunals by the Birmingham Institute of Judicial Administration also showed a similar process to operate among Trades Council officials.[89] The names of potential appointees are sent from the local to Departmental Headquarters via a selection process at the regional office; from conversation with regional officials it would seem that very few names are rejected, largely because of lack of numbers, although possibly some are 'mislaid'. Particular care, however, is taken not to antagonize the Trades Councils over their recommendations; one Insurance Officer stated that this would be to 'stir up a hornet's nest'. The policy of the old National Assistance Board was to search for 'men and women of standing in the area of the tribunal who have, for example, administrative experience in local government (whether as elected representatives or as officials) or in the running of important voluntary organisations, or who have experience as justices of the peace, or are clergymen'.[90] Indeed, little change seems to have taken place in this recruitment policy since the 1930s, when appointments for U.A.B. tribunal members were sought from 'responsible persons and bodies both official and otherwise who might be expected to have trustworthy knowledge of suitable persons'.[91] Originally, the 1911 structure had set up a system of voting in wards for insured workers to select their own representatives on the Courts of Referees, in an attempt to gain fair representation of differing trades and local areas.[92] However, this democratic but ungainly procedure was discontinued when the insurance scheme grew rapidly in the period following the First World War, and the workmen's representatives were appointed by the Board of Trade after consultation in the same manner as the employers' representatives had been selected.

One advantage with Local Appeal Tribunals, and to a certain extent with Industrial Tribunals, has been that there are recognizably 'two sides' of industry who can be approached for appointments. A balance of competing interest groups is therefore possible, but with Supplementary Benefit Appeal Tribunals such lines are more difficult to draw and, although the present system includes a working class representative, in practice he may by no means represent the interests of claimants; in fact workpeople's representatives are on occasion extremely harsh in their judgements of those from the same background; a number of commentators have detected here a notable differentiation between 'working class respectables' and others whom this group regards as 'working class roughs'. The *Supplementary Benefits Handbook* states that Minister's members are appointed 'as persons with knowledge of the problems encountered by claimants'.[93] But this can only mean in an empathetic sense, as they are clearly unrepresentative of the strata of society from which the majority of appellants come; Ruth Lister found in her study of London Supplementary Benefit Appeal Tribunals that some Minister's members came from welfare advisory jobs, but many seemed to be virtually identical to employers' representatives on Local Appeal Tribunals in that 'a good proportion were in personnel and managerial posts'. She adds that 'it is debatable how far such positions give their holders an awareness of the problems faced by the poor'.[94] Similar problems of course exist elsewhere in the administrative and judicial structure. For example, the Royal Commission on Justices of the Peace in 1948 found that at that time only 15 per cent were wage or salary earners of any kind.[95] With formal workpeople's representatives on both Local Appeal Tribunals and Supplementary Benefit Appeal Tribunals, the proportion of wage earners to other groups such as the retired, or landed gentry, has never been as low; but the same kind of problems exist in that both petty sessions and tribunals generally sit in the morning and few manual, skilled or clerical workers can take time off without proper remuneration.

In relation to tribunal chairmen, active party affiliation is a standard bar to appointment, but in keeping with the 'balance' concept members of Local Appeal Tribunals are often highly active in local party politics and public affairs. Trade union branch and district committee members, who form the bulk of the workpeople's panels, are in the nature of things prominent in Constituency Labour Parties, and likewise employers' representatives in the Local Appeal Tribunals are frequently to be found making political statements in the local press in other capacities. With Minister's members in Supplementary Benefit Appeal Tribunals, this public espousal of political beliefs is rare but not unknown; 25 per cent of the lay membership of Supplementary Benefit Appeal Tribunals in one regional study claimed active participation in a political organization, but such a subjective term on a self-reporting questionnaire is of course very imprecise.[96] One region included was Wales, where in most constituences Labour allegiance is strong but active participation tends to be restricted to rather few individuals, while many Conservative voters and indeed some Conservative Association officeholders like to regard themselves as apolitical. Some of those surveyed wanted more 'working class members' and 'poor people', but a large number, particularly Conservative voters, 'deprecated the appointment of what they saw as "politically-minded persons" to the lay ranks'.[97] Professor Bell in her study of Local Appeal Tribunals in the Northern Region found that other tribunal members sometimes accused workpeople's representatives of having a pro-appellant bias. However, this was not generally borne out by observation of the hearings, although workpeople's representatives claimed to see themselves as more sympathetic to appellants than other tribunal members.[98] It is suggested that, provided 'political' interest in its widest sense does not spill over to intrude as bias in tribunal adjudication, participation in local political and civic affairs is desirable as keeping tribunal members who are actively aware of questions of social and public concern. However, again it is crucial that some form of adequate training provide all tribunal members with some simple rules of judicial conduct enabling them to act as impartial adjudicators.

Unlike chairmen, the other tribunal members are not paid fees but are reimbursed their travelling expenses and any direct loss of earnings.[99] In general, it seems that the latter sum is not claimed by many wingmen, although there is a considerable difference here between the practice of trade unionists and other wingmen. Some more enlightened employers give a 'public service' time allocation for justices and tribunal members in the same way as they normally allow local government representatives to attend day-time Council meetings, although this is by no means general practice. One reason for the high proportion of lower-echelon but full-time trade union officials on Local Appeal Tribunals is that their unions regard their services as in the widest sense a part of their duties and in effect subsidize the system. In any case, many wingmen are over retirement age, and seem often more than willing to serve for no remuneration at all. At times in fact it seems that retired people are becoming 'a part-time judiciary' in many forms of tribunals[100]. In 1972, the total cost of fees to Local Appeal Tribunal chairmen was £72,400, and expenses paid to tribunal members, including chairmen, totalled £12,000. The accounts of Supplementary Benefit Appeal Tribunals did not separately identify members' expenses, but the figure given for total expenditure on fees and expenses was £54,025.[101] In comparison with the costs of a fully judicialized system, these are remarkably low figures and remain a strong argument for retaining the present largely lay system.

Training of tribunal members, as we have seen, is non-existent, apart from the preliminary talk with the local D.H.S.S. manager and the receipt of a skimpy departmental explanatory leaflet by Local Appeal Tribunal members only. Ironically, the original U.A.B. Appeal Tribunal members were given the instructions for U.A.B. officers on the exercise of discretionary powers; these were made public in a White Paper for their benefit, but were presumably also available to anyone who wished to purchase a copy.[102] The absence of a legally qualified chairman in Supplementary Benefit Appeal Tribunals means that the lack of any form of training for other tribunal members in this body of final jurisdiction is a serious defect. In Ruth Lister's study of London Supplementary Benefit members, respondents gave as their justification for not consulting the Supplementary Benefit Act, which governs their adjudicatory powers, that 'it was not really necessary as the chairman usually knew it and the clerk and presenting officer were there to advise them if a legal point came up'.[103] The incongruity of such dependence on Departmental officials in a supposedly 'independent' tribunal is self-evident, and it is furthermore clear from observation that few Supplementary Benefit tribunal members, including many chairmen, grasp the crucial distinction between what is law and what is merely departmental policy. Ruth Lister states that in her interviews with tribunal members 'some still did not understand even after it had been explained to them'.[104]

As with chairmen, knowledge of the applicable law is by no means the sole requirement of tribunal members; they must also assist in the conduct of business in an informal but fair and courteous manner. Unfortunately, through partial knowledge of how judicial officers in courts behave, some wingmen feel the need to behave on occasions with the formality they mistakenly imagine Lord Justices of Appeal to utilize.

One of the most notable distinctions between the British and other systems of administrative law is the amount of lay participation in the tribunal process. In the United States, for example, lawyers sitting alone decide most administrative disputes, and in particular the 'fair hearing' procedures in relation to termination or disqualification from welfare benefits. These 'examiners' are usually also employees of the agency under review, which leads many commentators to the view that this supposed appeal channel for the remedy of grievances 'starts with the administrative agency and, for all practical purposes, ends there [although] it is patterned after the judicial, adversary remedy'.[105] Certainly lay participation in the form of a jury, a lay magistracy or lay wingmen can give a certain assurance to an appellant or defendant that he is being judged by his peers. Such a view has of course long been a part of British constitutional practice in the criminal courts, and the extension of the principle to administrative justice is viewed with envy by a number of commentators in other countries who regard their own systems as 'over-judicialised'.[106]

At the least, lay participation means a considerable economic saving on highly-priced judicial manpower when the sums involved may be relatively small, although often very important to appellants in marginal terms. When so many people are willing to give their services virtually free—a factor which is absent in many other countries—then any assurance lay participation can give to appellants is eminently worthwhile conserving and upgrading. With recent trends towards earlier retirement, it can also provide opportunities for public service to those well qualified to serve, provided there is some control on upper age limits and care is taken to recruit younger members so as to balance tribunals in terms of age. Professor Bell's study of the Northern and Scottish Supplementary Benefit tribunals found that members were predominantly above 44 years, whereas 68 per cent of appellants were below that age.[107] Unfortunately, untrained wingmen, who sit mute because of lack of knowledge of their powers on the applicable law and whose few questions are only directed at categorizing claimants into stereotypes, are of little use. In Professor Bell's study two-thirds of Supplementary Benefit appellants interviewed felt that their hearing was fair, although 'sadly, they frequently had not even been able to identify the workpeople's representative and generally felt that the tribunal was remote from their world'.[108] This may, however, be just another manifestation of an often ill-justified high level of contentment or at least resignation among claimants. There is too the possibility, always the bane of such surveys, that appellants, feeling the need 'to play it safe' with information that could conceivably hurt their future eligibility, merely shrug their shoulders and say a wary 'OK'.

The author's study of a smaller sample of consecutive appellants, which was clearly unofficial and unconnected with the S.B.C., had an entirely different response. Only one appellant out of fifty responded favourably to a similar question—the appeal in his case had been allowed—and negative comments alleging bias and prejudice were common. A typical response was, 'they weren't listening. They had made up their minds before the case.' Another comment was, 'they were all far too old, I didn't like the look of them, they made me feel begging, made me feel bad'.[109] Similar reactions were found in a Nuffield study of tribunal appellants.[110] In Professor Bell's study this hostility did not seem to be apparent, but there was an expression of sadness with the lay members who it was felt had not played their full part in the proceedings.[111]

In recent years the use of lay participation in judicial dispute settlements has been tried with success in terms of adjudication in the now abandoned Industrial Relations Court, and with conspicuous success in the Restrictive Practices Court, where three High Court judges sit with two industrialists, an accountant and a trade union official.[112] Lay assessors also sit in Admiralty and Commercial Court sessions. In these cases, the lay court members normally bring to bear on the decision a specialist viewpoint, and as with many tribunals the lawyer chairman or judge is present to advise them of legal points. However, it is suggested that, as was the case with lay magistrates, it is essential to introduce compulsory training for all lay tribunal members, particularly in relation to social security tribunals, in an effort to help them deal with issues in a knowledgeable and judicial manner. Over-judicialization and the avoidance of petty legalism at the local appeal level can certainly be avoided by continuing to appoint lay wingmen, but to achieve the full benefit of their participation this should be coupled with sufficient training to ensure effective adjudication. Lack of training leads easily to disorder and a kind of narrowness and rigidity of thought, which is a far more troublesome vice than court room formality.

Although so far only a few local studies have been done on the composition of tribunal panels, it is abundantly clear from observation that, in the words of the first Child Poverty Action Group *Poverty* pamphlet, 'members are generally of late middle-age or retired. In terms of legal expertise and representativeness of the population they leave something to be desired.'[113] And although the 1965 National Insurance Act stated that 'in any case in which the claimant is a woman at least one of the members of the tribunal, if practicable, shall be a woman',[114] women are very much under-represented. This is one facet of tribunal membership that the Council on Tribunals is presently investigating, following a 1971 questionnaire sent to Departments.[115] Ruth Lister's study of fifty-five London Supplementary Benefit Appeal Tribunal members out of a total of 214, showed how clear the under-representation of women as well as that in the younger age groups is; for example, none of the chairmen and only one of the workpeople's representatives in her sample was a woman.[116] This figure, however, varies regionally and was possibly under-represented in the London study because of sampling error due to refusals of interview, as, nationally in 1973, 18.4 per cent of Supplementary Benefit chairmen were women and 21.8 per cent of those on the Supplementary Benefit panels were women. A slightly higher 27.7 per cent of those on the Local Appeal Tribunals were women, although as mentioned there were only six women chairmen in the whole country for Local Appeal Tribunals.[117] Few coloured people—only one in Ruth Lister's study—seem to be on the panels, although no precise figures are obtainable.

In general there seems to be a considerable overlap of tribunal members on different types of tribunal and also on a wide variety of public bodies: Professor Bell terms this phenomenon a 'local squire-archy'.[118] One study of Supplementary Benefit and Rent Tribunal members in the Midlands and Welsh regions showed that 12 per cent of Supplementary Benefit members had experience on other tribunals —about half of this was in relation to Local Appeal Tribunals. One-third of the Supplementary Benefit members surveyed were also on advisory committees such as police authorities and tourist boards. Twenty-five per cent of Supplementary Benefit Minister's members were magistrates, 18 per cent were councillors and 12 per cent were on hospital committees.[119] In terms of academic attainment, it is perhaps illogical to include workpeople's representatives with other tribunal members to make a general statement, as many of them had no great educational opportunities; although academic attainment does not always of course equal intellectual calibre, it is unfortunately true that, apart from some shining exceptions, the intellectual acuity of many tribunal wingmen is not high. This is partly because those with outstanding abilities are quickly brought on to other more prestigious bodies or are retained on union or managerial work of more immediate importance. However, despite this it is clear that recruitment is failing to attract many of the most able people in the community, particularly in Supplementary Benefit adjudication; additionally, in the last few years, a number of people in the community have gained considerable expertise in social security matters, but as yet few are being asked to join tribunal panels. With considerable overlap of tribunal membership it is interesting to find that a survey of Mental Health and Rent Tribunals, both generally regarded as high in status, nevertheless found 'relatively few lay members with low or medium level qualifications'.[120] Whatever the nature of qualifications, however, it is readily apparent to anyone attending tribunals that wingmen in Supplementary Benefit Appeal Tribunals rarely ask pertinent questions, and in Local Appeal Tribunals only intervene cogently when they have direct knowledge of an industrial situation. Lay participation in tribunal adjudication has been an excellent British invention. But to ensure its most effective utilization, adequate training by an independent source must be given to all tribunal members before and during the performance of their duties, and there should also be a thorough review of the whole procedure of the nomination and appointment of tribunal members.

The Clerk

The role of the clerk in social security tribunal proceedings has long been a controversial one, and concern about his impartiality and intrusion into tribunal adjudication has been expressed on numerous occasions. The Franks Committee stated categorically that 'the duties of a clerk should be confined to secretarial work, the taking of notes of evidence, and advice on the tribunal's functions. Unless sent for to advise he should be debarred from retiring with the tribunal'.[121] However, this standard is not generally adhered to in social security tribunals, and indeed the recommendation that clerks be debarred from retiring with the tribunals seems to be universally ignored. Most tribunals do not in fact retire in a literal sense (as do magistrates), but send the appellant, Presenting Officer and any members of the public out of the tribunal room when considering their decision. The regulations at present are somewhat ambiguous in Supplementary Benefit Appeal Tribunals in that it is stated that the clerk should be present at all sittings, but also that a tribunal 'may order any person to withdraw'.[122] The invariable practice is for everyone but the clerk to be asked to leave, even until recently visiting members of the Council on Tribunals. In Local Appeal Tribunals, too, clerks remain in the room, although often walking in and out on various errands, but their role is more easily perceived as secretarial. The Council on Tribunals reported in 1964 that the Lord Chancellor proposed to seek their advice on the question of retirement,[123] but the issue has as yet not been resolved. In comparison with tribunal experience, it should be noted that the Lord Chief Justice in 1952 put forcibly the view that in relation to magistrates,

> if the Clerk retires with the justices, the inevitable conclusion that people will form is that he may influence the justices or may take some course which it is for the justices alone to take. Justices can always send for the Clerk if they require advice on a point of law . . . but it is not desirable, and it is irregular, for a Clerk to retire with justices as a matter of course.[124]

There is undoubtedly a real difference between the practice of Local Appeal Tribunals and Supplementary Benefit Appeal Tribunals on this point. Where the chairman is a qualified lawyer, as in Local Appeal Tribunals, the Franks position of a clerk purely confined to paperwork, calling appellants and witnesses and making tea for the tribunal members, is generally adhered to. It is normally the case that Local Appeal Tribunal clerks are women whose demeanour shows them to be of secretarial status, whereas Supplementary Benefit clerks are generally men who act and are treated as if they have the same status as tribunal members. In Supplementary Benefit practice, the clerk may often be the expert to whom the chairman turns for information and advice. In five studies involving observation of Supplementary Benefit hearings, this was seen to be standard practice, although varying considerably with the qualities of the chairman and the personal qualities of the clerk.[125]

Observation of Supplementary Benefit Appeal Tribunals has only been allowed officially since July 1971; it is still circumscribed by administrative and procedural obstacles, and by the normal practice of asking observers to leave the room when there is a deliberation on a case where the appellant has been physically present or represented at the hearing.[126] Professor Herman, who during his study (before the 1971 regulations were changed) was allowed to remain in the tribunal room while decisions were made, states that 'clerks frequently interpret Commission policies to tribunal members when this seems to them to be useful'.[127] And in a Scottish study, the clerk intervened on his own initiative only in two out of sixty-six Supplementary Benefit cases observed, 'but these two cases were serious violations of the principle of fairness'.[128] In fact, the incidence of intervention by the clerk is, according to tribunal members, far higher when the appellant (and observers) are out of the room, possibly because there is a hesitancy by clerks to give open advice, but also because cases where the appellant has put in an appearance can engender prolonged debates among tribunal members, in which the clerk may intervene to, at the least, keep the tribunal on schedule. In Local Appeal Tribunals this kind of activity is rare, but even here there are unfortunate lapses, and the 'appearance' factor of a clerk remaining behind when the tribunal confers is crucial to the attitude of appellants towards the impartiality of the tribunal.[129] In the N.A.B. evidence to the Franks Committee, the Secretary of the Board admitted that he 'would not put it past [a Clerk] to speak if he is not asked',[130] but it is clear that this was a considerable understatement, in that in Supplementary Benefit Tribunals it is still 'common practice for him to point out reasons why the tribunal could not make a decision they might be contemplating'.[131] The former Director of Check!, an advice agency in Liverpool, reports that a barrister appearing for a client whose case fell directly under the *Simper* ruling by the Divisional Court, was met with the clerk 'waving the 1966 Act in the air [saying] "We go by the *law* here" '. Despite a brief lecture to the tribunal on the role of statute and common law, the appeal was disallowed.[132]

Even more questionable is the existing practice of the Supplementary Benefits clerk to write out the Record of Proceedings and the reasons for decisions. The procedure with the better Supplementary Benefit chairmen and all Local Appeal Tribunal chairmen is for the chairman himself to write out the decision and the reasons for it in longhand and then for the clerk to type this up and post copies to the parties concerned. One chairman of Industrial Tribunals has apparently gone a step further in excluding the clerk from the room during deliberations, and using a dictaphone to record decisions and reasons, whose tape can be transcribed later, not necessarily by the clerk.[133] The dangers of interference are clear, and it is disturbing to find in Professor Bell's study that, with weak Supplementary Benefit Appeal Tribunal members, the clerk has to 'press' for clearer reasons for the Record, or when he feels reasons are 'woolly' he articulates them himself, or occasionally clerks have 'found' reasons for what the tribunal wanted to do.[134]

One factor creating the difference between practice in the two types of tribunal is that Local Appeal Tribunal clerks are generally seconded from among Clerical Officers at a local office in a neighbouring town or district for relatively short periods, whereas Supplementary Benefit clerks are normally of Executive Officer rank and for a period of several years are full-time clerks travelling a weekly circuit of tribunals and therefore building up considerable expertise. Where needed, part-time or temporary clerks are used, who are normally assigned to general duties at Regional Headquarters. Often they will be mainly concerned with aiding the travelling clerk in the preparation of case lists and hearings, and so are not totally unfamiliar with tribunal work. However, Professor Bell's study found them much more inclined to be sympathetic to the S.B.C.'s point of view, and she urges that temporary clerks 'only be used when completely unavoidable circumstances make this necessary'.[135] It must also be stated that the legacy of the U.A.B. clerks, who were senior Board officials achieving a dominant position in relation to the tribunals, still lingers.[136] It is from this period that the practice of the clerk being present when tribunals conferred originated—indeed, this was specifically laid down in the U.A.B. regulations.[137] Incredible as it may seem, the U.A.B. clerk was sometimes the officer who had made the original adverse decision on the appellant's benefit claim.[138] Tony Lynes has discovered the Board's instructions to clerks, which state that the rules were 'designed to give to the Clerk a special standing and it is hoped that the Chairman and the Tribunal will look to him for guidance in consistent practice and in the avoidance of arbitrary findings unrelated to the broad practice of Tribunals . . . should be in a specially favourable position to give counsel and advice where they are needed'.[139] Further research by Tony Lynes in the Public Records Office has revealed that when the Manchester U.A.B. Appeal Tribunal ruled adversely to the Board on the question of onus of proof in a 'constructive household' case,[140] the manager of the office attended a session before the hearing of two similar cases and successfully lectured the tribunal to reach a contrary decision. A clerk similarly intervened in a Liverpool 'constructive household' case, but other tribunals were not always as compliant, as can be seen from U.A.B. correspondence.[141] Intervention by a senior member of the Department under review is unfortunately not entirely a matter of historical interest; the Council on Tribunals Report for 1970 disclosed a 'rare case' where a member of the D.H.S.S. legal staff had acted as *amicus curiae* in a Supplementary Benefit Appeal Tribunal.[142]

Before 1930, similar criticisms had been levelled at the Ministry of Labour in respect of senior officers appointed to act as clerks or 'appeals officers' to the Courts of Referees; this represented a change from the previous allocation in the 1911 structure of low-level officials from the Divisional Office, and seems to have been brought about by the surge of appeals in the 1920s, resulting in a policy to cut them back by using the clerk to influence decision-making. However, when the Morris Committee in 1929 found that these officers 'not infrequently participate . . . and in some cases question claimants . . . [and] that in some cases, after the claimant had withdrawn, the appeals officers remained whilst the Court were discussing their decision',[143] the Ministry of Labour voluntarily gave up the practice and undertook to appoint only junior officers as clerks with their duties confined to paperwork.

The Franks Committee rejected the proposal for a central corps of clerks to service all tribunals under the supervision of the Lord Chancellor, largely on the grounds of career prospects.[144] They also stated that it would be difficult to keep the clerks fully occupied, and that it would mean the end of training for D.H.S.S. staff who were seconded for a period to gain experience of tribunal work; this, according to the Committee was 'doubtless valuable in developing the outlook appropriate to the administration of a social service'.[145] One may perhaps wonder whether it is valuable in developing an outlook appropriate to the administration of justice. The other reasons, it is suggested, are also somewhat unconvincing, when it is noted that Supplementary Benefit clerks often remain in their positions for several years, and that since 1957 there has been a 'boom' in tribunal work, in particular the new polyglot jurisdiction of the Industrial Tribunals created in 1964. One estimate is that the number of clerks in the principal tribunals is now upward of 1,200, with at least 350 operating in the social security tribunals alone.[146] Allowing for pluralism between tribunals, an independent body of full-time tribunal clerks would seem now to be a feasible proposal worth implementing. Certainly an independent body of clerks, divorced from the Departments whose work the tribunal examines, would do much to promote an impression of impartiality. Clerks are at present quite naturally concerned with the furtherance of their own Department's policy as full-time employees, and it is simply not sufficient for them to be told 'to dissociate themselves from their former roles while they are fulfilling these special assignments'.[147] The D.H.S.S., in response to criticism, and after pressure from the

Council on Tribunals, has now specifically instructed clerks not to take an active part in tribunal proceedings, but to divert tactfully any questions from the tribunal members to the Presenting Officer from the S.B.C.

Also, since the instructions were issued in 1971, Supplementary Benefit clerks are no longer of Higher Executive Officer rank, but of Executive Officer rank; this reform, however, has its counter-productive nature as, although a senior officer of the agency as an 'impartial' clerk was clearly inadvisable, the Presenting Officer at the tribunal is usually of Higher Executive Officer rank, and an Executive Officer clerk can naturally be expected to defer to his opinions or at least reinforce them. The solution must surely be to adopt the Local Appeal Tribunal approach, and have a Clerical Officer as clerk, whose work is confined to the routine administration connected with the tribunal. In Professor Bell's study, Northern Region Supplementary Benefit chairmen who had served before the 1971 changes were asked if they had detected any change in the role of the clerks: none had.[148]

Professor Calvert has recently advanced the creation of a new career structure for social security adjudication, where promotion would be made through a series of specific tasks, such as adviser and clerk to tribunal chairman and eventually to Commissioner.[149] While it may be cynical to point out that such a hierarchical structure invites the onset of the 'Peter Principle' where everyone will eventually be promoted to operate at the level of their incompetence, it is suggested that clerks should never be placed in a situation where their performance will be judged for promotion. Based on observation of the two existing tribunal structures, it would seem preferable to have a clerk in the role of performing routine clerical duties under a strong tribunal, as is theoretically the case with Local Appeal Tribunals, rather than attempt a 'magistrates' clerk' approach as with the Supplementary Benefit Appeal Tribunals. As well as problems with a clerk in the promotional structure, and subordinate to advisers and chairmen whose recommendations would presumably count towards his promotion, it would also seem much more desirable to have advocates and advisers totally divorced in career terms from a system they would be challenging. And although Professor Calvert rightly criticises the rigidity of some members of the legal profession, he surely underestimates the rigidity of the near-watertight promotional bureaucracy which he wishes to create.

One difficulty which is sometimes not appreciated is the power of influence which the clerk may exercise on tribunal members in informal discussion prior to the hearing of a case. The author, sitting as an observer in one Local Appeal Tribunal, heard a clerk tell the members of a case due to be heard later that morning, in which 'the claimant has such a vile temper that *they* have stopped him coming and are going to send his wife instead . . . he nearly caused a fight at the office . . . he is up to no good anyway'. In this incident, no attempt was made by the chairman (a barrister) to stop the outburst, although no doubt he would have done so if it had occurred during the hearing. This again underlines the need for effective control on the part of the chairman; Professor Street, himself a Local Appeal Tribunal chairman, has questioned the belief that there are any 'indiscretions' on the part of Local Appeal Tribunal clerks, stating that he has 'never met one who made the least attempt to interfere either during the hearing or when the tribunal has been deliberating'.[150] Such a statement, it is suggested, is more of a compliment to Professor Street's powers of chairmanship than to Local Appeal Tribunal clerks, and also illustrates the difficulty of relying on evidence from those who are themselves active participants in the tribunal process; every tribunal advocate or member has his stock of 'battle stories', but only when there has been a great deal more academic observation than has been done at present will a full evaluation be possible.

A further power which can be a potential source of abuse is that which the clerk has in selecting tribunal members for a hearing, although most clerks rotate through the list of panels. In fact the Social Security Act, covering the Local Appeal Tribunals, states that 'so far as practicable, each member of a panel shall be summoned in turn to serve upon a local tribunal'.[151] Some Trades Council representatives complain that they only rarely serve, because they are known to be 'militant', and one Local Appeal Tribunal clerk admitted to the author that certain members are not put on together because 'they don't mix too well'. Generally in Supplementary Benefit Appeal Tribunals, Minister's members seem to sit about eight to twelve times a year, chairmen twelve to eighteen times, and workpeople's representatives five to eight times. This varies of course with the local caseload, and in major urban areas it is apparently possible for some members to sit as many as seventy times a year.[152] A small study in the Merseyside area showed that a workpeople's representative considered by the Local Trades Council to be subservient to the views of the S.B.C. was asked to sit much more frequently than other panel members, and in Ruth Lister's study one workpeople's representative stated that a Communist Party wingman had been asked to sit only once in three years.[153]

Many clerks of course perform their duties impeccably, but standards vary considerably, and it would be helpful both for clerks and for appellants if the position were regularized, and some form of adequate training introduced. The situation at present in Supplementary Benefit Appeal Tribunals is a disgrace. Because chairmen have no legal qualifications, the clerk is looked to for expertise on how the Supplementary Benefit Act should be interpreted, and yet he himself has no legal qualifications and his only experience of how the law works is entirely through his work in the administration of the agency under review. Further instructions to clerks on how to perform their duties may be helpful, but it is only a partial answer while the Supplementary Benefit Appeal Tribunal structure remains weak and members are incapable of decision-making on the basis of their own expertise.

The Presenting Officer

The Presenting Officer is the representative of the administrative agency under review at the tribunal hearings. As with the position of the clerk, there is considerable difference between practice in the Local Appeal and Supplementary Benefit Tribunals. In Local Appeal Tribunals, the representative is sometimes the local Insurance Officer who adjudicated on the case papers when the claim was first made. This somewhat ambivalent position of combining both initial administrative decision-maker and then Presenting Officer at the appeal tribunal seems nonetheless to work well in practice; however, with increasing numbers the Insurance Officer at the tribunal in urban areas is likely to be a specialist in tribunal work. This system of initial administrative adjudication certainly prevents tribunal overload which earlier occurred when all disqualification cases went automatically to the Court of Referees.[154] No oral hearing is made at the Insurance Officer stage, although a request for interview by the claimant is sometimes granted to help 'sort out things'. A 'dissatisfaction procedure' of a more formal nature exists where an Insurance Officer decides on a topic defined as a Minister's Question on which there is an exact precedent; notice of the precedent is given to the claimant, and only when a claimant remains dissatisfied 'after any appropriate investigations and explanations have been made' is the decision treated as adverse to the claimant and he is notified of his right to appeal to a Local Appeal Tribunal. Where there is a contribution or other Minister's Question not covered by a precedent, then there is immediate notification of a right to apply for a determination by the Secretary of State.[155] Insurance Officers and Local Appeal Tribunals can make use of a special device, local referees, drawn from the tribunal panels and resident in the neighbourhood, to investigate and report on questions of fact; however, this approach is rarely used in relation to unemployment benefits, although in relation to industrial injury benefits such reports are frequently crucial.[156]

As a general rule, there is discouragement by the National Insurance Commissioners of personal contact or discussion between Insurance

Officers and claimants, so that the initial administrative judgement is limited to questions of fact ascertainable 'on the papers' rather than based on the appearance, degree of articulateness or background of the claimant.[157] This posture is aided by guidelines to other departmental officers such as counter clerks that all claims should be posted, or channelled through them to the Insurance Officer, and that claimants should be politely directed away from seeking an interview with the Insurance Officer. In fact 'difficult' cases are occasionally discussed with the Insurance Officer, more so in relation to sickness and industrial injury benefits than with unemployment benefits, although there is a reasonable amount of insulation of the Insurance Officer from judgement on other matters than the facts and the law; unfortunately, occasional pieces of gossip via the departmental grapevine affect the Insurance Officer's attitude towards appellants at the tribunal, but short of quarantine this is bound to occur. Dr. Farmer criticizes this 'façade of independence' as being of doubtful value at any point in the administrative process,[158] but even if only of psychological importance it would seem useful to retain it if, as it probably does, it helps Insurance Officers to adopt a 'judicial mind' when deciding claims.

An attempt was made by the D.H.S.S. in the National Superannuation and Social Insurance Bill, which lapsed with the 1970 election, to write in a general 'dissatisfaction procedure' for all claims handled by Insurance Officers, but this idea has not yet been revived. Informally, something akin to a 'dissatisfaction procedure' is often utilized, but it is questionable whether it should be expressly written into pre-tribunal procedure. Dr. Farmer believes it can be a useful means of preventing tribunal overload,[159] but this is not a particular problem at the moment, and the potential for abuse which would exist if the procedure were adopted formally must give rise to a certain anxiety. An unrepresented and unadvised claimant is no negotiating match for an experienced civil servant, however pleasant, who is armed with knowledge of the statute law and the relevant commissioner's decisions. If the 'dissatisfaction procedure' veers towards the Insurance Officer saying discouragingly, 'appeal if you want, but you'll lose anyway and just waste your own time', then the appellant may be denied the basic right of his 'day in court'.[160] The Insurance Officer is a 'statutory official', usually of Executive Officer rank, and is appointed by the Secretary of State for Health and Social Services, subject to the consent of the Minister for the Civil Service as to numbers. In relation to unemployment benefits, the Insurance Officer is appointed with the concurrence of the Secretary of State for Employment.[161] In fact, the decisions as to personnel are made at local level by the managers of the local offices of the Department of Employment and the D.H.S.S. In conversation with managers it seems that on the employment side, the job of Insurance Officer is seen as fairly low priority in which mechanistic decisions can be taken on Commissioners' precedents. Once appointed, however, the independence of the Insurance Officer is strongly protected, and he is responsible solely to the Chief Insurance Officer in London whose independence is also guaranteed from departmental pressures. The chairman of the Local Appeal Tribunal is specifically instructed to ensure that 'the Insurance Officer does not act in the capacity of an advocate',[162] and this is a statement which is frequently repeated by the chairman of Local Appeal Tribunals to put appellants at their ease at the start of the hearing.

In the Supplementary Benefit Appeal Tribunal, the Presenting Officer is normally of more senior rank, usually a Higher Executive Officer or Assistant Manager at least. One D.H.S.S. official known to the author moved with promotion from being an Insurance Officer presenting sickness benefit cases on behalf of the S.B.C. to the Supplementary Benefit Appeal Tribunal in the same town.[163] Furthermore, in departmental terms the Presenting Officer in the Supplementary Benefit Appeal Tribunal is normally senior to the clerk, which has led to some conjecture that the clerk would be unlikely to uphold certain points of fair procedure against a contrary view put forward by a Presenting Officer. The Supplementary Benefits Presenting Officer has generally little prior knowledge of the case before he is asked to defend the S.B.C.'s decision at the tribunal; this is particularly true when presentation is administered, as it is in large metropolitan areas, on a regional basis. Professor Bell states that the Presenting Officer is 'a specialist officer engaged full-time in this work';[164] this may be so in some urban localities, but elsewhere tribunal presentation is rarely the sole duty of the Presenting Officer who often seems ill-prepared on the tribunal cases because of other office commitments.

The administrative review of appeals by S.B.C. officers has the same advantages as on the insurance side, but unfortunately there have been many allegations that a 'dissatisfaction procedure' is used here to thwart a successful appeal.[165] Certainly this was true of practice under the U.A.B., where it was required policy to interview an appellant when an appeal had been lodged. Tony Lynes quotes one U.A.B. official who stated that there was little doubt that this process had 'the effect of stifling appeals'.[166]

By observation it becomes clear that S.B.C. Presenting Officers generally view their role as adversary; the difference between the two tribunals can perhaps be characterized by saying that in general the S.B.C. Presenting Officer sees his role as an advocate for a disallowance of the appeal, whereas the Insurance Officer acts as *amicus curiae*, assisting the tribunal with questions of fact and bringing National

Insurance Commissioners' decisions to the notice of the chairman.[167] One startling discovery in Ruth Lister's study of London Supplementary Benefit Appeal Tribunal members was that they considered it a positive advantage for the Presenting Officer to be more knowledgeable of tribunal procedure and the law 'because the tribunal relied on him for information and guidance; they found him very kind and helpful'.[168] This reliance for impartial advice on a partisan member of the agency under review is of course yet another illustration of slipshod adjudication. In fact, under S.B.C. guidelines, the Presenting Officer is supposed to be an 'unbiassed presenter of all the facts, both favourable and unfavourable to the appellant', but as Professor Bell has pointed out, in the present state of Supplementary Benefit adjudication, this is an unrealistic expectation except in rare circumstances.[169]

However, as with the role of clerks, much depends on the individual personality of the Presenting Officer and also on the control which the chairman exercises over the procedure of the tribunal. One Local Appeal Tribunal chairman observed by the author stopped a hearing to warn an Insurance Officer about his conduct and, following the morning's session, instructed his clerk to send a written reprimand to the officer outlining his displeasure at the aggressive attitude displayed towards the appellant. The National Insurance Commissioners have also been critical of misbehaviour on occasions, including one cohabitation case where the Insurance Officer had indulged in 'undesirable cajolery, bluff and threats' outside the tribunal hearing.[170] Criticisms are frequently made of the aggressive behaviour of S.B.C. Presenting Officers towards appellants, although these are often in generalized form. Nevertheless, the inequality of the two 'sides' is summed up by the following comment from an early C.P.A.G. pamphlet before any research had been done in relation to Supplementary Benefits adjudication:

> The representative of the S.B.C. is invariably well-briefed and may refer to regulations to which the appellant does not have access. He is usually allowed to develop his argument uninterrupted by the appellant or tribunal members. The appellant, however, is by no means always allowed to present his (or her) case without considerable interruptions.[171]

Sometimes this sort of behaviour will clearly lead to a denial of justice, particularly if it impedes proper cross-examination of witnesses or detailed investigation of departmental evidence. The refusal of proper cross-examination will normally be grounds for judicial review, although this has not yet been directly tested in relation to social security tribunals.[172] Since 1946, Local Appeal Tribunal regulations have specifically stated that the appellant 'may call witnesses and shall be given an opportunity of putting questions directly to any witnesses called at the hearing'.[173] In contrast, the only right given to Supplementary Benefit appellants was, until 1971, to 'ask questions', although the position in Supplementary Benefit Appeal Tribunals has now been changed to conform, in theory, with Local Appeal Tribunals.[174]

Another frequent difficulty in Supplementary Benefit Appeal Tribunals is that Presenting Officers quote S.B.C. policy as though it were legally binding authority, failing to make clear the crucial distinction between law and mere departmental policy. Perhaps also symptomatic of the difference in role between Local Appeal Tribunals and Supplementary Benefit Appeal Tribunals is that, in Local Appeal Tribunals, the appellant is usually asked to speak first, followed by the Insurance Officer's comments on the case, whereas in Supplementary Benefit Appeal Tribunals the Presenting Officer frequently starts in a 'prosecutory' vein and then freely interrupts the appellant while he attempts to rebut statements. Most serious, however, and a topic which will be examined later, is the use by S.B.C. Presenting Officers of unsubstantiated evidence, even anonymous letters in some cases, without any intervention by the chairman. In fact, much of a Presenting Officer's case before the tribunal seems often to be carried out in contravention of the rules of Evidence, particularly hearsay from a visiting officer's report, and with no opportunity given to an appellant to cross-examine such officials. The same lax standards are also applied to the presentation of the appellant's case, although it is rare that the appellant brings witnesses or is even articulate enough to use hearsay testimony. A pre-war case, which may now be unsound, allowed hearsay evidence to be brought before a war pensions tribunal, but the court stated that this was mainly because it was in writing and was notified in advance to the appellant; it is unfortunately clear that little S.B.C. evidence put forward by Presenting Officers conforms even with this slender protection.[175] Although the legal exceptions to the hearsay rule are voluminous, so that hearsay may sometimes have probative value in the courts, a great deal more must be done to ensure even basis evidentiary rules in social security proceedings. However, it should be noted that failure to maintain the correct standards of impartial and fair presentation of the facts is as much the fault of weak chairmanship as it is of improper conduct by the Presenting Officer.

Although superiors frequently stress that Presenting Officers do not need to chalk up 'convictions', it is unfortunately true that individual officers sometimes act, and talk to observers, as if they were required to do so. Professor Herman points out that, in some circumstances, promotion may depend on winning appeals; he also states that office managers 'dislike losing appeals and the paperwork required to prepare a case for appeal and tend to try to anticipate tribunal actions when reviewing decisions following receipt of an appeal'.[176] Partly this results from inadequate training, but a great deal depends on the attitude of the Presenting Officer to his work. Although Insurance Officers are in effect defending their own decisions before the Local Appeal Tribunal, on the whole there is an acceptance of the tribunal's judgement and of a claimant's right to appeal in the first place, whereas in relation to Supplementary Benefit Appeal Tribunals one commentator states that 'it is notable that employees of the Commission see it as a hostile act to appeal against a determination'.[177]

Most Presenting Officers learn their work 'on the job', by accompanying their predecessors to some tribunal hearings. Given the poor calibre of many departmental employees, professional standards of advocacy are not to be expected. But much more could be done in providing Presenting Officers with proper knowledge of technique and the rules of evidence and fair procedure.[178] Here again a real difference can be detected between Local Appeal Tribunals and Supplementary Benefit Appeal Tribunals. All departmental officials are by nature bound, as Professor Robson has pointed out, 'to adopt a defensive attitude towards their own handiwork',[179] but the degree to which this is taken, and the extent to which it conflicts with the principles of Natural Justice, are the important questions to consider in this area. One consideration which does not seem to have received serious investigation is the attitude of departmental officials towards what they consider to be 'abuse', although it is clear that personal beliefs held by the Presenting Officer as to the character of the appellant are most important in determining the presentation of the case.[180] Over a period of time, certain key words come to be used in the Supplementary Benefit tribunals, almost as a kind of shorthand, and it becomes difficult even for observers to break from the stereotype suggested. Particularly important is the question of a claimant's 'prior record'. This is often referred to by Presenting Officers in their opening remarks, usually in a prejudicial manner, and has the immediate effect of categorizing the case for the tribunal into a stock social cliché. Examples from the author's observation study of fifty consecutive Supplementary Benefit hearings were comments such as:

> 'a long history of temporary employment'; 'a frequent visitor to the office'; 'spasmodically on benefit . . . more on than off'; 'very bad work record'; 'he has a long history'; 'he tramps the country looking for work'; 'a well-known appellant'; 'often down at the office'.

But beyond this questionable use of background departmental information is the more disquieting use of value-laden euphemisms, used as a kind of shorthand by the Presenting Officer. Examples in the same study were:

> 'she used to cohabit' (unrelated to the claim in question); 'a squatter at one time'; 'lives in a commune' (sharing a kitchen with others in the same building); 'a vegetarian' (perhaps relevant if the case had concerned a special diet allocation but, in the context, an additional label); 'Mrs. or Miss is it now?'; 'he owns a colour TV, and keeps a big dog too'; 'his so-called employer is well-known to us as being unco-operative'; 'she cohabits' (again irrelevant to the case under discussion); 'she has a complex family structure'; 'since had a child by another man'; 'numerous HP and other commitments'.

Clearly the dividing line on relevant and unrelated matters depends on the precise circumstances of the case—no one would suggest that a charge of cohabitation would be irrelevant in a cohabitation disqualification case—but in general the Presenting Officer seemed determined to smear the reputation of certain appellants; as one put it (in the later follow-up survey) 'he threw as much mud at me as possible'.[181] Often an observer can fairly well predict the outcome of a case when such phrases are used, and similarly the occasional 'deserving' case, where the Presenting Officer, in the same survey, used such phrases as 'hard worker all his life' and 'retired couple living in a thatched cottage'. However, most comments were derogatory, and in many instances could, with proper representation, have given immediate grounds for judicial review by the courts, and possibly grounds too for a defamation action.

Surprisingly, Professor Bell's study of Supplementary Benefit Appeal Tribunals in the Northern Region does not mention any instances of prejudicial comment; she also states specifically that there was no evidence of an overbearing manner on the part of the Presenting Officer, adding that 'the common style was rather low key—courteous and reasonable. We saw few examples of hostility towards appellants although there were one or two instances where a presenting officer found it difficult to suppress his feelings.'[182] One conceivable explanation of divergence between this and all other Supplementary Benefit hearing observations is that there does not seem to have been a lawyer involved in Professor Bell's study; possibly legally prejudicial commentary was thought merely to be part of 'advocacy'. As a matter of law, it has long been axiomatic that a party to an administrative hearing must have an adequate opportunity of knowing the case he has to meet, of answering it and of putting his own case in reply. Statements in the leading text are, it is suggested, impossible to square with much of the hearsay testimony and prejudicial comment put forward by Presenting Officers in Supplementary Benefit Appeal Tribunals; as Professor de Smith put it:

> If prejudicial allegations are to be made against [the appellant], he must normally . . . be given particulars of them before the hearing so that he can prepare his answers [and the] right to be heard must not be stultified by constant interruptions.[183]

One reason perhaps for the 'prosecutory' role being so much less pronounced among Insurance Officers is that, being an officer whose independence is guaranteed by legislation, he is less prone to pressure from colleagues. But perhaps more importantly, his relationship with the tribunal is such that the Insurance Officer frequently refers cases to it himself when the claimant has not made an appeal,[184] and it is not unusual for him to support an appeal, often in the light of further or more complete information, when it comes on for hearing. Similarly, cases are supported by the Chief Insurance Officer before the National Insurance Commissioners where a Local Insurance Officer has made a mistake.

A number of commentators have urged legal aid for tribunal appellants on the grounds of inequality between the parties, which can lead to a denial of justice; 'without representation tribunal proceedings do tend to become something of a battle between David and Goliath'.[185] Perhaps as important as knowledge of law on entitlement is the experience gained from repeated appearances before the tribunal which enables Presenting Officers to adjust their advocacy, in the manner of all good advocates, to the social situation and the personalities of the tribunal members. Evidence from low-level court and tribunal adjudication shows, however, that representation can be decisive; for example, a survey of magistrates proceedings, county courts and rent tribunals concluded that 'the dice are likely to be loaded in favour of the side that can hire a professional advocate'.[186] In Local Appeal Tribunals, and where there is a strong controlling chairman who conducts some form of inquisitorial proceedings, there is perhaps little chance of real abuse by the Presenting Officer in the absence of proper representation for the appellant. There are of course other reasons for advocating the extension of legal aid to tribunals.[187] However, as one National Insurance Commissioner pointed out to the author, if lawyers were to represent claimants on other than a sporadic basis, a strong argument could then be made out that Presenting Officers were unfairly matched. The imbalance which could arise is at present suggested by occasional adversary situations between a Presenting Officer and a legal advice agency advocate, trade union official or other person experienced in tribunal work.

A number of disturbing cases present themselves in Supplementary Benefits jurisdiction, and it is to be hoped that proper and effective standards will soon be enforced on all Presenting Officers, and the occasionally aberrant Insurance Officer in Local Appeal Tribunals. A clear delimitation of the role of such officers, backed up by training, would go a long way towards rebutting criticism. No one who has talked to Presenting Officers and Insurance Officers would wish to accuse them generally of malicious intentions—in fact, their lapses into bias are often seen by them as doing a good job within the unofficial and official guidelines and expectations of their Departments. It is the structure within which they operate that needs extensive change. As Professor Herman makes the point,

> The ambiguity surrounding the relationship of the tribunals and their personnel to the Department places great strain upon all persons within the system who are sincerely committed to make these tribunals into effective instruments of administrative justice.[188]

Throughout this chapter one theme has been readily apparent; tribunal adjudication at its best demands that tribunal participants are properly aware of their function and have the necessary training to fulfil it. Many of the modern criticisms which can be made of Local Appeal and Supplementary Benefit Appeal Tribunals have a depressingly familiar ring to them, and yet no one can now doubt the efficiency and beneficial effects of the tribunals in the British welfare system. Recent empirical work for the D.H.S.S. by Professor Bell shows what a number of commentators have long believed, that the Local Appeal Tribunals and Supplementary Benefit Appeal Tribunals have a wide range of similar problems and needs. Possibly there has been of late too much concentration on the defects of the Supplementary Benefit Appeal Tribunal system, and in particular on its personnel, which has tended to view Local Appeal Tribunals as embodiments of adjudicative perfection. Such an analysis is unhelpful if the tribunal structure of both systems is to be overhauled, upgraded and made more responsive to the needs of appellants. Lack of awareness through inadequate training is probably the major defect of most panel members and many chairmen of social security tribunals, and this applies also to clerks and presenting officers. Professor Bell has perhaps best made out the case for legally qualified Supplementary Benefit chairmen by showing that in her study legally unqualified chairmen were criticized both by her tribunal observers on technical grounds and also by appellants because of the unfavourable attitudes displayed when there was bad chairmanship.[189]

The commitment of many tribunal participants in the present structures towards goals of equity and sympathetic adjudication is unfortunately marred by a general lack of knowledge of the basic tenets of justice, and by some clearly unsuitable participants in the tribunal process. It would be to the benefit of these dedicated tribunal members and departmental officers, and to appellants and the wider community, if structural and personnel changes could be made which would ensure that those ideals were carried out.

NOTES

1. *Report of the Committee on Administrative Tribunals and Enquiries* (1957), H.M.S.O. Cmnd. 218, p. 9.
2. *loc. cit.*
3. *ibid.*, p. 16.
4. *Evidence to the Franks Committee* (1957), p. 825.
5. See generally, William A. Robson, *Justice and Administrative Law* (1951).
6. *Report of the Council on Tribunals for 1959* (1960), p. 6.
7. Geoffrey Sawer, *Law in Society* (1965), pp. 72–3.
8. *Lord Chancellor's Committee on Ministers' Powers* (1932), H.M.S.O. Cmd. 4060, p. 111.
9. 'An organised and diligent minority. . . employing after a fashion part of the machinery of representative institutions, is steadily increasing the range and power of departmental authority and withdrawing its operations more and more from the jurisdiction of the courts'; Lord Hewart, *The New Despotism* (1929), p. 12. See for his strictures on the Unemployment Insurance Acts, *ibid.*, p. 60.
10. H. W. R. Wade, *Administrative Law* (1971), p. 7. Professors Griffith and Street have said of the concept of the Rule of Law that 'it has a valuable emotive content so long as its use is not too clearly examined'; J. A. G. Griffith and Harry Street, *Principles of Administrative Law* (1973), p. 21.
11. S. A. de Smith, *Judicial Review of Administrative Action* (1968), p. 10.
12. Tony Lynes, *New Society* **16**, (10 September 1970), p. 456.
13. Quoted in Susan McCorquodale, 'The Composition of Administrative Tribunals.' *Public Law*, (1962), p. 298.
14. See Harry Street, *Justice in the Welfare State* (1975), pp. 34, 38.
15. Quoted in Susan McCorquodale, *op. cit.*, p. 299.
16. para. 6, Memorandum of Conditions of Service for Local Appeal Tribunal Chairmen. The bar on M.P.s serving as chairmen derives from s. 1(1) (f) House of Commons Disqualification Act 1957. Other unstated but general disqualifications would include bankruptcy or a criminal record.
17. *Evidence to the Franks Committee* (1957), p. 40.
18. *Franks Committee Report* (1957), p. 12.
19. Harry Street, *op. cit.*, p. 13. In the earlier edition of Professor Street's book this was 'the views of a local advisory committee' (1968), p. 14. Although local advisory committees attached to the D.H.S.S. were abolished in 1971, there is still a manpower committee attached to the local office of the Department of Employment which can be approached.
20. *ibid.*, p. 61.
21. See generally for criticism of the haphazard appointments system, the stereotypical 'rubber-stamp', which used to exist for appointments to the lay magistracy; Roger Hood, *Sentencing in Magistrates' Courts* (1962).
22. R. E. Wraith and P. G. Hutchesson, *Administrative Tribunals* (1973), p. 111. Originally there had been twenty-two women out of a total of 138 chairmen and 215 reserve chairmen with the setting up of the U.A.B. tribunals in 1935; *Report of the U.A.B. for 1935* (1936), H.M.S.O., Cmd. 5177, p. 49.
23. *Annual Report of the Council on Tribunals 1969–1970* (1970), para. 44.
24. Report of a *Justice* sub-committee, *The Judiciary* (1972), pp. 27–8.

25. See generally on proposals for a judicial promotion structure, Julian Fulbrook, Rosalind Brooke, and Peter Archer, *Tribunals: a Social Court*? (Society of Labour Lawyers/Fabian Tract 1973), p. 13.

26. R. E. Wraith and P. G. Hutchesson, *op. cit.*, p. 115 f.

27. See the evidence of the National Assistance Board to the *Franks Committee* (1957), p. 30.

28. See *ibid.*, p. 33, and Sir Geoffrey King, *The Ministry of Pensions and National Insurance* (1958), p. 86.

29. para. 5, *Memorandum of Conditions of Service for Local Appeal Tribunal Chairmen.*

30. *Hansard*, **851**, H. C. Deb. (19 February 1973), col. 35.

31. See generally, the evidence of the Lord Chancellor's secretary, Sir George Coldstream, to the *Franks Committee* (1957), p. 200.

32. *Hansard*, **175**, H. L. Deb. (5 March 1952), col. 545. This was denied by Professor Haggen and his supporters; in fact, every member of the Leeds tribunal panels wrote a letter urging his re-appointment.

33. *ibid.*, col. 525.

34. D.H.S.S., *Notes for Chairmen of Local Tribunals* (LT Memo No. 1)

35. Harry Street, *Justice in the Welfare State* (1975), p. 27.

36. Susan McCorquodale, *op. cit.*, p. 305.

37. *Annual Report of the U.A.B.* (1936), H.M.S.O. Cmd. 5177, p. 49.

38. Susan McCorquodale, *op. cit.*, p. 304. In 1973, only twenty-two out of 254 chairmen had previously sat as workpeople's representatives; *Hansard*, **343**, H. L. Deb. (25 June 1973), col. 1832.

39. Ross Flockhart, 'Some Aspects of Tribunal Membership', in Michael Adler and Anthony Bradley (eds.), *Justice, Discretion and Poverty* (1976), p. 103.

40. See the recommendation that appointments 'should not rest with the Minister concerned with the subject matter of the adjudications'; *Franks Committee Report* (1957) paras. 45–8. See now s. 7 Tribunals and Inquiries Act 1971, and, for the change-over, National Assistance Board, *Annual Report 1959* (1960), H.M.S.O. Cmnd. 1085.

41. Melvin Herman, *Administrative Justice and Supplementary Benefits* (1972), p. 22.

42. *Franks Committee Report* (1957), p. 12.

43. Sir Geoffrey King, op. cit., p. 85. There were three non-lawyers as chairmen in 1957, all of whom had been chairmen of Courts of Referees; *Oral Evidence of the Ministry of Pensions and National Insurance to the Franks Committee* (1957), p. 30.

44. R. S. W. Pollard, *Administrative Tribunals at Work* (1950), p. 47.

45. Jonathan Stein, 'Protecting the Right to Supplementary Benefit', unpublished draft London LLM dissertation (1968). Susan McCorquodale, *op. cit.*, p. 304.

46. Hansard, **343**, H. L. Deb. (25 June 1973), col. 1832, and Sir Harold Fieldhouse, Secretary of the N.A.B. in *Evidence to the Franks Committee* (1957), p. 45.

47. Ruth Lister, *Justice for the Claimant* (1974), p. 8.

48. Evidence to the Franks Committee (1957), p. 311 — 'we consider that people who are not lawyers but whose special experience makes them suitable for appointment should not be excluded'.

49. *Annual Report of the Council on Tribunals for 1966* (1967), p. 7.

50. H. W. R. Wade, *Towards Administrative Justice* (1963), p. 43.

51. H. J. Elcock, *Administrative Justice* (1969), pp. 50, 53.

52. Ruth Lister, *op. cit.*, pp. 8, 10.

53. Kathleen Bell, *Research Study on Supplementary Benefit Appeal Tribunals: Review of Main Findings: Conclusions: Recommendations* (D.H.S.S. 1975), pp. 6, 7, 23.

54. See in particular Ruth Lister, 'Supplementary Benefit Appeal Tribunals: an Urgent Case for Reform', in Michael Adler and Anthony Bradley (eds.), *op. cit.*, p. 176.

55. Ruth Lister, *Justice for the Claimant* (1974), p. 25.

56. *Franklin* v. *Minister of Town and Country Planning* [1948] A.C. 87, 103.

57. Ruth Lister, *op. cit.*, p. 27.

58. Melvin Harman, *op. cit.*, p. 46.

59. Julian Fulbrook, *The Appellant and his Case: the Appellant's View of Supplementary Benefit Appeal Tribunals* (1975), p. 8.

60. The rates in 1973 were £9.45 for a half-day session by a Supplementary Benefit Appeal Tribunal chairman and £11 for a half day session by a National Insurance Local Appeal Tribunal chairman. Comparative rates for the chairman of Rent and Industrial Tribunals were a daily fee of £27 and £30 respectively. Full-time chairman of Industrial Tribunals were paid an annual salary of £9,350; figures given in a written answer by the

Attorney-General *Hansard*, **851**, H. C. Deb. (19 February 1973), col. 34.

61. The tribunals were the Mental Health Review Tribunal, Industrial Tribunals and Rent Assessment Panels; W. E. Cavanagh and D. Newton, *Public Administration* [1971], p. 218.

62. Kathleen Bell, *op. cit.*, p. 23. See also the views of one of Professor Bell's researchers on the special difficulties of work-people's representatives on Local Appeal and Supplementary Benefit Tribunals; Steve Turner, 'The Trade Union Role in Tribunals', *Poverty*, No. 32 (1975), pp. 31–2.

63. R. E. Wraith and P. G. Hutchesson, *op. cit.*, pp. 102–3. See also the similar comments of Professors Schwartz and Wade: 'It is obvious that chairmen ought to have legal qualifications: tribunals have to administer law which is often complex, they may have qualified advocates appearing before them, and they must know the elements of procedure. . . But dispensing relief to the poorest people in the community is in some ways well suited to an experienced lay chairman'; Bernard Schwartz and H. W. R. Wade, *Legal Control of Government* (1972), p. 161.

64. Harry Street, 'Tribunals: Two New Publications', Legal Action Group *Bulletin* (1974), p. 128. Supplementary Benefit Appeal Tribunals have one short paragraph devoted to them in J. A. G. Griffith and Harry Street, *Principles of Administrative Law* (1973), pp. 161–2.

65. Harry Street, 'Judicial Review Refused', Legal Action Group *Bulletin* (1975), p. 118.

66. Norman Lewis, 'Supplementary Benefits Appeal Tribunals', *Public Law* (1973), p. 257; 'They appear to operate in marked contrast to the national insurance local appeal tribunals which are usually a model of balancing informal expertise with order and legality'; *ibid.*, p. 259.

67. Kathleen Bell, *op. cit.*, pp. 5, 25. For the study on local Appeal Tribunals see Kathleen Bell, Peter Collison, Stephen Turner and Susan Webber, 'National Insurance Local Appeal Tribunals: A Research Study', *Journal of Social Policy* **3** (1974), p. 289, and **4** (1975), p. 1.

68. See progress reports in the *Annual Reports* for 1968 (1969), p. 4, and for 1969–1970 (1970), p. 6.

69. See George Lach in R. S. W. Pollard (ed.), *Administrative Tribunals at Work* (1950), p. 46.

70. *Annual Report of the Council on Tribunals for 1971–1972* (1972), p. 6.

71. R. E. Wraith and P. G. Hutchesson, *op. cit.*, p. 168.

72. Ruth Lister, *op. cit.*, p. 45; Kathleen Bell, *op. cit.*, p. 7; thirteen out of seventeen Northern Region chairmen thought conferences could be of real value mentioning feelings of isolation and 'being out on a limb'. 78 per cent of all tribunal members surveyed wanted training for new members, and 50 per cent were in favour of training for serving members; *loc. cit.*

73. *Notes for Chairmen of Local Tribunals* (LT Memo No. 1) and *Notes for Members of Local Tribunals* (LT Memo No. 1A).

74. s. 97, SS Act 1975.

75. The latter is from the phrase in the *Supplementary Benefits Handbook* (1974), p. 64; 'and the other from a panel appointed by the Secretary of State'.

76. See the discussion on p. 165.

77. See para. 3(1), Schedule 5, National Assistance Act 1948.

78. William A. Robson, *Justice and Administrative Law* (1951), p. 227.

79. Personal communication from Tony Lynes.

80. para. 3, Schedule 3. SB Act 1966.

81. Eric Briggs and Alan Deacon, 'The Creation of the Unemployment Assistance Board', *Policy and Politics* **2** (1973), p. 51, quoting the Minutes of a Cabinet Unemployment Insurance Committee (1927).

82. *ibid.*, pp. 51–2.

83. See generally, George Lach in R. S. W. Pollard. (ed.)), *Administrative Tribunals at Work* (1950).

84. Susan McCorquodale, *op. cit.*, p. 303.

85. H. J. Elcock, *op. cit.*, p. 37.

86. A tribunal advocate quoted in Tony Gould and Joe Kenyon, *Stories from the Dole Queue* (1972), p. 156.

87. D.H.S.S., *Notes for Chairmen of Local Tribunals* (LT Memo No. 1), and *Notes for Members of Local Tribunals* (LT Memo No. 1A). See also evidence of the Ministry of Pensions and National Insurance to the *Franks Committee* (1957), para. 273, stating that tribunal members have no security of tenure.

88. The complete figures for wingmen in 1972 were 4,563 for national insurance tribunals and 1,229 for supplementary benefit tribunals; written answer by the

Attorney-General, *Hansard*, **851**, H. C. Deb. (19 February 1973), col. 34.

89. *New Society* **24** (26 April 1973), p. 193.

90. *Evidence to the Franks Committee* (1957) p. 30.

91. *Annual Report of U. A. B.* (1936), p. 50. See also the virtually identical method of selecting wingmen for the Courts of Referees at that time; evidence of the Ministry of Labour to the *Royal Commission on Unemployment Insurance* (1932), H.M.S.O. Cmd. 4185, p. 66.

92. See generally the report entitled *Courts of Referees* (1913), House of Commons Papers 527.

93. *Supplementary Benefits Handbook* (1974), p. 64.

94. Ruth Lister, *op. cit.*, p. 7. In a study of Scottish Supplementary Benefit tribunal members, only one of 148 respondents was judged to be in the Registrar General's Category V, and only one Minister's member and ten workpeople's representatives in Category IV; Ross Flockhart, *op. cit.*, p. 100.

95. *Royal Commision on the Justices of the Peace* (1948) H.M.S.O. Cmd. 7463, para. 32. See also Roger Hood, *Sentencing in Magistrates' Courts* (1962), p. 6.

96. W. E. Cavanagh and G. N. Hawker, 'Laymen on Administrative Tribunals', *Public Administration* **52** (1974), p. 220.

97. *loc. cit.*

99. See generally, Steve Turner, 'The Trade Union Role in Tribunals', *Poverty* **32** (1975), p. 31.

99. The powers of reimbursement are contained in para. 3(1) and (3), Sched. 10, SS Act 1975, and in para. 4, Sched. 3, SB Act 1966.

100. R. E. Wraith and P. G. Hutchesson, *op. cit.*, p. 115.

101. Figures given in a written answer by the Attorney-General, *Hansard*, **851**, H. C. Deb. (19 February), col. 34.

102. *Memorandum on the Unemployment Assistance (Determination of Need and Assessment of Needs) Regulations 1934* (1935), H.M.S.O., Cmd. 4791, see generally Tony Lynes, 'Unemployment Assistance Tribunals in the 1930s', in Michael Adler and Anthony Bradley (eds.) *op. cit.*, pp. 17–18.

103. Ruth Lister, *op. cit.*, p. 33.

104. *ibid.*, p. 35.

105. Joel F. Handler, 'Justice for the Welfare Recipient: Fair Hearings in AFDC', *The Social Service Review* **43** (1969), p. 12. See also Joel F. Handler, *Reforming the Poor* (1972).

106. See for example Bernard Schwartz and H. W. R. Wade, *Legal Control of Government* (1972), pp. 108, 131.

107. Kathleen Bell, Peter Collison, Stephen Turner and Susan Webber, 'National Insurance Local Tribunals: A Research Study — Part I', *Journal of Social Policy* **3** (1974), p. 311.

108. Kathleen Bell, *Research Study on Supplementary Benefit Appeal Tribunals* (1975), p. 18.

109. Julian Fulbrook, *The Appellant and his Case: The Appellant's View of Supplementary Benefit Appeal Tribunals* (1975), p. 14.

110. See generally, Coral Milton, 'Appellants' Perceptions of the Tribunal Process', in Michael Adler and Anthony Bradley (eds.), *op. cit.*, p. 129 *et seq.*

111. Kathleen Bell, *op. cit.*, p. 18.

112. See generally, R. B. Stevens and B. S. Yamey, *The Restrictive Practices Court* (1965) and s. 4, Restrictive Trade Practices Act 1956.

113. Rosalind Brooke *et al.*, *A Policy to Establish the Legal Rights of Low Income Families* (1969), p. 3.

114. s. 77(5) (c) NI Act 1965. This is now merely a request to the clerk, para. 1(4) (c), Schedule 10, SS Act 1975. One commentary states that in the 1925 National Insurance Local Appeal Tribunal structure 'Men cannot vote on women's cases and women cannot vote on men's cases'. The account is somewhat confused and is in other respects unreliable, so it is possible that this may mean unofficial guidelines in the Rota Panels rather than practice in the Courts of Referees; J. J. Astor *et al.*, *Unemployment Insurance in Great Britain: A Critical Evaluation* (1925), p. 10.

115. *Annual Report of the Council on Tribunals for 1971–1972* (1972), p. 24.

116. Ruth Lister, *op. cit.*, p. 5.

117. R. E. Wraith and P. G. Hutchesson, *op. cit.*, p. 111.

118. Kathleen Bell, Peter Collison, Stephen Turner and Susan Webber, 'National Insurance Local Tribunals: A Research Study — Part I', *Journal of Social Policy* **3** (1974), p. 315.

119. W. E. Cavanagh and G. N. Hawker, 'Laymen on Administrative Tribunals', *Public Administration* **52** (1974), p. 215.

120. W. E. Cavanagh and D. Newton, 'The Membership of Two Administrative

Tribunals', *Public Administration* **48** (1970), p. 449, and 'Administrative Tribunals: How People Become Members', *Public Administration* **49** (1971), p. 197.

121. Franks' recommendation No. 7. See also *Franks Committee Report* (1957), p. 14.

122. para. 11(1) and 11 (8) Supplementary Benefit (Appeal Tribunal) Regs. (1971) SI 1971, No. 680.

123. *Annual Report of the Council on Tribunals for 1963* (1964), Appendix A, p. 29.

124. Per Lord Goddard C. J. in *R* v. *East Kerrier Justices, ex p. Mundy* [1952] 2 Q.B. 719 at 723. See also the Lord Chief Justice's Practice Direction at [1953] 2 All E.R. 1306.

125. Kathleen Bell, *Research Study on Supplementary Benefit Appeal Tribunals* (1975), p. 10; Melvin Herman, *op. cit.*, p. 24; Ruth Lister, *op. cit.* p. 15, Michael Adler, Elizabeth Burns and Rosemary Johnson, in Michael Adler and Anthony Bradley (eds.), *op. cit.*, p. 115

126. See Julian Fulbrook, *op. cit.*, pp. 1–2, where in an interview to obtain permission to attend one Supplementary Benefit Appeal Tribunal, the regular chairman remarked, 'There are far too many damned academics poking their noses into places where they don't belong'.

127. Melvin Herman, *op. cit.*, p. 23.

128. Michael Adler, Elizabeth Burns and Rosemary Johnson, *op. cit.*, p. 115.

129. A letter from a Local Appeal Tribunal appellant in the *Shropshire Star* (18 July 1967), quoted in H. J. Elcock, *Administrative Justice* (1969), p. 46, states that not just the clerk but also the Insurance Officer stayed in the room when the tribunal was deliberating, and that the latter presumably 'put in his fourpence-worth'.

130. *Evidence to the Franks Committee* (1957), p. 47. Interestingly, Sir Harold Fieldhouse, the Secretary of the N.A.B., had attended only one tribunal session, but could report that the clerk intervened to say 'You cannot do that' during a hearing; *loc. cit.*

131. Ruth Lister, *op. cit.*, p. 15.

132. Steve Burkeman, 'We Go By the Law Here', in Michael Adler and Anthony Bradley (eds.). *op. cit.*, pp. 92–3.

133. H. J. Elcock, *op. cit.*, p. 9.

134. Kathleen Bell, *op. cit.*, p. 9.

135. *ibid.*, p. 21.

136. See the discussion at p. 166.

137. See generally, George Lach in R. S. W. Pollard, *op. cit.*, p. 60, and the Unemployment Assistance (Determination of Need and Assessment of Needs) Regs. (1936) S.R.&O. 1936 No. 776.

138. R. S. W. Pollard, *Oral Evidence to the Franks Committee* (1957), p. 528.

139. Quoted in Tony Lynes 'Unemployment Assistance Tribunals in the 1930s', in Michael Adler and Anthony Bradley (eds.), *op. cit.*, p. 13.

140. Alleged collusion in switching beds or claiming a member of the family had left home. See earlier at p. 168.

141. Tony Lynes, *op. cit.*, pp. 20–1.

142. Council on Tribunals, *Annual Report for 1970–71* (1971), para. 70.

143. *Committee of Inquiry under Sir Harold Morris K.C.* (1929), H.M.S.O. Cmd. 3415, p. 70.

144. *Franks Committee Report* (1957), p. 14.

145. *ibid.*, para. 60.

146. R. E. Wraith and P. G. Hutchesson, *op. cit.*, p. 123.

147. D.H.S.S. policy quoted in Melvin Herman, *op. cit.*, p. 24.

148. Kathleen Bell, *op. cit.*, p. 10.

149. Harry Calvert, 'Appeal Structures of the Future', in Michael Adler and Anthony Bradley (eds.), *op. cit.*, p. 185 *et seq.*

150. Harry Street, 'Tribunals: Two new publications', Legal Action Group *Bulletin* (1974), p. 128. One of the publications reviewed by Professor Street states of Local Appeal Tribunals, wrongly in the author's opinion, that 'it should be said at once that the close departmental connection cannot be detected by the outside observer except when hearings are actually held in local offices of the Department'; R. E. Wraith and P. G. Hutchesson, *op. cit.*, p. 122. The other publication states that 'the indiscretions of some clerks have on occasions led to flagrant breaches of Natural Justice'; Julian Fulbrook, Rosalind Brooke, and Peter Archer, *op. cit.*, p. 10.

151. para. 1(4), Schedule 10. SS Act 1975. An additional point which few clerks seem to adhere to is the injunction that 'in any case in which the claimant is a woman, at least one of the members of the tribunal, if practicable, shall be a woman' para. 1(4) (c), *ibid.* With so few women on the panels, no doubt it is often not 'practicable'.

152. W. E. Cavanagh and G. N. Hawker, 'Laymen on Administrative Tribunals', *Public Administration* **52** (1974), p. 209.

153. See *New Society* **24**, No. 548 (5 April 1973), and Ruth Lister, *op. cit.*, p. 5.

154. For example, in 1938, 500,000 cases were dealt with by the Courts of Referees; Ministry of Labour, *Annual Report 1938* (1939), H.M.S.O. Appendix XXIII. 98 per cent of all Social Security cases are now dealt with at the initial level of an Insurance Officer's decision; R. E. Wraith and P. G. Hutchesson, *op. cit.*, p. 277.

155. paras. 9(1), (2) and (4) The Social Security (Determination of Claims and Questions) Regs. (1975) SI 1975, No. 558.

156. para. 14, The Social Security (Determination of Claims and Questions) Regs. (1975) SI 1975, No. 558. See generally, J. Bell, *How to get your Industrial Injury Benefit* (1966), p. 244.

157. See, for example, R(G) 3/62.

158. J. A. Farmer, *Tribunals and Government* (1974), p. 104.

159. *ibid.*, p. 106.

160. Such a sentiment was expressed in the author's presence by an Insurance Officer to a Local Appeal Tribunal appellant; the appeal in fact succeeded.

161. See generally, s. 97 SS Act 1975.

162. D.H.S.S., *Notes for Chairmen of Local Tribunals* (LT Memo No. 1), p. 9. See also for comments on the passive role of the Insurance Officer before the tribunal, the *17th Report of the Lord Chancellor's Advisory Committee on Legal Aid and Advice* (1968), p. 71.

163. It was interesting to note that he regarded the National Insurance Commissioners' decisions and the A Code as of similar weight for the tribunals, clearly not understanding the distinction between law and policy, although he stated that he preferred reading Commissioners' decisions as the A Code was often 'incomprehensible'.

164. Kathleen Bell, *op. cit.*, p. 11.

165. See earlier at p. 200.

166. R. M. Gould, quoted by Tony Lynes, *op. cit.*, p. 25.

167. A member of the *New Society* editorial staff who attended a Supplementary Benefit Appeal Tribunal received a courteous but revealing comment from a Presenting Officer when talking with an appellant's representative in the waiting room: 'At one side of the room was a man with a pile of papers on his knee. "I don't like to eavesdrop," he said suddenly, "but I think you ought to know that I'm the opposition"'; Paul Harrison, 'The Tribunals of the Welfare State', *New Society*, **26**, No. 581 (22 November 1973), p. 462.

168. Ruth Lister, *op. cit.*, p. 14.

169. Kathleen Bell, *op. cit.*, p. 11.

170. C(G) 1/74; see the Note in Legal Action Group *Bulletin* (1974), p. 299.

171. Rosalind Brooke *et al.*, *op. cit.*, p. 2. See for more recent CPAG criticism, Henry Hodge, 'Techniques for Tribunals', Legal Action Group *Bulletin* (1973), p. 271, and Ruth Lister, *op. cit.*, p. 11.

172. See S. A. de Smith, *op. cit.*, pp. 111, 200.

173. Now para. 3(3) The Social Security (Determination of Claims and Questions) Regs. (1975) SI 1975, No. 558.

174. para. 10(1) Supplementary Benefit (Appeal Tribunals) Regs. (1966) SI 1966, No. 1066; para. 3(2) Supplementary Benefits (Appeal Tribunals) Regs. (1971) SI 1971, No. 680.

175. *R.* v. *War Pensions Entitlement Appeal Tribunal, ex parte Bott* (1933) 50 C.L.R. 228. See also *Wilson* v. *Esquimalt & Nanaimo Ry* [1922] 1 A.C. 202.

176. Melvin Herman, *op. cit.*, p. 27 and p. 16. See also the experience of a former N.A.B. officer, now a University researcher, whose local office manager disliked continually losing appeals because of a Supplementary Benefit chairman who was critical of the Board, and so anticipated the tribunal decision whenever possible; M. J. Hill, 'The Exercise of Discretion in the National Assistance Board', *Public Administration* (1969) p. 75.

177. Richard White in Pauline Morris, Richard White and Philip Lewis, *Social Needs and Legal Action* (1973), p. 27.

178. See generally on the status of social security officials, D. V. Donnison and Valerie Chapman, *Social Policy and Administration* (1967), p. 73. See for anecdotal and polemical discussion of Presenting Officers and departmental employees generally, Tony Gould and Joe Kenyon, *Stories from the Dole Queue* (1972), p. 12.

179. W. A. Robson, *The Governors and the Governed* (1964), p. 19.

180. The Fisher Committee contented themselves with the comment that, with regard to the training of social security officers, 'sympathetic treatment of claimants need not derogate from a proper degree of vigilance against abuse'; *Report of the Committee on Abuse of Social Security* (1973), H.M.S.O. Cmnd. 5228, p. 12. See

for the attitude of an SBC officer in an extreme form, Robin Page, *The Benefits Racket* (1971).

181. Julian Fulbrook, *op. cit.*, pp. 9–10. An advocate for the Lane Neighbourhood Centre in Birmingham told the author of an incident where he represented a claimant on an appeal for an Exceptional Needs Payment which had been awarded but not paid by the S.B.C. During lengthy discussions about furniture prices, the Presenting Officer suddenly intervened to say, 'Of course, the children aren't all from the same father'. In one case involving a West Indian woman, observed by the Nuffield Legal Research Unit, she was asked if the same father was responsible for both her children; Coral Milton, *op. cit.*, p. 140.

182. Kathleen Bell, *op. cit.*, pp. 10–11.

183. S. A. de Smith, *Judicial Review Administrative Action* (1968), pp. 190, 199.

184. In 1974, 585 insurance claims were so referred; D.H.S.S., *Annual Report 1974* (1975), p. 101. This figure, approaching 2 per cent of all appeal cases, was about average for the preceding five years.

185. H. J. Elcock, *op. cit.*, p. 65. The proceedings at a Supplementary Benefit Appeal Tribunal were once characterized by two social workers as 'a battle between ill-matched opponents out of which is generated resentment against "the winner" and whoever is "the loser" in the contest'; *Case Conference*, **14** (1967–8), pp. 413, 415, quoted in G. Ganz, *Administrative Procedures* (1974), p. 35.

186. Michael Zander and Cyril Glasser, "A Study in Representation", *New Law Journal* **117** (1967), p. 816.

187. See later discussion at p. 276 *et seq.*

188. Melvin Herman, *op. cit.*, p. 29.

189. Kathleen Bell, *op. cit.*, p. 17.

10

Tribunal Adjudication

As well as the requirements of judicial impartiality to ensure that tribunals are freed from the influence, real or imagined, of the Departments concerned with tribunal adjudication, the Franks Committee in 1957 also demanded two other requirements from the tribunal process —openness and fairness. They characterized these as follows:

> Openness seems to us to require the publicity of proceedings and knowledge of the essential reasoning underlying the decisions [and] fairness to require the adoption of a clear procedure which enables parties to know their rights, to present their case fully and to know the case which they have to meet.[1]

The tribunal hearing may of course confirm the initial decision of the administrative agency, but the right to a fair hearing has been stressed repeatedly as a fundamental tenet of administrative justice; the following discussion is an analysis of the observance of such standards, and generally of the rules of Natural Justice, by social security tribunals.

Tribunal Premises

Two important initial factors in the proper hearing of appeals are the interrelated questions of the location of the tribunal and the internal seating arrangements for tribunal participants in relation to the appellant. The Franks Committee pointed out that in 1957 nearly all Local Appeal and Supplementary Benefit tribunals were held in Ministry buildings, which, as well as creating an impression of dependence, were also considered by the Committee to be 'sometimes rather bleak'.[2] Since then the work of the Council on Tribunals has succeeded in moving all the Local Appeal Tribunals to more 'neutral' premises

For notes see p. 305

such as community and church halls. But many Supplementary Benefit Tribunals remain in some form of 'official' building, and the alternative of using County Court rooms, which is often tried, is perhaps just as unsuitable when the word 'Court Room' is written on the door. The Council on Tribunals was in fact asked by the newly-created S.B.C. in 1966 if the existing practice of holding N.A.B. tribunals on Ministry premises was acceptable, and their response was to urge immediate removal as a matter of principle;[3] it had of course been an earlier policy of the U.A.B. to have tribunal hearings on its own premises, as a further means of control over decision-making.[4] Unfortunately, the Council's directive has still not been adhered to completely, and the stigma which undoubtedly attaches to Ministry offices still remains to give appellants the image of dependence; a comparison here might be made with the old connotations that attached to the term 'Police Court'. As Professor Robson has pointed out, the siting of the tribunal not only affects the attitude of the appellant, but also that of tribunal participants, in that 'the mental association of a particular place with the exercise of judicial functions may help to produce an atmosphere in which a man feels more impartial and independent'.[5]

The Franks Committee also thought that the positioning of tribunal participants in the tribunal room itself was important, and that, in Local Appeal Tribunals, the practice of Insurance Officers sitting 'to one side of the tribunal . . . could give an unfortunate, though unjustified, impression that the Insurance Officer occupies a privileged position at the hearing'.[6] Such a practice was also found to exist with the siting of Presenting Officers in the National Assistance tribunals, and the Committee recommended that the practice 'should be avoided unless no other arrangement is possible'.[7] In fact, the seating of Insurance Officers and Presenting Officers to one side of the appellant, usually facing the clerk on the other side of a large table or across the floor, is the usual practice. Professor Rose states that

> The observable tendency of presenting officers even when placed on the same side of the conference table, to slide round to the end so that they almost parallel the position of the tribunal clerk, literally upstaging the clerk, reaffirms the presenting officer's identification with the tribunal and not as someone of equal status with the appellant.[8]

Psychologically such points are of course very important and only by attending to them can subliminal impressions of the tribunal as a 'club', of which the Presenting Officer is a full member, be dispelled.

Some commentators have put forward the idea of having local tribunal hearings all under one roof. This would include sessions of

Industrial and Rent Tribunals as well as those of the social security tribunals. The proposal may be feasible in urban areas with a reasonable case-load and ease of transportation to a central location, but there would be a serious possibility of under-use in rural areas where the existing arrangements for Local Appeal Tribunals holding sessions at 'neutral' church premises provide a more flexible answer. However, the attractions of a tribunal centre are considerable; as well as providing a common address, library facilities for appellants and their representatives, toilet and refreshment facilities, it could also be custom-built to deal with problems of easy access for disabled and elderly appellants, and parking. Initial building costs would have to be weighed not only with savings gained by increased administrative efficiency, but also the considerable social costs which would be gained by appellants.

Difficulties discussed before in relation to D.H.S.S. claiming facilities, such as flights of stairs and uncomfortable waiting room conditions, also apply to tribunal locations.[9] The attitude and sensitivity of the clerk in the waiting room situation is also a critical factor which affects an appellant, but even if the personality of the clerk cannot be dramatically altered, something should certainly be done to provide a degree of physical comfort. Steve Burkeman points out that there is rarely the facility of a separate conference room at social security tribunals for representatives and their clients, away from other appellants and the Presenting Officer; he also makes a plea for magazines for adults and toys or books for children accompanying their parents.[10] In the author's observation of a Supplementary Benefit Appeal Tribunal, with a follow-up of the appellants whose cases had been heard, a respondent who had multiple sclerosis reconnoitred the tribunal premises beforehand with her social worker and found that, although a lift was available to take her to the third floor tribunal room, she was unable to face the flight of steps to get up to the bottom of the lift; another with arthritis received a ticket for parking nearby, but subsequently wrote to the police explaining the situation and was excused.[11] These kinds of problems, which clearly have an impact on attendance rates and also on the state of mind of an appellant in the hearings, should of course be dealt with as far as possible in relation to existing tribunal premises, but a new tribunal centre would make it easier to cater for groups with special difficulties of movement; these are quite naturally involved with appeals for sickness, disability or industrial injury benefits.

It has also been estimated by the D.H.S.S. that over seventy copy-typists are nationally employed full-time in work relating to social security tribunals.[12] With a centralized corps of tribunal clerks, there would also be a strong argument for shared copy, secretarial and office facilities, both as a saving in cost but also as a further move towards increasing the independence of appeal tribunals from the Departments whose decisions are under review.

Time Limits

The factor of speed of decision is clearly important, both to the appellant and to the administrative machinery under review, and certain legal requirements have been built up to ensure reasonable efficiency. In Social Security adjudication, an Insurance Officer must dispose of a claim within fourteen days of it being lodged,[13] with a further time limit of twenty-one days following his written decision within which the claimant may make an appeal.[14] The notice of appeal must be in writing and at the minimum 'shall contain a statement of the grounds upon which the appeal is made';[15] administratively this is not interpreted as demanding precise citations of National Insurance Commissioners' decisions or sections in the relevant legislation or statutory instruments, but merely a statement of the general grounds for appeal. The Chairman of a Local Appeal Tribunal is able to extend the twenty-one day limit for 'good cause', which has been defined by the Commissioners as

> some fact which, having regard to all the circumstances (including the claimant's state of health and the information which he had received and that which he might have obtained), would have probably caused a reasonable person of his age or experience to act (or fail to act) as the claimant did.[16]

Generally, the most common reason for a late claim is ignorance of the law; in 1961, for example, the Commissioners found 'good cause' when a woman had been misled by reading the official departmental leaflets.[17] However, although the Commissioners make allowances for an appellant's intellectual abilities, this can also be taken into account against an appellant as when in a recent case the Commissioners were clearly influenced by an appellant's above average abilities.[18] The time limit for an appeal to the National Insurance Commissioners is three months from the date of the decision of the Local Appeal Tribunal, and similarly this can be extended for 'special reasons' at the discretion of the Commissioner. Appeals can also be made by a trade union or similar organization when the appellant was or is a member.[19]

A number of local offices dealing with insurance claims, both in the D.H.S.S. and in the Department of Employment, have internal instructions that an appellant must be written to with a fixed date for the hearing and a summary of the case against him on the day his appeal is lodged. However, the former Chief National Insurance Commissioner, Sir Robert Micklethwait, in evidence to the Council on Tribunals, stated that the average time taken for an appeal to be disposed of by a Local Appeal Tribunal was still fourteen weeks.[20] An estimate on the time taken to secure a further appeal to the National Insurance Commissioners is anything up to a year, although some of the delay is accounted for by the three month time limit for appeal and also the gathering in industrial injury cases of medical information. Unemployment cases are estimated by the Commissioners to be dealt with usually in about four months from the appeal at the local tribunal. In Supplementary Benefits adjudication, there is a similar time limit for the claimant to appeal within twenty-one days, with a similar discretion for an extension if the chairman believes there is just cause.[21] The S.B.C. may also review a decision after an appeal has been made out of time, where there has been ignorance of the law, a mistake of material fact, or a relevant change of circumstances.[22] However, the S.B.C. also sets itself an internal target of clearing cases through appeal inside three weeks although this is assessed as overly optimistic by most observers. This can sometimes involve sending appellants to tribunals some distance away, if the local tribunal sits only sporadically or has a full case-load in its scheduled sessions, which is not entirely satisfactory in that few appellants seem at present to realize that they can claim travel expenses.[23]

Thorough and fair adjudication must of course be balanced with swiftness of decision. However, the administrative problems of processing claims are considerable when coupled with factors such as staff shortage, poor communications in rural areas, and the increasing complexity of internal regulations and statutory rules on social security matters. Certainly some delay is due to bureaucratic sluggishness, which may, as Rosalind Brooke says, ‘stem(s) from low status and pay for the officials . . . and inadequate training and supervision’.[24] Further delays may arise, not from slack administration, but from such factors as adjournments or the incomplete constitution of a tribunal. Both social security tribunals are able to proceed in the absence of one member, but only if the appellant agrees to their continuing.[25] Professor Bell, in her study of Northern Region Supplementary Benefit tribunals was critical of a number of hearings where one member was absent; in fact one entire session had to be cancelled because neither of the wingmen showed up.[26] In such circumstances, consent by the appellant to have his case heard by two members rather than three is notional when taken in the context of his anxiety to have a quick decision and the possibility that he may have to take another day off work to attend the reconvened tribunal. However, on occasion, appellants will object to a wingman being present and, although there is no right of *voire dire* or peremptory challenge in theory, wingmen in these circumstances normally retire. At one Local Appeal Tribunal session observed, the tribunal discovered at the completion of the case list that, owing to an error by the clerk, both wingmen were representatives from the Trades Council. It is perhaps a commentary on the lack of communication, both among tribunal members and in local Trades Councils, that they were unknown to each other before.

In a 1952 survey, the National Insurance Advisory Committee summed up the question of appeal time limits by stating that

> While the time limit allowed should not be so long as to encourage laxness on the part of claimants it should be long enough to allow any insured person, able to take a normal interest in his affairs, conveniently to do all that needs to be done in preparing and making his claim.[27]

As will be discussed, the preparation of a case is not helped by difficulties over obtaining the rules on which departmental decisions are made in the first instance, but it would seem that little theoretical criticism can be made of the present position, which maintains a reasonable balance of speed and fairness, except in certain isolated cases. Certainly the administrative agencies concerned are well aware that excessive delay can lead to considerable hardship on the part of claimants whose only means of support is through some form of welfare payments. This arises in a particularly acute form with unemployed claimants denied benefit under the old four-week rule or its continuing associated disqualifications from benefit. Another similar area is that of claimants accused of cohabitation, whose benefit is cut off pending appeal, and who may have to go to the extreme of putting their children into care before the hearing comes on. Arguments have been made that in cohabitation cases benefit should only be stopped when an appeal has been disallowed, but the Fisher Committee rejected this as a general rule, although they added the strange, and surely unrealistic, rider that 'the S.B.C. could be more generous with urgent needs payments to cover this period'.[28] One minor internal administrative change has been the continuance of benefits for any children for a period. However, a woman's order book can still be withdrawn on the spot by an inspector or investigator, before any proper inquiry has been made or an appeal lodged; such a power is of course extremely threatening to an appellant. In contrast, appellants in cases where there has been a Social Security s. 20 disqualification followed by an automatic 40 per cent reduction in Supplementary Benefit, still continue to draw some benefit; women accused of cohabitation, sometimes on very flimsy grounds, get nothing. Similarly, if a single person is brought under the Social Security s. 19 trade dispute disqualification, he is totally disqualified and may only apply for emergency relief under s. 13 of the Supplementary Benefit Act 1966. This is difficult to obtain for the single striker but normally impossible for the accused cohabitee, because, as the D.H.S.S. put it in evidence to the Fisher Committee, she is already getting money from another source.[29]

In the United States, the Supreme Court has ruled that the termination of welfare assistance before an evidentiary hearing is a denial of Due Process, the American constitutional equivalent of the rules of Natural Justice.[30] Generally, if an appeal is received by the Division of Appeals within ten days of the date on the notification letter announcing reduction, termination or suspension, assistance is continued without reduction until the Fair Hearing. It is suggested that this should be a model for the British to emulate, if we are concerned about justice for appellants who may very well win their appeals but who, because of the present procedure, may suffer weeks of severe anxiety.

Non-Appearance

One of the most troubling questions in social security tribunal adjudication is that many appellants fail to attend the scheduled oral hearing on their case. This not only defeats the theoretical purpose of a tribunal appeal process founded on an oral re-examination of the facts, but is particularly serious in that appellants often lack the educational background to write effectively about the merits of their case. Precise national figures, broken down into benefit categories, seem to be unobtainable, but general estimates for social security tribunals given by various commentators would seem to be somewhat optimistic, certainly if applied to unemployment benefit cases. Professor Street, for example, estimates that 'almost one half' of Local Appeal Tribunal appellants fail to appear,[31] but the precise figure varies considerably between regions. Observation by the author of a Midland Region Local Appeal Tribunal over a period of three years showed just over 30 per cent of the appellants appearing at the 180 hearings attended, although it was interesting that the regular chairman made an estimate that about half made an appearance. The Newcastle/Edinburgh analysis of Local Appeal Tribunal case-papers showed attendance in 1970 to have been just over 50 per cent in Scotland and 54 per cent in the Northern Region. This study demonstrates the great variability of attendance when related to benefit category; for example, attendance on industrial disablement claims was 83 per cent, no doubt due to the critical importance of such a claim to the injured worker and also because he is more likely to be represented and not have other commitments, such as a job, intervening.[32]

In Supplementary Benefits adjudication, similar estimates are made of 50 per cent attendance, but again there are considerable variations. Professor Herman's study of 101 London Supplementary Benefit Appeal Tribunal hearings found just under half the appellants (forty-six) appearing, whereas another study in a tribunal serving a rural area found only eleven out of fifty consecutive appellants called for hearing actually coming to put their case. Three others sent close relatives such as a wife or son to appear on their behalf. And in Professor Bell's study of Northern Region Supplementary Benefit tribunal case-papers in 1973, only 43 per cent of appellants attended.[33]

Nevertheless, it can be stated with some confidence that non-appearance has a significant effect on the outcome of a case, and tribunal members repeatedly lament the lack of appellants coming before them to explain 'their side of the story'. One chairman of a Local Appeal Tribunal commented to the author after disallowing an appeal —'We wanted to know what he looked like and whether he seemed to us to be honest'. Similar statements, some worthy of Lombroso, are frequently made by tribunal members. In Ruth Lister's interview study of London Supplementary Benefit Appeal Tribunal members, the great majority considered non-attendance to affect an appellant's chances adversely, and in a Scottish study, 70 per cent of tribunal members acknowledged that non-attendance affected their decision; one member in fact made the remark that 'non-attendance indicates a weak appeal'.[34] Perhaps the best illustration of the effect that non-appearance has was observed in one Local Appeal Tribunal case, where the appellant arrived late for the hearing, having been held up by traffic. The appeal had already been disallowed with little comment by the tribunal members, but with her belated appearance the case was re-opened and, on hearing her evidence, even the Insurance Officer changed his view so as to support an allowance of the appeal. An additional factor to be weighed here is the usual practice of Presenting Officers and Insurance Officers to remain behind in the tribunal room during the deliberation on a case, usually perfunctory, when an appellant is not present; this of course gives them an opportunity to interject comments whenever the decision is going against them, so that a tribunal to uphold an appeal must literally out-argue the Presenting Officer with the possibility of upsetting personal relationships. In some tribunals, non-attendance cases are left to the end and dealt with summarily, although occasionally putting back the case to the end of the session may be justified in case the appellant may turn up. Certainly, tribunal members feel a measure of irritation when few or no appellants appear for sessions, and, as Professor Rose states, 'thus not only is the claimant handicapped by not being present in that his arguments are not heard, but also his absence seems to signify that his case and situation cannot be very serious'.[35] In terms of impartial adjudication, it is of course extremely difficult to evaluate an appellant's case when the sole written statement ascribed to him is the counter clerk's shorthand 'I want to appeal', as opposed to the Presenting Officer's written and oral submissions.

The Newcastle/Edinburgh research for the D.H.S.S. on Local Appeal Tribunals shows how statistically significant attendance is for a successful appeal. In the two regions whose case-papers were studied for 1970, the overall success rate for attenders was 35 per cent, and only 8 per cent for non-attenders. In the accompanying postal questionnaire, 72 per cent of chairmen thought it a 'big disadvantage' to the appellant's case if he did not attend the tribunal session.[36] Professor Bell's subsequent study on Supplementary Benefit Appeal Tribunals in the Northern Region showed a similar distinction in success rates: where the appellant appeared alone he was successful in 31.1 per cent of cases; and where he was not present the success rate was only 6.9 per cent.[37] An unpublished study by the D.H.S.S. in 1968 similarly showed that nationally appeals were only successful in 8 per cent of Supplementary Benefit cases where the claimant did not appear, compared with 29 per cent when he did, and a D.H.S.S. survey five years later showed a virtually identical result in that 25.5 per cent of those attending were successful, compared to only 8 per cent of appellants who did not attend.[38]

The usual reason advanced intuitively by most tribunal members to explain non-appearance seems to be that, having 'appealed in a fit of pique', claimants lose interest in their cases. However, research shows other more mundane factors to be operative. The author's follow-up study of fifty Supplementary Benefit appellants showed that a major cause of non-appearance was misunderstanding over the payment of expenses and compensation for time lost at work. This is at present subject to a maximum of £5.50 per day, and it is also possible to claim expenses for representatives. Only one non-appearing appellant had knowledge of this right, having purchased a copy of the *Supplementary Benefit Handbook*; most of those who actually came for the hearing seemed to be surprised, and even embarrassed, when the clerk asked them to tell him their expenses. Other difficulties mentioned in the follow-up interviews were disablement, deafness, and the lack of a baby-sitter; but the single most important reason for non-appearance was that the appellant was now back at work.[39] Such a factor would seem to be even more important amongst those making appeals to Local Appeal Tribunals, many of whom can be classified as 'short term' unemployed or temporarily sick, and who quickly go back to work. In Professor Bell's study of Local Appeal Tribunal appellants, 31 per cent of non-attenders mentioned difficulties connected with work.[40] Being back at work not only brings on a misguided fear of loss of pay to appellants—although some will still lose money if they have to take a whole day off because the allowance is inadequate for their hourly rate—but also brings with it the problem of summoning up the courage to ask for time off. By the time the hearing comes on, some appellants will have settled into a new job and do not want 'to start off on the wrong foot'; one Supplementary Benefit appellant stated that he had only finally obtained a job after a total cut in benefit by 'telling a pack of lies to cover up my past record and I didn't want to expose myself by asking for time off to attend a social security tribunal'.[41]

Other factors involved in non-attendance seem to be varied. Twenty per cent in Professor Bell's Local Appeal Tribunal study referred to illness in the family, having other appointments, being away from home or looking for a job, with the result that 'non-attendance resulted from a combination of pessimism about the outcome and practical difficulties'.[42] In the related Supplementary Benefit Appeal Tribunal study, 80 per cent of non-attenders were found to have practical reasons for not appearing, which included family circumstances, health, shortage of money or suitable clothes in which to appear, and travel problems.[43] Similar factors were found in the author's Supplementary Benefit appellant study, as well as problems connected with a farm worker who 'couldn't leave the animals', deafness, A level examination commitments, hospitalization, court appearance and 'social commitments' which were difficult to break.[44] Some of these reasons are clearly weighty matters, but one welfare rights advocate reports a number of cases where, despite intensive preparation with an appellant and his knowledge that an advocate will be present at the hearing, there is still non-appearance; subsequently, the appellant, often well-known to the advocate, makes a patently flimsy excuse such as 'I didn't have time'. One causative factor may be 'a sort of resigned defeatism that wants to confirm itself or at least justify the pessimism',[45] but it is clear that there is considerable scope for a social psychological study in this area.

However, many claimants couple their specific reason for non-attendance with a general expression of disillusionment about the appeal process itself; this is linked also with a misunderstanding of the relevance of following through with a personal appearance at the tribunal. A typical comment in the author's study was that 'It wouldn't have made much difference if I had gone anyway'. Others were:

> 'I couldn't be bothered after five or six letters without action . . . it was all becoming too much trouble'; 'It was not worth bothering with'; 'I had lost interest'; 'By the time the tribunal came around, I had got over the bad spell'; 'It might have been a waste of time to go'; 'They all work hand in glove with each other'; 'Pointless'; 'I couldn't have said any more about it'; 'Enough questions had been asked'; 'I'm fed up with all the letters . . . I was a shop steward last year and often attended with others, but we always lost. They never took a sympathetic view.'[46]

However, it was interesting to find that a majority, on thinking back and hearing of a possible claim for expenses, wished that they had attended.

Subjective feelings of what will happen at the tribunal clearly play a large part in non-appearance. A disconcerting finding of Professor Bell's empirical research on social security tribunals is that appellants more or less abandon hope after receiving a copy of the tribunal papers through the post. Thirty-two per cent of non-attenders in the Local Appeal Tribunal sample decided at this point not to go to the tribunal.[47] This might be seen as support for the belief that appellants appeal in the heat of the moment and later realize they do not have a case; but such a perspective must be treated with caution when viewed in relation to the social context. Few appellants are able to obtain proper advice on their appeal, so that discouragement at this stage may be very much uncalled for. Certainly the tribunal documents are of an official nature, and seem to be daunting to most appellants, but the evidence is that they read carefully if perplexedly through them. Seventy-three per cent of Professor Bell's Local Appeal Tribunal sample read the documents, many spending considerable time at it, but 31 per cent said they had difficulty in understanding them and 10 per cent gave answers suggesting that they had in fact had difficulty although not admitting it.[48] On the standard form sent by the Local Appeal Tribunal clerk there is a 'tear-off' section asking if the appellant wishes to be present, and 68 per cent replied in the affirmative in the Scottish and Northern Regions in 1970; however, 35 per cent of the returns were missing, having been either lost or destroyed, or never sent.[49] Nevertheless, this would seem to signify a high intent to appear even at this stage, which is subsequently not realized. Unfortunately, there is evidence that some appellants do not receive the official papers, particularly in relation to Supplementary Benefit Appeal Tribunals, where the clerk should also send Form LT 204 B 'Notes on Appeal Tribunals'. Twenty-one per cent of Professor Bell's Supplementary Benefit appellants stated that they did not receive this official leaflet,[50] and a number of commentators have criticized the receipt of tribunal documents at the last moment. Often the Notice of Hearing for a Supplementary Benefit appeal will arrive only a day or two before the scheduled hearing which leaves little time for getting advice on the appeal.

Professor Bell's studies seem to have found little overt hostility towards social security tribunals, and even a high rate of belief in their independence and impartiality, although in the Local Appeal Tribunal survey it was perhaps significant that 37 per cent of appellants did not realize that the tribunal was an independent body.[51] Such a finding contrasts dramatically with all other evidence we have from social security tribunal appellants, and it is suggested that this must throw some doubt on the respondents' view of the Newcastle study as an 'independent' study, clearly backed as it was by the D.H.S.S. Negative comments of bias and prejudice were common in the author's study of Supplementary Benefit appellants; many in the sample were entirely pessimistic about their chances before a tribunal, and similar views can be seen in an earlier sample of mothers on National Assistance, and in a study of appellants by the Nuffield Legal Research Unit.[52] Such views of disillusionment and enmity are not of course new, and can be found in the earlier years of experience with the Courts of Referees and U.A.B. Appeal Tribunals.[53] And it is also clear that many older appellants still find it abhorrent to get involved with any form of public relief, remembering childhood experiences and cautionary tales about Workhouses.[54] Often such attitudes surface as 'nervousness' or a reluctance to discuss 'private matters in public', which reinforce the need to be sensitive to all forms of stigmatizing pressure, open or subliminal, in dealing with tribunal appellants.

If notification of non-appearance because of difficulties about the time of the hearing reaches the clerk of a social security tribunal, then he will normally adjourn the case to a later date, particularly when one is suggested by the appellant. Regulations in fact require a Local Appeal Tribunal to adjourn the case for at least one month, but there is a discretion to bring the case on before this time if an appellant requests it.[55] However, appellants often seem not to understand this procedure and it would certainly help if the case papers displayed this right more prominently and perhaps gave a telephone number, to be called reverse charges, which would assure that the adjournment was relayed to the clerk. Unfortunately, because Supplementary Benefit Appeal Tribunal clerks are often away travelling their circuits, notification can sometimes be mislaid. Similarly, another way of significantly increasing the appearance rate of claimants at hearings would be to make absolutely clear the position on travel and work-related expenses by a prominent notification on the forms sent out by the clerk. Such a statement could be boldly printed on the front page of the respective Supplementary Benefit B/O 22 and Local Appeal Tribunal LT2A forms, which are the basic tribunal documents.

Much more imagination and effort needs to be applied to this problem of non-appearance. Certainly, the first time there is non-attendance, it is suggested that a case be automatically adjourned for a month and a personal letter be sent to the appellant stressing the importance of attendance, mentioning an expenses claim and a local advice agency which could help with the appeal, as well as urging generally that he come to the new hearing to put his case. One further possibility would be to hold evening hearings once a month after normal working hours; this would have the additional attraction of being a means towards attracting capable chairmen and wingmen reluctant to take time off day-time work. Additionally, the expenses notification might include a claim for 'babysitting' expenses on the lines of the present allowance for representative's expenses.

Privacy and the Right to a Reasoned Decision

The retention of total privacy in Supplementary Benefit Appeal Tribunal hearings has probably been instrumental in keeping this area, in Tony Lynes's phrase, a 'backwater of British justice'. Only recently has this shroud of secrecy been lifted to the extent that academic observers or even members of the Council on Tribunals could see what went on at tribunal hearings, and here only if the chairman and the appellant agree.[56] Previously the only way for observers to attend a Supplementary Benefit Appeal Tribunal was to act as the representative or 'friend' of the appellant, but here of course the 'observer' became an active participant in the hearing and could not judge how typical his case was. The theoretical justification for this secrecy, as stated by the Franks Committee, was that, 'if any or all of these appeals were to be heard in public many applicants might be deterred from appealing or even from applying for assistance and the purpose of the legislation might thus be frustrated'.[57] Such a statement needs, however, careful scrutiny.

It is interesting to note from the outset that the majority of appellants have very little idea of how social security tribunals are constituted, and certainly do not know whether they hold hearings in public or in private; in the author's study, guesses were made by appellants that Supplementary Benefit Appeal Tribunals consisted of two social security officers, or that it was a divorce court judge sitting alone, and in another study of Local Appeal Tribunal appellants, only 22 per cent knew that the chairman was a lawyer and 8 per cent thought the tribunal consisted of departmental officials.[58] Discussing private matters with anyone, including strangers sitting as tribunal members, might be thought to be just as deterrent as having an observer present as well. The use of the privacy argument by S.B.C. officers is also on occasions misleading; they seem sometimes to have little compunction in breaching privacy by putting as evidence to a tribunal a personal letter about which the appellant clearly feels embarrassed. This happened in one case where the author represented a claimant, and made the strongest objections to the introduction of a letter included in the tribunal documents, whose contents were irrelevant to the appeal but which were also highly likely to inculcate prejudice in the minds of the tribunal members. Unfortunately, the label 'privacy' has come to be used in much welfare litigation, not in relation to the client's interests, but, in the words of an American commentator, 'as a device to insure the privacy of the functionary and to conceal his activities'.[59]

Until the Franks Report, Local Appeal Tribunal hearings were similarly held *in camera*, although Industrial Injury Tribunals, constituted in 1946 as a result of the Beveridge Report, have always been held in public; the present rule is that the chairman of the amalgamated Local Appeal Tribunal has a discretion to exclude the public, 'if he is of the opinion that intimate personal or financial circumstances may have to be disclosed or that considerations of public security are involved';[60] if there is exclusion this is generally in fact at the request of appellants rather than by the direction of the chairman. This right is very rarely exercised, even though the Local Appeal Tribunals have to deal on occasions with similarly 'intimate' questions, such as cohabitation; of course such sensitive matters are dealt with daily in public in the Family Division of the High Court. In fact, not all Supplementary Benefit litigation is kept secret, as some matters such as recovery actions are heard by magistrates, trade dispute cases go straight to the Local Appeal Tribunals, and tribunal cases can be reviewed in the High Court, all with the possibility of full publicity. Fears as to extensive press coverage, often expressed by Supplementary Benefit tribunal participants, and S.B.C. officials, seem to be groundless in the light of Local Appeal Tribunal practice. The date, time and location of such hearings are normally displayed at the local town hall, or are freely available at the local D.H.S.S. office. Generally, however, local newspapers have little space or time to cover tribunals, except where there is a trade dispute test case covering the disqualification of a number of workers. The National Insurance Commissioners apparently, however, 'keep in close touch with the press',[61] but this is not very evident in national newspaper coverage. Publication of the National Insurance Commissioners' reports is carefully constructed so that the identity of the claimant is not revealed, and the numbered form of citation also ensures some degree of further protection.

It is urged here that in the interests of openness, Supplementary Benefit Appeal Tribunals should also hold all their hearings in public, subject to a right by the appellant, which should be notified to him at the start of the hearing, to exclude observers. If there is a fear of excessive numbers, it is very unlikely that hordes of interested citizens will suddenly start to attend, judging from the experience since 1965 of Local Appeal Tribunals. But it would facilitate observation by those with a legimate interest in the workings of tribunals, who at present must negotiate a series of obstacles to secure admission. During the author's observation of Supplementary Benefit hearings, one chairman insisted on asking questions obviously calculated to persuade appellants to ask for the removal of observers; not one made the request. Indeed, some even suggested to the chairman that such an independent presence was helpful to them. It should be added that in the author's observation of Local Appeal Tribunals no appellant at any time objected to his presence. If the change to public hearings were to result in fewer claims, which it is doubted, this would be more than offset by the beneficial impression of openness which could make a major contribution towards creating confidence in the minds of potential appellants in the independence of tribunals. A famous dictum by Mr. Justice Brandeis is perhaps apt: 'publicity is justly commended as a remedy for social and industrial diseases. Sunlight is said to be the best of disinfectants; electric light the most efficient policeman'.[62]

A further extension of the 'secrecy syndrome' which affects Supplementary Benefit tribunals is the lack of a full and reasoned decision given to the appellant on the refusal of his appeal. The Franks Committee believed that, in the interests of justice, a tribunal must set out reasons for a decision 'to the fullest paracticable extent' and in writing, so as to ensure that they have been properly thought out: 'a decision is apt to be better if the reasons for it have to be set out in writing because the reasons are then more likely to have been properly thought out'.[63] Until 1957 very few tribunals, and certainly not the social security tribunals, gave reasons for a decision, even though the Donoughmore Committee, erroneously, thought that this was contrary to the principles of Natural Justice.[64] In fact, it would seem that in the case-law only the Medical Appeal Tribunal was under an obligation to set out its findings on material facts.[65] However, despite a strong recommendation, the legislation following the Franks Report merely stated that the tribunal should 'furnish a statement, either written or oral, of the reasons for the decision if required',[66] thereby leaving the onus on the claimant to request such a statement. Nevertheless, in Local Appeal Tribunals, the practice is for the chairman always to record in writing both the evidence submitted and the reasons for a decision, apparently for the simple reason that an official form is provided for this, at the instigation of the National Insurance Commissioners, so as to facilitate a hearing of a possible second appeal. The *Notes for Chairmen* prepared by the D.H.S.S. also suggest that he follow this procedure, and the statutory regulations now require that the chairman record in writing all decisions and a statement of the grounds for them as well as all findings of material fact.[67] Practice as to oral notifications of the decision varies, but generally the Local Appeal Tribunal chairman will re-call an appellant from the waiting-room to explain the tribunal's decision.

Some tribunals apparently have the clerk inform the appellant of the decision in the waiting-room. Occasionally there seem to have been outbursts of cursing on the part of an aggrieved appellant,[68] but this is rare, and particularly so when a tribunal has shown itself to have adjudicated impartially on the case, even though the result is adverse to the appellant. Following the hearing, a typed copy of the decision, and the chairman's notes on the evidence given, is sent to the appellant; if the tribunal was not unanimous, then the reasons given by the dissenting members are also recorded. This practice, which was not required by law until 1967, seems to have grown up in the period after the 1946 reform.[69] Such a procedure contrasts favourably with Supplementary Benefits practice, where, until 1971, no reasons whatsoever were given for a decision except, and this only after 1958, at the express request of the appellant.[70] However, many chairmen seem only even now to write a one-sentence comment such as 'Commission decision upheld', and even this is normally handwritten and seems often to be difficult to read. Evidence submitted by the parties is not normally summarized, and there is no mention of a dissent. A study carried out on Supplementary Benefit Appeal Tribunal decisions in the Citizens Rights Office showed that in only twenty-one out of forty cases were adequate reasons given for a decision, despite the fact that in most cases there had been a C.R.O. advocate present stressing adjudication on the basis of the Supplementary Benefit Act and the statutory regulations.[71] Furthermore, claimants are not normally informed of the decision except by post following a delay, in several instances, of some days.

A proper notification of the reasons for a decision, and preferably a summary of the evidence submitted, is of course an essential prerequisite for further appeal or review by the courts. Unfortunately, this may account for the paucity of writing given by some chairmen insecure enough to worry about their decision being overturned on appeal. As

Professor Street puts it, every tribunal chairman knows that 'if you want to evade judicial scrutiny, don't put in writing any more than you can help'.[72]

In the United States, long criticized for its use of lengthy transcripts in the administrative appeal process,[73] the new and reasonably inexpensive alternative of tape-recording lower court trials and administrative hearings has replaced the older method of having a stenographer at every hearing. Cassette tapes are kept until after the appeal date has expired and are then re-used. Having a tape-recorder running also allows a chairman to be more selective in his note-taking and therefore to be more aware of physical inter-action rather than attempting a verbatim transcript. Such a system also allows speedy replay of testimony for tribunal members if they are uncertain of a point later during the course of deliberations.

As until recent times Supplementary Benefit appeals were most unlikely to go any further, little was done to provide adequate information, usually on the grounds of the administrative time saved. But, as Lord Denning has pointed out, the practice of giving full reasons for a decision reached in private is 'to command the confidence of the public'.[74] It is urged that it has become essential to provide an adequate 'speaking order' on the lines of that given routinely by the Local Appeal Tribunals. However, perhaps a more important reason for requiring a written statement of both evidence and decision is that of its effect on the proper adjudication of a case, in that, as Professor Robson states, such a discipline quite obviously develops 'the mental capacity and sense of fairness of the adjudicator'.[75]

Burden of Proof and the Principles of Natural Justice

Many of the practical problems surrounding social security tribunal adjudication stem from the difficulties inherent in deciding such intractable questions as the 'genuineness' of unemployment. In a survey of ninety-two unemployed men, Adrian Sinfield concluded that 'the distinction between voluntary and involuntary termination of a job—so important in deciding eligibility to state benefits and public attitudes towards unemployment—was often a shadowy and arbitrary one'.[76] And these difficulties become more acute as adjudication moves from the area of fixed contribution requirements to the completely subjective assessment of individual motives in relation to disqualification. E. Wight Bakke doubted, in his 1933 study of British unemployment, as to

> whether a Court [of Referees], no matter how carefully chosen and how thoroughly respected, can apply fairly and adequately

> tests which will show the genuineness of a person's unemployment or industrial status, if it is not possible to formulate contribution or automatic employment record tests which will determine that fact. The determination of industrial status, or the 'genuineness' of the unemployment before a Court of Referees is surrounded by many and perhaps insurmountable difficulties.[77]

The problems of adjudication in Supplementary Benefit Appeal Tribunals are perhaps even more magnified, in that, as well as determining the genuineness of unemployment—often without the immediate link with employers and the local industrial situation which the Department of Employment can provide for the determination of unemployment insurance claims—difficult policy decisions must be made on such claims as 'cohabitation' and discretionary Exceptional Needs awards. Cohabitation questions occur in both tribunals, but much more rarely in Local Appeal Tribunal jurisdiction, where it is in relation to widows' benefits. This form of 'compulsory marriage' has not as yet been judicially or statutorily defined with any precision; a recent National Insurance Commissioner's formulation is clearly at odds with internal policy standards laid down by the S.B.C. and publicized in the *Supplementary Benefits Handbook*.[78] Terms such as 'unemployment' and 'cohabitation' are not, in relation to welfare law, simply economic or social descriptions. They carry a number of moral presumptions as to the beneficial effects of work and the nature of family life. And it is clear from observation of the tribunals at work that these moral views are an integral part of the decision-making process in both initial determination and tribunal adjudication. Repeatedly, examples of operative personal beliefs occur in areas of alleged welfare abuse. For instance, the real hardship and deprivation found among the unemployed in Adrian Sinfield's empirical survey contrasts starkly with the following confident assertion, typical of its type, made by a 'Director of Welfare Services' writing in *The Times*:

> Certainly one of the major defects of the welfare state is the choice extended to the unskilled between working if they feel like it, or living on their fellows if they do not . . . Such words as poverty and hardship are glibly bandied about . . . as though academics like Professor Abel-Smith and Professor Townsend have proved that chronic indigence is the settled state of large groups in the community . . . In any search for those in the greatest need few, if any, will be found in the ranks of the unemployed.[79]

Such views obviously operate in the minds of tribunal members; Ruth Lister reports that from her interviews with London Supplementary Benefit Appeal Tribunal members it was clear that 'the law was seen as largely irrelevant and decisions were made on the merits of the appellant rather than of the appellant's case'.[80] Views as to whether an appellant is or is not 'deserving', the basic standard in the Poor Law administration of welfare benefits, seem unfortunately still to be the basis of much decision-making in the social security tribunals. Where this is so, it becomes very difficult for an appellant to win a claim on the merits of his case, and consequently negates the judicial nature of both the original appeal and later attempts to remedy an unjust decision. As Professor Handler points out, clarification of the issues on appeal will be virtually impossible because the original decision is 'shrouded in a fog of judgemental impressions that will prevent administrative or judicial reversal'.[81]

Clearly, personal beliefs will affect, in some way, the administration of any system of determination of claims, and particularly so in questions concerning such concepts as work and welfare.[82] The very real difficulties of correct and impartial adjudication on such fluid, and emotive, terms as 'misconduct' and 'voluntary unemployment' should not be underestimated. In these circumstances, the requirements of tribunal procedure in complete accordance with the principles of Natural Justice is crucial in order to ensure a full and fair hearing for the appellant's case; this will decrease to the minimum possible any chance of operative bias.

Unfortunately, a breach of Natural Justice has come to be, in much recent debate on tribunals, a devalued term applied indiscriminately to any situation where unfairness is alleged. Simply stated, the rules of Natural Justice, as formulated by the courts, are a form of scrutiny maintained over bodies exercising some kind of judicial function. Although their precise limits are still a matter of uncertainty, and perhaps necessarily so, their fundamental principles have long been judicially defined.[83] For example, it has been laid down that the members of the review body or appellate tribunal 'must act in good faith and fairly listen to both sides . . . giving a fair opportunity to those who are parties in the controversy for correcting or contradicting any relevant statement prejudicial to their view'.[84] This aspect was further developed in the leading case by Lord Haldane, who stated that members of any body exercising judicial functions 'must deal with the question referred to them without bias, and they must give to each of the parties the opportunity of adequately presenting the case made'.[85]

The head of bias, contained in the rule *nemo judex in causa sua* and connoting, as the judges have refined the concept, prejudice,[86] direct financial interest,[87] or personal bias,[88] should perhaps be only of marginal importance in social security tribunals, as members normally have no personal interest in the case before them. On occasion wingmen disqualify themselves from sitting in a particular case; for example, where in one case the employer's representative in a Local Appeal Tribunal case was in fact the personnel officer who had dismissed the appellant. Only a very strong bias which is 'an operative prejudice, whether conscious or unconscious',[89] will disqualify, but it would seem that at the least the personal and moralistic viewpoints of some tribunal members are inimical to good adjudication.

However, the second head of Lord Haldane's definition, which contains the *audi alteram partem* rule that both sides should be given a full opportunity to be heard, brings into question the whole nature of the tribunal process, and the fact that claimants are generally unrepresented, which forms the basis of this discussion. Under the rule, whose principles are necessarily fluid, Professor de Smith stated that the following points can be extrapolated for procedures in administrative tribunals as well as courts: they

> must conduct oral hearings; the judges are personally identifiable; only one who has heard all the evidence may participate in the decision; the parties are entitled to legal representation; the rules of evidence must be observed; cross-examination of witnesses (if they are called to give oral evidence) must be permitted; the decision must be based on evidence.[90]

Unfortunately, both Local Appeal and Supplementary Benefit Appeal Tribunals fail to qualify on several points. As we have seen, there are full oral hearings in only about 50 per cent of all cases, because appellants are not present for a variety of reasons, many of which are beyond their control. Very few chairmen in Supplementary Benefit Appeal Tribunals introduce themselves or their wingmen, or make any sort of informative statement about what interests they represent; this is also not standard practice in Local Appeal Tribunals.[91] Sometimes, astonishingly, a tribunal member who is late is nevertheless allowed to join a case while it is proceeding and takes part in the subsequent decision.[92] Basic rules of evidence are, as we have seen, rarely known let alone observed by most Supplementary Benefit chairmen. The device of cross-examination, as stated in a leading American text, 'is beyond any doubt the greatest legal engine ever invented for the discovery of truth',[93] but its use in relation to social security tribunals is sporadic, often denied because of the lack of witnesses physically present whose testimony is nevertheless introduced by hearsay and, even when utilized by a few welfare rights advocates or lawyers, sufficient time is not allowed for its proper deployment.[94] Also, as Professor de Smith pointed out, 'often a party cannot effectively exercise his right to cross-examine unless he is represented by a lawyer'.[95] And finally, many decisions in social security tribunals can be easily seen to be based, not on evidence, but on rumour, social background and even physiognomy.

One critical point in all judicial procedures is where the burden of proof is attached. It has long been a principle of criminal trials in the Anglo-American system that the prosecution must establish its case beyond a reasonable doubt, whereas in civil litigation the plaintiff must establish a case on the lower standard of a 'balance of probabilities'. This second standard is the one applicable to tribunals, but there are a number of difficulties involved in its use in social security tribunals. Firstly, in a civil appeal situation in the courts, onus of proof is placed on the appellant, but here there has been no prior hearing so that logically the onus should rest on the administrative agency to defend its decision. This is the view taken by the National Insurance Commissioners even when there has been a prior hearing at the local level, and it is suggested that this is the best approach for all tribunals. However, because of the laxity of tribunal procedure, often an appellant may be faced with a heavy burden of proof; for example, in many tribunal hearings on a disqualification for failure to take up employment, a number of Presenting Officers and Insurance Officers are content to state that in the area generally there are suitable vacancies. Chairmen unfortunately do not often insist on documentary evidence of this in the way of newspaper advertisements or Department of Employment vacancy lists, and the appellant is then thrown into a position of defending his conduct without advice, representation or prior warning. Certainly most appellants will not have kept records of their job applications. Once again, this sort of abuse of procedure is more prevalent in Supplementary Benefit Appeal Tribunals, and in fact the Fisher Committee recommended that, before disqualification from benefit, the S.B.C. should show specific job refusal which would not be less remunerative than remaining on benefit.[96] This point was rejected by the then Government, but it would seem eminently sensible.

In relation to cohabitation disqualifications, the procedures of social security tribunals also do not normally make clear to the appellant that the administrative agency must prove its charges, although a National Insurance Commissioner's decision states clearly that, for Local Appeal Tribunals, 'the burden of proof of . . . cohabitation rests with the Insurance Officer'.[97] One recent commentary admits that there are difficulties in this area, but goes on to say of Supplementary Benefit Appeal Tribunals that 'since most of the proceedings are not adversarial in nature the question where the burden of proof lies has little importance'.[98] Such a statement could clearly never come from someone who has watched a Supplementary Benefit Appeal Tribunal cohabitation case, where the procedure is often not only adversarial but accusatorial in a literal sense. Professor Street, using his own experience of Local Appeal Tribunals, seems also to think the onus of proof question is in fact properly dealt with in social security tribunals, and further points out somewhat disingenuously that there is always the possibility of an appeal.[99] But as one former student of his, with considerable experience as an advocate in tribunals not so capably chaired, points out, in most such cases

> There is a presumption of guilt and, therefore, a transferred burden of proof on to the claimant, because *his benefit has already been suspended* before the appeal is lodged or heard. And if Professor Street is right, and the tribunal *does* commit an error of law, how many claimants are in a position to recognise it or have the resources to follow it up by an appeal to the Commissioner?[100]

Ruth Lister, from her observation of London Supplementary Benefit Appeal Tribunal hearings, believes that in effect the onus of proof is placed on the appellant 'to persuade the tribunal that she is telling the truth'. She suggests that, because of the present abuse of procedure, where an appeal involves total withdrawal of benefit, then a higher standard of proof, such as proof beyond a reasonable doubt, should apply.[101] While it is true that social security tribunal procedure leaves a lot to be desired, this extra burden would probably prove too complicated in administration. It would perhaps also be unnecessary if there were firstly a rule against any cut-off in benefit until after an appeal was heard and, secondly, if the already existing theoretical safeguards on onus of proof and basic rules of evidence were strictly enforced. However, another of Ruth Lister's proposals, establishing basic rules of procedure by statutory instrument, would seem eminently worthwhile. These would be set out in simple language and sent to every appellant with the tribunal documents. Most of the points she suggests for inclusion are already buried in the existing regulations or are implicit in the rules of Natural Justice, but a clear statement of principles to which all tribunal participants could refer would be very helpful.[102]

Professor Laski stated that, in constitutional terms, 'executive discretion is an impossible rule unless it is conceived in terms of judicial standards'.[103] But given that under the rules of Natural Justice an appellant must know the case he has to meet, how far can it be said that in social security tribunals this standard is observed? Most important here is the position of the secret Codes operated by the S.B.C. in determining claims, which have already been referred to in other connections.[104] These internal rules, now covering some 900 or so loose-leaf pages, do not of course have the effect of binding law before the appeal tribunals or in a court, as would legislation or statutory instruments; they are also not directly available to tribunal members. However, there is often real confusion in practice as to how much effect the internal Codes should have, and, where the appellant is not present, there is an observable tendency for the tribunal to act as a 'rubber stamp' for decisions based on the Departmental rules. These internal policy guidelines do, however, have the quality of law in that they provide the source of authority and the norms for initial administrative decision-making, so that in knowing their content one can reasonably predict the outcome of the S.B.C.'s decision on the claim. In the light of the small fraction of claims appealed, this framework of secret rules therefore is the 'law' on the bulk of claims. Their secrecy has been partly mitigated since 1970 by the publication of the summary of certain rules in the *Supplementary Benefits Handbook*, but the availability of this booklet to claimants is clearly limited by a number of social factors, even if its language and context could be understood by someone coming to tribunal work for the first time. The motives for this secrecy are somewhat difficult to understand; Tony Lynes puts forward the view that:

> The real reason for keeping the A Code secret . . . is that supplementary benefits are for the poor and only for the poor. They are a form of communal charity, and the essence of charity is that it is concerned not with people's rights but with their welfare. To publish detailed rules about the administration of the scheme would conflict with this view of its essential nature.[105]

The continuing debate over rights as against charity contains a number of theoretical questions, but also for those interested in boosting the position of the poor the dilemma as to which strategy can in the long run provide more benefit for the poor. As Professor Jowell points out, if welfare policy is exposed to public criticism, it is of course debatable 'whether or not the outcome of the criticism will ultimately enure to the benefit of welfare claimants'.[106] The S.B.C.'s view is that, although the 1966 Supplementary Benefit Act laid emphasis on a concept of right to benefit, 'the distinctive feature of the Supplementary Benefits Scheme is its discretionary element . . . a claimant's "rights" go further than legal entitlement . . . a "right" to courtesy and understanding relationships . . .'[107] But the extension to a 'right to courtesy' is merely capitalizing on the imprecise nature of the term 'right' in general usage, although the statement perhaps serves to emphasize some of the confusion which has arisen in trying to place 'rights' and 'charity/discretion/flexibility' as diametrically opposed concepts.[108] The subtleties of a Hohfeldian analysis are perhaps unnecessary to point out that the right to entitlement under the 1966 Act is a very different thing from the expectation of courtesy when making a claim at the S.B.C. counter.

It is interesting to find, in relation to Tony Lynes's charge of a 'charity' mentality, that members of the Supplementary Benefit Appeal Tribunals have recently expressed dissatisfaction with their role in respect to the Family Income Supplement scheme, because in their view 'there is little room for the exercise of any discretion in the implementation of the Scheme'.[109] From observation it is clear that Supplementary Benefit Appeal Tribunal members often regard themselves as performing a charitable function, and generally appear uncomfortable when advocates appear before them quoting statutory rules and regulations. As Ruth Lister states, any observer of Supplementary Benefit Appeal Tribunals must be struck by how often appellants are 'subjected to interrogation by the chairman and members on matters not strictly relevant to the content of the appeal'.[110] However, the developing nature of the British system seems to have been a movement away from flexible internal rules towards defined rights with an element of knowledge by the claimant and a general consistency of decision-making. The single most important development here was of course the setting up of the unemployment insurance scheme to remove some of the unemployed from the almost wholly discretionary receipt of Poor Law relief. It is nevertheless interesting to find one writer in 1943 contrasting the 'legalistic interpretations' of the U.A.B. tribunals with the 'superior' discretion of the old Public Assistance committees.[111]

Such a movement has been mirrored in many other countries where welfare benefits have moved from being regarded as 'largesse' or a 'privilege' to the status of a 'right'. For example, in a New York case in 1921 a court cut off Old Age Assistance to an appellant because he chose to live in rags in an old barn—'he has no right to defy the standards and conventions of civilised society while being supported at public expense'—whereas in a landmark decision in 1969 the Supreme Court stated that 'the constitutional challenge cannot be answered by the argument that public assistance benefits are a "privilege" and not a "right" '.[112]

However, the goal here must be, as Professor K. C. Davis states, to 'cut back unnecessary discretion',[113] and not totally to eliminate all discretion. Care should certainly be taken not to move social security adjudication to the opposing vice of excessive technicality and rigidity. As an American commentator on the British system has pointed out in comparison with experience in the United States, 'the goal of the elimination of all discretion in public assistance is both illusory and self-defeating. The search for equity and adequacy does not require the elimination of discretion but rather the elimination of unnecessary discretion'.[114] It was of course this aim of removing unnecessary discretion which prompted the change from National Assistance to Supplementary Benefits in 1966.[115]

However, linked with the discussion on discretion is a more fundamental discussion of the right of Natural Justice to knowledge of the case against the appellant. This of course presupposes that the appellant has access to the rules on which the initial determination is made, but also more importantly to the rules on which the tribunal makes its decision. In relation to Local Appeal Tribunals, these rules are contained partly in statute and in delegated legislation under them, and partly in the published decisions of the National Insurance Commissioners, neither of which are normally available in Public Libraries. In certain cases, reliance will be placed on unreported decisions, and these are only available at the National Insurance Commissioners' National and Regional Headquarters. An appellant will on rare occasions ask the Insurance Officer if he can look at the reported decisions. But, as one Insurance Officer commented to the author, 'He wastes a day poring through them, and I waste a day trying to explain it all to him . . . I have never known it to do them one bit of good.' However, in relation to Supplementary Benefits, the precise rules on which the initial decision is made are totally unavailable, and the statutory rules and regulations on which the Supplementary Benefit tribunals should make their decisions are, like those of the Local Appeal Tribunals, generally unavailable to claimants, and are in many cases unintelligible without proper advice. Not only must incisive questions be asked about the availability of information on the applicable law, but also on the need for some form of advice to make it comprehensible to appellants, as well as representation to aid him in making the best of any available arguments at the oral hearing of his case.

Representation, Advice and Legal Aid

Perhaps the most important, and certainly the most controversial, question concerning tribunals is whether full legal aid should be extended to appellants, particularly those contesting social security determinations; or whether some form of advice and representational facilities should be made available to appellants, either as an interim measure before full legal aid becomes available, or as an alternative. Before 1958 there had in fact been a total ban on all legal representatives before the social security tribunals, which was only lifted when the Franks Committee showed itself to be of the opinion that the ban was inappropriate and possibly in breach of the rules of Natural Justice.[116] The Franks Committee also recommended that legal aid should be extended to all tribunals, with an immediate extension to final appellate bodies such as the National Insurance Commissioners;[117] but this suggestion was not approved by the then Government. An Opposition spokesman, James Griffiths, pointed out in the House of Commons that, in removing the ban on lawyers, 'we shall be giving nothing unless the Government are prepared to extend the legal aid service'.[118]

At the time of writing, this whole matter is under full consideration by the Lord Chancellor's Office, so that changes may soon be made to the present situation. The historical background is that both the Rushcliffe Committee and the 1949 Legal Aid and Advice Act clearly contemplated the extension of legal aid to tribunals, but as yet the full provisions of the Act have been made available only to appellants before the Lands Tribunal and the Commons Commissioners. In 1968, the Lord Chancellor's Advisory Committee raised the topic, but decided to postpone full consideration until further research had been carried out. This Report echoed the traditional view that Supplementary Benefit cases 'almost invariably contain no matter of law'.[119] Subsequently, however, the Lord Chancellor's Advisory Committee reversed its opinion and recommended the extension of legal aid and advice to all tribunals under the aegis of the Council on Tribunals.[120] The proposal was to extend the existing green form legal aid scheme to cover representation at tribunals. This scheme, which allows up to £25 to be spent in obtaining advice from a solicitor (about three hours' work for the average solicitor), had previously only been available for the preparation of a brief, although it was possible for a solicitor to act as a 'McKenzie Man' when he assisted as an adviser to the appellant at a tribunal hearing. Although the High Court objected to a layman appearing as a representative in the courts rather than merely advising litigants, in practice the green form scheme has been used by some solicitors to represent clients both at courts and in tribunals.[121]

Unfortunately, very few solicitors have utilized the green form scheme for tribunal work; figures quoted by Lord Elwyn-Jones at the Law Society Conference in 1974 were that 60 per cent of green form work currently concerned matrimonial matters, 10 per cent criminal work and only 1 per cent concerned work in connection with all the listed statutory tribunals under the oversight of the Council on Tribunals.[122] A Legal Action Group survey in 1974 of its own solicitor members, clearly a group which will be highly motivated to use the green form scheme, showed that only 48 per cent had given assistance for a tribunal appeal. And of this work, 59 per cent concerned Rent Tribunal matters, 36 per cent Industrial Tribunals, and only 17 per cent in connection with Local Appeal Tribunals.[123] Perhaps most damning is the information from the Nuffield study that 78 per cent of appellants connected with Rent, Local Appeal and Supplementary Benefit Appeal Tribunals, had never heard of the green form scheme, and others claiming knowledge were very confused.[124]

Another initial difficulty here is the nature of the present legal aid system, which is solely geared to individualized litigation. At present the test for a legal aid grant is whether 'a prudent unassisted party who had adequate but not over-abundant means of his own would choose to risk them by bringing or defending the action'.[125] As Richard White points out, this has the effect of excluding legal aid in cases where the applicant's interest is fairly small, but a class or group interest is considerable.[126] Such 'test case' or 'impact litigation' work by Legal Assistance Programmes in the United States has achieved dramatic changes in the welfare process and in relation to the rights of the poor generally. This question of individualized as opposed to group interest is generally based on cost-effectiveness, and of course when only individual benefits are taken into consideration then statements such as the following, in a recent study on administrative tribunals, can be made:

> Legal representation is only necessary in exceptional cases; and because the sums of money are for the most part small the cost of universal legal representation would be disproportionate; in any case, as matters stand, there is no incentive for the legal profession to specialise in tribunal law and practice.[127]

The last remark is inevitably an entirely circular argument. But the sums of money gained in benefit may be in a marginal sense extremely important, and may also amount to a considerable figure when available to a whole class or group of beneficiaries. The comment also ignores the fact that legal representation does not just involve advocacy at the tribunal, but also matters such as advice, counselling, drafting of appeals and negotiation with the welfare administration; often representation is much more important, and time-saving, in the pre-hearing process of application and administrative review than at the hearing itself.

The basic argument for the extension of legal aid to social security tribunals is that without it appellants are at a considerable disadvantage. This is partly so because of their lack of skill in advocacy techniques, partly because of their lack of knowledge of the law involved in their case, and partly because of unfamiliarity with the tribunal setting.[128] It is quite clear that, in any adversary situation, appellants who are properly represented by skilled and competent advocates will be more likely to win their appeals. In Professor Bell's study of Northern Region Supplementary Benefit appeals in 1973, the success rate for unrepresented appellants appearing on their own was 31.1 per cent compared with 42.4 per cent when appearing with a representative; the success rate was only 6.9 per cent where neither representative nor appellant attended. However, these figures only refer to sixteen cases where there was a representative out of 1,274 in the Northern Region that year.[129] In the related study of Northern and Scottish Region Local Appeal Tribunals in 1970, unrepresented appellants on their own had a success rate of 22 per cent, whereas with a representative the rate was 50 per cent, and without any appearance at all the rate was only 8 per cent.[130] The D.H.S.S. survey in 1968 previously quoted showed that, when Supplementary Benefit appellants appeared, decisions in their favour were 29 per cent; but when represented, their success rate was 35.8 per cent. Such figures are confirmed by observation in many other areas of adversary legal process.[131]

From observation in social security tribunals it is also clear that very few claimants can make their own case out in any adequate sense. In most instances, their appeal consists of a simple protest or blurted plea for help, without any basis in the legal rules applicable and usually with little fluency. Professor Whitmore, a visiting Australian who observed a number of tribunal hearings, states that

> The commonest situation before tribunals—very common indeed—is that the claimant or party is completely inarticulate. Sometimes he or she is literally trembling before the tribunal. How justice can be accorded to someone who fails to say anything, or merely mumbles a few words, I fail to see.[132]

Such a view seems to be disputed by Professor Bell in her recent work, where she believes that in Supplementary Benefit Appeal Tribunals many appellants were 'not completely incapable of coping—many did surprisingly well'.[133] This has not been the conclusion of other observers, where practically all appellants without exception were seen to be visibly floundering. In an observational study of fifty consecutive Supplementary Benefit appeals, conducted by the author,

> the observers at the hearings were quite clear that *no* appellant had exhibited sufficient knowledge of the law and the process, and that only one representative had done so. In the follow-up survey, 31 out of 38 appellants contacted admitted no knowledge of the legal rules, and in many circumstances, utter bewilderment; 'I just couldn't manage'; 'I'm not very good at coping with these sorts of things'; 'the legalistic jargon in the papers was incomprehensible'; 'I was floundering'; 'I was distraught . . . put the whole

> matter into the hands of my bank manager'. From the written appeals on the hearing papers from other appellants, it was also possible to see the same kind of reaction: 'I have wife and three children—please help'; 'I just cannot afford to live on this amount'. In the majority of cases, it was impossible to define the precise nature of the appeal . . . Facts relating to the claim were often difficult, if not impossible, to disentangle from the family history of the appellants, but no interviewee showed any real appreciation of the requirements of the law, or how he or she could have adapted the case-presentation to fit them. Seven interviewees thought that, by themselves, they had been able to cope with the tribunal process, although none was thought to have done so adequately by the observers; indeed, they had often been the most grotesque examples of helplessness and lack of knowledge. Four of them had made a personal appearance at the tribunal, one of them being a former tribunal presenting officer who, although articulate, displayed a total incomprehension of any regulation or principle relating to his case. He lost the appeal. Similarly, another appellant who claimed to understand what was involved had not turned up, and had merely written on his appeal form, with no further detail, 'I wish my case to go further'.[134]

Some commentators have suggested, however, that lawyers might not be the best kind of advocates for appellants who are in this sort of difficulty. They lay emphasis on the need for assistance with advocacy techniques rather than knowledge of the law. For example, Professor Bell, a social scientist, thinks that 'it is by no means certain that legal representation is always the most appropriate form of help'[135] and, from a series of questions in her empirical work for the D.H.S.S., believes that appellants want a representative who is

> a person with knowledge and experience of supplementary benefits and tribunal procedure, yet one who was accessible, approachable and able to explain points in the language of everyday life. He or she was not envisaged as a remote, rather impersonal professional who would take over the case completely leaving the appellant in a purely passive role. Rather he was seen as an extension of the appellant, assisting him, speaking up for him, acting in conjunction with him.[136]

In fact, such a description sounds very much like the ideal which conscientious lawyers strive after in their work, although the point is taken that few of them achieve this standard. However, such a statement by itself hardly makes out the case for another non-lawyer advocacy group to take up representational work on a wide basis, and, if anything, should increase pressure for lawyers interested in tribunal advocacy, and sensitive to issues such as client-domination, to be properly remunerated for their work.

It is certainly true that in the present legal aid vacuum a great deal of valuable work has been done by welfare agencies and non-lawyer advocates. However, although such advocates may be initially without legal training, their knowledge of the way tribunals operate rapidly becomes a knowledge of the substantive law applied. This skill is in many cases far superior to that at present prevalent among lawyers, so that associated with an argument for introducing lawyers in any major way into tribunal adjudication must be a recognition that they will need proper training in this specialized field. It would of course be unpardonable if, in bringing lawyers more fully into the tribunal process, no adjustment were made to the way in which they traditionally think and work, with the result that features long criticized in court proceedings —such as delay, unnecessary tactical adjournments, technicality, formality and excessive rigidity—were reproduced in the tribunals. The only advantage of lawyers over other advocates is their prior training in general rules of evidence and procedure, and possibly their experience in general advocacy techniques. But perhaps the most important question to ask is, what *kind* of lawyer will be introduced into tribunal work by some further extension of legal aid. Professor Whitmore stresses that it should certainly not be 'the "above it all" type who is at pains to establish to the tribunal, and to his audience, if any, that administrative jurisdiction is really beneath his dignity'.[137] Professors Abel-Smith and Stevens point out that 'some lawyers can do more harm than good to their client's interests when appearing before tribunals',[138] and Professor Street warns that, if legal aid is fully introduced into tribunals, 'chairmen . . . will have to be very firm indeed in handling the barrister who seeks to conceal his ignorance by "bouncing" the tribunal and to impose on it the alien procedures of other courts'.[139] There is also the fairly obvious assumption that lawyers in unaccustomed forums do not perform well for their clients; in a study of Juvenile Courts in the United States, it was found that when retained on an individualized basis 'private attorneys . . . are unfamiliar with the non-courtlike procedures and atmosphere, are not welcome, do not like the work, and often fumble'.[140] Such difficulties will of course affect anyone speaking in a strange situation, but there may be some truth in the view that many lawyers are pedantically immune to changes in setting, and fail to perceive a need to alter their speaking style. As well as alerting lawyers to avoid this sort of unhelpful and irritating behaviour in tribunals, it would perhaps be useful also to note here the natural and widespread reluctance among many sections of the community, but particularly the poor, to have any dealings at all with lawyers. As Professor Laski remarked,

> There is a widespread feeling among the disinherited that the lawyer is their natural enemy; that he embodies, both in his principles and in his technique, the main protective armament of the present social system . . . The poor, I think, could be pardoned if they had the impression that the law was an instrument more for their control than for their service.[141]

One present form of representation before tribunals is that provided by trade unions. This help, usually by the district official of the union, has existed since the creation of social security tribunals, but has always been very much less pronounced on the assistance side, now known as Supplementary Benefits.[142] An estimate made in 1961 was that 80 per cent of industrial injury claimants before local tribunals were assisted by representatives from trade unions,[143] but this figure would seem to be considerably lower in unemployment insurance cases. The figure was less than 1 per cent in the author's study of one Local Appeal Tribunal over three years, but this was in an area of low unionization and the figure no doubt varies considerably. Professor Bell's study, for example, showed 20 per cent of all Local Appeal Tribunal appellants in the Scottish and Northern Regions in 1970 having a representative, and of these 75 per cent were trade unionists. Breaking this down into categories, 61 per cent of industrial injury cases involved a representative, 89 per cent of industrial death grant cases, 16 per cent of sickness benefit cases, and only 13 per cent of unemployment benefit cases.[144] One L.S.E. study of trade union legal services estimates that representation is provided at over ten thousand appeals each year.[145] Trade union representation in Supplementary Benefit Appeal Tribunals seems, however, to be rare; in Professor Herman's study, five out of fourteen represented cases were by trade unionists, but this may be a London phenomenon, as in a C.P.A.G. observation of fifty Midland Region appeals no trade union representatives appeared, and in an analysis of Supplementary Benefit appeals in the Northern Region for 1973, only one involved a trade union representative.[146]

Generally, trade unions will not unnaturally support only those cases which they think have real merit, and the Local Appeal Tribunal will often attach considerable weight as to whether a claimant who is a union member is being backed by his union. There is a space on the notification reply form, sent to appellants before the hearing, asking if they wish another copy of the papers to be sent to any organization to which they belong, and this may result in a number of cases being notified to the unions which otherwise would not have been referred by the appellant himself during his preoccupation with other matters such as finding a job. It has long been known that unions have fairly good success rates in Local Appeal Tribunals when dealing with industrial injury matters, but an analysis of 1970 figures for the Northern and Scottish Regions shows that a success rate for trade union representation of 38 per cent in industrial injury cases is matched by one of 39 per cent in unemployment benefit cases, and there are even higher rates of 51 per cent for sickness benefit and 54 per cent for industrial disability benefit. However, only 7 per cent of all appellants for unemployment benefit had a trade union representative, although such claims accounted for 55 per cent of all claims before the Local Appeal Tribunals.[147] An important factor here seems to be that when there is a trade union representative, the appellant also attends the tribunal in most cases, and it was found that the success rate was 47 per cent when the appellant was with his trade union representative and only 22 per cent when he was absent, so that, as Professor Bell comments, it would 'appear from the statistical analysis that attendance is at least as important as representation'.[148] Particular groups with low unionization, such as women, the young, and the long-term unemployed, all do poorly with appeals. As a member of Professor Bell's research team points out, 'there is no reason why they should bring weaker cases to appeal; the answer is much more likely to be that unions have not succeeded in extending their services to major groups of the unemployed'.[149]

Representation by trade unionists is sometimes of a high standard, particularly if the trade union officer also sits as a tribunal member, and therefore knows the procedure involved, although the argument is rarely couched in legal terms, but relies principally on natural wit. Often it appears to be more in the nature of 'interpretation' between the appellant and the tribunal members rather than advocacy of a case, but trade union representation can on occasions have an important effect by presenting the facts concisely and relevantly. The factor of previous knowledge of tribunal procedure is clearly important in reducing the natural diffidence of appellants or their representatives, but it is by no means decisive; one of the most nervous appellants seen by the author in a Local Appeal Tribunal was a former Presenting Officer, with forty-three years service in relation to social security matters. Trade union representation before the National Insurance Commissioners is much more important, and some larger unions, such as the G.M.W.U., retain solicitors to act on their behalf in all industrial injury cases before the Commissioners. Generally, the social insurance officer of the union will handle most appeals before the Commissioners.

Although in recent years, trade unions have become much more aware of their role as representatives before tribunals, particularly in relation to Industrial Tribunals, there is still little formal training offered to trade unionists who may be involved as representatives or tribunal members. The Social Insurance Departments of the major unions have built up considerable knowledge on the National Insurance Commissioners' decisions, particularly in relation to industrial injury benefit, and often help in the preparation of an important case at the local level; but they are generally very short of resources and time to do much more than concentrate on test cases or those that they think may set important precedents. A certain amount of information is given in courses for full-time organisers and shop stewards, and since 1956 the T.U.C. Training College has provided a week-long course in general social security matters, including tribunal work, but there is considerable room for improvement. The Workers' Educational Association and some University Extra-Mural Departments and Polytechnics have given sporadic courses because of local demand, but clearly, given the importance of this work to trade union members, the T.U.C. would be well advised to co-ordinate training, both for representatives and for the many workpeople's representatives serving on tribunals.

Another group undertaking occasional advocacy before tribunals consists of social workers, but the number of cases involved varies considerably with the region, internal guidelines and training. In Professor Bell's postal study of Northern Region Local Appeal chairmen, 85 per cent had never encountered a social worker representing an appellant, and there were only two social workers in the whole analysis of case-papers for the Northern and Scottish Regions in 1970.[150] More social workers seem to appear with appellants in Supplementary Benefit Appeal Tribunals, often classified by the clerk as 'friend', but here too their appearance is a comparative rarity. Part of this may be due to lack of knowledge of social security matters; in 1968 and 1969 a study of social work associations by Olive Stevenson, then the Social Work Adviser to the S.B.C., found that in response to questions about whether social workers 'adequately understand' the Supplementary Benefit system, 'the short, unequivocal answer to this question is "No"—an answer given by nearly all of the associations consulted and amply borne out by interviews with social workers and by evidence from other sources'.[151] Since that time, a number of efforts by the social work associations and Local Authorities, in conjunction with groups like the Child Poverty Action Group, have succeeded in putting on courses designed to give social workers basic training in social security law and in some cases in tribunal advocacy techniques. There has also been a realization among social workers that knowledge of social security law can dramatically increase the income available to their clients, if only because at the least they will be able to recognize potential claims and refer their clients to other enabling agencies if they themselves are unable to give advice or act as representatives.[152]

Another reason for the limited role of social workers in tribunal advocacy may be because of ongoing relationships between social workers and welfare administrators. There is necessarily a fear by many social workers that, if they 'rock the boat' by fearlessly supporting the case of one client, this may jeopardize the legitimate claims of other clients in their case-load. A victory may prove to be a pyrrhic one when it is followed by retaliation and hostility; such a phenomenon is well-documented in the United States, and seems to be basic in any representational welfare system.[153] As Richard White points out, Local Authority social workers will 'happily enter into negotiations with officers of the [S.B.C.] over particular claims but are reluctant to lodge appeals as this is frowned on by their own superiors as "not playing the game" '.[154]

Unfortunately, much tribunal 'representation' is little more than physical presence alongside the appellant; this may be comforting and may conceivably enable the appellant to speak more coherently than he otherwise would, but generally it is of little value in formulating and arguing a case which will counter that put forward by the Presenting Officer. This type of representation is normally classified by the clerk on the tribunal papers as being in the category 'friend', although this may include everyone from social worker to welfare rights advocate or even lawyer if no other designation is advanced or requested. In the three months up to 1 May 1973, the figures show that out of 8,575 Supplementary Benefit appellants attending hearings, only 1,560 were represented and in 1,137 of these cases this was by a 'relative' or 'friend'.[155]

Additionally, there is the possibility that some types of 'representation' positively damage the appellant's chances. This is unfortunately often the case with representatives from the Claimants' Unions, who can easily be seen to have a markedly adverse effect on most tribunal members.[156] Ruth Lister's interviews of London Supplementary Benefit Appeal Tribunal members found, for instance, that half were in favour of extending representation before their tribunals, 'though some excluded representation by the claimants' unions'.[157] The widespread nature of this belief can be seen in the low success rate of Claimants' Unions, which cyclically reinforces their hostility towards tribunals and makes them even less endearing. However, in their own terms, it should be pointed out that Claimants' Union members are often not so much intent on winning appeals, unlike for example the National Welfare Rights Organisation in the United States, as in making other claimants more politically aware of the 'underclass movement'. Nevertheless, the imaginative use by some Claimants' Union representatives of exhibits could be usefully employed by other advocates; disintegrating sheets, shredded underwear and gaping shoes provide testimony often far more eloquent than any display of representational pyrotechnics.

Certainly the middle-class welfare rights advocate can generally more easily relate to tribunal members, although on occasions it is notable that Supplementary Benefit Appeal Tribunal members are determined to take a well-educated professional 'down a peg or two'. Professor Rose also points to the danger of 'a form of middle class co-option . . . whereby the educated and the expert enter into a compassionate complicity, where the chairman and the well-briefed middle-class representative retreat into an expert's world, leaving the appellant no longer an actor in his own destiny but merely the object of the case at issue'.[158] One interesting point here is that an increasing number of 'middle-class' representatives have at one time experienced the claimant status themselves, usually during a temporary period as students. However, the effective tribunal advocate, of whatever background, must clearly avoid the vice of having a 'spectator' client. But it is also unfortunately true that some advocates who become totally involved in an individual's case will reach the point where their advocacy turns into a general inveighing against the welfare system, for which tribunal members are not responsible. Such conduct can easily become an irritant and often proves counter-productive in terms of a decision on the merits. Such vices are of course not just confined to welfare advocacy. Another common fault of advocates, particularly lawyers, is that those who spend their time poring over statutes and regulations tend to overestimate the interest and knowledge which others will have in the subject-matter. All these factors mean that any adviser who is self-critical of his work must inevitably wrestle with the ongoing problem of fully involving his client in decisions on the case.

Professor Bell, in relation to such common advocacy problems, seeks however to widen her criticism. She feels that her empirical research leads her 'to question a tendency to assume that on the whole people are not capable of managing welfare state situations and are anxious to hand over to brokers who will undertake the transactions on their behalf'.[159] She goes on to suggest a strategy for enabling citizens to know their own rights so that they can themselves 'become actively and effectively involved in the business of the Welfare State'. Such an analysis is very attractive at first sight, but it is suggested that it is misguided. Firstly, any sensitive trained advocate appreciates the dangers of 'brokerage'; this is something to guard against but not a reason by itself for dismissing representational advocacy. Secondly, this author would strongly dispute Professor Bell's implied assertion that many appellants are perfectly capable of handling welfare law problems, or should indeed be expected to do so. That idea seriously underrates the complexities of the welfare process, which, being related to the endless variety of human needs, is necessarily complicated. No one would in modern times expect a well-educated layman to defend himself when charged with a serious criminal offence, or to pursue any but the most trivial of civil actions without adequate legal advice and representation. Similarly, no one should be expected to defend himself against a cut in benefit or petition for welfare grants without skilled assistance. In reply to those who claim welfare law is 'straightforward', it should perhaps be stated that that too is the original view of many lay litigants before their 'simple problem' goes on appeal to the House of Lords. Thirdly, Professor Bell's comment implies that claimants are anxious to take on 'transactions' themselves, whereas from experience it would seem much more likely that most claimants would very much like a good 'broker' if one were available. Finally, successful lawyering is itself a device which enables clients, and the social community in contact with them, to learn a great deal more about their legal rights. When the lawyer/client relationship is open and mutual this can lead to considerable creativity in response to needs which were not perceived by the client as 'legal' in nature. There are not two diametrically opposed alternatives on this question, of extending legal aid or of doing what Professor Bell suggests in 'developing [a] strategy for enabling citizens to exercise their rights'; as can be seen from recent experience in Britain and elsewhere, the involvement of lawyers with the legal problems of the poor can have a 'ripple' effect in informing many others in the community of previously under-utilized legal rights and remedies.

One critical component of any form of representation is pre-hearing advice to the client. In Professor Bell's empirical work on Local Appeal Tribunals, 75 per cent of respondents in her sample received absolutely no advice at all on their appeals; 14 per cent had consulted a trade union official; 4 per cent a relative or friend; 1 per cent a claimants' union, and there was a miscellaneous group of 1 per cent who had consulted advisers such as a doctor or a Citizens' Advice Bureau. Additionally, 50 per cent could not think of any source of help for their claims, 14 per cent thought of a trade union, 5 per cent of a Citizens' Advice Bureau (although presumably 4 per cent had not been able actually to consult one), and 3 per cent of an M.P. or councillor.[160] These figures, bad as they are, were good when compared with the Supplementary Benefit Appeal Tribunal sample—for example, only one out of 235 appellants consulted a trade unionist about his appeal and none of the others thought of contacting a trade union, although over 50 per cent of the sample would have welcomed advice and representation.[161]

Given the seemingly insurmountable problems associated with condensing complex welfare legislation into simple reading material for claimants, the abstruseness of many official leaflets is perhaps understandable. Also, with the recent revelations about the unsuspected extent of non-literacy in the British population, oral explanation of welfare rules by a competent adviser may well be more effective than further attempts to simplify the leaflets; in fact, at present some leaflets can be misleading through the well-intentioned desire of welfare administrators to make them 'readable'. In the Oxford Unemployment Study it was found that 10 per cent of the sample in Newcastle and 15 per cent of that in Coventry and Hammersmith could not read or write well.[162] It would seem safe to assume that low take-up of benefits or potential appeals not utilized, due to factors stated by claimants as 'couldn't be bothered', should be translated as 'could not cope' because of literacy problems; Rex Halliwell has suggested that it is at this juncture that social workers can best function as enablers in the welfare system.[163] Associated with the factor of poor reading levels among many welfare claimants is the requirement of the appellate structure to have some form of written appeal statement which gives tribunal members an indication of what the appeal is about. This statement is of course their only knowledge of the appellant's case when he is unable to attend the oral hearing, and inevitably the typical comment 'I wish to appeal' stands little chance of success against the detailed oral and written statements of the Presenting Officer. A high proportion of appellants are from working-class backgrounds and are unaccustomed to speaking in public situations, and also to putting their ideas down on paper. Industrial Tribunals have adopted the helpful device of a questionnaire to be completed on the appeal form rather than leaving a large blank space to fill in with reasons for an appeal; this policy has proved to be a considerable help to those not able to marshal facts on paper with any ease. As a recent National Survey of the Unemployed has shown, 'all the evidence combines to show the unemployed being heavily concentrated among unskilled and semi-skilled manual workers'.[164] In these circumstances, it is hardly to be expected that welfare claimants will display a high degree of leaflet comprehension, or be able to draft complex appeal statements without advice, or be able to argue their cases forcefully and with relevance before an appeal tribunal.

At present there is a notable tendency on the part of many working-class appellants to go to the D.H.S.S. office to 'sort things out', rather than read leaflets and draft an appeal claim at home. In the United

States this tendency has been formalized into a pre-hearing investigation where a district welfare supervisor will talk over a case to get the claimant's version, and will also give a verbal explanation of the Fair Hearing procedure. Unlike administrative reconsideration in the British welfare system, there is a face-to-face meeting which is an attempt to get the facts for the later oral appeal hearing. However, there is the potential for a supervisor to settle the case on the spot, and inevitably there are criticisms that an unexpected claimant with no proper advice can be 'sold short'.

Skilled advice can have remarkable results. In one case, where a family put in a claim to the S.B.C., much of which was carefully tied to that permissible under the A Code guidelines, the result was an Exceptional Needs payment of £317.54. This sum covered 105 items of clothing and thirty-seven of bedding listed on the S.B.C.'s internal B/O 44 form, along with fifteen articles of sportskit, three beds and various household articles.[165] However, although this was clearly helpful for the family involved, it points up the deprivation suffered by many other similar families who have not had the good fortune to be put in contact with a capable and well-informed adviser who had access to features of the internal administrative guidelines or the tenacity to pursue an imaginative claim.

The author's study asked the appellants themselves what kind of representative they would ideally like if taking up another appeal to a Supplementary Benefit Appeal Tribunal. The choices listed were: 'would not want a representative'; 'a free properly qualified lawyer'; 'social worker'; 'trade unionist'; 'a voluntary organisation such as the Child Poverty Action Group or a Claimants' Union'; 'a supportive friend'; 'other person'. Twenty of the thirty-eight respondents chose the option of a lawyer, two wanted their own social worker, one specified a 'lawyer stroke social worker', three wanted a trade union representative, two wanted someone from the claimants' union, and one wanted his former prison welfare officer. Significantly, a number of non-appearing appellants would have gone to the hearing if they could have had a representative of some kind. One appellant felt that he would need a representative in any future case 'because I am just of average intelligence and not brilliant', another because it would have been 'just somebody to speak for me', and a third, and successful, appellant was adamant that 'we would not have won without representation'. One feature of the responses was that the preference for a lawyer was much more marked among middle-class appellants; a television script-writer in the sample, who had been highly articulate at the hearing, although obviously floundering in the regulations and what he described as 'endless red tape', stated afterwards that 'to have got anywhere I would have needed a battery of competent lawyers'.[166] It is suggested that, in the midst of the theoretical and financial debate on the extension of full legal aid to tribunals, it should be considered significant that, when asked, Supplementary Benefit appellants clearly wanted the extension.

One argument against legal aid for tribunals that is often advanced is that, in a well-run tribunal, the chairman will ensure that an inarticulate or incoherent claimant is helped along with his or her case. Some dubious theories sometimes advanced by commentators at this juncture are that, firstly, the tribunal will always be sympathetic towards a helpless, tongue-tied appellant; and that, secondly, the presence of a competent lawyer appearing on behalf of an appellant will always have the opposite effect of hardening the hearts of tribunal members towards the merits of the case. Such views are in fact often expressed by tribunal members, as in Ruth Lister's study of London Supplementary Benefit Appeal Tribunal members, where the respondents clearly believed that they were dealing with 'human problems' and that 'with a sympathetic and helpful tribunal the appellants could put their case best themselves'.[167] Certainly a well-ordered tribunal will enable an unrepresented appellant to put his points without interruption, and an adept chairman or sometimes a workpeople's representative will be able to prod a nervous or confused appellant into some form of useful utterance. Occasionally the chairman, if he is a lawyer, may even suggest useful questions for the cross-examination of a witness; a frequent comment of chairmen in Local Appeal Tribunals is to say, 'If I were you I would want to ask . . .', but it is clear from observation that this is an entirely inadequate approach to the safeguarding of a claimant's rights or to his making out a proper case. This is particularly so when an adversary situation develops, as it is perhaps bound to with the presence of a Presenting Officer briefed to uphold the initial decision of the Department under review; unfortunately, with bad chairmanship, this can further develop into chaos, especially if feelings are running high. In a general directive of the National Insurance Commissioners, one of the duties of Local Appeal Tribunals is to help unrepresented appellants;[168] this however can be particularly difficult when the case has almost gone by default in terms of the case-papers, which tribunal members will have read before the hearing. Representation and advice on strategy in the pre-hearing process are often just as decisive as representation at the tribunal itself. One witness to the Franks Committee stated bluntly that, in the light of his experience, 'to suppose that ordinary people can represent themselves is complete nonsense and to suppose that the chairman of a tribunal can do an advocate's job for him is simply not correct'.[169]

The distinction in function between impartial adjudicator and advocate for the appellant makes any reliance on this method most unsatisfactory, although in the present situation it is clearly superior to leaving the appellant entirely to his own resources. National Insurance Commissioners, generally having considerably more time to hear a case, often expend a great deal of patience in drawing evidence out from an unrepresented appellant. In relation to this point, it is interesting to find a novel procedure adopted in a War Pensions Tribunal case, where the tribunal members met the unrepresented appellant *before* the hearing and, according to an observer of one such case, 'it was the expertise of the Tribunal, both legally and medically, that won the case for the appellant'.[170] However, the difficulties involved in this area can perhaps best be seen in relation to experience in the United States, where administrative law judges in Fair Hearings use the metaphor of 'three hats' for their role—representing unrepresented claimants, then representing the case of the Social Security Administration, and finally judging the case on the merits.[171] When it is noted that the judge first reviews the case on the papers, including the claimant's confidential welfare file, and is employed by the Social Security Administrative Bureau of Hearings and Appeals, it is understandable that Fair Hearings are often viewed by appellants and legal services lawyers as merely explaining administrative actions in a friendly manner. As a general principle, the words of Sydney Smith in 1826 would still seem to merit attention: 'of all false and foolish dicta, the most trite and the most absurd is that which asserts that the Judge is counsel for the prisoner. We do not hesitate to say that this is merely an unmeaning phrase, invented to defend a pernicious abuse'.[172]

A most encouraging sign of change in the British legal system has been the growth in recent years of voluntary legal advice agencies, many of them handling tribunal cases, in an attempt to cater for an unmet need for legal assistance among the poor. Some form of free legal advice has of course existed for many years with the 'Poor Man's Lawyer'—the Toynbee Hall legal advice centre has existed since 1893—and since 1939 with the services of the Citizens' Advice Bureaux.[173] But a report by the Legal Action Group in 1972 showed a dramatic increase in the number of voluntary legal advice centres attempting 'to fill the gaps in the statutory provision of legal services for people of limited means', and their study located sixty-one British legal advice agencies of which only thirteen existed before 1968.[174] Much of the impetus for this movement has come from the American example of Neighbourhood Law Firms, set up in 1964 as part of the War on Poverty programme, which attempt in an aggressive manner to seek out the legal disabilities of the poor.[175] A number of other agencies have been set up with similar aims in relation to tribunal work, such as the Citizens' Rights Office based in London and Edinburgh, which has perhaps the most expertise in handling tribunal cases, dealing with over 3,000 enquiries a year. A Free Representation Unit for social security cases was launched by bar students in 1972, which claims a 50 per cent success rate on appeals, and in response to this the Bar Council has changed professional practice rules which prevented barristers and pupils from appearing at tribunals without a fee or instructions from a solicitor. However, the Free Representation Unit has lately changed its main emphasis away from Local Appeal and Supplementary Benefit Appeal Tribunal cases, because of appellant demand, and is now very heavily involved in representation before Industrial Tribunals; on a conservative estimate F.R.U. now provides assistance to 4 per cent of all London based applicants to Industrial Tribunals.[176] And in other localities away from London, local groups have set up social security advice centres and in some cases have pressurized local authorities into appointing their own welfare rights officers: Newcastle, for example, has appointed four such officers who will spend part of their time advising social workers, giving advice directly to the public and acting as advocates at tribunal hearings.[177]

However, it is clear that a great deal more effort must be made in this direction before equal justice can be provided for all those with rights involving the legal process. A number of imaginative schemes have been proposed along the lines of an overall 'consumer shop' catering for a wide range of social and legal problems.[178] Another more recent scheme called for a national network of registered Local Tribunal Agencies, funded by block grants, and providing advice and representation as an immediate access point for tribunal appellants; these agencies would also channel cases to solicitors where there was a need for specialized legal skills. Representation would be provided by licensed, paid lay representatives who would have passed a recognized training course in the law and practice of the tribunal in which they work. Allied to the agencies, which would be initially based on existing organizations such as the C.R.O. and other local advice groups, there would be tribunal officers whose role would be to publicize such facilities and establish agencies where needed.[179] This would seem to ensure independence rather more effectively than to have the adjudicative service itself contain its own advice and advocacy staff, as has been put forward by Professor Calvert.[180] Although superficially it would seem attractive to graft on an advice agency, this is to ignore the fact that many of the legal disabilities of the poor are not compartmentalized, and an advocate may need to range over many areas outside the social security field for his client. As the Legal Action Group pointed out, such a proposal 'would not substitute for the services of solicitors but would provide a gateway and a supplement to those services' along the lines of the present liaison system between legal advice agencies and local Law Societies. At present, as the Legal Action Group often comments, solicitors cannot even cope with the existing demand on more conventional legal matters due to the fact that as a per capita proportion there are fewer solicitors now than in 1900.[181] Unfortunately, the Law Society seems to view this proposal as creating a third, and possibly competitive, branch to the profession, so that for the moment the Lord Chancellor's Advisory Committee has rejected systemized lay assistance in tribunals.[182]

Occasionally, an argument is made against the extension of legal aid by stating that lawyers generally are not interested in or are ignorant of tribunal work. Clearly without the provision of full legal aid, lawyers have little pecuniary incentive to involve themselves in this type of work, and therefore little chance to learn the substantive law and the procedural aspects of advocacy before tribunals. If lawyers can adapt themselves, as many have shown themselves capable of doing on a *pro bono* basis, then their presence in tribunals, performing the lawyer's traditional role of safeguarding the rights of appellants and putting forward the most cogent case possible on their behalf, would be of considerable benefit to the furtherance of justice in the system. This is of course not to exclude other forms of advice and representation—in any case, there are just not enough good, adaptable lawyers to go around—but, as Lord Gardiner framed the central question on legal aid: 'it is no good people having legal rights if they cannot afford to enforce or defend them'.[183]

The Second Tier Appeal

A major advantage of Local Appeal Tribunals over their Supplementary Benefit counterparts lies in the right of a second appeal to the National Insurance Commissioners. The possibility of further appeal is helpful in maintaining high standards of procedure at the first stage of appeal, but perhaps its more important attribute is that the policy rules on which initial administrative decisions and local appeals are made become subject to full scrutiny by specialists in social security law. It is not statutorily laid down that Local Appeal Tribunals must follow Commissioners' decisions, although, as Professor Street points out, any chairman who systematically disregarded them would be liable to have his appointment terminated.[184] However, generally this loose form of precedent percolates to the lower levels of both administrative and tribunal adjudication, with considerable benefit to the appeal process.

Having the National Insurance Commissioners' precedents to guide them, and the fact that these carry more authority than internal policy guidelines, also ensures considerable independence for Insurance Officers from their departmental framework. This case-law has also had a world-wide impact on other welfare systems; for example, in the formative years of the American system, the Social Security Board issued a volume of selected Umpires' decisions which form the basis of much later administrative decision-making.[185]

National Insurance Commissioners are senior barristers, earning, as the Franks Committee pointed out, salaries higher than County Court judges;[186] and a study of their work reveals impeccable standards of impartial adjudication, and considerable understanding of industrial and social situations. Hearings are held in public, although no one is usually present other than the interested parties. However, oral hearings are not as of right, but only if the Commissioner believes it necessary after a request has been made, so that 75 per cent of cases are decided on the basis of the Local Appeal Tribunal papers and new submissions from each side.[187] The proceedings are formalized to the extent that there is a set procedure and interruptions are not allowed unless immediately relevant; in fact an approximate comparison can be made with proceedings in the County Courts, which by High Court standards are very informal. The D.H.S.S. or Department of Employment is normally represented by a departmental lawyer, and there are none of the questionable activities seen in relation to Presenting Officers and Insurance Officers at the local tribunals. Similarly the clerks, who are lawyers, have an attitude beyond reproach, assisting the Commissioners hearing the case by taking a note of the arguments and testimony. The appellant is also often represented, even in unemployment benefit cases, by a trade union official, generally from the national office and often experienced in this type of work. In industrial injury cases, the appellant may also have a lawyer representing his case, whose fee will be paid by the union. National Insurance Commissioners are not necessarily bound by the strict rules of Evidence applicable in the courts,[188] but from observation it is clear that few legal commentators would find their conduct of cases anything but exemplary.

It was mooted before the Franks Committee that there should be a further appeal from the National Assistance Appeal Tribunal to the National Insurance Commissioners, or a similar appellate body,[189] but the argument of the Committee was that no second appeal was needed as 'by their very nature questions of assistance require to be finally determined as quickly as possible'.[190] However, although delay is certainly a factor to guard against on initial appeal, it is perhaps not so important on second appeal unless it is of an excessive nature. This is for the simple reason that if there is a chance of review a claimant who lost initially will not mind waiting; and if the claimant has won, then ordinarily there will not be a second appeal, and certainly he will not initiate it. Generally, the Insurance Officer does not appeal to the National Insurance Commissioners unless he feels there is an important point of law at issue. As we have seen, both the Insurance Officer and the S.B.C. have the instant right to review a case following appeal, with very wide powers of alteration. The fact that this is so rarely exercised in Supplementary Benefits jurisdiction would lead one to suppose that if a second appeal were created the S.B.C. would rarely use it—one point here would be that, if they lost a second time, a Commissioner's decision would create a precedent for other tribunals which they might not wish to have.

Subject to the prerogative orders of certiorari, prohibition and mandamus, decisions of the National Insurance Commissioners are final.[191] Owing to the nature of administrative tribunals, review is generally only available through certiorari, which may be granted as a discretionary remedy in four main circumstances: where a tribunal exceeds its jurisdiction or does not have jurisdiction; where there has been a breach of the rules of Natural Justice; where there is fraud or duress in procuring a decision, and where there is an error of law on the face of the record.[192] The cost and complexity of bringing such an application to the courts is, however, prohibitive for most appellants, and there has been in recent years a great deal of criticism of what Lord Justice Scarman calls in relation to administrative law, 'our legal apparatus originating in the battles of the seventeenth century'.[193] During 1974 there were five such applications to the High Court for an order of certiorari from a National Insurance Commissioner's decision.[194] But without a proper study it is impossible to gauge whether this was due to general satisfaction with the adjudication of the case, or whether this is a low figure due to the legal and financial obstacles in pursuing the matter further. Such obstacles are even more important in relation to Supplementary Benefit cases, where there has until now been no second appeal on the original case. A further difficulty here is that by the nature of certiorari, the High Court can in fact only quash a decision, not decide it as if it were an appeal. A formulation of the law by the High Court will automatically be incorporated into a new decision on a Social Security case when it is retried by a Commissioner, but, as Ruth Lister points out, a Supplementary Benefit Appeal Tribunal has such an amorphous jurisdiction that it could simply repeat its original decision, 'taking care not to make another error of law in giving its reasons'.[195] And as was perfectly clear in the aftermath of the *Simper* case, the S.B.C. is capable of ignoring a High Court formulation of a legal point while continuing to enforce its own policy directive and pressing for legislation to change the law.[196]

The National Insurance Commissioners decide on average about 1,500 cases a year, but only a small fraction of these decisions are published, although an unreported 'numbered' decision is occasionally relied upon.[197] The selection of cases to be reported is made by the Chief Commissioner, and in 1974 he selected thirty-nine decisions as being of special importance;[198] this is a fairly typical figure, and there is a conscious policy to limit the case law and prevent it from undue proliferation. Unreported but numbered decisions are circulated among the Commissioners, and are available for inspection in the ante-room of the Commissioners' headquarters in London, and at their Edinburgh and Cardiff offices. Unnumbered decisions are very rarely cited, but are also available if needed. The loose-leaf digest of Commissioners' decisions, known generally as the *Jenkins Index*, is published by the Stationery Office and contains only reported decisions.

Lay assessors can be utilized by the Commissioners to assist in cases, but at present this practice is never used in unemployment cases and only rarely in industrial injury cases.[199] It is also possible for especially difficult cases to be heard by a tribunal of three Commissioners sitting together, who are therefore able to decide a case by a majority decision.[200] Few cases have been dealt with by a tribunal of three in recent years, but for example in 1972 some decisions on the Trade Dispute disqualification in relation to lay-offs caused by the miners' strike were so heard.[201]

The Commissioners have a considerable advantage over the ordinary courts in not being strictly bound by their own previous decisions, although care is taken to establish reasonable 'certainty'.[202] Professor Calvert describes the Commissioners as 'a judiciary of innovators', and in regard to two decisions, which quickly and effectively changed long-standing interpretations of the law, Professor Wedderburn comments that 'there are judges who will envy this power' to overrule obsolete decisions so easily.[203]

Although the introduction of a further appeal in Supplementary Benefit cases would introduce some delay, it is suggested that the beneficial effects of a full analysis of the law, and its feedback into the administrative machinery, would more than outweigh this. At present of course Supplementary Benefit tribunal decisions are open to review by the Courts, a process which normally takes much longer than an appeal to the Commissioners. Additionally, there would be the important advantage of introducing a real element of consistency into Supplementary Benefit Appeal Tribunals on a national scale.

It is curious how the S.B.C. on the one hand prides itself on its unlimited freedom of discretion, which legally applies equally to the Supplementary Benefit Appeal Tribunals, and yet on the other hand, through its Presenting Officers and clerks, frequently tries to prevent the tribunals from making a generous grant in case this action 'sets a precedent', In fact a very rudimentary form of *stare decisis* already exists, both internally when Departmental officials take note of how its local tribunal reacts to cases, and externally through the spread of information by such organizations as the Citizens' Rights Office and the Legal Action Group. When a Presenting Officer flatly tells a Supplementary Benefit Appeal Tribunal that some course of action is impossible, it is always helpful for an advocate to be able to produce some account of a previous occasion on which a tribunal decided to the contrary. Also, in the minds of the tribunal members themselves, there is quite naturally what Howard Elcock calls 'a vast submerged body of precedent',[204] in that they are likely to analogize with previous decisions, and will often spontaneously declare a particular policy in relation to certain types of cases, although there is rarely an associated conscious reasoning about why this should be so. In the light of these factors, quasi-precedent is already powerfully operative, but it is of course sporadic, often illogical and rarely closely related to the existing statutory rules and regulations. Justice as a concept has always implied the notion of equal treatment and, it is suggested, only when Supplementary Benefit adjudication is based on independent appellate decision-making, guided by independent precedents, can the tribunal structure be regarded as satisfactory.

Another important reason for having a second tier appeal for Supplementary Benefit cases is that at present any form of recourse to the courts through a petition for review is fraught with difficulties. Firstly, as has been mentioned, the legal machinery is cumbersome and costly. But, secondly, the judges have made it quite clear in recent years that they do not wish to get involved at all in tribunal cases. Lord Denning, despite his past willingness to interfere with the adjudication of private or domestic tribunals,[205] has recently indicated that judicial review should only be used as an extreme rarity in tribunal cases. Clearly the difficulties which the courts at one time experienced with the morass of litigation on Workmen's Compensation are an important factor in the formation of such an attitude. As Professor Robson has described the huge volume of appeals, there was 'a veritable jungle of case law, through which neither light nor warmth could penetrate'.[206] Despite frequent protests from the House of Lords, each new case seemed only to add to the number of 'competing analogies' rather than consolidating the law, and fear of a recurrence of such litigation is implicit in what one commentator has called Lord Denning's 'avalanche phobia'.[207] As Lord Denning put it himself in relation to the Workmen's Compensation legislation,

> One of the principal mistakes was to interfere too much with the decisions of the arbitrators to whom the legislature had entrusted the administration of compensation . . . I should like to say today that it would be unfortunate if, by means of applications for certiorari, the court should become involved in a stream of cases under the present Act.[208]

In relation to industrial injury adjudication, such sentiments may be sensible policy where there exists a second tier appeal structure of the standard of the National Insurance Commissioners, as well as a reasonably capable local appeal structure—in the *Culverwell* case this was a Medical Appeal Tribunal, but the same would apply to a Local Appeal Tribunal. However, in Lord Denning's most recent pronouncement, that the courts 'should leave the tribunals to interpret the Act in a broad, reasonable way, according to the spirit and not to the letter', he was referring to the decision of an entirely lay Supplementary Benefit Appeal Tribunal which had been required to determine the meaning of the term 'householder' in relation to the Supplementary Benefit Act 1966. In this situation no lawyer had been involved in the adjudication of the case, and there had been no possibility of a second appeal other than a petition for review to the courts. Lord Denning, although admitting that the tribunal's decision was 'erroneous in point of law', denied certiorari on policy grounds, because he feared that the courts might become 'engulfed with streams of' Supplementary Benefit cases.[209] As Professor Street has pointed out, the Court of Appeal decision is in fact so vague that it gives no clear indication when certiorari will be available in the future.[210] Such a situation must inevitably lead to an impasse; if the courts retreat from their general review role in Supplementary Benefit cases, even when there is clearly an erroneous decision on the law, then there is no other avenue of legal redress for an aggrieved appellant.

The answer for Supplementary Benefit cases is clearly to introduce immediately a strong second tier appeal. This would certainly go a long way to reduce the possibility of further applications for certiorari about which Lord Denning is worried. Having a specialist second tier authority would also cut down considerably the time involved before redress is made; too much can sometimes be made of the advantages of specialization in adjudicatory work, although certainly there would be no need for tutoring in the fundamentals of social security law as apparently had to be done by counsel in the *Moore* case before the Court of Appeal.[211] Much of the ordinary work of the courts involves points of great complexity on which judges would not presume to consider themselves as possessing the necessary expertise. Social security law is no more difficult than, for example, cases involving revenue or family law which have associated subject matter. However, no National Insurance Commissioner could fail to build up a considerable range of knowledge on industrial matters, in a manner analogous to that of a judge in the Family Division. Similarly, a second tier appeal adjudicator on Supplementary Benefit cases would quickly build up expertise on the kind of social and industrial problems involved in the law.

One of the major flaws of the British tribunal system is its tendency to have a proliferation of tribunals; each time new legislation is passed, a new tribunal has been set up. The Franks Committee drew attention to this phenomenon and urged that 'whenever it is proposed to establish a new tribunal consideration should first be given to the possibility of vesting the jurisdiction in an existing tribunal'.[212] Unfortunately, this advice has only been heeded sporadically. The Industrial Tribunal, which has gathered extended jurisdiction seemingly year by year, is an obvious exception; in fact this has reached such a point that a number of years ago Professor Wedderburn wondered if 'much more work and many more issues of legal complication may break their backs'.[213] The Local Appeal Tribunals have also added to their jurisdiction since their former incarnation as Courts of Referees: they now decide, as well as unemployment benefit cases, appeals on sickness benefits, industrial injury benefits, retirement pensions, widows and orphans benefits and family allowances. These jurisdictions were all at one time decided by a separate tribunal, as in the case of industrial injuries benefit, or by a system of referees chosen from a panel of barristers and solicitors. Nevertheless, trends in the opposite direction can easily be discerned; for example, when in 1969 the Government proposed in a National Superannuation and Social Insurance Bill that the anomalous 'Minister's Questions' be moved fully out of the control of the administrative structure, it suggested a new tribunal be set up with a right of appeal to the High Court. As was pointed out by the Ministry in evidence to the Franks Committee, the original reason for the separate adjudication of 'Minister's Questions' was 'largely historical and no longer necessarily valid'.[214] When the Government's proposal was sent to the Council on Tribunals for comment, the Council strongly urged that 'Minister's Questions' should go into the normal Local Appeal Tribunal system, with an appeal to the Commissioners.[215] In fact there is no clear borderline at present because contribution and related questions in Social Security are handled both in the Local Appeal Tribunal structure as well as by the Department as 'Minister's Questions'; occasionally there are awkward and protracted difficulties with the division of functions.[216] With the change of Government, rather than because of pressure from the Council on Tribunals, the Bill was unsuccessful, but it is hoped that transfer of the jurisdiction to the Local Appeal Tribunal system will be made at an early stage, as suggested by the Council. The present situation is unduly fragmented and unsatisfactory.

Inconsistent decisions on the Trade Dispute disqualification in social security law are avoided at present by having, as we have seen, all such appeals in Supplementary Benefit cases go directly to the Local Appeal Tribunals to be decided on the basis of National Insurance Commissioners' decisions. It was also one of the Fisher Committee's recommendations that cohabitation cases should similarly be transferred to the Local Appeal Tribunals, so as to be judged on the basis of legally reasoned criteria. Given that there should be a second tier appeal system for Supplementary Benefit cases, it would seem efficacious to open up the National Insurance Commissioners to hear the total jurisdiction, rather than create yet another appeal tribunal. This is the recommendation of Professor Bell in her work for the D.H.S.S.,[217] and it is suggested that this would be the best solution to existing problems. An interesting Edinburgh study of Supplementary Benefit hearings has recently shown the relatively few cases that could possibly involve a 'discretion' element, and the many common factors between the two tribunals in terms of decision-making.[218] It is suggested that the disqualification and voluntary unemployment controls work of the Supplementary Benefit Appeal Tribunals could easily be overseen by the Commissioners, as this is virtually identical in nature to the Social Security disqualifications. Cohabitation cases are already determined by the Commissioners in relation to widows' benefits, and it is suggested that the Family Income Supplement work of Supplementary Benefit Appeal Tribunals is little different in qualitative terms from adjudication on matters such as Family Allowances. Only determination of Exceptional Needs payment would be a distinct new field, and some regulated guidelines by an independent source would most definitely be a real asset to adjudication.

The Child Poverty Action Group, which has, like the Society of Labour Lawyers, long advocated a second tier appeal for Supplementary Benefit cases, seems somewhat ambivalent on incorporating Supplementary Benefit appeals into the National Insurance Commissioners structure. Ruth Lister advocates a second tier authority, but is not emphatic about wanting it to be the National Insurance Commissioners,[219] and in a recent letter to the Lord Chancellor, the Director of C.P.A.G. wrote that 'there should be a second tier appeal body similar to the National Insurance Commissioners.[220] In an earlier memorandum to the Lord Chancellor, the Group makes the point that they would 'not like to see the membership of such a body confined to established barristers as in the National Insurance system. A growing number of practising and academic lawyers have experience in this field and their expertise could be drawn on'.[221] An additional reason for reservations about extending jurisdiction to the National Insurance Commissioners, in their comment on Professor Bell's work, is that the Group would 'like to see the body made more accessible to people outside London and would thus recommend that it be regionally based'.[222] At present there are of course regional National Insurance Commissioners for Scotland and Wales, but this system could easily be extended, particularly if with the addition of Supplementary Benefit jurisdiction there were to be a greater caseload. As to the inclusion of other lawyers, this could be partly accomplished by an activation of the role of assessors sitting with the Commissioners. A revolving panel of part-time academic lawyers and local appeal tribunal chairmen to sit with the Commissioners on an individual basis would mean a beneficial influx of new perspectives as well as providing some experience for chairmen of appellate work; this could be the foundation of later appointment to a Commissionership. The system of assessors could also, it is suggested, be extended in time to the occasional use of lay wingmen from the local tribunals as part of their ongoing training experience. This experience of sitting with the Commissioners would assist a critical effect of a new second appeal in Supplementary Benefit cases, which would be to strengthen adjudication at the local level. As has been pointed out by Henry Hodge, when appeals to the National Insurance Commissioners were allowed in attendance allowance cases, the quality of the initial decision-making, made by delegated authority from the Attendance Allowance Board, improved remarkably.[223]

About half the administrative tribunals under the oversight of the Council on Tribunals have now adopted a Presidential system, and a number of suggestions have been made that this should be extended to Local Appeal and Supplementary Benefit Appeal Tribunals. The Chief National Insurance Commissioner's functions are at present entirely adjudicative and there is no central day-to-day administrative direction of Local Appeal Tribunals. One recent commentary has pointed out the advantages of a Presidential system in the following terms:

> First its manifest independence, which gives tribunals a *persona* in the public mind comparable to that of the courts, and removes the suspicion that they are part of the departmental mechanism; and second, the ease of communication which enhances both efficiency and morale.[224]

Professor Herman in his study of Supplementary Benefit Appeal

Tribunals advocates a full-time President of the tribunals, who would have responsibility for supervising clerks and tribunal members, as well as convening meetings and conferences for chairmen and members.[225] Following this approach, it is suggested that the National President, who would himself sit as a local tribunal chairman as his other duties permitted, should, like the President of Industrial Tribunals, issue administrative and practice directions to other chairmen. Until such time as the Local Appeal and Supplementary Benefit Appeal Tribunals merge, there should be a President for each system. The Chief Commissioner is far too occupied with adjudicative responsibilities to take on this task, and the President should be someone closely in touch with local tribunal adjudication. He would be in a position to examine such questions as the siting of tribunals and internal seating, the selection of chairmen and wingmen, the selection and duties of clerks, and he would have full responsibility for all training and conferences. Professor Bell's idea of regional senior chairmen would help to localize the effect of this regrouping,[226] and these senior chairmen could assist in selecting new members for the wingmen panels, and could also make suggestions to the President for the appointment of new tribunal chairmen by the Lord Chancellor.

In any reform of the present social security tribunal structure, the setting up of a second appeal for Supplementary Benefit cases must play a central role. The lack of co-ordination and direction which is apparent in any observation of Supplementary Benefit Appeal Tribunals at work is largely due to the absence of strong independent directives on basic definitional aspects of the law and the elements of impartial adjudication. Professor Bell believes that only at a third stage, when senior chairmen have been appointed and the Supplementary Benefit Appeal Tribunals have achieved a modicum of adjudicative strength should a second appeal be instituted.[227] But as the Child Poverty Action Group's comments on her proposals point out, if the right of appeal is available at a first stage of reform, this would have the salutary effect of immediately ensuring that the Supplementary Benefit Appeal Tribunals examined their procedure and decisions in the light of their new accountability.[228]

As to additional expense, present estimates are that a Local Appeal Tribunal hearing costs approximately £16 a case, whereas a case at the level of the National Insurance Commissioners costs £165–195. There are no available estimates on Supplementary Benefit hearings, but these are probably a little less costly than Local Appeal Tribunals.[229] Certainly, adding a second appeal to Supplementary Benefit cases would initially mean a rise in cost, but it is suggested that considerable savings could be made if the local tribunals were amalgamated and

Minister's Questions transferred to the tribunal structure, thereby avoiding considerable duplication of resources. Additionally, with a more professional outlook and a centralization of administrative control of tribunals under a President, there would be a considerable cutting of waste and inefficiency over the long term. Delay in the initial stages of reform may also be a factor to contend with if there is a sudden spate of appeals, but this should be soon reduced as more guidelines are laid down, and are acted on at the stage of initial administrative determination as well as in the local tribunals. Some advance planning, and perhaps prior issuance of directives on the law by the Commissioners, would be a useful safeguard against such an occurrence.

In recent years a number of more radical suggestions have been made to change the nature of British welfare adjudication. One proposal recommended that a change of name from social security tribunals to 'a Social Court' might bring the system more into the open and perhaps rid it of the legacy of second-rate justice.[230] This had been the thinking behind the successful change to a Restrictive Practices Court, which would have been a tribunal but for pressure on the Government to create an 'impartial court' in contrast to the unpopular tribunal known as the Monopolies Commission.[231] Clearly the nature of the system is of far greater importance than its name and, as we have seen in the historical development of the present system, a name-change by itself solves little. What is needed are some sweeping changes in the structure of social security tribunals, particularly in the Supplementary Benefit Appeal Tribunals, to turn the system as a whole into what Henry Hodge has characterized as 'a decent poor person's court',[232] where justice is on a par with that administered in other parts of the judicial system. The extension of legal aid and advice is, it is suggested, as important and necessary as these structural changes, but if a hard choice has to be made because of limited funds, then the extension of full legal aid should be postponed and perhaps introduced gradually through the funding of Law Centres and Tribunal Advocacy Groups. It is structural change along the lines suggested that is imperative.

The Public Watchdog

Before the Franks Committee Report, little attention had been paid to the issues of administrative justice, and it was a major recommendation of this committee that a permanent body should be set up to supervise the workings of all tribunals.[233] This body, known as the Council on Tribunals, consists of part-time members and meets usually once a month; an Annual Report is issued, which Professor de Smith rightly characterized as 'illuminating but tardy'.[234] Members of the Council are also encouraged to visit tribunal sessions, but, given that the number of tribunals under their oversight is now over 2,000, this is clearly impossible except on an occasional *ad hoc* basis. Numerous criticisms, right from its creation, have been made of its cautious approach to the issues, and its lack of thought on long-range strategy. Professor Griffith, for example, called its first Annual Report a 'timorous and platitudinous document'.[235] Professor Street in his Hamlyn lectures thought that the Council was playing no role in ensuring that personnel discharged their duties competently, and suggested that 'in order to assess the quality of the chairman's paper work random examination of decision files would have to be made . . . not only does the Council not do this, it has not even the power'.[236]

However, there are signs that the Council has, within its very limited range, achieved a number of important changes on particular small-scale issues, and also that it has helped to focus attention on some problems common to all tribunals. The Council's role, however, is purely advisory, although it does act as a kind of 'clearing house' or 'ombudsman' for complaints about tribunals. The Council unfortunately seems to use the number of complaints it receives as a kind of barometer on the effectiveness of tribunals. But, as the Council's first chairman pointed out, very few people are aware of its existence, and unfortunately this has continued to be the case so far as social security claimants are concerned.[237] There is some overlap between the work of the Parliamentary Commissioner for Administration and the Council, but again the Ombudsman is a relatively little known figure to those actually using tribunals and can only be approached through an M.P.[238] However, as Martin Partington has shown, there is considerable potential in the use of the Parliamentary Commissioner as a means of exercising 'quality control' which can have the effect of altering internal administrative and adjudicative practice.[239] One considerable advantage is that the Commissioner is able to look at all internal records of the case and all applicable rules and regulations. Complaints on individual cases, such as those referred to the Council by the Child Poverty Action Group, have met with little success,[240] simply because there is not the staff to follow them up with any effectiveness. Similarly, although there has been Parliamentary and Press exposure on the few cases referred to the Parliamentary Commissioner, there is no possibility of effective overall supervision of tribunal adjudication, but only a report on individual cases of 'maladministration'.

The Council's consultative and monitoring function on all new draft regulations and constitutions for tribunals is perhaps its most important work, but as an instrument of effective change it is severely handicapped. Professor Garner, after a study of the Council, points out in reply to criticism 'that the Council is a watchdog that does not bite. One answer to this point is, of course, that it cannot bite'.[241] Additionally, for the first decade of its existence up until 1968, the Council was very much preoccupied with the activities of Tribunals of Inquiry, which had of course been the original subject matter of the Franks Committee after the Crichel Down affair.[242] Useful as the Council's work has been in developing interest in the tribunal process, it is clear that many issues remain unresolved. Certainly, substantial changes will be required before justice in social security tribunals can be fully equated with justice in the courts, and it is clearly unrealistic to look to the Council as a means for this sort of change; this can only be achieved by the actions of Parliament or by directives from the Lord Chancellor's Office.

NOTES

1. *Report of the Committee on Administrative Tribunal and Enquiries* (1957), H.M.S.O. Cmnd. 218, p. 10 (hereafter referred to as *Franks Committee Report*).

2. *Franks Committee Report* (1957), p. 19.

3. *Annual Report of the Council on Tribunals for 1966* (1967), p. 7.

4. See for example the comment in U.A.B., *Annual Report* (1937), H.M.S.O. Cmd. 5526, p. 49. Location of welfare 'fair hearings' in H.E.W. offices in the United States has been a point of criticism for some time.

5. W. A. Robson, *Justice and Administrative Law* (1951), p. 598.

6. *Franks Committee Report* (1957), p. 20.

7. *loc. cit.*

8. Hilary Rose, 'Who can de-label the claimant?' *Social Work Today* (1973), p. 410.

9. See earlier, p. 65.

10. Steve Burkeman, 'We Go By the Law Here', in Michael Adler and Anthony Bradley (eds.), *Justice, Discretion and Poverty* (1976), p. 96.

11. Julian Fulbrook, *The Appellant and his Case: The Appellant's View of Supplementary Benefit Appeal Tribunals* (CPAG 1975), p. 5.

12. Quoted in R. E. Wraith and P. G. Hutchesson, *Administrative Tribunals* (1973), p. 308.

13. s. 99(1) Social Security Act 1975 (hereafter SS Act 1975).

14. s. 100 (4) SS Act 1975.

15. s. 100 (5) SS Act 1975.

16. C(S) 371/49.

17. R(I) 21/61.

18. C(S) 197/73. See Peter Moore, 'A Lawyers Guide to National Insurance — Some Overall Legal Concepts', Legal Action Group *Bulletin* (1974), p. 240. See also R(P) 10/59 and R(S) 2/63.

19. s. 101(3) and (5) SS Act 1975.

20. Quoted in the *Annual Report of the Council on Tribunals for 1969–1970* (1970), p. 6.

21. para. 4, Supplementary Benefits (Appeal Tribunal) Regs. (1971) SI 1971, No. 680.

22. para. 5, Supplementary Benefit (General) Regs. (1966) SI 1966, No. 1065. See also generally, Peter Moore, 'Supplementary Benefit: Reviews and Late Claims', Legal Action Group *Bulletin* (1974), p. 165.

23. See at p, 260. The power to redirect cases is contained in para. 7, Supplementary Benefit (Appeal Tribunal) Regs. (1971) SI 1971, No. 680.

24. Rosalind Brooke, 'Social Administration and Human Rights', in Peter Townsend and Nicholas Bosanquet (eds.), *Labour and Inequality* (1972), p. 252.

25. para. 11(3), The Social Security (Determination of Claims and Questions) Regs. (1975) SI 1975, No. 558, and para. 10(2), Supplementary Benefits (Appeal Tribunal) Regs. (1971) SI 1971, No. 680;

in Supplementary Benefit tribunals, the chairman must not be the missing member.

26. Kathleen Bell, *Research Study on Supplementary Benefit Appeal Tribunals: Review of Main Findings: Conclusions: Recommendations* (D.H.S.S. 1975), p. 5. (here after referred to as SBAT Study.)

27. 'Time Limits', *Report of the National Insurance Advisory Committee* (1952). H.M.S.O. Cmnd. 8483, p. 9.

28. *Report of the Committee on Abuse of Social Security Benefits* (1973), H.M.S.O. Cmnd. 5228, p. 228 (hereafter referred to as the *Fisher Committee Report*).

29. See generally, the Note on the Fisher Committee Report by Judith Reid in *Industrial Law Journal* **2** (1973), p. 175. Investigators of social security abuse apparently spend about 38 per cent of their time on suspected cohabitation cases.

30. *Goldberg* v. *Kelly* 397 US 254 (1970).

31. Harry Street, *Justice in the Welfare State* (1975) p. 16.

32. Kathleen Bell, Peter Collison, Stephen Turner and Susan Webber, 'National Insurance Local Tribunals: A Research Study — Part I', *Journal of Social Policy* **3** (1974), p. 300 (hereafter referred as *LAT Study—Part I*).

33. Melvin Herman, *Administrative Justice and Supplementary Benefits* (1972), p. 42; Julian Fulbrook, *op. cit.*, p. 5; Kathleen Bell, *SBAT Study*, p. 16.

34. Ruth Lister, *Justice for the Claimant* (1974), p. 28, and Ross Flockhart, 'Some Aspects of Tribunal Membership', in Michael Adler and Anthony Bradley (eds.), *op. cit.*, p. 106.

35. Hilary Rose, *op. cit.*, p. 410.

36. Kathleen Bell, et al., *LAT Study — Part I*, p. 289.

37. Kathleen Bell, *SBAT Study*, p. 15.

38. First study quoted in Melvin Herman, *op. cit.*, p. 40; the second in *Hansard*, **855**, H. C. Deb. (1 May 1973), cols. 264–5.

39. Julian Fulbrook, *op. cit.*, p. 5.

40. Kathleen Bell, Peter Collison, Stephen Turner and Susan Webber, 'National Insurance Local Tribunals: A Research Study — Part II', *Journal of Social Policy* **4** (1975), p. 6 (hereafter referred to as *LAT Study — Part II*).

41. Julian Fulbrook, *op. cit.*, p. 6.

42. Kathleen Bell *et al.*, *LAT Study — Part II*, p. 6.

43. Kathleen Bell, *SBAT Study*, p. 16.

44. Julian Fulbrook, *op. cit.*, p. 6.

45. Howard Mason, Lane Neighbourhood Centre, Birmingham. Personal communication to the author.

46. *loc. cit.*

47. Kathleen Bell *et al.*, *LAT Study — Part II*, p. 6.

48. *ibid.*, p. 3.

49. Kathleen Bell *et al.*, *LAT Study — Part I*, p. 300.

50. Kathleen Bell, *SBAT Study*, p. 12.

51. Kathleen Bell *et al.*, *LAT Study — Part II*, p. 3.

52. Julian Fulbrook, *op. cit.*, p. 6; Dennis Marsden, *Mothers Alone* (1969), p. 205; Coral Milton, 'Appellants' Perceptions of the Tribunal Process', in Michael Adler and Anthony Bradley (eds.), *op. cit.* p. 134.

53. See for example, E. Wight Bakke, *The Unemployed Man: A Social Study* (1933), p. 104; John Hilton, *Rich Man, Poor Man* (1944), p. 93; Hilda Jennings, *Brynmawr* (1934), p. 141.

54. For an example of one contemporary reminiscence about queuing up at the workhouse for out-relief, and all that this implied, see the autobiographical account in George Brown, *In My Way* (1971), p. 20. The present author's grandfather, when a terminal patient, begged his family not to let the authorities take him 'up the Hill'; in fact he was already in a bed in what used to be the local Workhouse, which has now been modernized to serve as a hospital.

55. para. 10(2), The Social Security (Determination of Claims and Questions) Regs. (1975) SI 1975, No. 558.

56. para. 11(6), Supplementary Benefits (Appeal Tribunal) Regs. (1971) SI 1971, No. 680.

57. *Franks Committee Report* (1957), pp. 41–2.

58. Julian Fulbrook, *op. cit.*, p. 12; Kathleen Bell et al., *LAT Study — Part II*, p. 1.

59. Richard M. Elman, *The Poorhouse State* (1966), p. 14.

60. para. 11(1), The Social Security (Determination of Claims and Questions) Regs. (1975) SI 1975, No. 558.

61. R. E. Wraith and P. G. Hutchesson, *op. cit.*, p. 193.

62. Quoted by Bernard Schwartz and H. W. R. Wade, *Legal Control of Government* (1972), p. 77.

63. *Franks Committee Report* (1957), p. 24.

64. *Committee on Ministers' Powers* (1932), H.M.S.O. Cmd. 4060, p. 80.

65. See *R.* v. *Medical Appeal Tribunal at*

London, ex p. Burpitt [1957] 2 QB 584.

66. s. 12(1) Tribunals and Enquiries Act 1958, now s 2 1971 Act.

67. para. 12, The Social Security (Determination of Claims and Questions) Regs. (1975) SI 1975, No. 558.

68. H. J. Elcock, *Administrative Justice* (1969), p. 92.

69. See the evidence of the Ministry of Pensions and National Insurance to the *Franks Committee* (1957), p. 45. See now para. 12(1) (c), The Social Security (Determination of Claims and Questions) Regs. (1975) SI 1975, No. 558.

70. The 1971 change was made by para. 12(1), Supplementary Benefits (Appeal Tribunal) Regs. (1971) SI 1971, No. 680, where Supplementary Benefit Appeal Tribunals must now 'record every determination and provide a statement of the reasons therefor in writing'.

71. Unpublished study by students at the London School of Economics, quoted in Ruth Lister, *op. cit.*, p. 43. The same sort of problems exist at the initial administrative stage of adjudication, where few appellants get adequate written notice of the reasons for disqualification or denial of benefit; see Ivor Abelson, 'Getting Written Decisions from the S.B.C.', Legal Action Group *Bulletin* (1975), p. 213.

72. Harry Street, *Justice in the Welfare State* (1975), p. 61.

73. See for a comment on 'the gigantic written records which clog the American administrative machine', Bernard Schwartz and H. W. R. Wade, *op. cit.*, p. 147.

74. Lord Denning, *Freedom Under the Law* (1949), pp. 91–2.

75. W. A. Robson, *Justice and Administrative Law* (1951), p. 381.

76. Adrian Sinfield, 'Poor and Out of Work in Shields', in Peter Townsend (ed.), *The Concept of Poverty* (1970), p. 223.

77. E. Wight Bakke, *The Unemployed Man: A Social Study* (1933), p. 102.

78. See R(G) 3/71 and the five criteria for S.B.C. decision-making in the *Supplementary Benefits Handbook* (1974), pp. 7–8. See for the recommendation that Supplementary Benefit Appeal Tribunals be bound by National Insurance Commissioners' decisions, *Fisher Committee Report* (1973), para. 341. See generally, Henry Hodge, *New Society* **24** (26 April 1973), p. 191, and Ruth Lister, *As Man and Wife*? (CPAG 1973) In the United States, the similar 'man in the house' rules in welfare law have been struck down as unconstitutional by the Supreme Court; *King* v. *Smith* 392 US 302 (1968).

79. 'Sponging on the State', *The Times* (22 March 1966).

80. Ruth Lister, *Justice for the Claimant* (1974), pp. 62–3.

81. Joel F. Handler, *The Coercive Social Worker* (1973), p. 148.

82. See generally, Aaron Levenstein, *Why People Work* (1962).

83. See for one area where the principles have been much explored, though perhaps little clarified, the question of trade union discipline and expulsion: *Huntley* v. *Thornton* [1957] 1 All E.R. 234; *Leary* v. *N.U.V.B.* [1970] 2 All E.R. 713; and generally, K. W. Wedderburn, *The Worker and the Law* (1971) pp. 451–65. See for a general summary of the principles, Paul Jackson, *Natural Justice* (1973), and the earlier H. H. Marshall, *Natural Justice* (1959).

84. per Lord Loreburn L. C. in *Board of Education* v. *Rice* [1911] A.C. 179 at 182.

85. per Viscount Haldane in *Local Government Board* v. *Arlidge* [1915] A.C. 120 at 132.

86. See on this point *R.* v. *Deal Justices, ex. p Curling* (1881) 45 L.T. 439; *Franklin* v. *Ministry of Town and Country Planning* [1947] 1 All E.R. 612; and the decision of Justice Frank, *In re Linaham* (1943) 138 F 2d 650.

87. See on this point *Dimes* v. *Grand Junction Canal* (1852) 3 H.L.C. 759; and *R.* v. *Sunderland Justices* [1901] 2 K.B. 357.

88. See on this point, *R.* v. *Camborne Justices* [1955] 1 Q.B. 41; and *R.* v. *Barnsley Licensing Justices* [1960] 2 Q.B. 167.

89. *R.* v. *Queens County JJ* [1908] 2 I.R. 285 at 294, per Lord O'Brien CJ.

90. S. A. de Smith, *Judicial Review of Administrative Action* (1968), p. 180.

91. A study in Edinburgh in fact found that Supplementary Benefit Tribunals in the area were marginally more helpful in this respect; Michael Adler, Elizabeth Burns and Rosemary Johnson, 'The Conduct of Tribunal Hearings', in Michael Adler and Anthony Bradley (eds.) *op. cit.*, p. 114.

92. See the report by Richard White in Pauline Morris, Richard White and Philip Lewis, *Social Needs and Legal Action* (1973), p. 29.

93. Wigmore, *Evidence* (1974 Chadbourn Revision), vol. V, p. 32, s. 1367.

94. The relevant Local Appeal Tribunal regulations make it clear that there is a right to put questions directly to any witnesses called at the hearing, but not to subpoena witnesses or ensure expenses for them; para. 3(3), The Social Security (Determination of Claims and Questions) Regs. (1975) SI 1975, no. 558.

95. S. A. de Smith, *op. cit.*, p. 201.

96. Fisher Committee Report (1973), paras. 269, 491.

97. R(G) 1/53.

98. R. E. Wraith and P. G. Hutchesson, *op. cit.*, p. 267.

99. Harry Street, 'Tribunals: Two new Publications', Legal Action Group *Bulletin* (1974), p. 129.

100. Steve Burkeman, Director of Check! Legal Action Group *Bulletin* (1974) p. 170.

101. Ruth Lister, *op. cit.*, pp. 40, 41.

102. Ruth Lister, 'Supplementary Benefit Appeal Tribunals: an Urgent Case for Reform', in Michael Adler and Anthony Bradley (eds.) *op. cit.*, p. 177.

103. Harold Laski, *A Grammar of Politics* (1938), p. 301.

104. Secrecy is maintained under s. 2, Official Secrets Act 1911, although, as has been stated, the *Supplementary Benefits Handbook* attempts to enable advisers of claimants to be able to give 'advice on a fully informed basis'; *ibid.*, p. 2.

105. Tony Lynes, *Welfare Rights* (1969), p. 6.

106. Jeffrey Jowell, 'The Legal Control of Administrative Discretion', *Public Law* (1973), p. 178. See also for a useful discussion of this point, John Veit Wilson, 'Rights or Charity?' (unpublished paper, 1973).

107. *Supplementary Benefits Handbook* (1972), p. 1.

108. See earlier discussion on p. 33.

109. *Annual Report of the Council on Tribunals for 1971–1972* (1972), p. 23.

110. Ruth Lister, *Justice for the Claimant* (1974), p. 11.

111. Herbert W. Marshall in William Robson (ed.) *Social Security* (1943), p. 42. See also on the relative nature of comparisons here, Michael J. Hill, 'The Exercise of Discretion in the N.A.B.', *Public Administration* **47** (1969), p. 75.

112. *Wilkie* v. *O'Connor* 25 N.Y.S. 2d 617 (Sup. Ct. 1921) and *Shapiro* v. *Thompson* 394 US 618 at 626 (1969).

113. K. C. Davis, *Discretionary Justice* (1971), p. 232.

114. Melvin Herman, *op. cit.*, p. 9.

115. See in particular the speeches by Margaret Herbison, Minister of Pensions and National Insurance, and Norman Pentland, the Parliamentary Secretary; *Hansard*, **729**, H.C. Deb. (24 May 1966), cols. 336, 411.

116. It was removed by the National Insurance (Determination of Claims and Questions) Amendment Regs. (1958) SI 1958, No. 701, and the National Assistance (Appeal Tribunals) Amendment Rules Confirmation Instrument Regs (1958) SI 1958, No. 714. See on Natural Justice in relation to domestic tribunals J. E. Alder, 'Representation before Tribunals', *Public Law* (1972), p. 278.

117. *Franks Committee Report*, para. 89 and Recommendation 16.

118. *Hansard*, **575**, H. C. Deb. (31 October 1957) col. 510.

119. *17th Report of the Lord Chancellor's Advisory Committee on Legal Advice and Assistance* (1968), H.M.S.O. Cmnd. 373, p. 73. See for a critique, Rosalind Brooke, *Modern Law Review* **33** (1970), p. 436.

120. *24th Legal Aid and Advice Report of the Law Society and Comments and Recommendations of the Lord Chancellor's Advisory Committee 1973–1974* (1974), H.M.S.O.

121. See generally, Davies LJ in *McKenzie* v. *McKenzie* [1970] 3 All E.R. 1034 at 1036; *Mercy* v. *Persons Unknown* (*Times* Reports, 4 June 1974). See for a recommendation by the National Insurance Commissioners for the use of the green form scheme in relation to Commissioners' appeals, *Law Society Gazette* (13 February 1974).

122. Legal Action Group *Bulletin* (1974), p. 260.

123. 'How has the Green Form Scheme Worked?,' Legal Action Group *Bulletin* 1974), p. 234.

124. Coral Milton, *op. cit.*, p. 139.

125. E. J. T. Matthews and A. D. M. Oulton, *Legal Aid and Advice* (1971), p. 124 f.

126. Richard White, *op. cit.*, pp. 18–19.

127. R. E. Wraith and P. G. Hutchesson, *op. cit.*, p. 264.

128. An ingenious argument for the extension of legal aid to tribunals has also been advanced by Professor Atiyah, but from different motives. He believes that such an extension would make 'politically more palatable' his proposals for the elimination of all personal injury litigation and its replacement by a universal insurance

scheme; P. S. Atiyah, *Accidents, Compensation and the Law* (1970), p. 619.

129. Kathleen Bell, *SBAT Study*, p. 15.

130. Kathleen Bell *et al.*, *LAT Study — Part II*, p. 18.

131. See generally, Robert Egerton, *Legal Aid* (1945); Suzanne Dell, *Silent in Court* (1971); J. Bell, *How to get Industrial Injuries Benefits* (1966), p. 233; Allen Potter, *Organised Groups in British National Politics* (1961), p. 181.

132. Harry Whitmore, 'The Lawyer in Administrative Justice', **33** *Modern Law Review* (1970), p. 485.

133. Kathleen Bell, *SBAT Study*, p. 18.

134. Julian Fulbrook, *op. cit.*, pp. 12–13.

135. Kathleen Bell, 'Administrative Tribunals since Franks', *Social and Economic Administration* **4** (1970), p. 295. See also the same author's *Tribunals in the Social Services* (1969).

136. Kathleen Bell, *SBAT Study*, p. 16.

137. Harry Whitmore, *op. cit.*, p. 488.

138. Brian Abel-Smith and Robert Stevens, *In Search of Justice* (1968), p. 320. See also the comment on English barristers in Judith Shklar, *Legalism* (1964), p. 14.

139. Harry Street, 'Tribunals: Two new Publications', Legal Action Group *Bulletin* (1974), p. 129. Howard Elcock also notes that lawyers often delay proceedings because they 'feel that they must be seen by their clients to earn their fees'; H. J. Elcock, *Administrative Justice* (1969), pp. 64–5.

140. See generally, Anthony Platt and Ruth Friedman, 'The Limits of Advocacy: Occupational Hazards in Juvenile Court', *University of Pennsylvania Law Rev.* **116** (1968), pp. 1156–84, and Joel F. Handler, 'The Juvenile Court and the Adversary System: Problems of Function and Form', *Wisconsin Law Rev.* (1965), pp. 7–51.

141. Harold Laski, *Studies in Law and Politics* (1932), pp. 282, 290. See also generally on attitudes towards lawyers, Brian Abel-Smith, Michael Zander and Rosalind Brooke, *Legal Problems and the Citizen* (1973).

142. See for example a report on this practice in the *Annual Report of the U.A.B.* (1937), H.M.S.O. Cmd. 5526, p. 43.

143. Allen Potter, *Organised Groups in British National Politics* (1961), p. 180. A comparison was made with War Pensions Appeals where 72 per cent of all claims were supported by the British Legion, which gives free legal advice to all former servicemen.

144. Other categories of representative involved were 14 per cent 'relative'; 5 per cent 'legal'; 3 per cent 'friend'; 1 per cent 'political' (including local government councillors, M.P.s and officers of political parties) and 3 per cent 'other'; Kathleen Bell *et al.*, *LAT Study — Part I*, p. 289.

145. Roy Lewis and Geoff Latta, 'Union Legal Services', *New Law Journal* **123** (1973), p. 387. See also Geoff Latta and Roy Lewis, 'Trade Union Legal Services', *British Journal of Industrial Relations* **12** (1974), p. 56.

146. Melvin Herman, *op. cit.*, p. 42; Julian Fulbrook, *op. cit.*, p. 7; Kathleen Bell, *SBAT Study*, p. 16.

147. Kathleen Bell *et al.*, *LAT Study — Part II*, p. 15.

148. *ibid.*, p. 18.

149. Steve Turner, 'The Trade Union Role in Tribunals', *Poverty* **32** (1975), p. 29.

150. Kathleen Bell *et al.*, *LAT Study — Part I*, p. 301, *Part II*, p. 20.

151. Olive Stevenson, *Claimant or Client?* (1973), p. 206.

152. See for a text designed for use in social work training, Michael Zander, *Social Workers, Their Clients and the Law* (1974).

153. See generally, Joel F. Handler, *The Coercive Social Worker* (1973).

154. Richard White, *op. cit.*, p. 27.

155. *Hansard*, **855**, H.C. Deb. (1 May 1973), col 264. Unfortunately, the connotation of 'friend' can prove counter-productive; the Nuffield study found appellants who stated, 'on the letter you weren't allowed a solicitor, you could just take a friend;' Coral Milton, *op. cit.*, p. 138.

156. See for an unintended account of how not to conduct a tribunal case, Bill Jordan, *Paupers: The Making of the New Claiming Class* (1973); see also James Graham, *The Enemies of the Poor* (1970).

157. Ruth Lister, *op. cit.*, p. 21.

158. Hilary Rose, *op. cit.*, p. 409.

159. Kathleen Bell *et al.*, *LAT Study — Part II*, p. 24.

160. Kathleen Bell *et al.*, *LAT Study — Part II, p. 1.*

161. Kathleen Bell *SBAT Study*, p. 15. See also Steve Turner, *op. cit.*, p. 30.

162. See generally M. J. Hill, R. M. Harrison, A. V. Sargeant, and V. Talbot, *Men out of Work* (1973).

163. See Rex Halliwell, 'The Use of Social Workers', *Poverty* **27** (1973), p. 8.

164. W. W. Daniels, *A National Survey of the Unemployed* (1974), p. 11.

165. David Bull, *The Guardian* (7 December 1973). See also David Bull, 'Supplementary Benefit Appeals: Advocacy Against Policy Decisions', Legal Action Group *Bulletin* (1975), p. 18.

166. Julian Fulbrook, *op. cit.*, pp. 13–14. See also Coral Milton, *op. cit.*, p. 138.

167. Ruth Lister, *op. cit.*, p. 22.

168. R(1) 6/69.

169. R. S. W. Pollard in *Evidence to the Franks Committee* (1957), p. 535.

170. Seth Otuteye, 'Some Aspects of Social Security Law — A Comparison Between English and French Legal Methods' (unpublished Cambridge Ph.D. thesis, 1971).

171. See for the 'three hats' concept, *Rausch* v. *Gardiner* 267 F. Supp. 4, 6 (E. D. Wis. 1967). 42 U.S.C. s. 405 is the statutory section covering requests for a Fair Hearing. See also Joel F. Handler, 'Justice for the Welfare Recipient: Fair Hearings in the AFDC', *The Social Service Review* **43** (1969), p. 12.

172. Quoted in Robert Egerton, *Legal Aid* (1945), p. 92.

173. See generally on the background of such services, the Society of Labour Lawyers Report, *Justice for All* (1968), and Rosalind Brooke, *Information and Advice Services* (1972). CABx in London now employ over ten full-time salaried lawyers and are doing considerable work in tribunal representation; *New Society* **33** No. 672, (21 August 1975) p. 439.

174. Legal Action Group, *Legal Advice Centres — An Explosion*? (1972), p. 7.

175. See for a survey, Daniel H. Lowenstein and Michael J. Waggoner, 'Neighbourhood Law Offices: The New Wave in Legal Services for the Poor', *Harvard Law Review* **80** (1967), p. 805, and Earl Johnson, *Justice and Reform*: *The Formative Years of the Office of Economic Opportunity Legal Services Program* (1974).

176. See Bill Rees, 'The Free Representation Unit — Current Progress', Legal Action Group *Bulletin* (1973), p. 240; Note in *ibid.*(1974), p. 150, and Robin Allen and Richard Drabble, 'The Free Representation Unit in Industrial Tribunals', *ibid.* (1975), p. 311.

177. See letter from Geoff Fimister, Welfare Rights Officer, Newcastle-upon-Tyne, in Legal Action Group *Bulletin* (1975), p. 327: 'I'm sure that we're still only scratching the surface as far as the need for representation is concerned; but at least we're scratching it rather harder these days'. See also an earlier note on the Newcastle C.A.B. representation scheme, *ibid.*, pp. 284–5.

178. Lucy Syson and Rosalind Brooke, 'The Voice of the Consumer', in Brian Lapping and Giles Radice (eds.), *More Power to the People* (1968), pp. 57–75.

179. 'Tribunal Representation: LAG calls for a National Network', Legal Action Group *Bulletin* (1974), p. 27.

180. Harry Calvert, 'Appeal Structures of the Future', in Michael Adler and Anthony Bradley (eds), *op. cit.*, p. 202.

181. 'Current Events in Legal Aid', Legal Action Group *Bulletin* (1974), p. 289.

182. See generally, *24th Legal Aid and Advice Report of the Law Society and the Lord Chancellor's Advisory Committee 1973–1974* (1974).

183. Lord Gardiner, the Lord Chancellor, in *Hansard*, **309**, H.L. Deb. (18 June 1969), col. 1041.

184. Harry Street, *op. cit.*, p. 28.

185. See Unemployment Compensation Interpretation Service, *Benefit Decisions of the British Umpire*, Benefit Series, General Supplement No. 1 (June 1938). See generally, Ralph Altman, *Availability for Work* (1950) on jurisdictional similarities. See also for a comment on European plagiarism, P. R. Kaim-Caudle, *Comparative Social Policy and Social Security* (1973), p. 203.

186. *Franks Committee Report* (1957), p. 26.

187. See generally para. 13, The Social Security (Determination of Claims and Questions) Regs. (1975) SI 1975, No. 558.

188. For example, the courts have suggested *obiter* that the rules of Natural Justice need not be strictly applied in industrial injury cases; *R.* v. *National Insurance Commissioners, ex parte Viscusi* [1974] 1 WLR 649, [1974] KIR 197.

189. See the evidence of the Society of Labour Lawyers to the *Franks Committee* (1957) p. 514; and see also the view of Reg Prentice supporting this idea, *Hansard* **575**, H. C. Deb. (31 October 1957), cols. 459–60.

190. *Franks Committee Report* (1957), p. 42.

191. s. 117(1) SS Act 1975.

192. See generally, S. A. de Smith, *Judicial Review of Administrative Action* (1973,

3rd edition), and Bill Birtles, 'Remedies in Administrative Law', Legal Action Group *Bulletin* (*1973*), p. 273.

193. Sir Leslie Scarman, 'Administrative Law and the Legal Profession', Legal Action Group *Bulletin* (1974), p. 262, and generally his *English Law — the New Dimension* (1974). See also the Law Commission Working Paper, *Remedies in Administrative Law* (1971), and Bernard Schwartz, 'Forms of Review Action in English Administrative Law', *Colorado Law Rev.* (1956), pp. 203–26.

194. D.H.S.S., *Annual Report 1974* (1975), H.M.S.O. Cmnd. 6150, p. 102.

195. Ruth Lister, *op. cit.*, p. 56.

196. See earlier at p. 40.

197. For example, the leading decision, stating that the onus of proof in misconduct cases is on those who allege misconduct, is an unreported decision; C.U. 1/57.

198. D.H.S.S., *Annual Report 1974* (1975), p. 102.

199. s. 101(6) SS Act 1975.

200. s. 116(1) and (2) SS Act 1975.

201. See R(U) 12/72 and R(U) 13/72.

202. See generally an article by a former Chief Commissioner, Sir Archibald Safford, 'The Creation of Case Law under the National Insurance and National Insurance (Industrial Injuries) Acts', *Modern Law Review* **17** (1954), p. 197. See also the forthcoming Hamlyn lectures by Sir Robert Micklethwait.

203. Harry Calvert, *Social Security Law* (1974), p. viii; K. W. Wedderburn, *The Worker and the Law* (1971), p. 125.

204. H. J. Elcock, *op. cit.*, p. 80.

205. See, for example, his statements in *Annamunthodo* v. *Oilfield Workers Trade Union* [1961] 3 All E.R. 621 (PC); *Barnard* v. *National Dock Labour Board* [1953] 2 Q.B. 18.

206. William A. Robson, *Justice and Administrative Law* (1951), p. 210.

207. Judy Reid, Note in 4 *Industrial Law Journal* (1975), p. 185.

208. Lord Denning MR in *R.* v. *Industrial Injuries Commissioner, ex parte AEU* [1966] 1 All E.R. 97 at 101 (the Culverwell case).

209. See generally, Lord Denning MR in *R.* v. *Preston Supplementary Benefits Appeal Tribunal, ex parte Moore*; *R.* v. *Sheffield Suplememtary Benefits Appeal Tribunal, ex parte Shine* [1975] 1 W.L.R. 624 at 631.

210. Harry Street, 'Judicial Review Refused', Legal Action Group *Bulletin* (1975), p. 118.

211. See Henry Hodge, 'The Long Retreat' Legal Action Group *Bulletin* (1975), p. 86. See also the comment by Professor Atiyah that if lawyers became more generally involved as a profession in tribunal work it 'would not be necessary for counsel to spend half a day outlining the most elementary principles of the industrial injury system as happened when a recent case was taken to the House of Lords'; P. S. Atiyah, *Accidents, Compensation and the Law* (1970), p. 383.

212. *Franks Committee Report*, para. 139.

213. K. W. Wedderburn, *op. cit.*, p. 151.

214. Sir Eric Bowyer, Secretary to the Minister of Pensions and National Insurance, *Evidence to the Franks Committee* (1957), (Days 1–2) para. 304. See earlier discussion at pp. 138–9.

215. See *Report of the Council on Tribunals 1969–1970* (1970), p. 6.

216. See for example R(S) 3/68.

217. Kathleen Bell, *SBAT Study* (1975) p. 24.

218. Michael Adler, Elizabeth Burns and Rosemary Johnson, *op. cit.*, pp. 122–3.

219. Ruth Lister, *op. cit.*, p. 67, and a personal communication: 'I would still prefer a second tier body for Supplementary Benefit appeals . . . But I do not feel that strongly about it'.

220. Frank Field, Letter to Lord Elwyn-Jones from the Child Poverty Action Group (9 May 1975).

221. *Comment by the Child Poverty Action Group on the Proposals made by Kathleen Bell* (October 1975) (Appendix I, Memo 10, March 1975, para. 3).

222. *ibid.*, p. 4.

223. Henry Hodge, 'Really: Yet Another Tribunal?' Legal Action Group *Bulletin* (1975), p. 287.

224. R. E. Wraith and P. G. Hutchesson, op. cit., pp. 309–10. The authors in fact, think of the Chief National Insurance Commissioner as a 'President *primus inter pares*' (p. 84), but he is certainly very different from the administrative head of other tribunal systems such as, for example, the President of Industrial Tribunals. They also add in relation to policy reasons for the adoption of a Presidential system: 'Theoretical considerations apart, presidential systems are in vogue'; p. 310.

225. Melvin Herman, *op. cit.*, p. 60.

226. Kathleen Bell, *SBAT Study*, p. 20.

227. *ibid.*, p. 24.

228. *Comment by the Child Poverty Action*

Group on the Proposals made by Kathleen Bell (1975), p. 4.

230. See generally, Julian Fulbrook, Rosalind Brooke, and Peter Archer, *Tribunals: a Social Court?* (Society of Labour Lawyers/Fabian Society Tract, 1973). See for a criticism that the introduction of even the most informal 'court' may reduce attendance rates; Ruth Lister, 'Supplementary Benefit Appeal Tribunals', *Social Work Today* **6** (1975), p. 516.

231. R. B. Stevens and B. S. Yamey, *The Restrictive Practices Court* (1965), pp. 18–19.

232. Henry Hodge, *op. cit.*, p. 288.

233. *Franks Committee Report* (1957), p. 30.

234. S. A. de Smith, *op. cit.*, p. 46.

235. J. A. G. Griffith in Gerald Gardiner and Andrew Martin, *Law Reform NOW* (1963), p. 36.

236. Harry Street, *Justice in the Welfare State* (1975), p. 63.

237. Lord Reading, 'A Public Watchdog', *The Listener* (12 November 1959), p. 811.

238. See generally on the division of functions, Harry Street, *op. cit.*, p. 116, and s. 5(2) (a) The Parliamentary Commissioner Act 1967.

239. See generally, Martin Partington, 'Supplementary Benefits and the Parliamentary Commissioner' in Michael Adler and Anthony Bradley (eds.), *op. cit.*, p. 158 *et seq.*

240. See generally, Ruth Lister, *Council Inaction* (CPAG 1975).

241. J. F. Garner, 'The Council on Tribunals', *Public Law* (1965), p. 321.

242. *Crichel Down Inquiry* (1954), H.M. S.O. Cmd. 9176. R. E. Wraith and P. G. Hutchesson, *op. cit.*, p. 206; a consultant to this study, Alistair Macdonald, was Secretary to the Council for its first ten years — the book states, presumably as a result of his experiences, that 'much of great value has been unostentatiously achieved'; p. 221.

11

Conclusion

The most immediate effect of unemployment is loss of income, and the welfare administrative and appeal mechanisms providing cash payments to the unemployed through a complex system of regulations have been the subject of this study. In the present day, it is fully realized that unemployment is part of a whole spectrum of interrelated social, economic and industrial factors, which include such questions as the state of international trade and currency. But this appreciation of factors outside the control of the individual who becomes unemployed is, as we have seen, only of recent origin. The chief explanation of unemployment which was given just seventy years ago was that of the moral turpitude of the individual worker who refused to take up employment. For example, an editorial in the *Spectator* in 1908 stated that in relation to 'the major part of unemployment what is wanted is a moral, not an economic, remedy'.[1]

Often such views were linked with a eugenic perspective, which saw poverty in terms of Social Darwinism; Herbert Spencer, for instance, believed earlier that the Poor Law merely encouraged 'the multiplication of the reckless and incompetent by offering them an unfailing provision'.[2] Professor George has extrapolated four ideal types representing historical viewpoints towards poverty: as an ascribed status under feudalism; as vagabondage following the collapse of feudalism; as attributable to an individual's personal and moral failings; and finally as 'a social problem of physical subsistence and social inequality during this century'.[3] But, as he points out, none of these stages has had a clear delineation, and British public opinion—and therefore those concerned with welfare administration—can still be seen to retain many vestiges of an earlier pathological approach to poverty.

In what may be termed 'primitive' societies, economic security depends on factors almost exclusively concerned with agricultural

For notes see p. 317

output, such as climate, soil, control of pests, irrigation and drainage. But in modern Western societies, the job security of workers, and therefore the economic security of them and their families, depends firstly on the more intangible factors of economic climate creating demand for the goods which the worker produces. Tied to this is the factor of efficiency in the worker's firm, normally beyond his influence, but crucial to the long-term survival of his employment. Secondly, the worker's job depends on his avoiding personal hazards such as industrial injury, sickness or some disability which will reduce his working capacity. And finally, there is the possibility of job discrimination based not on efficiency but on prejudice relating to factors such as sex, class, race, religion or age. Social security questions cannot be seen in a vacuum away from such issues and, as Professor ten Broek remarked, any welfare system

> must be regarded, in modern time no less than in the Middle Ages, as an indispensable part of the overall system of labour legislation. Whatever might be said in welfare terms of the necessity to deal with the particular needs of the individuals and families, the unemployed segment of the population stands in an economic and social relationship to the employed segment. How the State regulates that relationship, through what machinery and for what ends, and the extent to which it leaves regulation to the operation of unregulated forces, are intricate problems of politics and general economics no less than of welfare.[4]

The ancient Poor Law had been a form of communal charity, given reluctantly, and with the minimal aim of keeping the destitute from starvation and death by exposure. Other spasmodic forms of assistance before the twentieth century had helped to ward off to some extent the distress suffered by the working classes, although the motivation seems often to have derived from fear of social disturbance rather than from considerations of humanity. However, such mechanisms were a long way from adequate maintenance and, furthermore, they were riddled with assumptions as to the need to prevent the onset of 'dependency' or 'chronic pauperism'. As one proponent of the C.O.S. viewpoint wrote in 1902,

> The first object of the Poor Law is the provision of relief for the destitute; the second object is the prevention of the evils and abuses caused by this provision of relief—in short, while the relief should be sufficient, it should not be attractive.[5]

The many factors which precipitated the movement away from such a system were partly due to economic changes in the labour market, but they were also due to the realization, through the work of social surveyors such as Booth and Rowntree, that a moral explanation of unemployment was simply not sufficient.

Portraying the role of individuals in social change is of course fraught with difficulties. But as Beveridge wrote of his first mentors in the field of social reform, 'it is not easy for any honest writer on the last sixty years to get away from the Webbs'.[6] The real impact of the Webbs, and of Beveridge himself, will remain a matter of debate. But the Minority Report of the 1909 Royal Commission still stands as one of the most important documents of the century; not so much for what it said in contrast to the Majority Report, nor for its immediate effect on legislation, which was minimal, but for its symbolization of a break with past dogmas. The old mixture of Poor Law, charity and relief works was exposed, even for the members of the Majority, as inadequate and also positively harmful. However, if the Webbs with their prodigious compilations of facts and figures were instrumental in the destruction of the old mechanisms, it was Beveridge who performed the constructive task of formulating a new system. Firstly through his advocacy of Labour Exchanges; then through his collaboration with Llewellyn Smith in setting up the 1911 unemployment insurance scheme, followed by his practical work in the inter-war period as chairman of the Unemployment Insurance Statutory Committee; and finally with his famous wartime Report, building on his experience and framing a blue-print for a comprehensive system of social security.

Beveridge's enduring mark on the British system has been the use of the insurance principle. And, although in relation to social security, insurance has taken on assumptions very different from its commercial form and has even on occasions brought the system close to foundering, its success has been, in the words of Professor Asa Briggs, to have 'removed the stigma of pauperism from a social service, reconciled "voluntary" and "compulsory" approaches to provision, and facilitated "public approval" of state expenditures which otherwise would have been challenged'.[7] The Beveridge Report's assumptions that supplementary forms of social assistance would wither away have not proved correct in the post-war situation, and indeed the inbuilt schism between contributory and non-contributory benefits is now proving in many respects to be somewhat of a liability.[8] However, the importance of the insurance principle has been that it acted as a catalyst between the old forms of charitable relief and an evolving modern system of comprehensive social security.

Although there have been many changes in the twentieth century schemes for the relief of the unemployed, it has been the argument of this study that there has been little fundamental change in the administrative and substantive law structures, and virtually none in relation to the appeal system. For example, in one of the most loudly trumpeted 'reforms', that of 1948, it is interesting to find that the U.A.B. Appeal Tribunals changed into the N.A.B. Appeal Tribunals without any change in personnel and with only minor changes in terms of duties and operating rules.[9] Furthermore, there has until recently been little proper investigation of how these structures, of great importance to so many people, function in practice, or of the legal problems and issues involved. The ideal of the appeal tribunals in social security adjudication has been to have 'a friendly talk round the table . . . less formal, less expensive and less time-consuming than courts of law'.[10] But the assumption of fairness and efficiency which often accompanied such statements must be increasingly open to question. One traditional British response to such criticisms in any sphere has always been to urge the appointment of an investigating Royal Commission,[11] but although this may be helpful for the overall planning of the British tribunal system, it is important to heed Professor Tawney's famous warning that the call for more and more research is often used as a reason for not doing what everybody knows ought to be done. Grave defects at present mar the hope of impartial adjudication in the social security tribunals, and these should be remedied by immediate and strenuous action on the part of the Lord Chancellor, the Departments involved and the Council on Tribunals.

The Poor Law system was based on a principle of deterrence, and it was the stated hope of the post-Beveridge reforms that this concept would be finally buried.[12] However, it has become clear that, in a social security system based on the underlying assumption that the primary means of acquiring income is that of going out to work, many of the old methods and formulae for preserving the financial incentive to work have remained. For example, in substantive terms, the law changed its name from 'less eligibility' to the recently repealed but not necessarily dormant 'wage stop'; however, the practical effect of all such work discipline controls has been very much the same. Moreover, the underlying philosophy of the welfare system, and that of many of its participants, would still seem often to have its roots directly in nineteenth century views of poverty, even though on the surface there has been a considerable change of emphasis in the theoretical nature of the system from complete reliance on charitable discretion towards the securing of legal and social rights. However, many issues remain unresolved, both in the overall structure of social security and its use as an instrument for redistributing wealth, as well as in the technical administrative and adjudicative areas of the determination of claims. As the peripatetic

New Zealand Royal Commission stated, in relation to its overseas study tour of 1971, 'nowhere did we find the aims of social security policy or of community responsibility clearly defined. Social security administrators are everywhere prisoners of history, tradition and political will'.[13]

Social security law, as Professor Kahn-Freund has remarked, is in a substantive sense, 'not only complex [but] extraordinarily kaleidoscopic, so that everything said today may very well have lost its validity tomorrow'.[14] This compounds the difficulties of a claimant seeking justice within the social security administrative and appeal process. Not only is it difficult for lawyers and other advisers to keep abreast of the technical law, but it is clear that the vast majority of claimants are ignorant of their rights, or do not know how to exercise them, or are unwilling to risk the disapproval of the welfare system by pressing an appeal; almost certainly they will lack access to competent advisers and representatives. Because of recent publicity given to welfare rights organizations and law centres, it is easy to exaggerate their effectiveness in relation to the claimant population as a whole. Professor Handler points out that, despite the much larger role of welfare rights advocacy in the United States, the vast majority of welfare recipients are 'passive, dependent, and interested in stability. Their ignorance of what they are entitled to combines with their low expectations, so that they do not perceive injustice or feel aggrieved'.[15]

A great deal more effort and critical attention by lawyers must be given to the scrutiny of welfare laws and practices so as to fill this vacuum. As Professor Reich pointed out during the early years of an American surge in the examination of the legal rights of the poor, 'the legal profession does not even know enough about agency practices in the welfare field to be able to identify possible denials of rights'.[16] It is suggested that a comparable situation exists in Britain today amongst the majority of lawyers. And yet welfare adjudication is often a critical and immediate point of contact between a large sector of society and the administration of justice.

It is imperative that a judicial appeal system reviewing welfare claims should guarantee a full, fair and proper hearing on each case. The clients of welfare systems are rarely in a position to know whether they are being wrongfully treated. It must be the concern of lawyers to ensure that they are given their full rights.

NOTES

1. *Spectator* (18 January 1908).

2. Herbert Spencer, *Social Statics* (1868), pp. 353–4. See also the Report of a Committee appointed to consider the Eugenic Aspect of Poor Law Reform, *Eugenics Review* **2** (1910), p. 193. See generally, T. R. Malthus, *An Essay on the Principle of Population* (1798, 1967).

3. Victor George, *Social Security and Society* (1973) p. 1.

4. Jacobus ten Broek, *Family Law and the Poor* (1971), pp. 16–17.

5. Sophia Lonsdale, *The English Poor Laws* (1902), p. 7.

6. Beveridge, *Power and Influence* (1953), p. 25.

7. Asa Briggs, "The Welfare State in Historical Perspective", in S. P. Aiyar, *Perspectives on the Welfare State* (1966), p. 38.

8. See for the aim of ridding social security of this sharp distinction, expressed by Margaret Herbison about the 1966 MoSS Act changes; Hansard, **729**, H. C. Deb. col. 335. See also on the 'myth' of insurance, John Hilton, "The State and the Unemployed", *Political Quarterly* **14** (1933), p. 16.

9. See *Report of the N.A.B. for 1948* (1949), H.M.S.O., Cmd. 7767, p. 41.

10. D. Scott Stokes in R. S. W. Pollard (ed.), *Administrative Tribunals At Work* (1950), p. 19.

11. See, for example, a call for a 'Beeching' on tribunals, R. E. Wraith and P. G. Hutchesson, *Administrative Tribunals* (1973), p. 319.

12. See for the "abolition of the policy of deterrence", Rosalind Chambers, "The National Assistance Act 1948", *Modern Law Review* **12** (1949), p. 69.

13. New Zealand Royal Commission of Inquiry, *Social Security in New Zealand* (1972), p. 11.

14. Otto Kahn-Freund in Eric Stein and Thomas L. Nicholson (eds.), *American Enterprise in the European Common Market* (1960), p. 298.

15. Joel F. Handler and Ellen Jane Hollingsworth, *The "Deserving Poor"* (1971), p. 200.

16. Charles A. Reich, "Individual Rights and Social Welfare: The Emerging Legal Issues", *Yale Law Journal* **74** (1965), p. 1256.

SELECT BIBLIOGRAPHY

(All titles published in London unless otherwise specified.)

ABBOTT, GRACE, *From Relief to Social Security* (Chicago, 1941).

ABEL-SMITH, BRIAN, *The Reform of Social Security* (Fabian Society, 1953).

——, *Freedom in the Welfare State* (1963).

——, *Labour's Social Plans* (1966).

——, and STEVENS, ROBERT, *Laywers and the Courts* (1967).

——, ——, *In Search of Justice* (1968).

——, and TOWNSEND, PETER, *The Poor and the Poorest* (1965).

——, ZANDER, MICHAEL, and BROOKE, ROSALIND, *Legal Problems and the Citizen* (1973).

ADLER, MICHAEL, and BRADLEY, ANTHONY (eds)., *Justice, Discretion and Poverty* (1976).

AIKEN, MICHAEL, FERMAN, LOUIS A., and SHEPPARD, HAROLD L, *Economic Failure, Alienation and Extremism* (Ann Arbor, 1968).

AIKIN, OLGA, and REID, JUDITH, *Employment, Welfare and Safety at Work* (1971).

AIYAR, S. P., *Perspectives on the Welfare State* (Bombay, 1966).

ALLEN, SIR CARLETON, *Administrative Jurisdiction* (1956).

——, *Courts and Judgements* (1959).

ALTMAN, RALPH, *Availability for Work* (Cambridge, Mass., 1950).

ALTMEYER, ARTHUR J., *The Formative Years of Social Security* (Madison, Wisc., 1966).

ANDERMAN, S. D., *Unfair Dismissals and the Law* (1973).

ARCHER, PETER (ed.), *Social Welfare and the Citizen* (Harmondsworth, 1957).

ARMYTAGE, W. H. G., *Heavens Below: Utopian Experiments in England 1560–1960* (1961).

ASHFORD, E. BRIGHT, and GLEN, A. P., *Glen's Law on Unemployment Assistance* (1934).

ASHLEY, SIR WILLIAM, *An Introduction to English Economic History and Theory, The Middle Ages* (1888, 2nd edit. 1925).

ASKWITH, LORD, *Industrial Problems and Disputes* (1920).

ASPINALL, A., *The Early English Trade Unions* (1949).

ASTOR, J. J. *et al., The Third Winter of Unemployment* (1923).

——, *Unemployment Insurance in Great Britain: A Critical Examination* (1925).

ATIYAH, P. S. *Vicarious Liability in the Law of Torts* (1967).

——, *Accidents, Compensation and the Law* (1970).

ATKINSON, A. B., *Poverty in Britain and the Reform of Social Security* (Cambridge, 1969).
AVINS, ALFRED, *Employee's Misconduct* (Allahabad, 1968).

BAGEHOT, WALTER, *The English Constitution* (1867, latest edit. 1971).
BAGLEY, J. J. and A. J., *The English Poor Law* (1966).
BAKKE, E. WIGHT, *The Unemployed Man: A Social Study* (1933).
——, *Insurance or Dole?* (New Haven, 1935).
——, *Citizens Without Work* (New Haven, 1940).
——, *The Unemployed Worker* (New Haven, 1940).
BALL, F. N., *National Insurance, and Industrial Injuries* (1948).
BARNETT, HENRIETTA O., *Canon Barnett, His Life, Work and Friends* (1919).
BEALES, H. L., and LAMBERT R. S., *Memoirs of the Unemployed* (1934).
BECKER, JOSEPH M., *The Problem of Abuse in Unemployment Benefits* (New York, 1953).
——, *Guaranteed Income for the Unemployed: The Story of SUB* (Baltimore, 1968).
——, *Shared Government in Employment Security* (New York 1959).
BELL, E. MOBERLY, *Octavia Hill* (1942).
BELL, J., *How to Get Industrial Injuries Benefits* (1966).
BELL, KATHLEEN, *Tribunals in the Social Services* (1969).
——, *Research Study on Supplementary Benefit Appeal Tribunals: Review of Main Findings: Conclusions: Recommendations* (D.H.S.S., 1975).
BELL, WINIFRED, *Aid to Dependent Children* (New York, 1965).
BELLOC, HILAIRE, *The Servile State* (1912).
BENDIX, REINHARD, *Work and Authority in Industry* (New York, 1956).
BENTHAM, JEREMY, *Constitutional Code for the Use of all Nations and all Governments professing Liberal Opinions* (1830).
BERNSTEIN, IRVING, *The Lean Years: A History of the American Worker 1920–1933* (Boston, Mass., 1960).
BESANT, WALTER, *London in the Nineteenth Century* (1909).
BEVAN, ANEURIN, *In Place of Fear* (1952).
BEVERIDGE, JANET, *Beveridge and his Plan* (1954).
BEVERIDGE, WILLIAM, *Unemployment, A Problem of Industry* (1909, latest ed. 1930).
——, *Insurance for All and Everything* (*Daily News* pamphlet, 1924).
——, *The Past and Present of Unemployment Insurance* (1930).
——, *Causes and Cures of Unemployment* (1931).
——, *Planning under Socialism* (1936).
——, *The Unemployment Insurance Statutory Committee* (1937).
——, *Social Insurance and Allied Services* (1942).
——, *The Pillars of Security* (1943).
——, *Full Employment in a Free Society* (1944).
——, *Voluntary Action* (1948).
——, *Power and Influence* (1953.)
——, *The London School of Economics and its Problems 1919–1937* (1960).

BLACKLEY, M. J. J., *Collected Essays* (1882).
——, *Thrift and National Insurance as a Security against Pauperism* (1906).
BLAU, PETER, M., *The Dynamics of Bureaucracy* (Chicago, 1955, 1965).
BLOM-COOPER, LOUIS, and DRURY, GAVIN, *Final Appeal* (1972).
BOOTH, CHARLES, *Life and Labour of the People of London* (17 vols., 1889–1903).
——, *Pauperism, A Picture* (1892).
——, *Poor Law Reform* (1911).
BOOTH, MARY, *Charles Booth, A Memoir* (1918).
BOOTH, WILLIAM, *In Darkest England and the Way Out* (1890, 6th ed. 1970).
——, *The Surplus* (1908).
——, *The Vagrant and the Unemployable* (1909).
BORRIE, GORDON, *Justice and the Administration* (Fabian Soc., 1957).
——, *Elements of Public Law* (1961, 2nd ed. 1970).
BOSANQUET, BERNARD, *In Darkest England On the Wrong Track* (1891).
BOSANQUET, HELEN, *The Strength of the People* (1902).
——, *Social Work in London* (1914).
BOTTOMLEY, VIRGINIA, *Families with Low Income in London* (C.P.A.G., 1971).
BOULTON, A. HARDING, *The Law and Practice of Social Security* (Bristol, 1972).
BOURDILLON, A. F. C., *Voluntary Social Services* (1945).
BOWLEY, A. L., and BURNETT-HURST, A. R., *Livelihood and Poverty* (1915).
——, and HOGG, MARGARET. *Has Poverty Diminished?* (1925).
BOYSON, RHODES (ed.), *Down with the Poor* (1971).
BRAITHWAITE, WILLIAM J., *Lloyd George's Ambulance Wagon* (1957).
BRANSON, NOREEN, and HEINEMANN, MARGOT, *Britain in the Nineteen-Thirties* (1971).
BRIGGS, ASA, *Social Thought and Social Action: A Study of Seebohm Rowntree* (1954, 1961).
——, *Chartist Studies* (1962).
BROCKMAN, J. St. L., *The Law Relating to Family Allowances and National Insurance* (continuing supps.).
BROCKWAY, FENNER, *Inside the Left* (1942).
BROOKE, ROSALIND, *Information and Advice Services* (1972).
——, *Rights in the Welfare State* (C.P.A.G. undated).
——, *et al.*, *A Policy to Establish the Legal Rights of Low Income Families* (C.P.A.G., 1969).
BROWN, LORD GEORGE-BROWN, *In My Way* (1971).
BROWN, J. C., 'Ideas concerning Social Policy and their Influence on Legislation in Britain 1902–1911' (unpublished London Ph.D. thesis, 1964).
BROWN, KENNETH D., *Labour and Unemployment 1900–1914* (Newton Abbot, 1971).
BROWN, R. G. S., *The Administrative Process in Britain* (1970).
BRUCE, MAURICE, *The Coming of the Welfare State* (1961, 4th ed. 1968).
——, *The Rise of the Welfare State* (1973).
BRYANT, RICHARD, and BRADSHAW, JONATHAN, *Welfare Rights and Social Action* (C.P.A.G., 1972).
BULL, DAVID, *Action for Welfare Rights* (C.P.A.G., 1970).

——, *Family Poverty* (1971, 2nd ed. 1972).

BULLOCK, ALAN, *The Life and Times of Ernest Bevin* (1960).

BURNET, GILBERT, *History of the Reformation of the Church of England* (1679–81, 2 parts, 2nd ed. 3 parts, 1681–1715).

BURNS, EVELINE M., *Towards Social Security* (New York, 1936).

——, *British Unemployment Programs 1920–1938* (Washington D.C., 1941).

——, *The American Social Security System* (Cambridge, Mass., 1949).

——, *Social Security and Public Policy* (New York, 1956).

BURNS, JOHN, *The Unemployed* (1893).

BURROWS, SIR JOHN, *Decisions in the Court of King's Bench upon Settlement Cases* (2 vols., 1786).

CALVERT, HARRY, *Social Security Law* (1974).

CARR, C. T., *Concerning English Administrative Law* (New York, 1941).

CAVAN, R. S. and RANCK, K. H., *The Family and the Depression* (1938).

CHALMERS, THOMAS, *Dr. Chalmers and the Poor Laws* (1911).

CHECKLAND, S. G. and E. O. A. (ed., with an Introduction), *The Poor Law Report of 1834* (Harmondsworth, 1974).

CHEGWIDDEN, SIR THOMAS, and MYRDDIN-EVANS, G., *The Employment Exchange Service of Great Britain* (1934).

CHEYNEY, E. P., *A History of England from the Defeat of the Armada to the Death of Elizabeth* (1914–1926).

CHURCHILL, WINSTON, *Liberalism and the Social Problem* (1909).

——, *The Second World War* (6 vols., 1948–1954).

CLAIMANTS UNION, *Claimants Handbook for Strikers* (1972).

CLARKE, CHARLES E., *Social Insurance in Britain* (Cambridge, 1950).

CLARKE, JOHN, *Social Administration* (1935, 4th ed. 1943).

——, *Social Welfare* (1953).

CLARKE, ORME, *The Law of National Insurance* (1912).

CLAYTON, G., *British Insurance* (1971).

CLOWARD, R. A., and PIVEN, FRANCES, *Regulating the Poor* (1972).

COHEN, JOSEPH. L., *Insurance Against Unemployment* (1921).

COHEN, MAX, *I Was One of the Unemployed* (1945).

COLE, DOROTHY, and UTTING, J. E. G., *The Economic Circumstances of Old People* (Welwyn, 1962).

COLE, G. D. H., *The Life of Robert Owen* (1925).

——, *A Short History of the British Working Class Movement 1789–1925* (1925–7, new ed. 1948).

——, *The Intelligent Man's Guide Through World Chaos* (1932).

——, *Chartist Portraits* (1941).

——, *Fabian Socialism* (1943).

——, *The Means to Full Employment* (1943).

——, and M. I., *The Condition of Britain* (1937).

——, and POSTGATE, RAYMOND, *The Common People 1746–1946* (1938, 4th ed. 1949).

COLE, MARGARET, *Beatrice Webb* (1945).

——, *The Story of Fabian Socialism* (1961).
——, *The Life of G. D. H. Cole* (1971).
——, (ed.), *The Webbs and their Work* (1949).
COLEMAN, R. J., *Supplementary Benefits and the Administrative Review of Administrative Action* (C.P.A.G., 1970).
COLLIE, JOHN, *Malingering and Feigned Sickness* (1913).
——, *Fraud in Medico-Legal Practice* (1932).
COMYNS CARR, A. S., GARNETT, STUART, and TAYLOR, J. H., *National Insurance* (1912).
COOPER, GEORGE, and DODYK, PAUL M., *Cases and Materials on Income Maintenance* (St. Paul, Minn., 1973).
CROSSMAN, R. H. S., *Socialism and the New Despotism* (1956).

DANIEL, W. W., *A National Survey of the Unemployed* (P.E.P., 1974).
DAVENANT, CHARLES, *Works* (1771).
DAVIDSON, ROGER, 'Sir Hubert Llewellyn Smith and Labour Policy 1886–1916' (unpublished Cambridge Ph.D. thesis, 1971).
DAVIS, KENNETH CULP, *Discretionary Justice* (1971).
DAVISON, RONALD, *British Unemployment Policy* (1938).
——, *The Unemployed, Old Policies and New* (1929).
——, *What's Wrong with Unemployment Insurance* (1930).
DAWSON, W. H., *Bismarck and State Socialism* (1890).
——, *Social Insurance in Germany 1883–1911* (1912).
DEARNLEY, I. H., *Public Assistance Adminstration and Accounts* (1931).
DEKKER, THOMAS, *Seven Deadly Sins of London* (1606, 1880).
DELL, SUZANNE, *Silent in Court* (1971).
DENNING, LORD, *Freedom under the Law* (1949, latest ed. 1968).
DENVIR, JOHN, 'Making Welfare Responsive: New Approaches to the Problem of Control' (Harvard Law School unpublished paper, 1972).
DEPARTMENT OF EMPLOYMENT, *British Labour Statistics, Historical Abstract 1886–1968* (1971).
DE SCHWEINITZ, KARL, *England's Road to Social Security 1349–1942* (Philadelphia, 1943).
——, *People and Process in Social Security* (New York, 1948).
DE SMITH, S. A., *Judicial Review of Administrative Action* (1959, 3rd ed. 1974).
DICKENS, CHARLES, *Oliver Twist* (1838).
DICKINSON, JOHN, *Administrative Justice and the Supremacy of Law* (Cambridge, Mass., 1927).
DISRAELI, BENJAMIN, *Sybil, or the Two Nations* (1845).
DODD, WALTER F., *Administration of Workmen's Compensation* (New York, 1936).
DONNISON, D. V., and CHAPMAN, VALERIE, *Social Policy and Administration* (1965, 3rd imprint 1970).
DOUGLAS, PAUL H., *Standards of Unemployment Insurance* (Chicago, 1933).
——, *Social Security in the United States* (1936).
DRAGE, GEOFFREY, *Public Assistance* (1930).
DRAKE, CHARLES D., *Labour Law* (1969, 2nd ed. 1973).

EDEN, FREDERICK, *The State of the Poor* (3 vols., 1797, repub. 1928).
EDSALL, NICHOLAS C., *The Anti-Poor Law Movement 1834–1844* (Manchester, 1971).
EGERTON, ROBERT, *Legal Aid* (1945).
ELCOCK, H. J., *Administrative Justice* (1969).
ELKS, LAURIE, *The Wage Stop: Poor by Order* (C.P.A.G., 1974).
ELMAN, RICHARD M., *The Poorhouse State: The American Way of Life on Public Assistance* (New York, 1966).
EMMERSON, H. C., and LASCELLES, E. C. P., *Guide to the Unemployment Insurance Acts* (5th ed. 1930).
ENGELS, FRIEDRICH, *The Condition of the Working Class in England* (Oxford 1845, 1958 trans.; 2nd ed. 1971).
ERVINE, ST. JOHN, *God's Soldier: General William Booth* (2 vols., 1934).
ESCOTT, T. H., *England, Its People, Policies and Pursuits* (1885).
EXLEY, C. H., *The Guide to Poor Relief* (1932).
——, *The Guide to the Law and Administration of the Needs Test* (1933).

FAMILY WELFARE ASSOCIATION, *Guide to the Social Services* (annual).
FARMER, J. A., *Tribunals and Government* (1974).
FAWCETT, HENRY, *Pauperism, Its Causes and Remedies* (1871).
FEILING, KEITH, *The Life of Neville Chamberlain* (1946, reissue 1970).
FELS, MARY, *Joseph Fels: His Life Work* (1920).
FIELD, FRANK, *Poverty: The Facts* (C.P.A.G., 1975).
——, and GRIEVE, MARGARET, *Abuse and the Abused* (C.P.A.G., 1971).
FINER, S. E., *Anonymous Empire* (1958).
——, *The Life and Times of Sir Edwin Chadwick* (1952).
FOOT, MICHAEL, *Aneurin Bevan* (vol. I, 1963).
FORD, P., *Incomes, Means Tests and Personal Responsibility* (1939).
FOWLE, T. W., *The Poor Law* (1881, 1890).
FULBROOK, JULIAN, *The Appellant and his Case: The Appellant's View of Supplementary Benefit Appeal Tribunals* (C.P.A.G., 1975).
——, BROOKE, ROSALIND, and ARCHER, PETER, *Tribunals— a Social Court?* (Fabian Soc., 1973).
FURNISS, EDGAR S., *The Position of the Labourer in a System of Nationalism* (Boston, 1920, reprinted New York, 1965).

GAGLIARDO, DOMENICO, *American Social Insurance* (New York, 1949).
GANZ, G., *Administrative Procedures* (1974).
GARDINER, GERALD, and MARTIN, ANDREW, *Law Reform NOW* (1963).
GEORGE, HENRY, *Poverty and Progress* (1880).
GEORGE, VICTOR, *Social Security, Beveridge and After* (1968).
——, *Social Security and Society* (1973).
——, and WILDING, PAUL, *Motherless Families* (1972).
GIBBON, I. G., *Unemployment Insurance* (1911).
GILBERT, BENTLEY B., *The Evolution of National Insurance in Great Britain* (1966).

——, *Britain Since 1918* (1967).
——, *British Social Policy 1914–1939* (1970).
GILLIN, JOHN LEWIS, *Poverty and Dependency* (New York, 1921, 3rd ed. 1937).
GLADDEN, E. N., *British Public Service Administration* (1961).
GLASSER, PAUL H., and LOIS N., *Familes in Crisis* (1970).
GLENNERSTER, HOWARD, *National Assistance: Service or Charity?* (Fabian Soc., 1962).
GOFFMAN, ERVING, *Stigma* (New Jersey, 1963).
GOODHART, A. L., *Essays in Jurisprudence and the Common Law* (1927).
GORDON, ALBAN, *Social Insurance* (1924).
GORDON, ANDREW, *A Guide to the National Insurance Act of 1946* (1946).
GORDON, M. S., *The Economics of Welfare Policies* (New York, 1963).
GOSDEN, P. H. J. H., *The Friendly Societies in England 1815–1875* (Manchester, 1961).
GOULD, TONY, and KENYON, JOE, *Stories from the Dole Queue* (1972).
GRAHAM, JAMES J., *The Enemies of the Poor* (New York, 1970).
GREAVES, H. R. G., *The British Constitution* (1938, 3rd ed. 1955).
GREENWOOD, ARTHUR, *Juvenile Labour Exchanges and Aftercare* (1911).
GREGG, PAULINE, *The Welfare State* (1967).
GRIFFITH, J. A. G., and STREET, HARRY, *Principles of Administrative Law* (5th ed. 1973).
GRIFFITHS, JAMES, *Pages from Memory* (1969).
GRUBB, ISABEL, *Quakerism and Industry before 1800* (1929).
GRUNFELD, CYRIL, *The Law of Redundancy* (1971).

HALL, M. PENELOPE, *The Social Services of England and Wales* (1952, 1969 ed. Anthony Forder).
HAMILTON, LORD GEORGE, *Parlimentary Reminiscences and Reflections 1886–1906* (1922).
HAMILTON, MARY AGNES, *Sidney and Beatrice Webb* (1933).
HAMMOND, J. L. and B. L., *The Village Labourer* (1912).
——, ——, *Lord Shaftesbury* (1923).
——, ——, *The Bleak Age* (Harmondsworth, 1947).
HANDLER, JOEL F., *Reforming the Poor* (New York, 1972).
——, *The Coercive Social Worker* (Chicago, 1973).
——, and HOLLINGSWORTH, ELLEN JANE, *The Deserving Poor* (Chicago, 1971).
HANES, DAVID G., *The First British Workmen's Compensation Act* (New Haven, 1968).
HANNINGTON, WAL, *The Problem of the Distressed Areas* (1937).
——, *Ten Lean Years* (1940).
——, *Unemployed Struggles* (1936, republ. 1973).
HARDIE, JAMES KEIR, *The Unemployment Problem* (1928).
HARRINGTON, MICHAEL, *The Other America* (Harmondsworth, 1963).
HARRIS, JOSÉ, *Unemployment and Politics* (1973).
HARRIS, R. W., *National Health Insurance in Great Britain 1911–1946* (1946).
HARVEY, AUDREY, *Casualties of the Welfare State* (1960).

HAW, GEORGE, *From Workhouse to Westminster* (1907).
HAY, WILLIAM, *Collected Works* (1794).
HECLO, HUGH, *Modern Social Politics in Britain and Sweden* (1974).
HEDGES, R. Y., and WINTERBOTTOM, A., *The Legal History of Trade Unionism* (1930).
HEPPLE, B. A., and O'HIGGINS, PAUL, *Individual Employment Law* (1971).
HERMAN, MELVIN, *Administrative Justice and Supplementary Benefits* (1972).
HEWART, LORD, *The New Despotism* (1929).
HIBBERT, CHRISTOPHER, *The Roots of Evil: A Social History of Crime and Punishment* (1963).
HILL, M. J., *Policies for the Unemployed: Help or Coercion?* (C.P.A.G., 1974).
——, HARRISON, R. M., SARGEANT, A. V., and TALBOT, V., *Men Out of Work: A Study of Unemployment in Three English Towns* (Cambridge, 1973).
HILL, POLLY, *The Unemployment Services* (1940).
HILTON, G. W., *The Truck System* (Cambridge, 1960).
HILTON, JOHN, *Rich Man, Poor Man* (1944).
HOBSBAWM, E. J., 'Fabianism and the Fabians 1884–1914' (unpublished Cambridge Ph.D. thesis, 1949).
——, *Labouring Men* (1964).
HODGE, HENRY, *Legal Rights* (1974).
HOHMAN, HELEN F., *The Development of Social Insurance and Minimum Wage Legislation in Great Britain* (New York, 1933).
HOOD, ROGER, *Sentencing in Magistrates' Courts* (1962).
HOOD PHILLIPS, O., *Constitutional and Administrative Law* (1967).
HORWITZ, JULIUS, *The Inhabitants* (New York, 1960).
HOUGHTON, DOUGLAS, *Paying for the Social Services* (Institute of Economic Affairs, 1967).
HOWARD, DONALD S., *The WPA and the Federal Relief Policy* (New York, 1943).
HOWITT, WILLIAM, *The Rural Life of England* (2 vols., 1838).
HUGHES, EMRYS, *Winston Churchill in War and Peace* (1950).
——, *Keir Hardie* (1956).
HUNTFORD, ROLAND, *The New Totalitarians* (New York, 1972).
HUTCHINS, B. L., and HARRISON, A., *A History of Factory Legislation* (1903, 3rd ed. 1926, reprint, 1966).
HYNDMAN, H. M., *The Record of an Adventurous Life* (1911).

INDERWICK, F. A., *The Interregnum 1648–1660* (1891).
INGLIS, BRIAN, *Poverty and the Industrial Revolution* (1971).
L'INSTITUTE SCIENTIFIQUE DE RECHERCHES ÉCONOMIQUES ET SOCIALES, *Le Chômage en France* (Paris, 1938).

JACKSON, C., *Unemployment and Trade Unions* (1910).
JACKSON, DUDLEY, *Unfair Dismissal: How and Why the Law Works* (1975).

JACKSON, PAUL, *Natural Justice* (1973).
JACKSON, R. M., *The Machinery of Justice* (Cambridge, 1972).
JENKINS, EDGAR, *Index and Digest of Decisions given by the Commissioners under the National Insurance Acts* (1964 and supps.).
JENKINS, ROY, *Mr. Attlee* (1948).
——, *Mr. Balfour's Poodle* (1954).
JENNINGS, HILDA, *Brynmawr: A Study of a Distressed Area* (1934).
JENNINGS, IVOR, *The Poor Law Code* (1930, 2nd ed. 1936).
——, *Cabinet Government* (Cambridge, 1936, 3rd ed. 1959, reprinted 1969).
JOHNSON, EARL, *Justice and Reform: The Formative Years of the OEO Legal Services Program* (New York, 1974).
JONES, MERVYN, *Life on the Dole* (1972).
JONES, P. d'ARCY, *The Christian Socialist Revival 1877–1914* (1968).
JORDAN, BILL, *Paupers: The Making of the New Claiming Class* (1973).
JORDAN, W. K., *Philanthropy in England 1480–1660* (1959).
JUSTICE, *The Citizen and the Administration* (1961).

KAHN-FREUND, OTTO, *Labour and the Law* (1972).
——, and HEPPLE, BOB, *Laws Against Strikes* (Fabian Soc., 1972).
KAIM-CAUDLE, P. R., *Comparative Social Policy and Social Security* (1973).
KEAST, HORACE, *Case Law on National Insurance and Industrial Injuries* (Hadleigh, Essex, 1952).
KEELING, FREDERIC, *The Labour Exchange in Relation to Boy and Girl Labour* (1910).
KIDD, ARCHIBALD T., *History of Tin-Plate Workers* (personal loan, 1949).
KINCAID, J. C., *Poverty and Equality in Britain* (Harmondsworth 1973).
KING, SIR GEOFFREY, *The Ministry of Pensions and National Insurance* (1958).
KLEIN, VIOLA, *Britain's Married Workers* (1965).

LAFITTE, FRANÇOIS, *Britain's Way to Social Security* (1945).
LALLEMAND, LÉON, *Histoire de la Charité* (Paris, 1902–1912).
LANSBURY, GEORGE, *Your Part in Poverty* (1917).
——, *My Life* (1928).
LAPPING, BRIAN, and RADICE, GILES (eds.), *More Power to the People* (Fabian Soc., 1968).
LASKI, HAROLD, *A Grammar of Politics* (1925, 4th ed. 1938).
——, *Studies in Law and Politics* (1932).
——, *Parlimentary Government in England* (1938).
LEGAL ACTION GROUP, *Legal Advice Centres—An Explosion?* (1972).
LEICESTER, JAMES, and FARNDALE, JAMES, *Trends in the Services for Youth* (1967).
LEONARD, E. M., *The Early History of English Poor Relief* (Cambridge, 1900, 2nd impression, London, 1965).
LEVENSTEIN, AARON, *Why People Work* (New York, 1962).
LEVY, ROBERT J., LEWIS, THOMAS P., and MARTIN, PETER W., *Social Welfare and the Individual* (New York, 1971).

LEWIS, R. A., *Edwin Chadwick and the Public Health Movement* (1952).
LIDBETTER, E. J., *Settlement and Removal* (1932).
LISTER, RUTH, *The Administration of the Wage Stop* (C.P.A.G., 1972).
——, *As Man and Wife?* (C.P.A.G., 1973).
——, *Council Inaction* (C.P.A.G., 1975).
——, *Justice for the Claimant* (C.P.A.G., 1974).
——, *Social Security: The Case for Reform* (C.P.A.G., 1975).
——, *Supplementary Benefit Rights* (1974).
——, (ed.), *National Welfare Benefits Handbook* (C.P.A.G., 1972 and updates).
LLOYD GEORGE, DAVID, *The People's Insurance* (3rd ed. 1912).
LOCH, C. S., *Charity and Social Life* (1910).
LONGMATE, NORMAN, *The Workhouse* (1974).
LONSDALE, SOPHIA, *The English Poor Laws* (3rd ed., 1902).
LYNES, TONY, *National Assistance and National Prosperity* (1961).
——, *Welfare Rights* (Fabian Soc., 1969).
——, *The Penguin Guide to Supplementary Benefits* (Harmondsworth, 1972).

MACUALAY, H. H., *Fringe Benefits and their Federal Tax Treatment* (New York, 1959).
MCBEATH, M. G., and RANDS, D. N., *Salary Administration* (1969, 2nd ed. 1970).
MCBRIAR, A. M., *Fabian Socialism and English Politics 1884–1918* (1962).
MCCABE, JOSEPH, *Robert Owen* (1920).
MCCULLOCH, J. R., *The Literature of Political Economy* (1845, 1938).
MACDONALD, J. RAMSAY, *The New Unemployed Bill of the Labour Party* (1909).
MACKAY, T., *The English Poor* (1889).
——, *A History of the English Poor Law* (1899).
——, *Working-Class Insurance* (1890).
——, *The State and Charity* (1898).
——, *Public Relief of the Poor* (1901).
MACKENZIE, NORMAN (ed.), *A Guide to the Social Sciences* (1966).
MACLEAN, F. J., *The Human Side of Insurance* (1931).
MALTHUS, T. R., *An Essay on the Principle of Population* (1798, 1967).
MARR, T. R., *The Example of Germany* (1904).
MARRIS, PETER, *Widows and their Families* (1958).
——, and REIN, MARTIN, *Dilemmas of Social Reform* (1967, 2nd ed. 1972).
MARSDEN, DENNIS, *Mothers Alone* (1969).
——, and DUFF, EUAN, *Workless: Some Unemployed Men and their Families* (1975).
MARSH, DAVID C., *National Insurance and National Assistance in Great Britain* (1950).
——, *The Future of the Welfare State* (1964).
——, (ed.), *Social Administration* (1965).
MARSH, LEONARD C., *Health and Unemployment* (Oxford, 1938).
MARSHALL, ALFRED, *Official Papers* (1888, ed. J. M. Keynes, 1926).

MARSHALL, DOROTHY, *The English Poor in the Eighteenth Century* (1926).
MARSHALL, H. H., *Natural Justice* (1959).
MARSHALL, J. D., *The Old Poor Law 1795–1834* (1968).
MARSHALL, T. H., *Class Citizenship and Social Development* (New York, 1964).
——, *Social Policy* (1965, 3rd ed. 1970).
MARSTON, MAURICE, *Sir Edwin Chadwick* (1925).
MARTIN, E. W. (ed.), *Comparative Development in Social Welfare* (1972).
MASTERMAN, N. (ed.), *Chalmers on Charity* (1900).
MATTHEWS, E. J. T., and OULTON, A. D. M., *Legal Aid and Advice* (1974 with supps.).
MAYER, JOHN E., and TIMMS, NOEL, *The Client Speaks* (1970).
MAYHEW, HENRY, *London Labour and the London Poor* (1851, new imprint, 1967)
MEACHER, MOLLY, *Rates Rebates* (C.P.A.G., 1972).
——, *Scrounging on the Welfare: The Scandal of the Four Week Rule* (1974).
MEADE, J. E., *Poverty in the Welfare State* (Oxford Economic Papers, vol. 24, 1972).
MEARNS, ANDREW, *The Bitter Cry of Outcast London* (1883, 1970).
MENCHER, SAMUEL, *Poor Law to Poverty Program* (Pittsburgh, 1967).
MENDELSOHN, RONALD, *Social Security in the British Commonwealth* (1954).
MERIAM, LEWIS, *Relief and Social Security* (New York, 1946).
MILLETT, JOHN D., *The Unemployed Assistance Board* (1940).
MILLS, H. V., *Poverty and the State* (1886).
MITCHELL, B. R., and DEANE, PHYLLIS, *Abstract of British Historical Statistics* (Cambridge, 1962, 2nd ed. 1971).
MITCHELL, WILLIAM LLOYD, *Social Security in America* (Cambridge, Maryland, 1964).
MONEY, L. G. CHIOZZA, *Insurance versus Poverty* (1912).
MONYPENNY, SIR WILLIAM, *The Life of Benjamin Disraeli, Earl of Beaconsfield* (6 vols., 1910–1920, new ed. 1929).
MOORE, PETER, *Students Rights: Social Security, Other Benefits and Housing* (C.P.A.G., 1975).
MORAN, LORD, *Winston Churchill, The Struggle for Survival* (1966).
MORLEY, FELIX, *Unemployment Relief in Great Britain* (1924).
MORRIS, PAULINE, WHITE, RICHARD, and LEWIS, PHILIP, *Social Needs and Legal Action* (1973).
MOSS, JOHN, *The National Assistance Act* (1948).
MOWAT, C. L., *Britain Between the Wars* (1955).
——, *The Charity Organization Society 1869–1913* (1961).
——, *Lloyd George* (1964).
MUGGERIDGE, KITTY, and ADAM, RUTH, *Beatrice Webb 1858–1943* (1967).
MUIRHEAD, JAMES F., *Land and Unemployment* (1935).
MUIRHEAD, JOHN H., *By What Authority?* (2nd ed. 1909).
MULLINS, GEO. W., *Unemployment: The Gateway to a New Life* (1926).
MYERS, CHARLES A., and SCHULTZ, GEORGE P., *The Dynamics of a Labour Market* (New York, 1951).
MYRDAL, GUNNAR, *An American Dilemma* (1944).

——, *Challenge to Affluence* (1963).

THE NATIONAL INNOVATIONS CENTRE, *Welfare Rights Stalls* (1972).

NATIONAL YOUTH EMPLOYMENT COUNCIL, *Unqualified, Untrained and Unemployed* (H.M.S.O., 1974).

NELSON, DANIEL, *Unemployment Insurance, The Amercian Experience 1915–1935* (Madison, Wis., 1969).

NEWMAN, T. S., and LEE, A. G., *Guide to Unemployment Insurance* (1947).

NICHOLLS, GEORGE, *A History of the English Poor Law* (1904).

NONET, PHILIPPE, *Administrative Justice* (New York, 1969).

NORTH, *Discourse on the Pernicious Tendency of the Laws for the Maintenance and Settlement of the Poor* (1753).

O'CONNOR, PHILIP, *Vagrancy* (Harmondsworth, 1963).

ORWELL, GEORGE, *The Road to Wigan Pier* (1937, 1959).

ORWIN, C. S., and C. S., *The Open Fields* (Oxford, 1938, 3rd ed. 1967).

OTUTEYE, SETH, 'Some Aspects of Social Security Law—A Comparison between English and French Legal Methods (unpublished Cambridge Ph.D. thesis, 1971).

OWEN, DAVID, *English Philanthropy 1660–1960* (Cambridge, Mass., 1965).

OXLEY, G. W., *Poor Relief in England and Wales 1601–1834* (Newton Abbot, 1974).

PAGE, ROBIN, *The Benefits Rackets* (1971).

PARKER, S. R., THOMAS, C. G., ELLIS, N. D., and MCCARTHY, W. E. J., *Effects of the Redundancy Payments Act* (H.M.S.O., 1971).

PASHLEY, ROBERT, *Pauperism and the Poor Laws* (1852).

PEACOCK, ALAN T., *The Economics of National Insurance* (1952).

PEASE, EDWARD R., *The History of the Fabian Society* (1925).

PECHMAN, JOSEPH A., AARON, HENRY J., and TAUSSIG, MICHAEL K., *Social Security: Perspectives for Reform* (Washington D.C., 1968).

PERCIVAL, TOM, *Poor Law Children* (1912).

PFAUTZ, HAROLD W., *Charles Booth on the City* (Chicago, 1967).

PIGOU, A. C., *The Economics of Welfare* (1920, 4th ed. 1932).

PILGRIM TRUST REPORT, *Men Without Work* (Cambridge, 1938).

PIMLOTT, J. A. R., *Toynbee Hall* (1935).

PINKER, ROBERT, *Social Theory and Social Policy* (1971).

POLANYI, KARL, *The Great Transformation* (1944).

POLITICAL AND ECONOMIC PLANNING, *Inquest on the Unemployment Act* (1935).

——, *The British Social Services* (1937).

——, *Advisory Committees in British Government* (1960).

POLLARD, R. S. W. (ed.), *Administrative Tribunals At Work* (1950).

PORT, FREDERIC, *Administrative Law* (1929).

POSTGATE, RAYMOND, *The Life of George Lansbury* (1951).

POTTER, ALLEN, *Organised Groups in British National Politics* (1961).

POTTER, DOUGLAS, and STANSFIELD, D. H., *National Insurance* (2nd ed. 1949).

POUND, JOHN F., *Poverty and Vagrancy in Tudor England* (1971).

POWER, EILEEN, *The Wool Trade in English Mediaeval History* (Oxford, 1941, reprinted London, 1949).

POYNTER, J. R., *Society and Pauperism* (1969).

PRETYMAN, J. R., *Dispauperisation* (1876, 2nd ed. 1878).

RATHBONE, ELEANOR, *Family Allowances* (*The Disinherited Family*, 1924) (1949).

RAYNES, HAROLD E., *Social Security in Britain* (1957, 2nd ed. 1960).

REASON, WILL, *University and Social Settlements* (1898).

REID, G. L., and ROBERTSON, D. J., *Fringe Benefits, Labour Costs and Social Security* (1965).

REIN, MARTIN, *Social Policy: Issues of Choice and Change* (New York, 1970).

REYNOLDS, GEORGE, *Dr. Barnardo's Homes: Startling Revelations* (1877).

RHODES, H. V., *Setting Up a New Government Department* (1949).

RIDEOUT, R. W., *Principles of Labour Law* (1972).

——, *Trade Unions and the Law* (1973).

RIMLINGER, GASTON V., *Welfare Policy and Industrilization in Europe, America and Russia* (New York, 1971).

ROBERTS, DAVID, *Victorian Origins of the British Welfare State* (New Haven, 1960).

ROBINSON, JOAN, *Theory of Employment* (1938).

ROBSON, WILLIAM A., *Justice and Administrative Law* (1928, 3rd ed. 1951).

——, *The Governors and the Governed* (1964).

——, (ed.), *Social Security* (1943, 2nd ed. 1948).

RODGERS, BARBARA (WITH GREVE, JOHN, and MORGAN, JOHN S.), *Comparative Social Administration* (1968).

RODGERS, BRIAN, *The Battle Against Poverty* (2 vols., 1969).

ROHRLICH, GEORGE F. (ed.), *Social Economics for the 1970's* (New York, 1970).

ROLPH, C. H., *The Life, Letters and Diaries of Kingsley Martin* (1973).

ROSE, HILARY, *Rights, Participation and Conflict* (1970).

ROSE, MICHAEL, *The English Poor Law 1780–1930* (Newton Abbot, 1971).

——, *The Relief of Poverty 1834–1914* (1972).

ROUTH, GUY, *Occupation and Pay in Great Britain 1906–1960* (Cambridge, 1965).

ROWNTREE, B. SEEBOHM, *Poverty: A Study of Town Life* (1901, 3rd ed. 1922).

——, *The Human Need of Labour* (1918).

——, *The Human Factor in Business* (1938).

——, *Poverty and Progress* (1941).

——, and LASKER, BRUNO, *Unemployment: A Social Study* (1911).

ROYAL INSTITUTE OF INTERNATIONAL AFFAIRS, *Unemployment: An International Problem* (1935).

RUBINOW, I. M., *Social Insurance* (New York, 1916).

RUBNER, ALEX, *Fringe Benefits: The Golden Chains* (1962).

RUDGE, THOMAS, *General View of the Agriculture of the County of Gloucestershire* (1807).

RUNCIMAN, W. G., *Relative Deprivation and Social Justice* (1966).
RUSSELL, JAMES E., *National Policies for Education, Health and Social Services* (New York, 1955).

SABATIER, WILLIAM, *Treatise on Poverty, Its Consequences and the Remedy* (1797).
SALTER, F. R., *Some Early Tracts on Poor Relief* (1926).
SANDER, F. E. A., *Materials on Public Welfare Law* (Harvard Law School photocopy, 1972).
SANDFORD, JEREMY, *Down and Out in Britain* (1971).
SAWER, GEOFFREY, *Law in Society* (1965).
SCARMAN, SIR LESLIE, *English Law: The New Dimension* (1974).
SCHLOSS, DAVID, *Insurance Against Unemployment* (1909).
SCHWARTZ, BERNARD, *Law and the Executive in Britain* (New York, 1949).
——, and WADE, H. W. R., *Legal Control of Government* (New York, 1972).
SCOTT, J. W., *Self-Subsistence for the Unemployed* (1935).
SEAGER, HENRY ROGERS, *Social Insurance* (New York, 1910).
SENIOR, NASSAU, *Political Economy* (1850, 6th ed. 1872).
——, (ed. SIMPSON, M. C. M.), *Correspondence with Alexis de Tocqueville from 1834 to 1859* (2 vols., 1872).
SEYMOUR, JOHN BARTON, *The British Employment Exchange* (1928).
SHKLAR, JUDITH, *Legalism* (Cambridge, Mass., 1964).
SHOWLER, BRIAN, *On to a Comprehensive Employment Service* (Fabian Soc., 1973).
SIDGWICK, HENRY, *Principles of Political Economy* (2nd ed. 1887, 3rd ed. 1901).
SIMEY, T. S. and M. B., *Charles Booth, Social Scientist* (Oxford, 1960).
SINFIELD, ADRIAN, *The Long-Term Unemployed* (O.E.C.D. Paris, 1968).
——, *Which Way for Social Work?* (Fabian Soc., 1969).
——, 'Unemployment Compensation and Employment Security' (unpublished Fabian Soc. paper, 1972).
SINGER, H. W., *Unemployment and the Unemployed* (1940).
——, *Can We Afford Beveridge?* (1943).
SKIDELSKY, ROBERT, *Politicians and the Slump* (1967).
SLACK, KATHERINE, *Social Administration and the Citizen* (1966, 2nd ed. 1969).
SLATER, GILBERT, *Poverty and the State* (1930).
SLAVICK, FRED, *Voluntary Quit Disqualification in Unemployment Insurance* (Princeton, New Jersey, 1954).
SMILES, SAMUEL, *Self Help* (1859, 1958 Centenary ed. with Intro. by Asa Briggs).
SMITH, ADAM, *An Inquiry into the Nature and Causes of the Wealth of Nations* (1776).
SMITH, CHRIS., and HOATH, DAVID C., *Law and the Underprivileged* (1975).
SMITH, N. J., *A Brief Guide to Social Legislation* (1972).
SOCIETY OF LABOUR LAWYERS, *Justice for All* (Fabian Soc., 1968).
SOMERS, JOHN, *A Collection of Scarce and Interesting Tracts, Tending to Elucidate Detached Parts of the History of Great Britain* (1795, 2nd ed. 1809–1815).

SPENCER, HERBERT, *Social Statics* (1868).

STARK, W., *Jeremy Bentham's Economic Writings* (1952).

STEELE, R. D., *The National Assistance Act 1948* (1949).

STEINBECK, JOHN, *The Grapes of Wrath* (New York, 1939).

STEINER, GILBERT Y., *Social Insecurity: The Politics of Welfare* (Chicago, 1966).

——, *The State of Welfare* (Washington D.C., 1971).

STEPHENS, HAROLD M., *Administrative Tribunals and the Rules of Evidence* (Cambridge, Mass., 1933).

STEVENS, R. B., and YAMEY, B. S., *The Restrictive Practices Court* (1965).

STEVENSON, E. F., *Unemployment Relief: The Basic Problem* (1934).

STEVENSON, OLIVE, *Claimant or Client?* (1973).

STEWART, BRYCE M., *Unemployment Benefits in the United States* (New York, 1930).

STOCKER, E. O. F., and NILSSON, P. G., *The Law Relating to Supplementary Benefits and Family Income Supplements* (continuing supps.).

STOCKS, MARY, *Eleanor Rathbone* (1949).

STOCKS, M. D., *Fifty Years in Every Street* (Manchester, 1945, 2nd ed. 1956).

STREATHER, JANE, and WEIR, STUART, *Social Insecurity: Single Mothers on Benefit* (C.P.A.G., 1974).

STREET, HARRY, *Justice in the Welfare State* (1968, 2nd ed. 1975).

SWANISH, PETER T., *Trade Disputes Disqualification Clause under the British Insurance Acts* (Chicago, 1937).

TAWNEY, R. H., *The Agrarian Problem in the Sixteenth Century* (1912).

——, *Religion and the Rise of Capitalism* (1926, Harmondsworth, 1938).

——, *Equality* (1931).

TEN BROEK, JACOBUS (ed. HANDLER, JOEL F.), *Family Law and the Poor* (Westport, Conn., 1971).

——, (ed.). *The Law and the Poor* (San Francisco, 1966).

THIEBLOT, ARMAND J., and COWIN, RONALD M., *Welfare and Strikes: The Use of Public Funds to Support Strikes* (Philadelphia, 1972).

THOMAS, DOROTHY, *Social Aspects of the Business Cycle* (1925).

THOMPSON, E. P., *The Making of the English Working Class* (1963).

TILLYARD, FRANK, *Unemployment Insurance in Great Britain* (1949).

TITMUSS, R. M., *Poverty and Population* (1938).

——, *Problems of Social Policy* (in the series *A History of the Second World War*) (1950)

——, *Essays on 'The Welfare State'* (1959, 2nd ed. 1969).

——, *Commitment to Welfare* (1968).

——, *Social Policy* (1974).

TOWNSEND, JOSEPH, *A Dissertation on the Poor Laws, By a Well-Wisher to Mankind* (1786, republ. 1971).

TOWNSEND, PETER, *The Family Life of Old People* (1957).

——, *Social Services for All?* (Fabian Soc., 1968).

——, (ed.), *The Concept of Poverty* (1970).

——, and Bosanquet, Nicholas (ed.), *Labour and Inequality* (Fabian Soc., 1972).

Townshend, Emily C., *The Case Against the C.O.S.* (Fabian Soc., 1911).

Trevelyan, Sir George, *English Social History* (1944, 3rd ed. 1946, Harmondsworth, 1967).

U.S. Department of Labor, *Comparison of State Unemployment Insurance Laws* (Washington D.C., 1972, plus supps.).

Vandyk, Neville, *Tribunals and Inquiries* (1965).

Vernon, R. V., and Mansergh, N., *Advisory Bodies* (1940).

Vulliamy, A. F., *The Law of Settlement and Removal of Paupers* (1895).

Wade, E. C. S., and Phillips, G., *Constitutional and Administrative Law* (1931, 8th ed. 1970).

Wade, H. W. R., *Administrative Law* (Oxford, 1961, 3rd ed. 1971).

——, *Towards Administrative Justice* (Ann Arbor, 1963).

Walker, Nigel, *Morale in the Civil Service: a Study of the Desk Worker* (Edinburgh, 1961).

Warburton, Edward, and Butler, Carl, *Disallowed: The Tragedy of the Means Test* (1935).

Ward, J. T., *The Factory System* (Newton Abbot, 1970).

Wasserstrom, Richard A., *The Judicial Decision* (1961).

Watson, Frank Dekker, *The Charity Organization Movement in the United States* (New York, 1922).

Webb, Beatrice, *My Apprenticeship* (1926).

——, (ed. Cole, Margaret), *Diaries 1924–1932* (1946).

——, (ed. Drake, Barbara, and Cole, Margaret), *Our Partnership* (1948).

Webb, Sidney and Beatrice, *The Break-up of the Poor Law: Part One of the Minority Report 1909* (1909).

——, ——, *English Poor Law Policy* (1910).

——, ——, *The Prevention of Destitution* (1911, reissue 1920).

——, ——, *The History of Trade Unionism* (1920).

——, ——, *English Poor Law History* (3 vols., 1927–1929, new ed. Part One, 1963).

——, ——, *Methods of Social Study* (1932).

Wedderburn, Dorothy, *White Collar Redundancy* (Cambridge, 1964).

Wedderburn, K. W., *The Worker and the Law* (Harmondsworth, 1965, 2nd ed. 1971).

——, *Cases and Materials on Labour Law* (Cambridge, 1967).

——, and Davies, P. L., *Employment Grievance and Disputes Procedures in Britain* (1969).

Wheare, K. C., *Maladministration and its Remedies* (1973).

Whitaker, Ben, *Participation and Poverty* (Fabian Soc., 1968).

WHITEHEAD, GEORGE, *Unemployment: Causes and Remedies* (1933).
WILKINSON, ELLEN, *The Town that was Murdered* (1939).
WILLIAMS, A. E., *Barnardo of Stepney: The Father of Nobody's Children* (1943, 3rd ed. 1966).
WILLIAMS, FRANCIS, *A Prime Minister Remembers* (1961).
WILSON, ARNOLD, and LEVY, HERMAN, *Workman's Compensation* (1939).
WILSON, JOHN VEIT, 'Rights or Charity?' (unpublished paper, 1973).
WOODWARD, E. GILBERT, *Archbold's Poor Law* (16th ed. 1930).
WRAITH, R. E., and HUTCHESSON, P. G., *Administrative Tribunals* (1973).
WRIGHT, R. P., *For Men Must Work* (1969).

YOUNG, A. F., and ASHTON, E. T., *British Social Work in the Nineteenth Century* (1956).
YOUNG, MICHAEL (ed.), *Forecasting and the Social Sciences* (1968).
——, (ed.), *Poverty Report 1974* (1974).

ZANDER, MICHAEL, *Social Workers, Their Clients and the Law* (1974).
ZWEIG, F., *Labour, Life and Poverty* (1948).
——, *Men in the Pits* (1948).

INDEX